STAR WARS

DARTH VADER

DARK LORD OF THE SITH

FORTRESS VADER

STAR WARS
DARTH VADER
DARK LORD OF THE SITH
FORTRESS VADER

Writer	**CHARLES SOULE**
Penciler	**GIUSEPPE CAMUNCOLI**
Inker	**DANIELE ORLANDINI** with **TERRY PALLOT** (#22)
Colorists	**DAVID CURIEL** (#19, #21-25), **DONO SÁNCHEZ-ALMARA** (#20, #23-24) & **ERICK ARCINIEGA** (#20)
Letterers	**VC's JOE CARAMAGNA** (#19, #21-25) & **TRAVIS LANHAM** (#20)
Cover Art	**GIUSEPPE CAMUNCOLI** & **ELIA BONETTI**
Assistant Editor	**TOM GRONEMAN**
Editor	**MARK PANICCIA**
Vader's Castle Concepts	**LUCASFILM'S ERIK TIEMENS, CHRISTIAN ALZMANN & MATT ALLSOPP**
Special Thanks	**ILMxLAB & ILM ART DEPARTMENT**
Editor in Chief	**C.B. CEBULSKI**
Chief Creative Officer	**JOE QUESADA**
President	**DAN BUCKLEY**

For Lucasfilm:

Assistant Editor	**NICK MARTINO**
Senior Editor	**ROBERT SIMPSON**
Executive Editor	**JENNIFER HEDDLE**
Creative Director	**MICHAEL SIGLAIN**
Lucasfilm Story Group	**JAMES WAUGH, LELAND CHEE, MATT MARTIN**

Collection Editor JENNIFER GRUNWALD
Assistant Editor CAITLIN O'CONNELL
Associate Managing Editor KATERI WOODY
Editor Special Projects MARK D. BEAZLEY
VP Production & Special Projects JEFF YOUNGQUIST
SVP Print, Sales & Marketing DAVID GABRIEL
Book Designer ADAM DEL RE

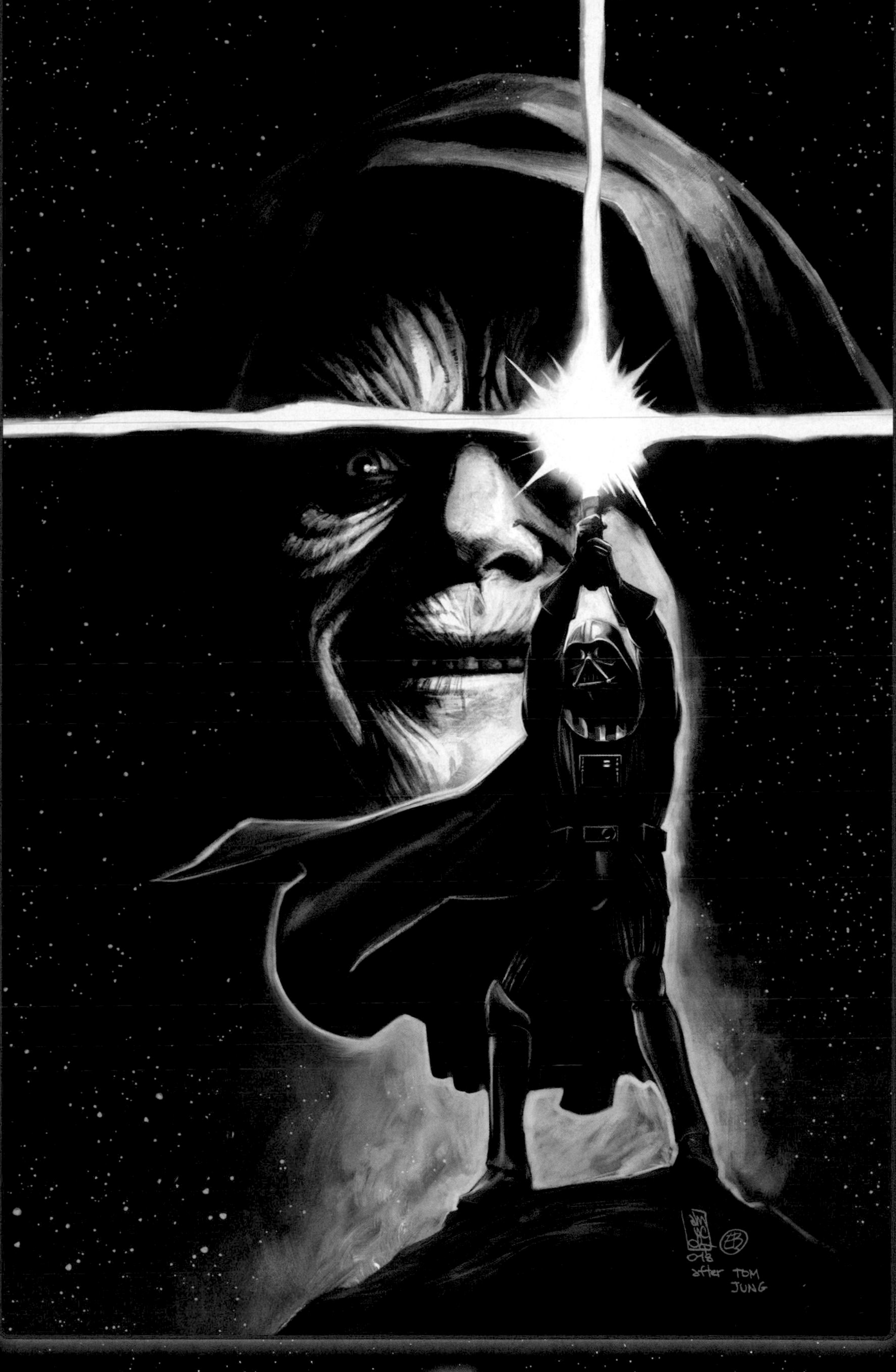
after TOM
JUNG

FORTRESS VADER

The Republic is overthrown. Emperor Palpatine rules the galaxy with an iron fist.

Second only to the Emperor is Palpatine's apprentice — the fearsome Darth Vader. Vader's fall to the dark side of the Force and defeat at the hands of Obi-Wan Kenobi leaves him confined to a suit of cybernetic armor to preserve his life. Now, he lives only to serve his master's Empire.

To ensure the survival of this New Order, Vader leads a squad of dark side adepts — the Inquisitorius — in routing out and destroying the greatest threat to Palpatine's rule — the remaining Jedi Knights....

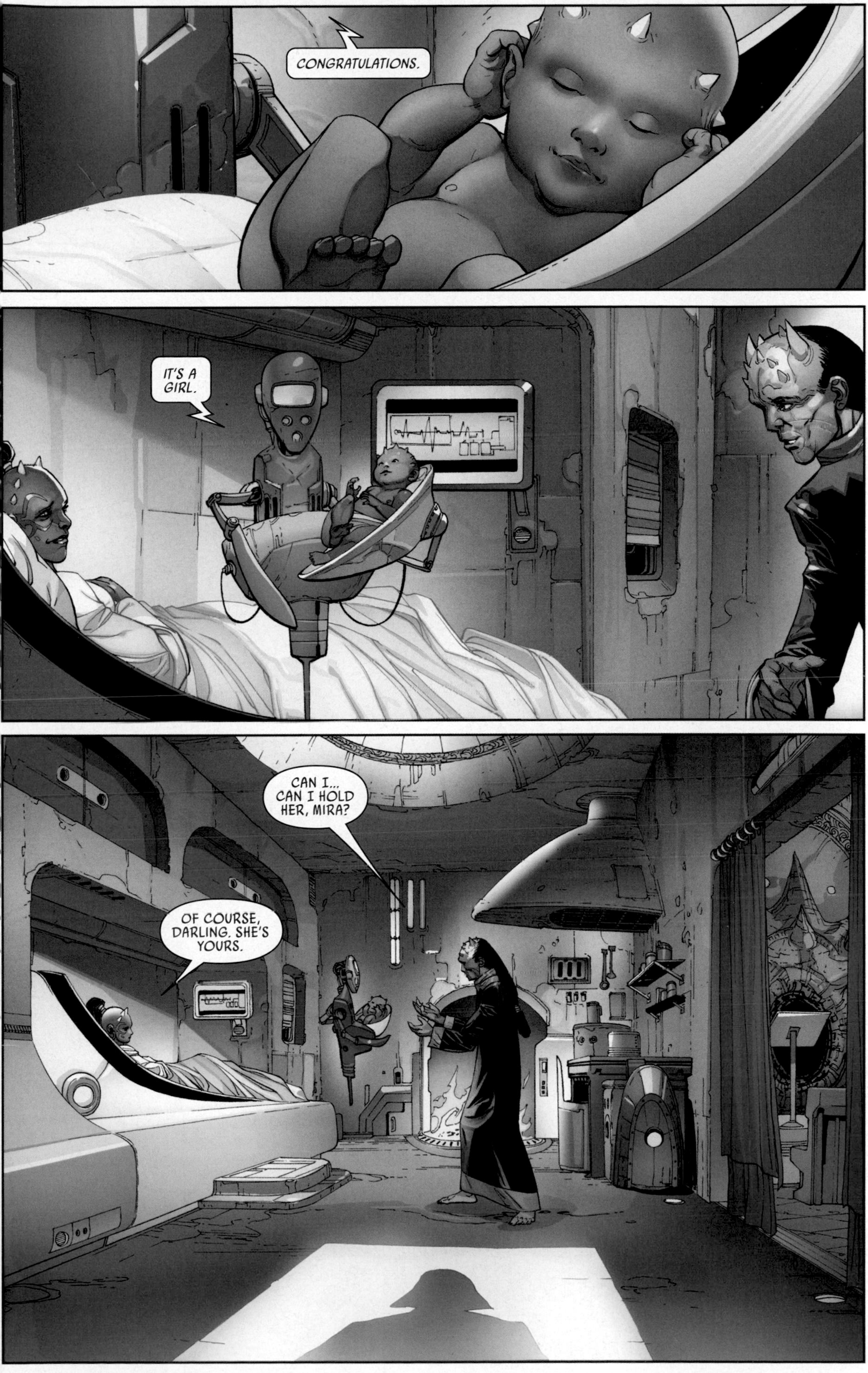
CONGRATULATIONS.
IT'S A GIRL.
CAN I... CAN I HOLD HER, MIRA?
OF COURSE, DARLING. SHE'S YOURS.

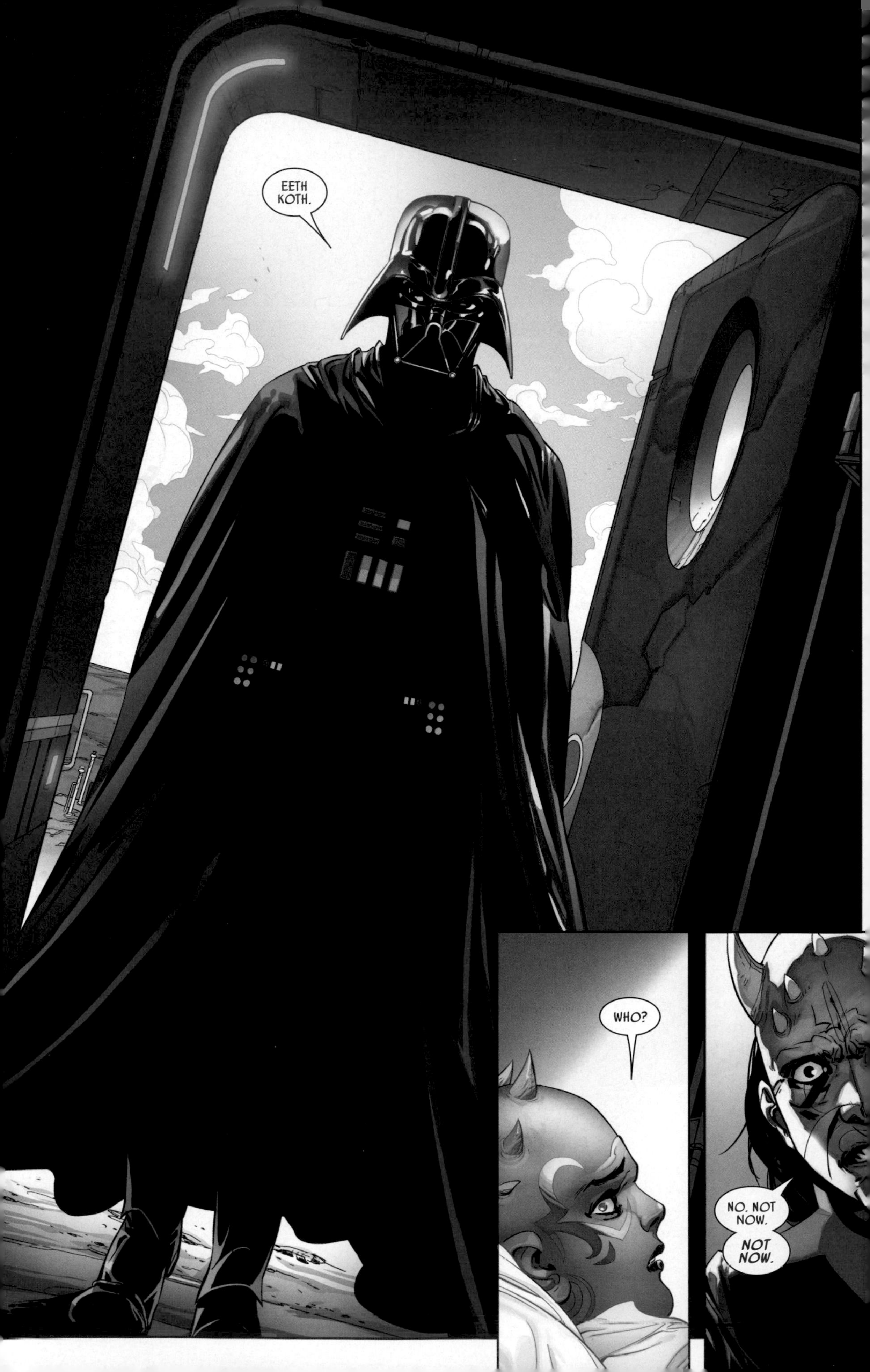
EETH KOTH.
WHO?
NO. NOT NOW.
NOT NOW.

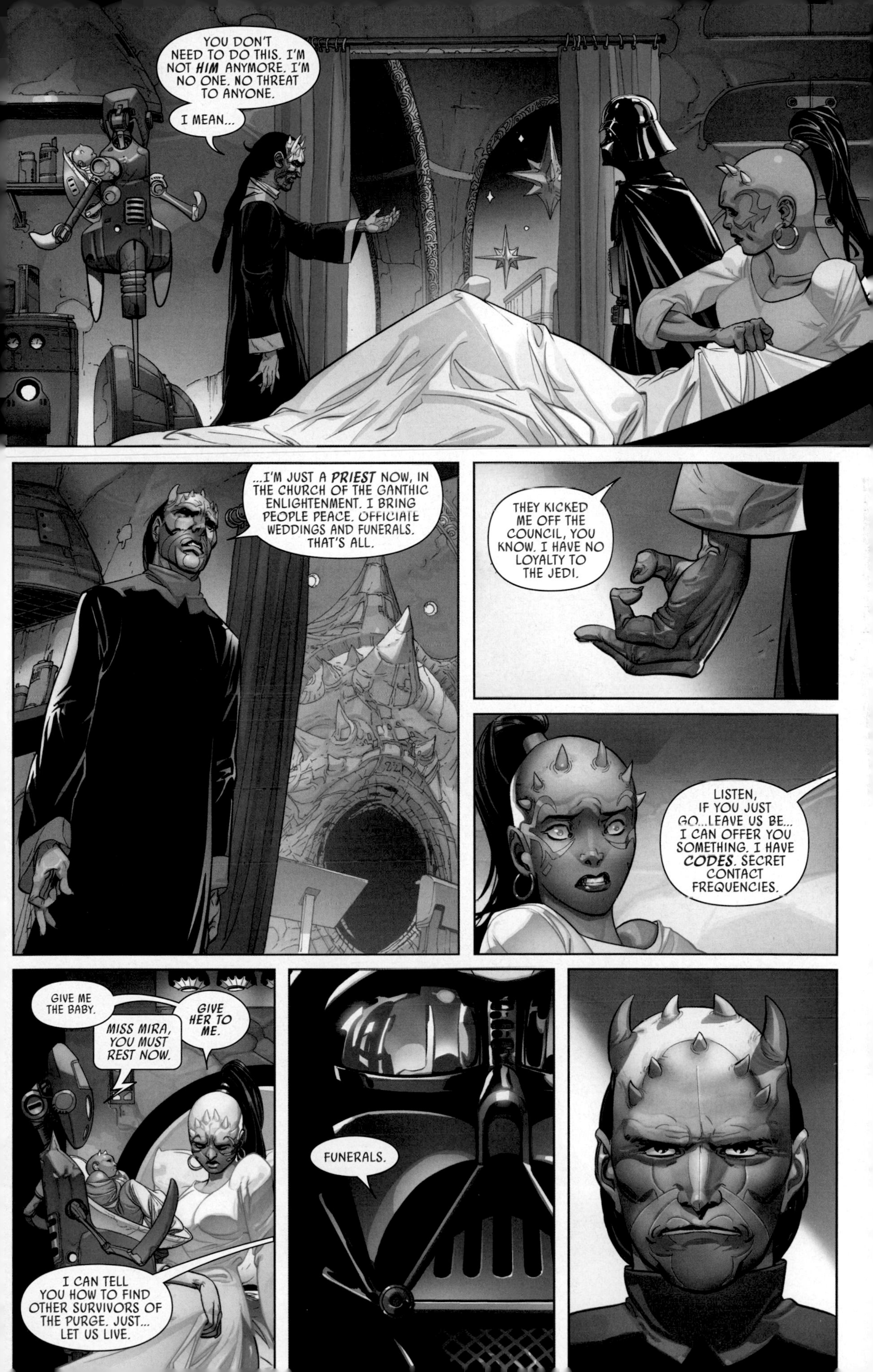

YOU DON'T NEED TO DO THIS. I'M NOT HIM ANYMORE. I'M NO ONE. NO THREAT TO ANYONE.
I MEAN...
...I'M JUST A PRIEST NOW, IN THE CHURCH OF THE GANTHIC ENLIGHTENMENT. I BRING PEOPLE PEACE. OFFICIATE WEDDINGS AND FUNERALS. THAT'S ALL.
THEY KICKED ME OFF THE COUNCIL, YOU KNOW. I HAVE NO LOYALTY TO THE JEDI.
LISTEN, IF YOU JUST GO...LEAVE US BE... I CAN OFFER YOU SOMETHING. I HAVE CODES. SECRET CONTACT FREQUENCIES.
GIVE ME THE BABY.
GIVE HER TO ME.
MISS MIRA, YOU MUST REST NOW.
I CAN TELL YOU HOW TO FIND OTHER SURVIVORS OF THE PURGE. JUST... LET US LIVE.
FUNERALS.

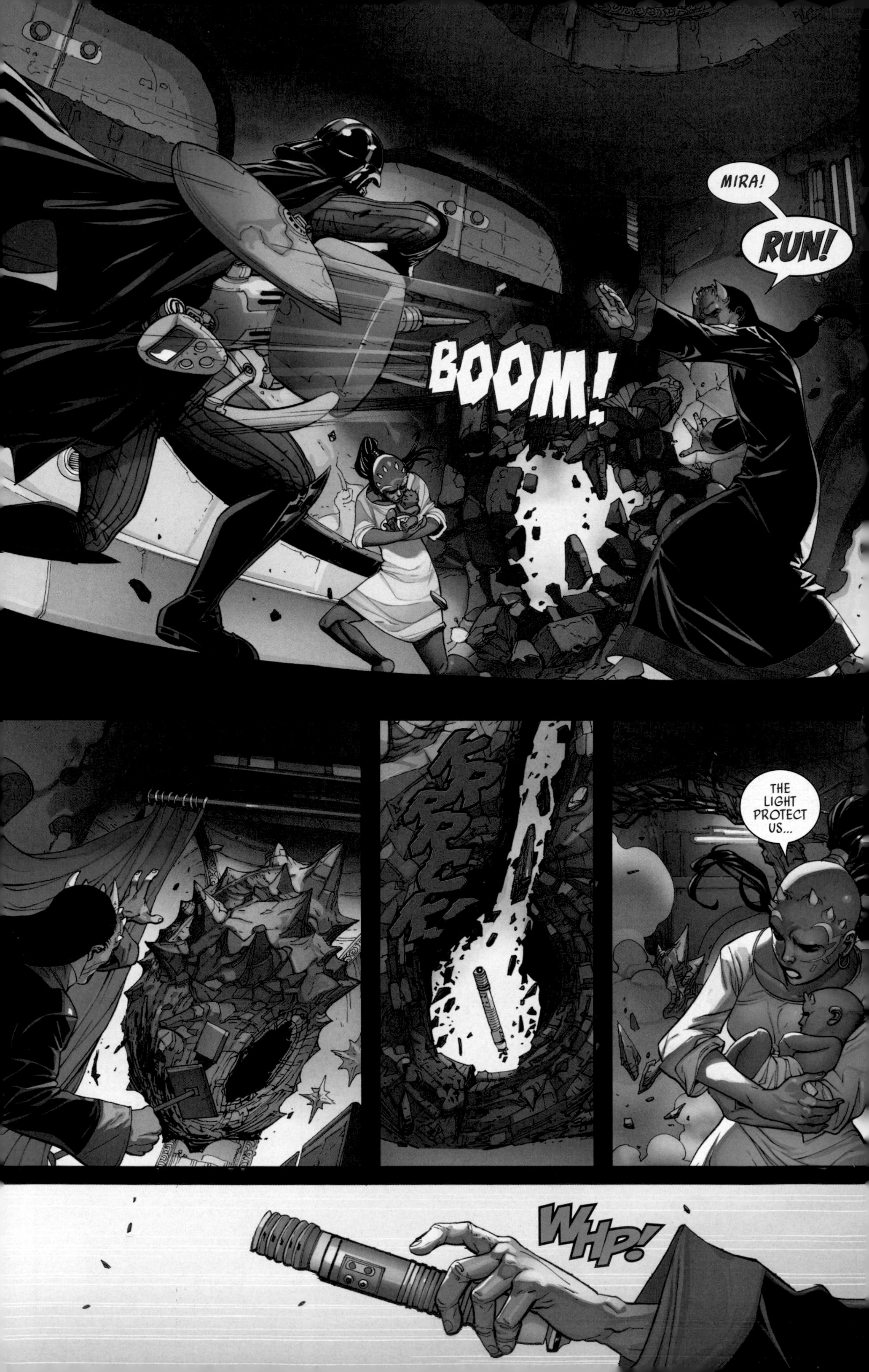
MIRA!
RUN!
BOOM!
THE LIGHT PROTECT US...
WHP!

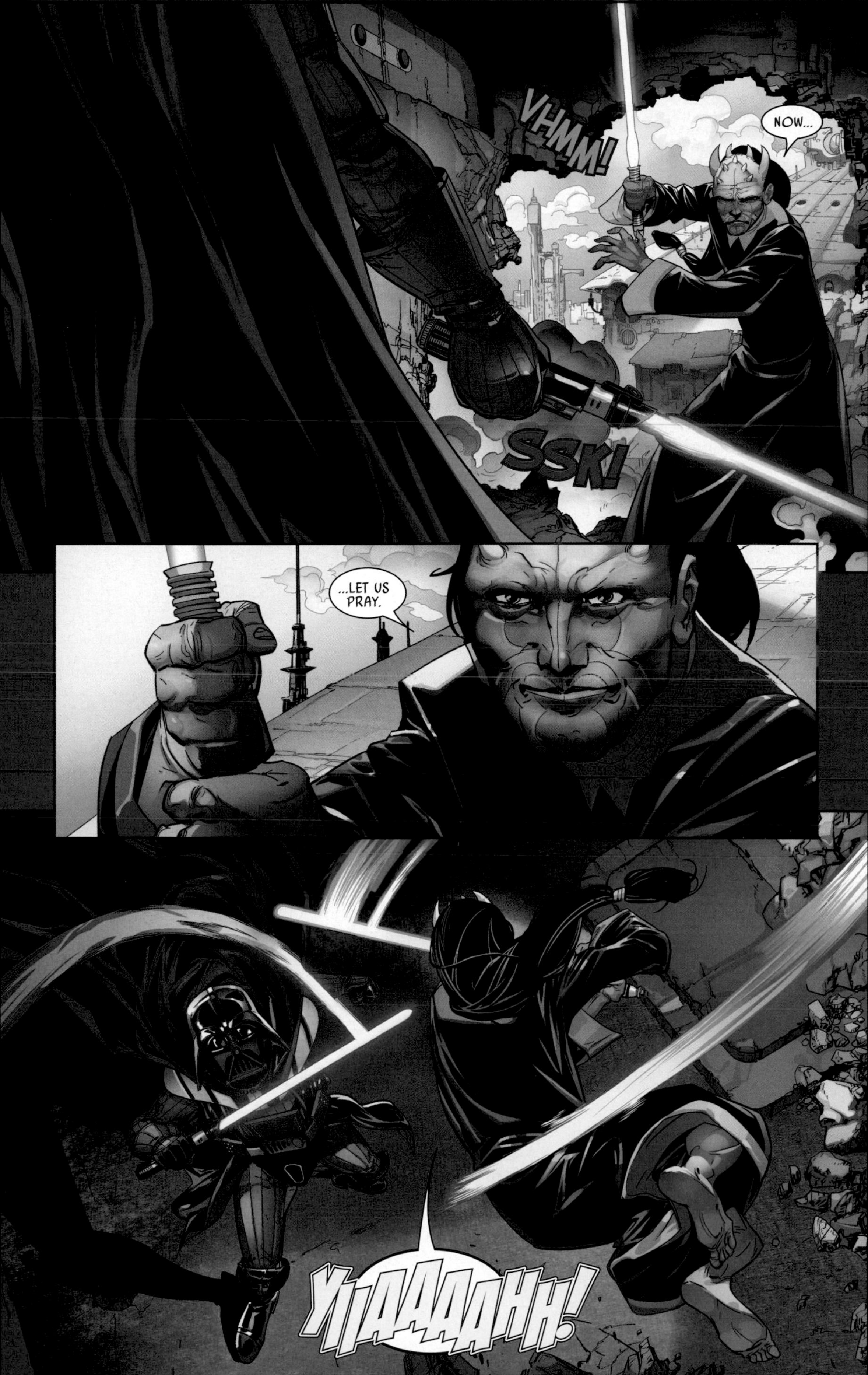
VHMM!
NOW...
SSK!
...LET US PRAY.
YIIAAAAAHH!

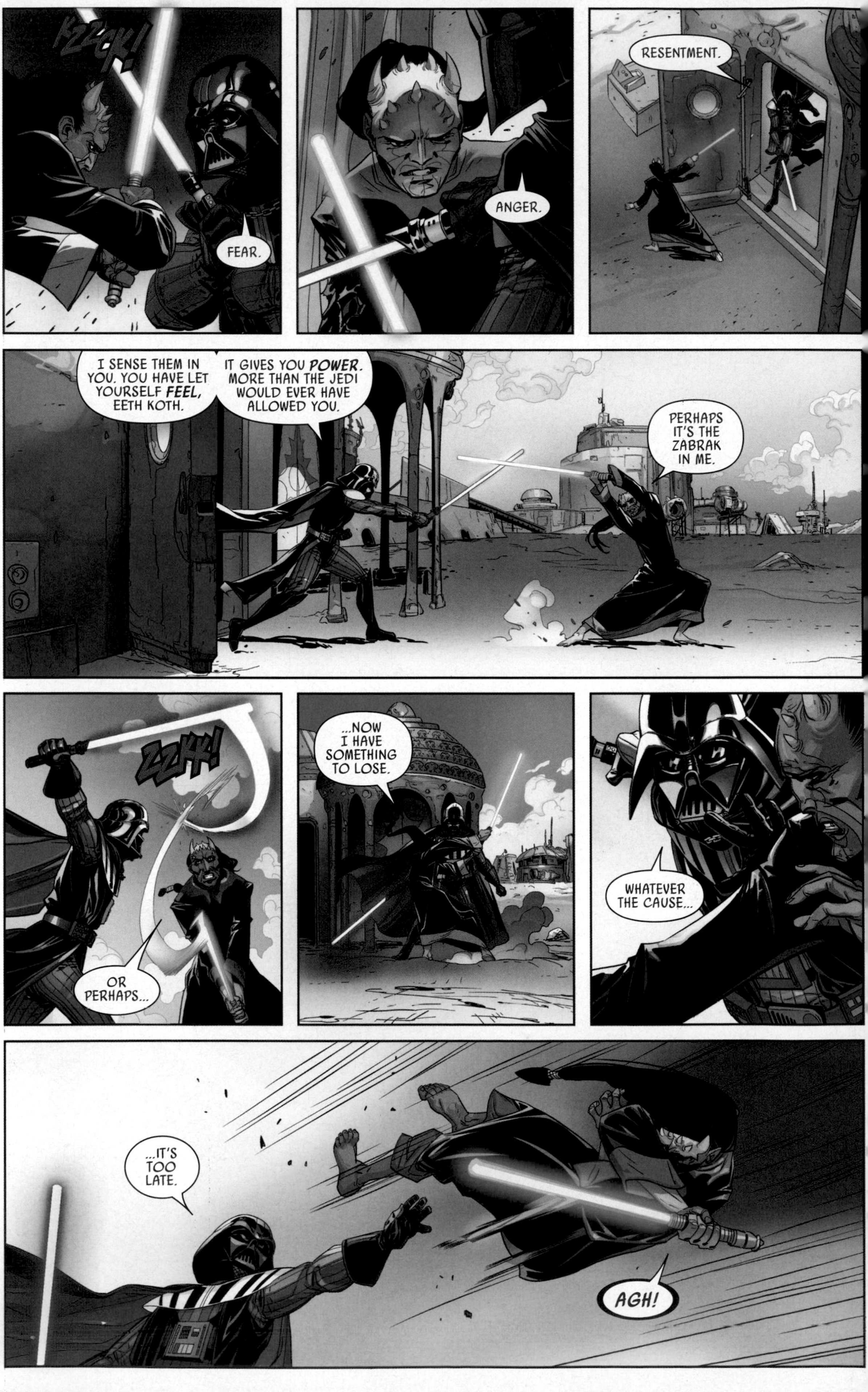
KZZCK!
FEAR.
ANGER.
RESENTMENT.
I SENSE THEM IN YOU. YOU HAVE LET YOURSELF FEEL, EETH KOTH.
IT GIVES YOU POWER. MORE THAN THE JEDI WOULD EVER HAVE ALLOWED YOU.
PERHAPS IT'S THE ZABRAK IN ME.
ZZKK!
OR PERHAPS...
...NOW I HAVE SOMETHING TO LOSE.
WHATEVER THE CAUSE...
...IT'S TOO LATE.
AGH!

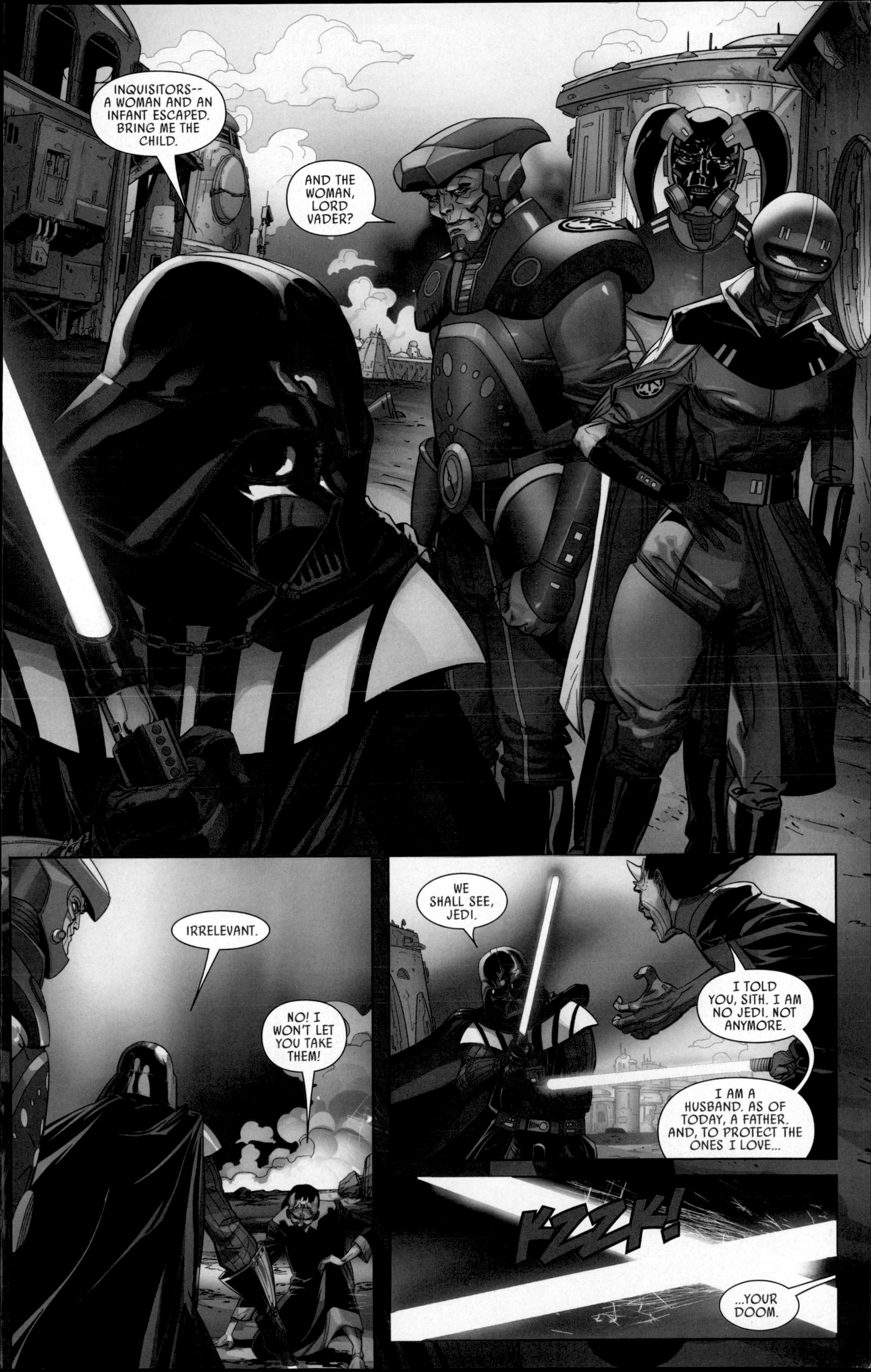
INQUISITORS-- A WOMAN AND AN INFANT ESCAPED. BRING ME THE CHILD.
AND THE WOMAN, LORD VADER?
IRRELEVANT.
NO! I WON'T LET YOU TAKE THEM!
WE SHALL SEE, JEDI.
I TOLD YOU, SITH. I AM NO JEDI. NOT ANYMORE.
I AM A HUSBAND. AS OF TODAY, A FATHER. AND, TO PROTECT THE ONES I LOVE...
KZZK!
...YOUR DOOM.

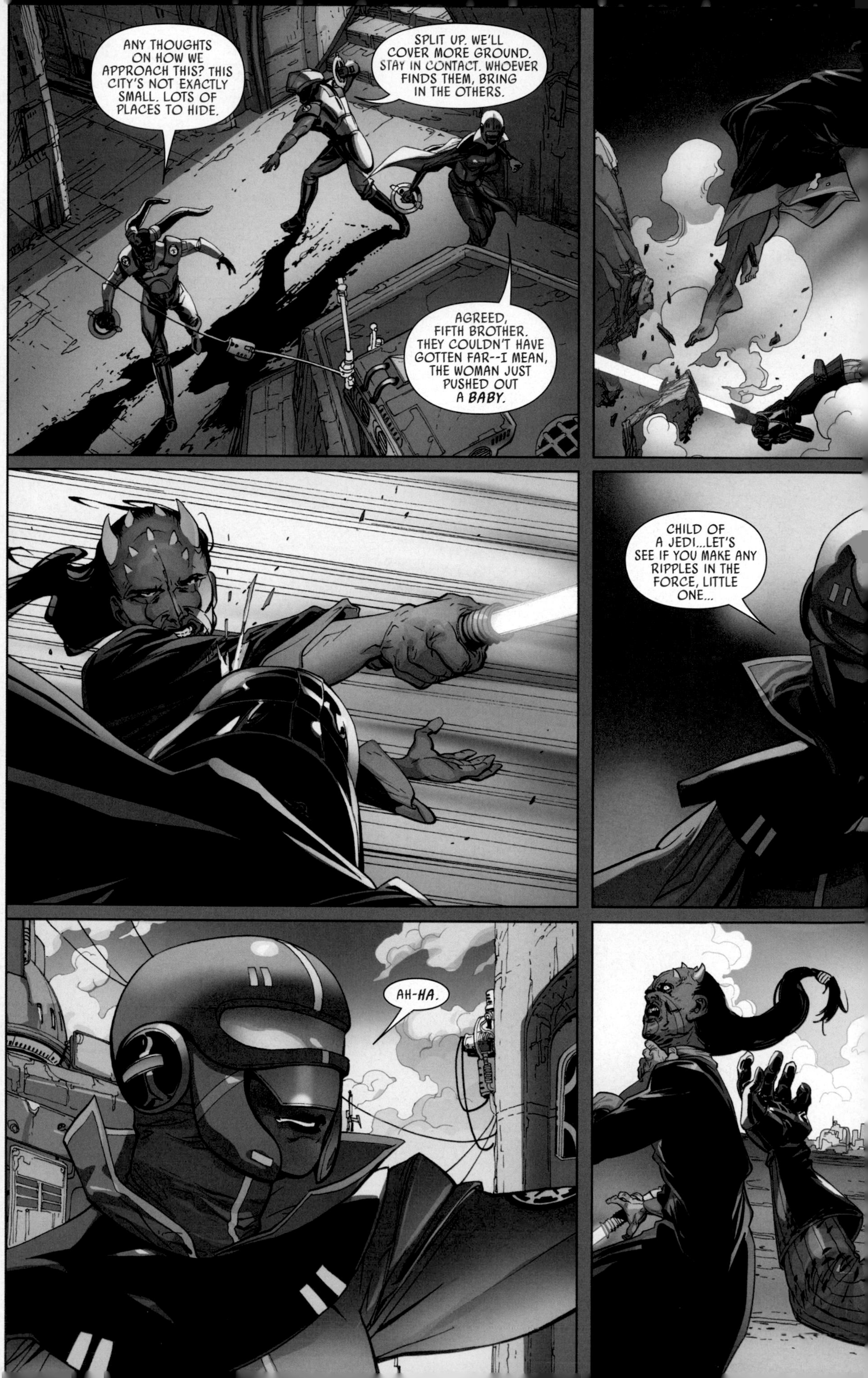
ANY THOUGHTS ON HOW WE APPROACH THIS? THIS CITY'S NOT EXACTLY SMALL. LOTS OF PLACES TO HIDE.
SPLIT UP. WE'LL COVER MORE GROUND. STAY IN CONTACT. WHOEVER FINDS THEM, BRING IN THE OTHERS.
AGREED, FIFTH BROTHER. THEY COULDN'T HAVE GOTTEN FAR--I MEAN, THE WOMAN JUST PUSHED OUT A BABY.
CHILD OF A JEDI...LET'S SEE IF YOU MAKE ANY RIPPLES IN THE FORCE, LITTLE ONE...
AH-HA.

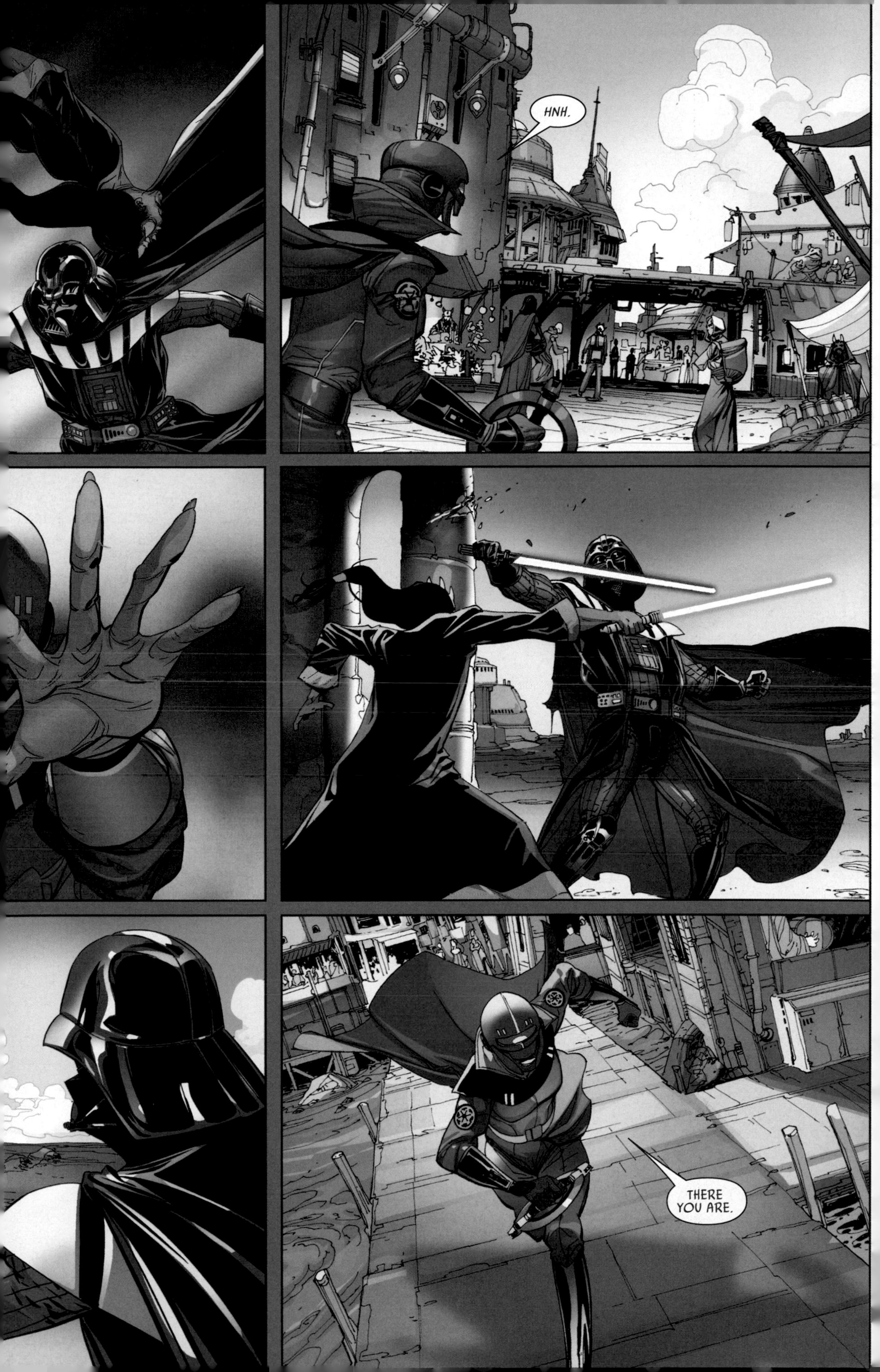
HNH.
THERE YOU ARE.

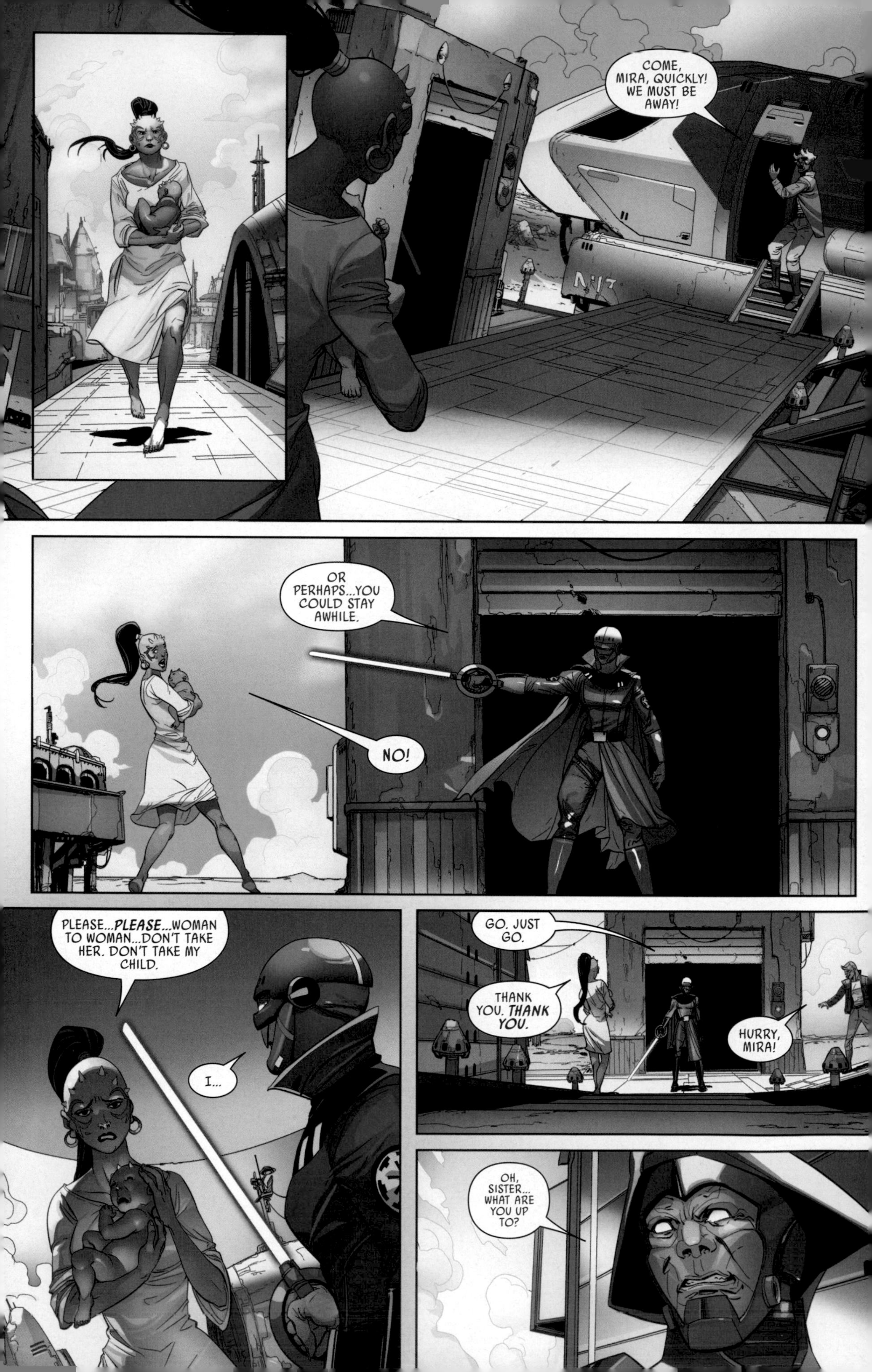
COME, MIRA, QUICKLY! WE MUST BE AWAY!
OR PERHAPS...YOU COULD STAY AWHILE.
NO!
PLEASE...PLEASE...WOMAN TO WOMAN...DON'T TAKE HER. DON'T TAKE MY CHILD.
I...
GO. JUST GO.
THANK YOU. THANK YOU.
HURRY, MIRA!
OH, SISTER... WHAT ARE YOU UP TO?

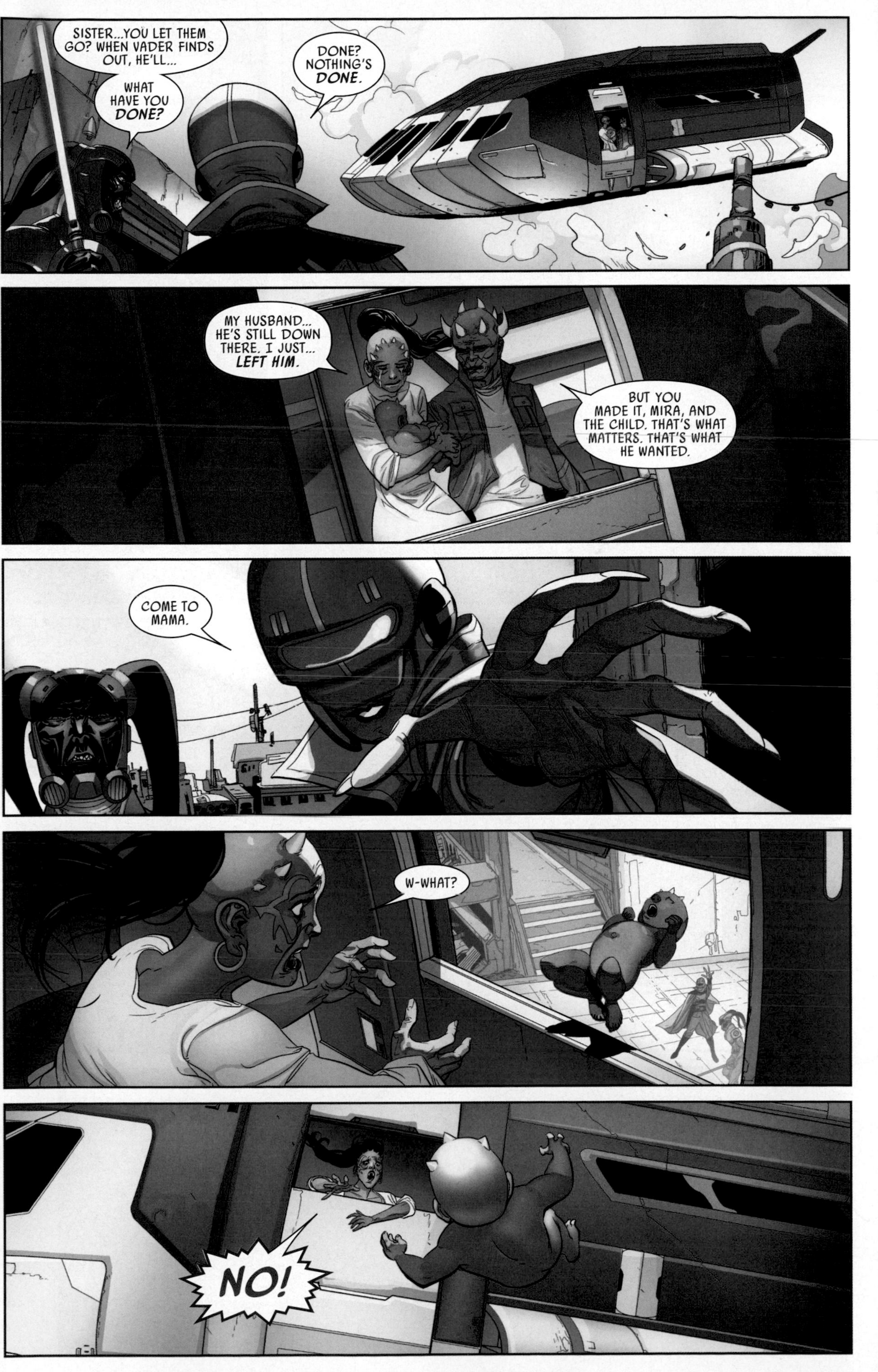
SISTER...YOU LET THEM GO? WHEN VADER FINDS OUT, HE'LL...
WHAT HAVE YOU *DONE?*
DONE? NOTHING'S *DONE.*
MY HUSBAND... HE'S STILL DOWN THERE. I JUST... *LEFT HIM.*
BUT YOU MADE IT, MIRA, AND THE CHILD. THAT'S WHAT MATTERS. THAT'S WHAT HE WANTED.
COME TO MAMA.
W-WHAT?
NO!

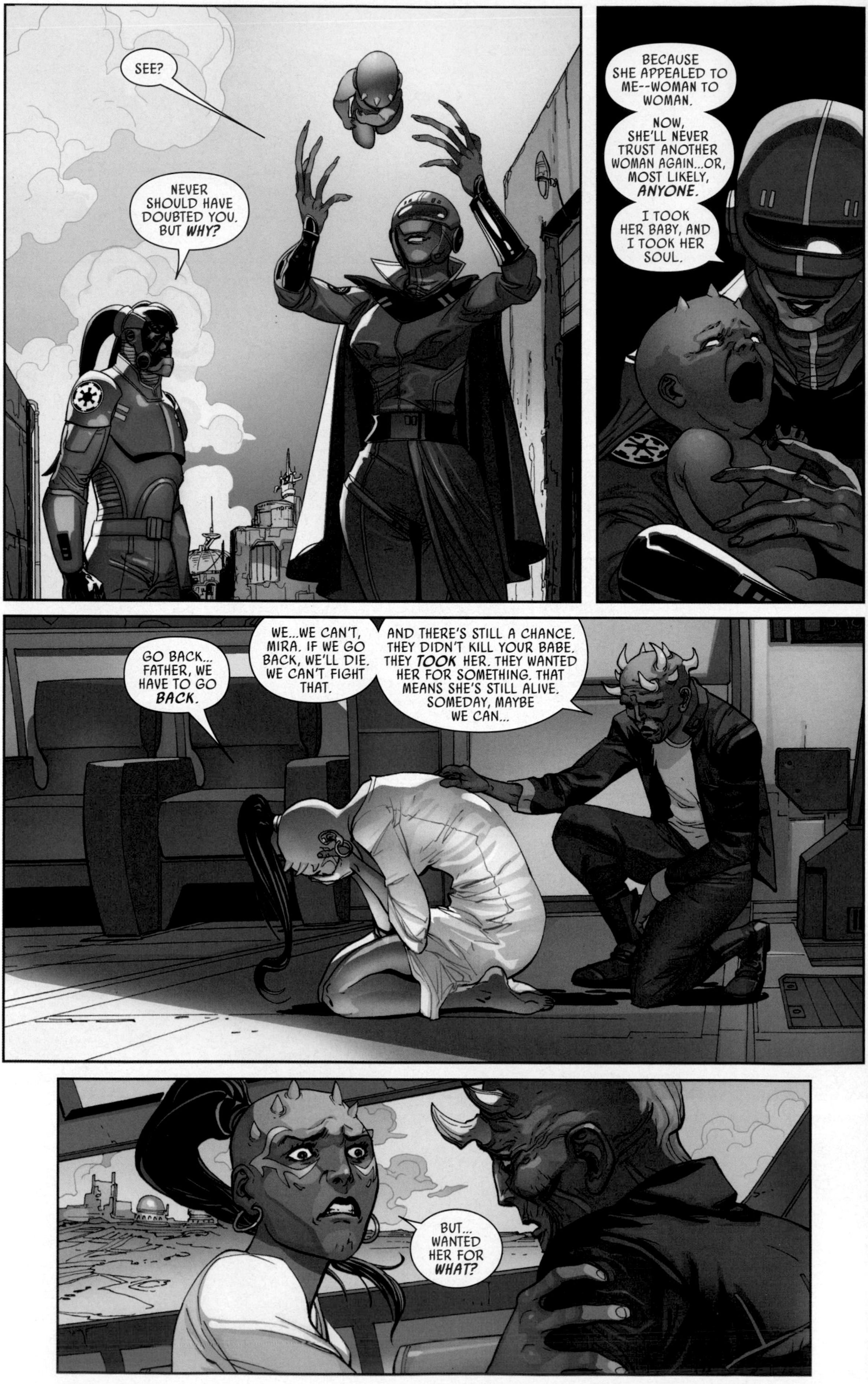
SEE?
NEVER SHOULD HAVE DOUBTED YOU. BUT WHY?
BECAUSE SHE APPEALED TO ME--WOMAN TO WOMAN.
NOW, SHE'LL NEVER TRUST ANOTHER WOMAN AGAIN...OR, MOST LIKELY, ANYONE.
I TOOK HER BABY, AND I TOOK HER SOUL.
GO BACK... FATHER, WE HAVE TO GO BACK.
WE...WE CAN'T, MIRA. IF WE GO BACK, WE'LL DIE. WE CAN'T FIGHT THAT.
AND THERE'S STILL A CHANCE. THEY DIDN'T KILL YOUR BABE. THEY TOOK HER. THEY WANTED HER FOR SOMETHING. THAT MEANS SHE'S STILL ALIVE. SOMEDAY, MAYBE WE CAN...
BUT... WANTED HER FOR WHAT?

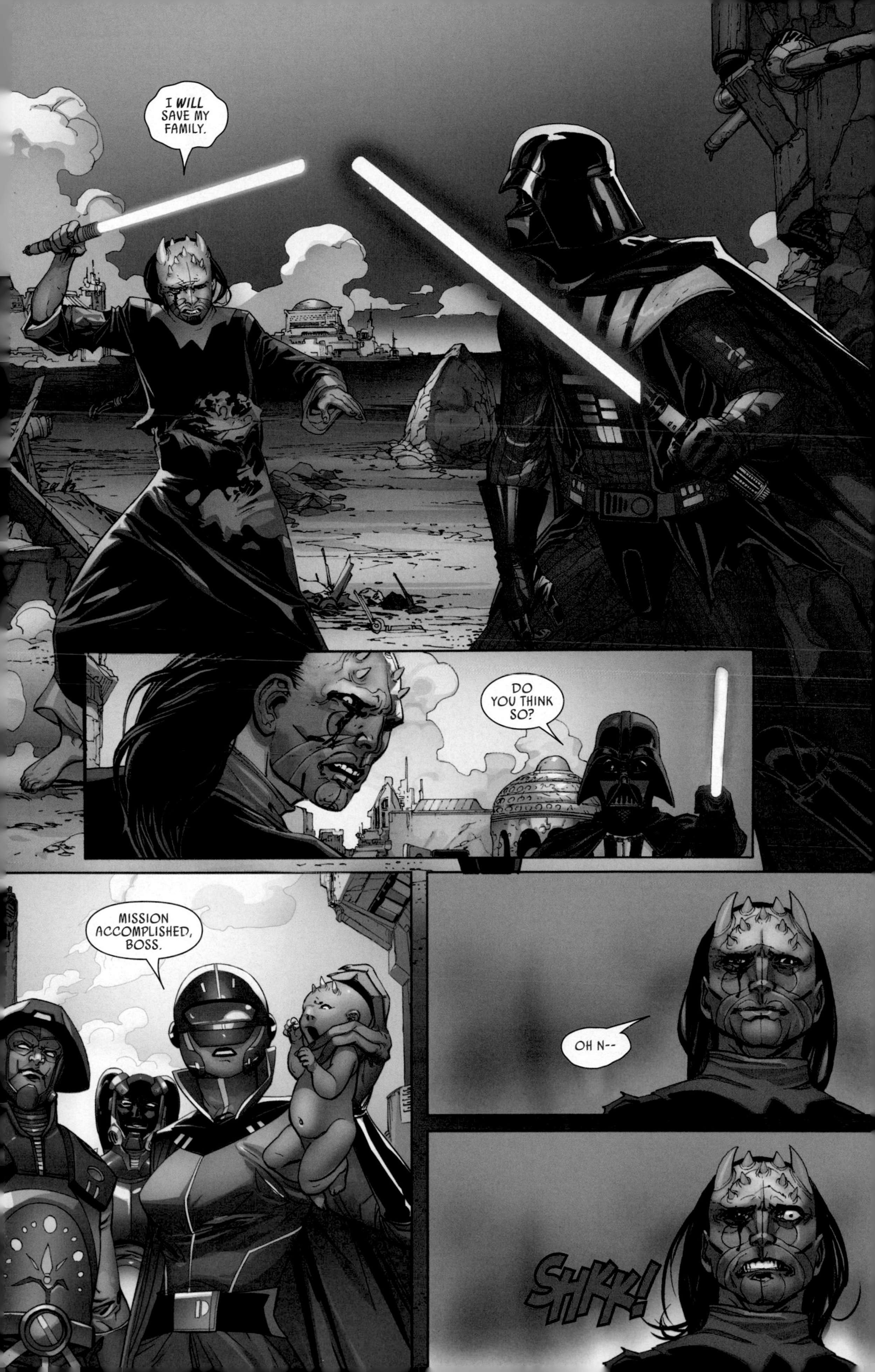
I WILL SAVE MY FAMILY.
DO YOU THINK SO?
MISSION ACCOMPLISHED, BOSS.
OH N--
SHKK!

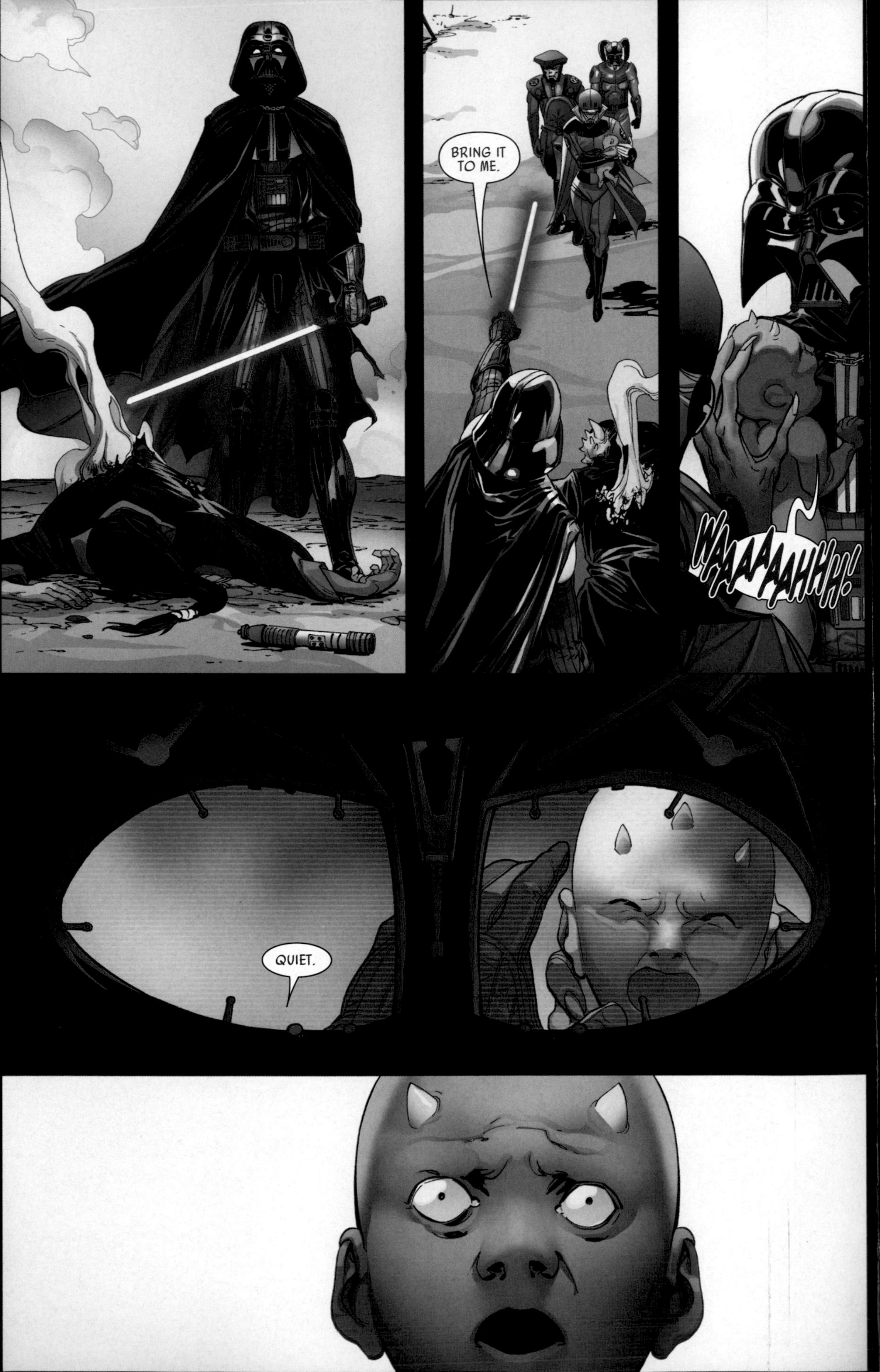
BRING IT TO ME.
WAAAAAAHHH!
QUIET.

Coruscant.

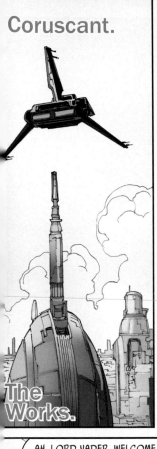

The
Works.

AH, LORD VADER. WELCOME BACK. IT SEEMS YOUR MISSION WAS SUCCESSFUL ON AT LEAST ONE LEVEL.

YOU BROUGHT A NEW CHILD. THE SEEKERS THEMSELVES COULD HAVE DONE NO BETTER.

I WAS SUCCESSFUL ON *EVERY* LEVEL, GRAND INQUISITOR.

EETH KOTH IS DEAD. YOUR INQUISITORS PERFORMED THEIR ROLES WELL.

WHAT IS THE NEXT TARGET?

LOOK AT THE PRETTY THING.

LOOK AT THE PRETTY, PRETTY THING.

THIS WAY, LORD VADER. WE SHOULD TALK.

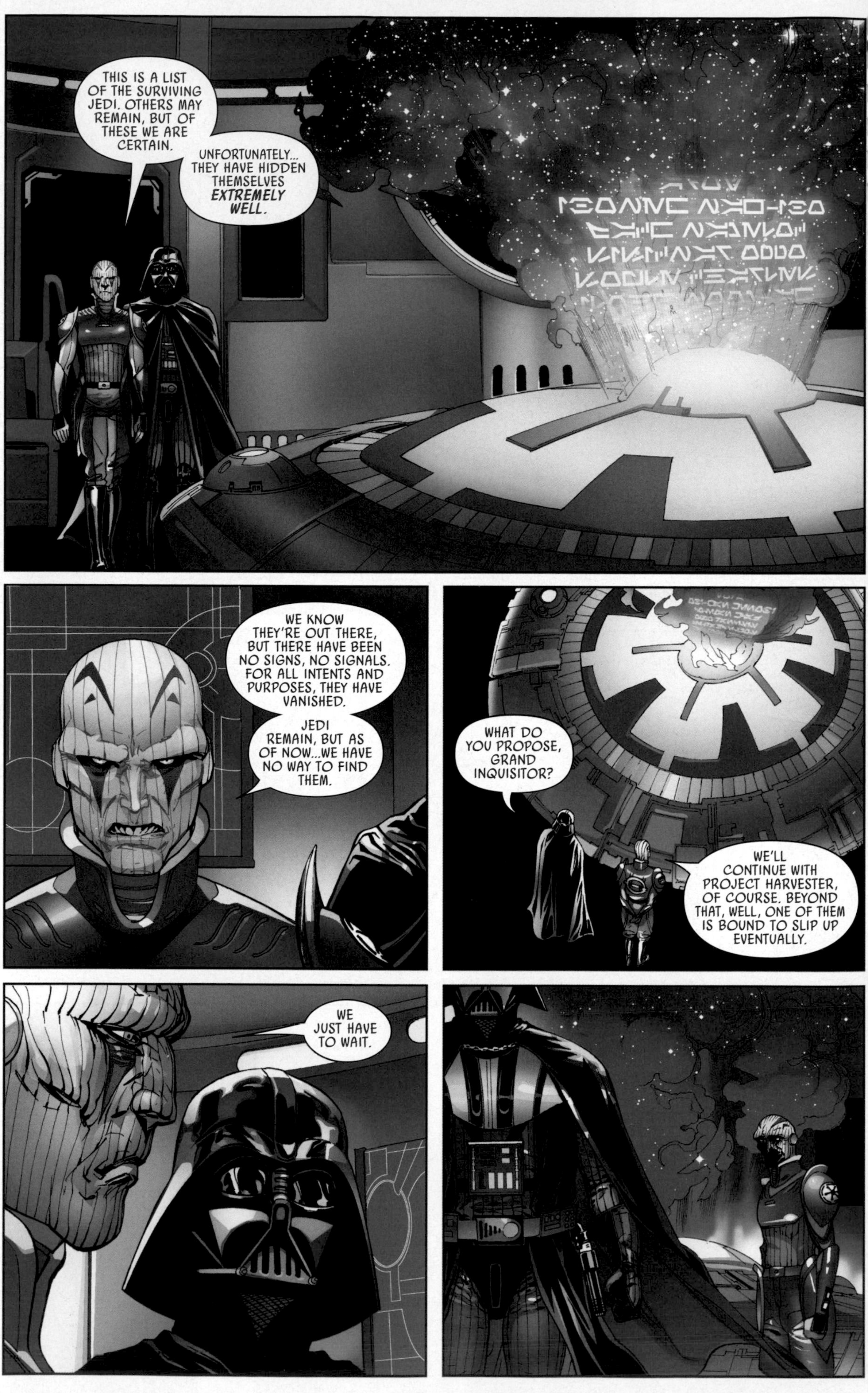
THIS IS A LIST OF THE SURVIVING JEDI. OTHERS MAY REMAIN, BUT OF THESE WE ARE CERTAIN.
UNFORTUNATELY... THEY HAVE HIDDEN THEMSELVES *EXTREMELY WELL*.
WE KNOW THEY'RE OUT THERE, BUT THERE HAVE BEEN NO SIGNS, NO SIGNALS. FOR ALL INTENTS AND PURPOSES, THEY HAVE VANISHED.
JEDI REMAIN, BUT AS OF NOW...WE HAVE NO WAY TO FIND THEM.
WHAT DO YOU PROPOSE, GRAND INQUISITOR?
WE'LL CONTINUE WITH PROJECT HARVESTER, OF COURSE. BEYOND THAT, WELL, ONE OF THEM IS BOUND TO SLIP UP EVENTUALLY.
WE JUST HAVE TO WAIT.

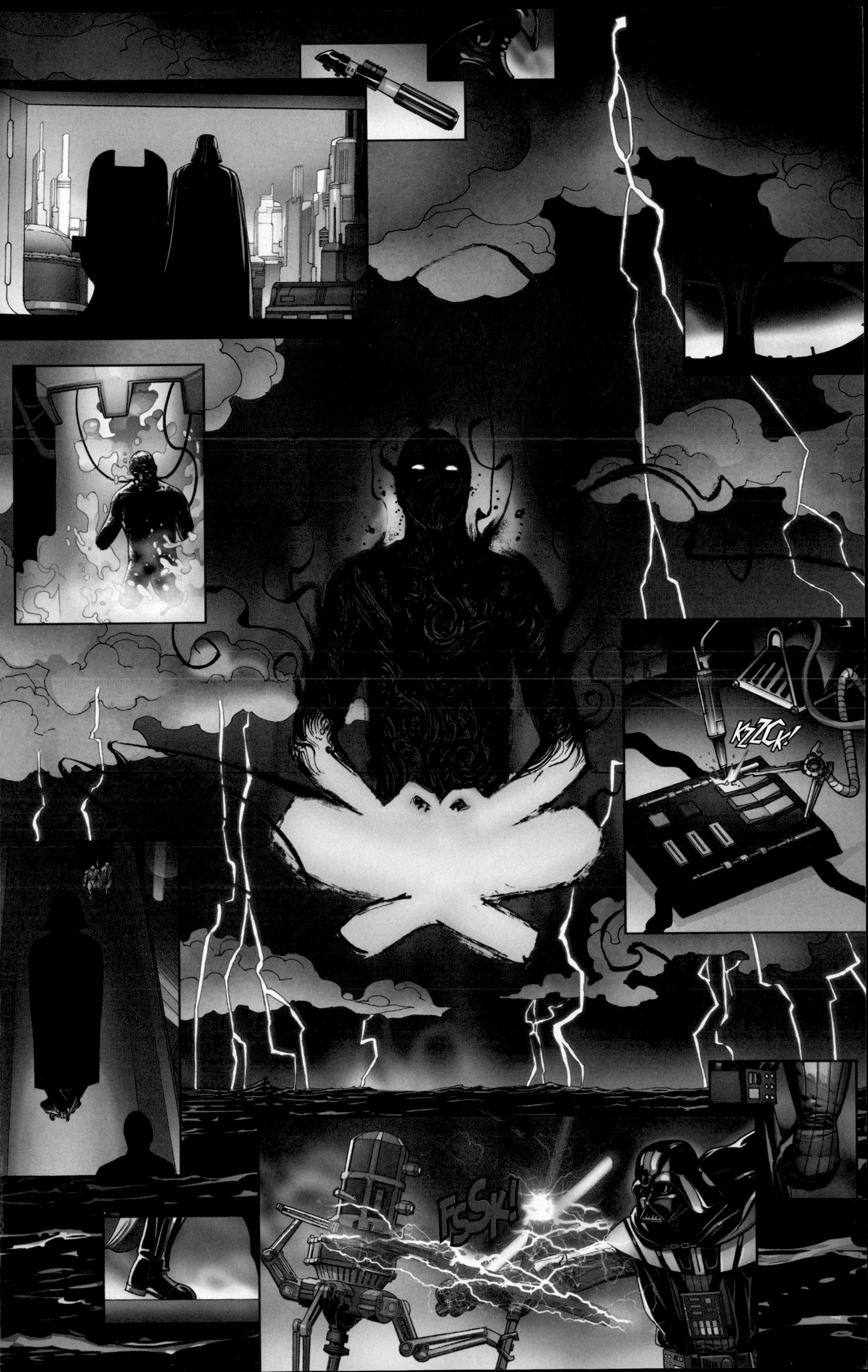
KZZCK!
FSSK!

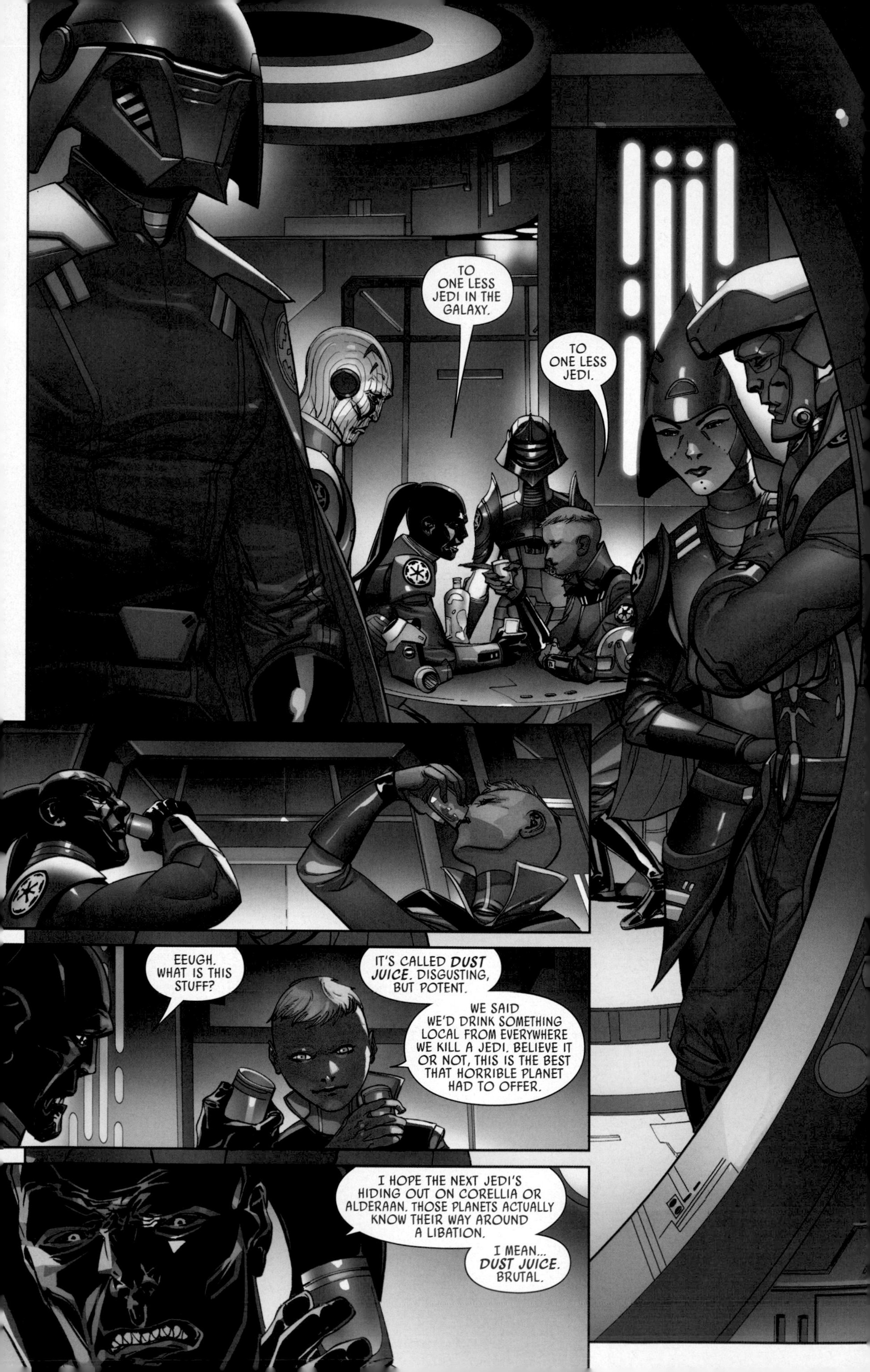

TO ONE LESS JEDI IN THE GALAXY.
TO ONE LESS JEDI.
EEUGH. WHAT IS THIS STUFF?
IT'S CALLED DUST JUICE. DISGUSTING, BUT POTENT.
WE SAID WE'D DRINK SOMETHING LOCAL FROM EVERYWHERE WE KILL A JEDI. BELIEVE IT OR NOT, THIS IS THE BEST THAT HORRIBLE PLANET HAD TO OFFER.
I HOPE THE NEXT JEDI'S HIDING OUT ON CORELLIA OR ALDERAAN. THOSE PLANETS ACTUALLY KNOW THEIR WAY AROUND A LIBATION.
I MEAN... DUST JUICE. BRUTAL.

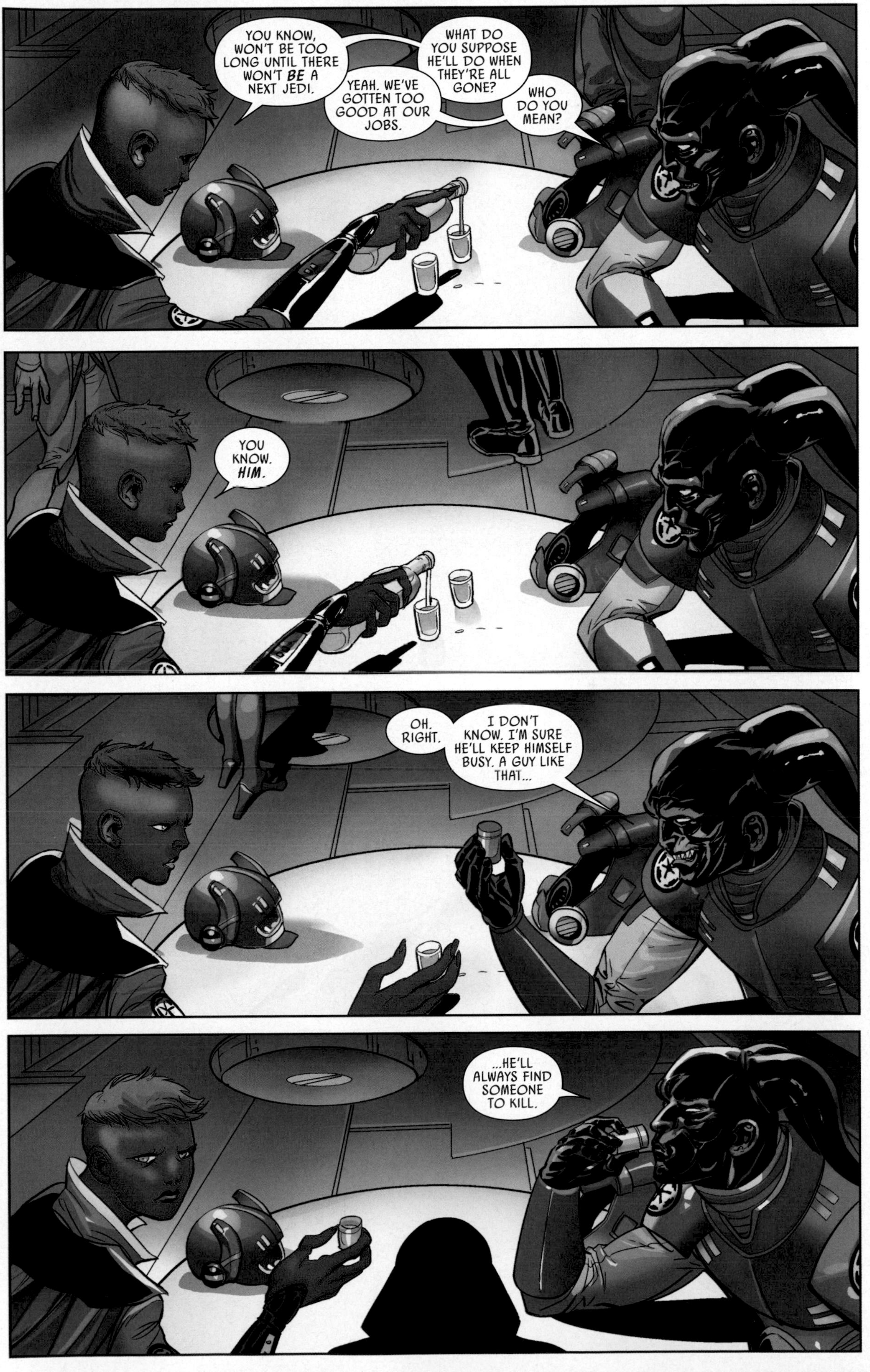

YOU KNOW, WON'T BE TOO LONG UNTIL THERE WON'T **BE** A NEXT JEDI.
YEAH. WE'VE GOTTEN TOO GOOD AT OUR JOBS.
WHAT DO YOU SUPPOSE HE'LL DO WHEN THEY'RE ALL GONE?
WHO DO YOU MEAN?
YOU KNOW. ***HIM.***
OH. RIGHT.
I DON'T KNOW. I'M SURE HE'LL KEEP HIMSELF BUSY. A GUY LIKE THAT...
...HE'LL ALWAYS FIND SOMEONE TO KILL.

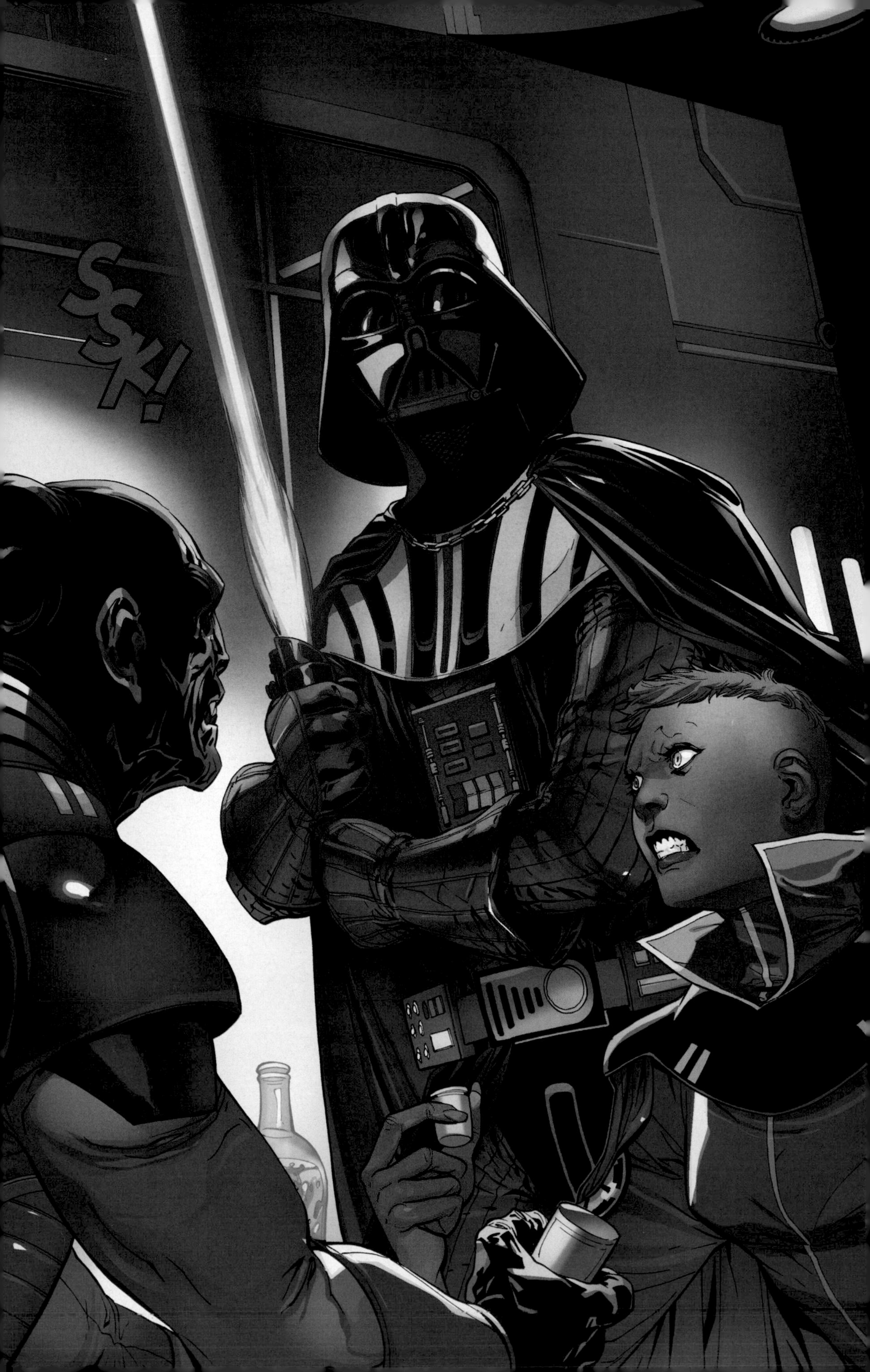
SSSK!

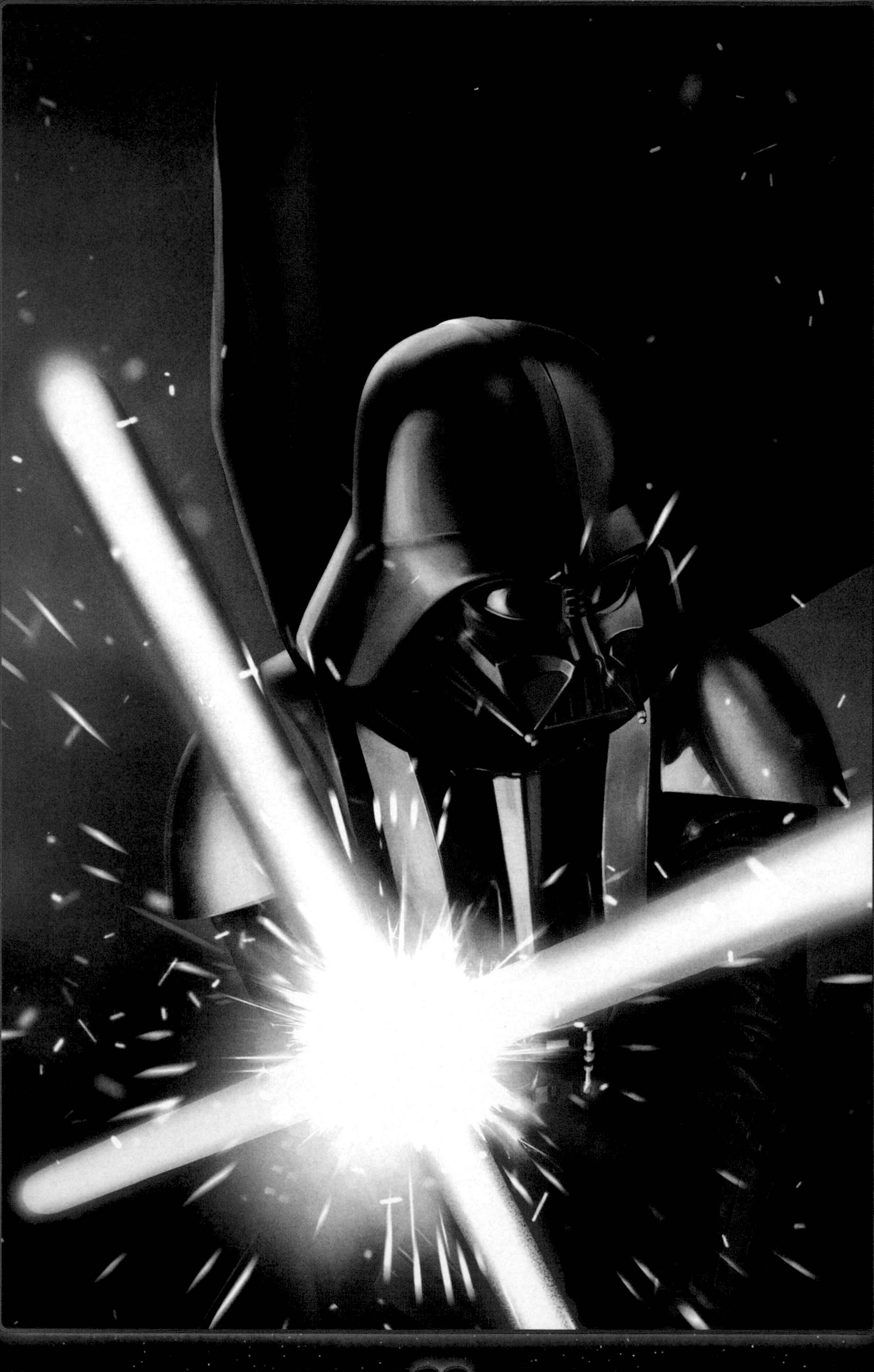

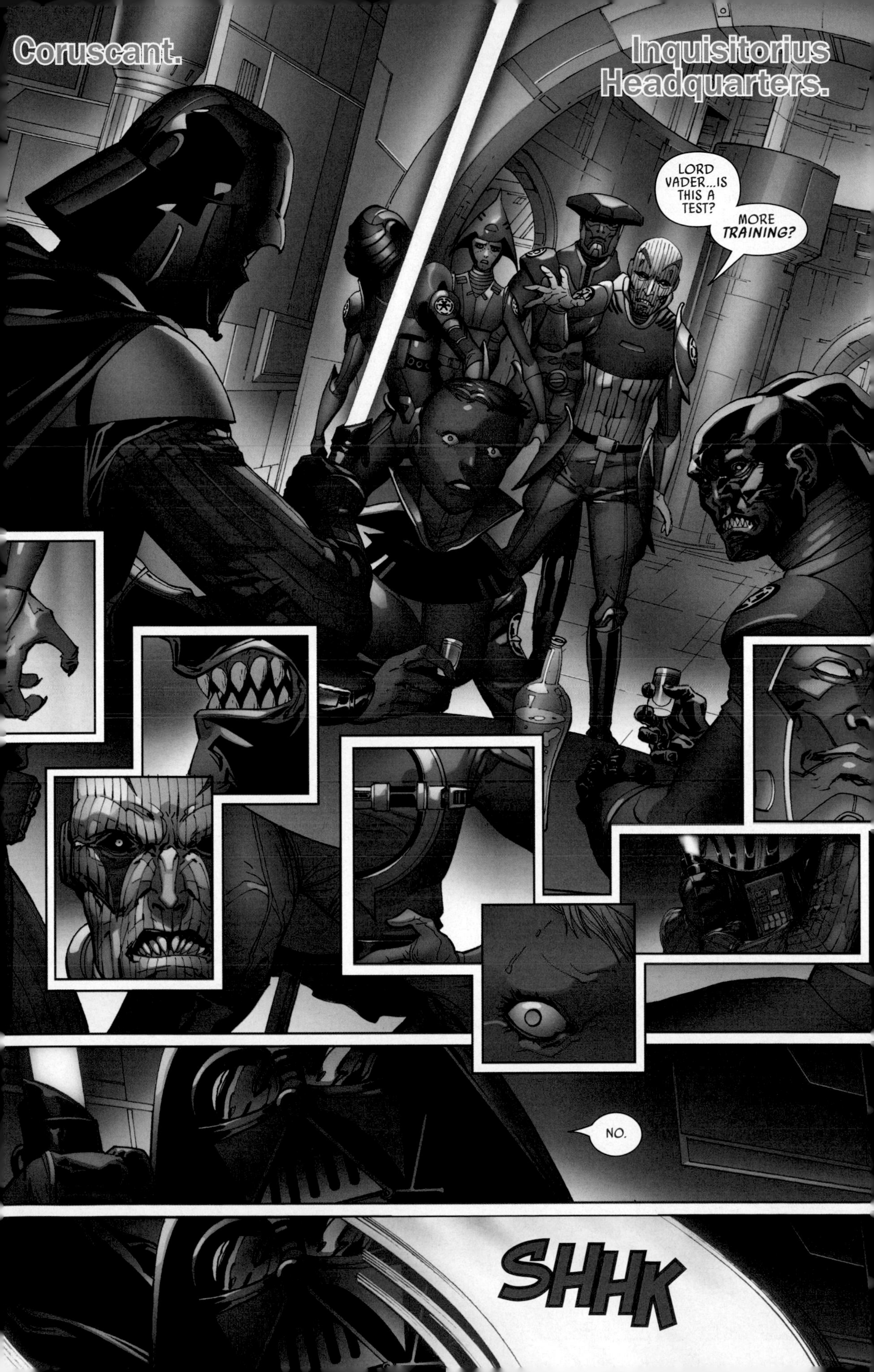
Coruscant.
Inquisitorius Headquarters.
LORD VADER...IS THIS A TEST?
MORE TRAINING?
NO.
SHHK

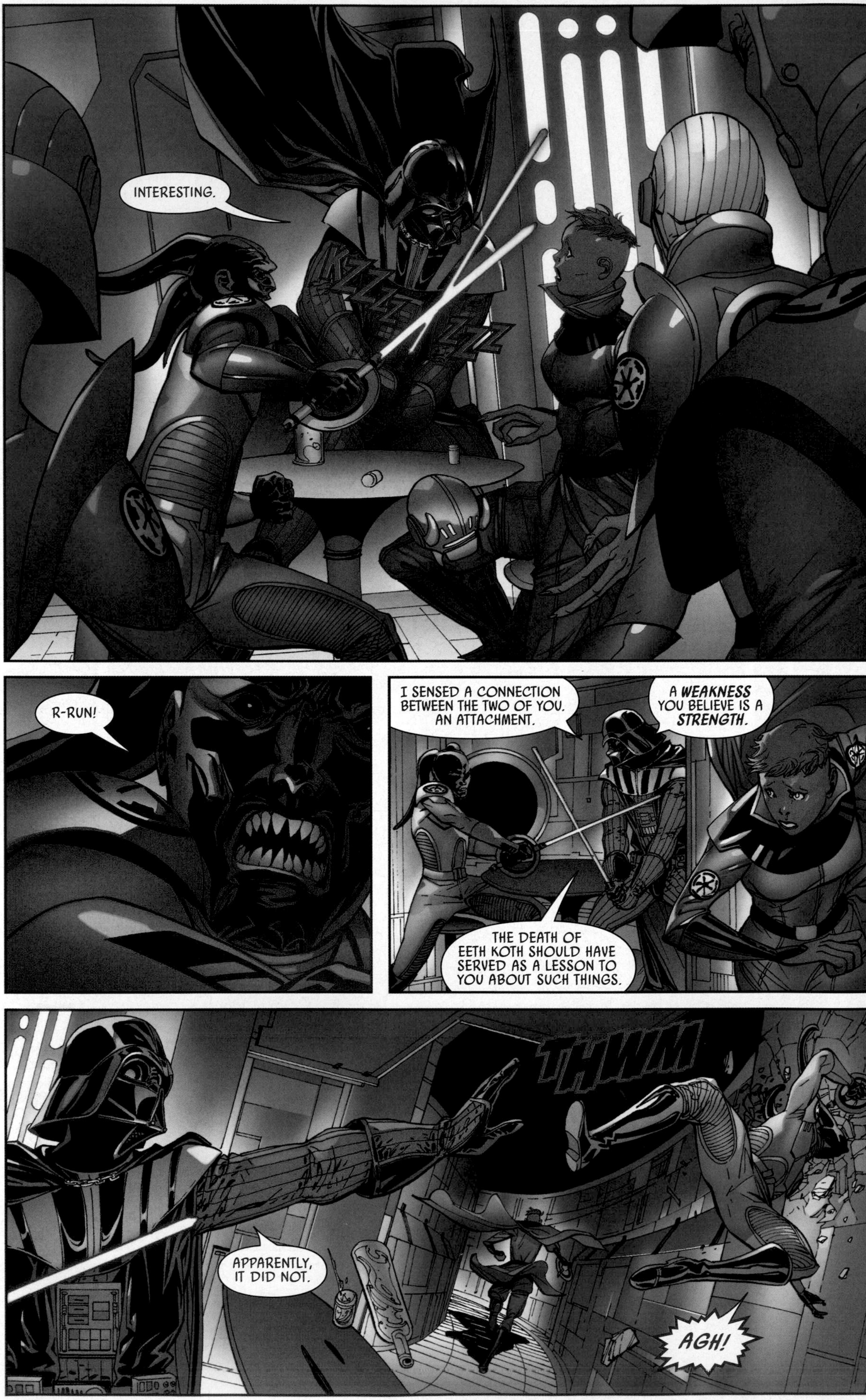
INTERESTING.
KZZZZZZZZZ
R-RUN!
I SENSED A CONNECTION BETWEEN THE TWO OF YOU. AN ATTACHMENT.
A WEAKNESS YOU BELIEVE IS A STRENGTH.
THE DEATH OF EETH KOTH SHOULD HAVE SERVED AS A LESSON TO YOU ABOUT SUCH THINGS.
THWM
APPARENTLY, IT DID NOT.
AGH!

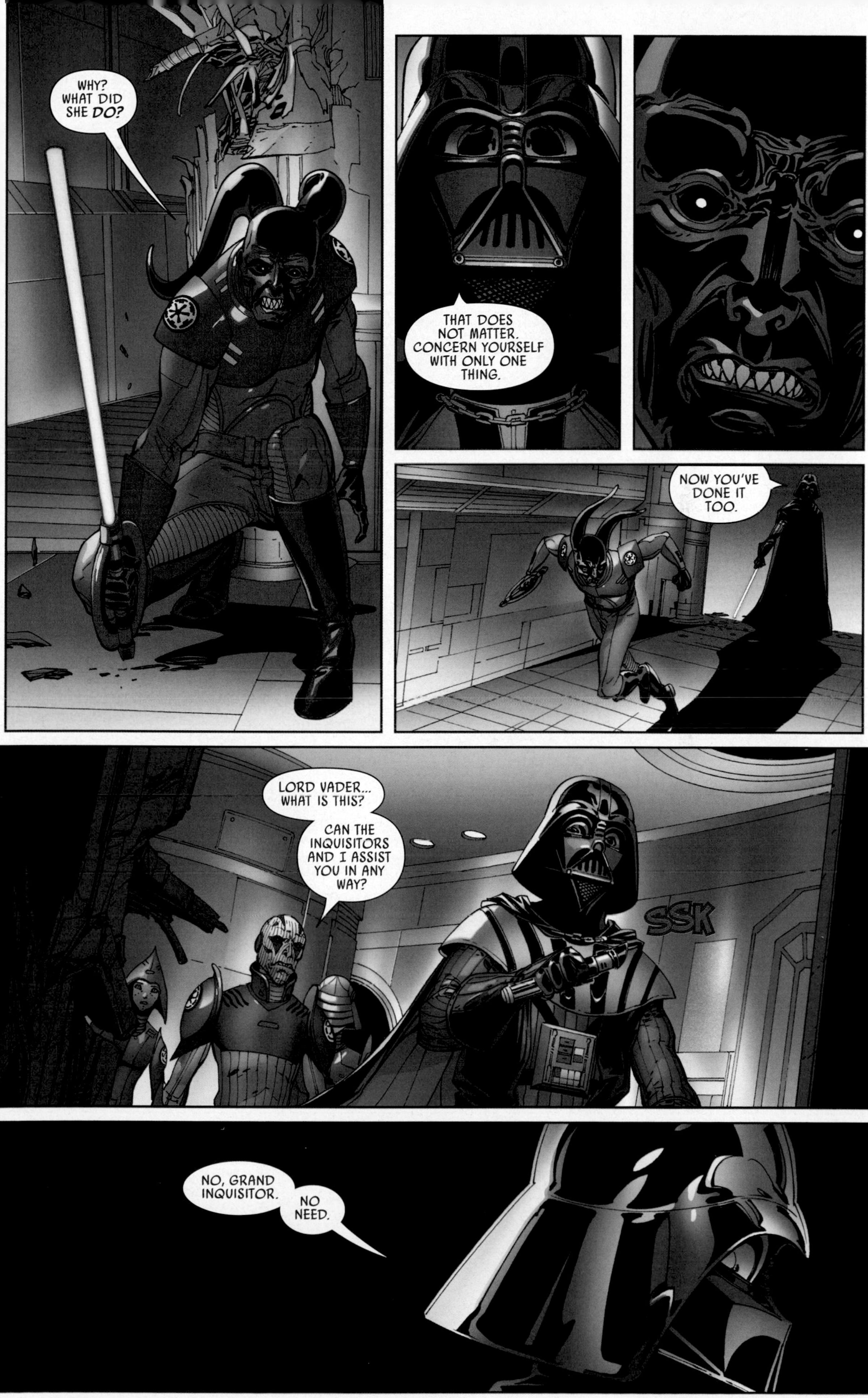
WHY? WHAT DID SHE *DO?*
THAT DOES NOT MATTER. CONCERN YOURSELF WITH ONLY ONE THING.
NOW YOU'VE DONE IT TOO.
LORD VADER... WHAT IS THIS?
CAN THE INQUISITORS AND I ASSIST YOU IN ANY WAY?
SSK
NO, GRAND INQUISITOR.
NO NEED.

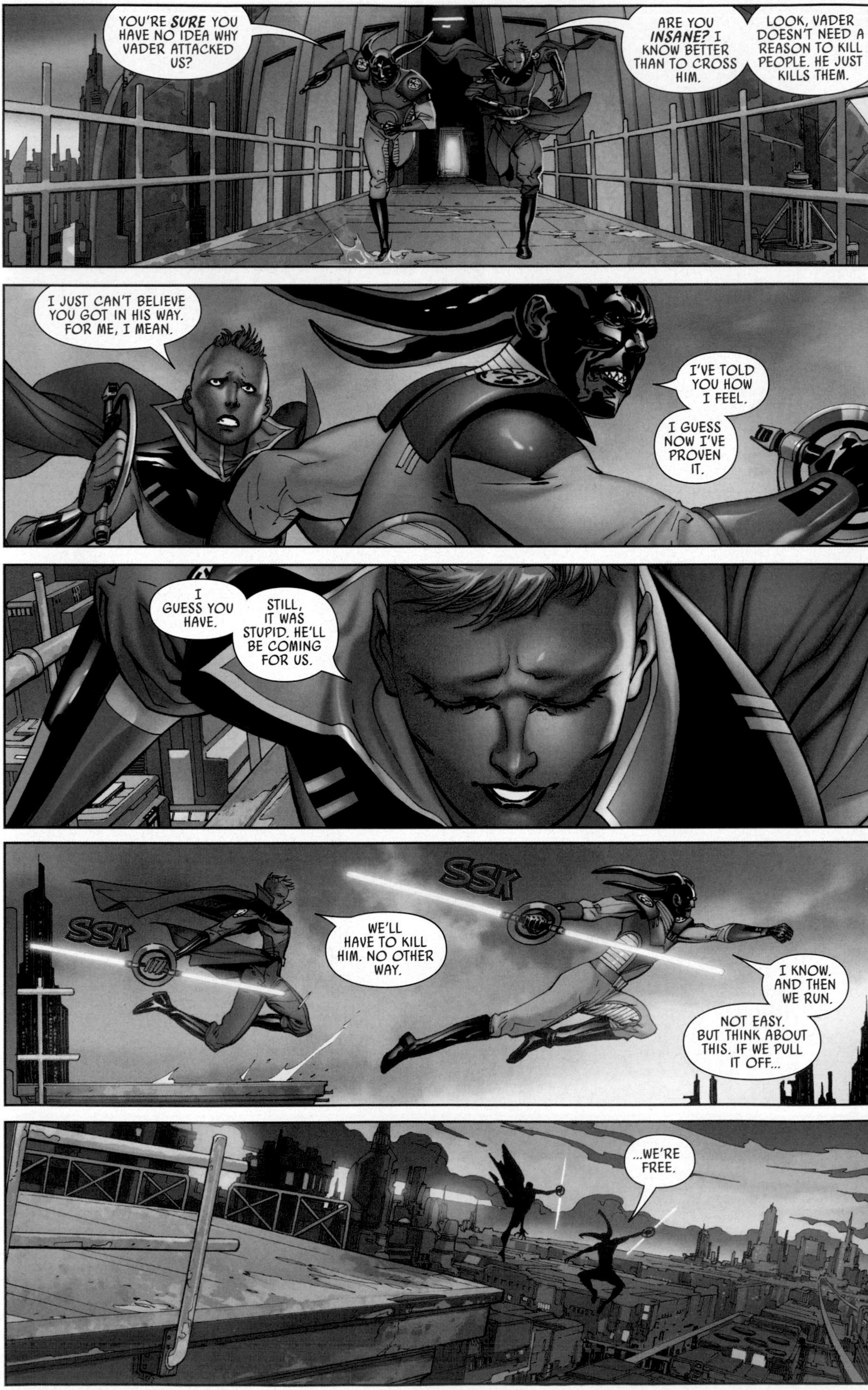
YOU'RE **SURE** YOU HAVE NO IDEA WHY VADER ATTACKED US?
ARE YOU **INSANE?** I KNOW BETTER THAN TO CROSS HIM.
LOOK, VADER DOESN'T NEED A REASON TO KILL PEOPLE. HE JUST KILLS THEM.
I JUST CAN'T BELIEVE YOU GOT IN HIS WAY. FOR ME, I MEAN.
I'VE TOLD YOU HOW I FEEL.
I GUESS NOW I'VE PROVEN IT.
I GUESS YOU HAVE.
STILL, IT WAS STUPID. HE'LL BE COMING FOR US.
SSK
SSK
WE'LL HAVE TO KILL HIM. NO OTHER WAY.
I KNOW. AND THEN WE RUN.
NOT EASY. BUT THINK ABOUT THIS. IF WE PULL IT OFF...
...WE'RE FREE.

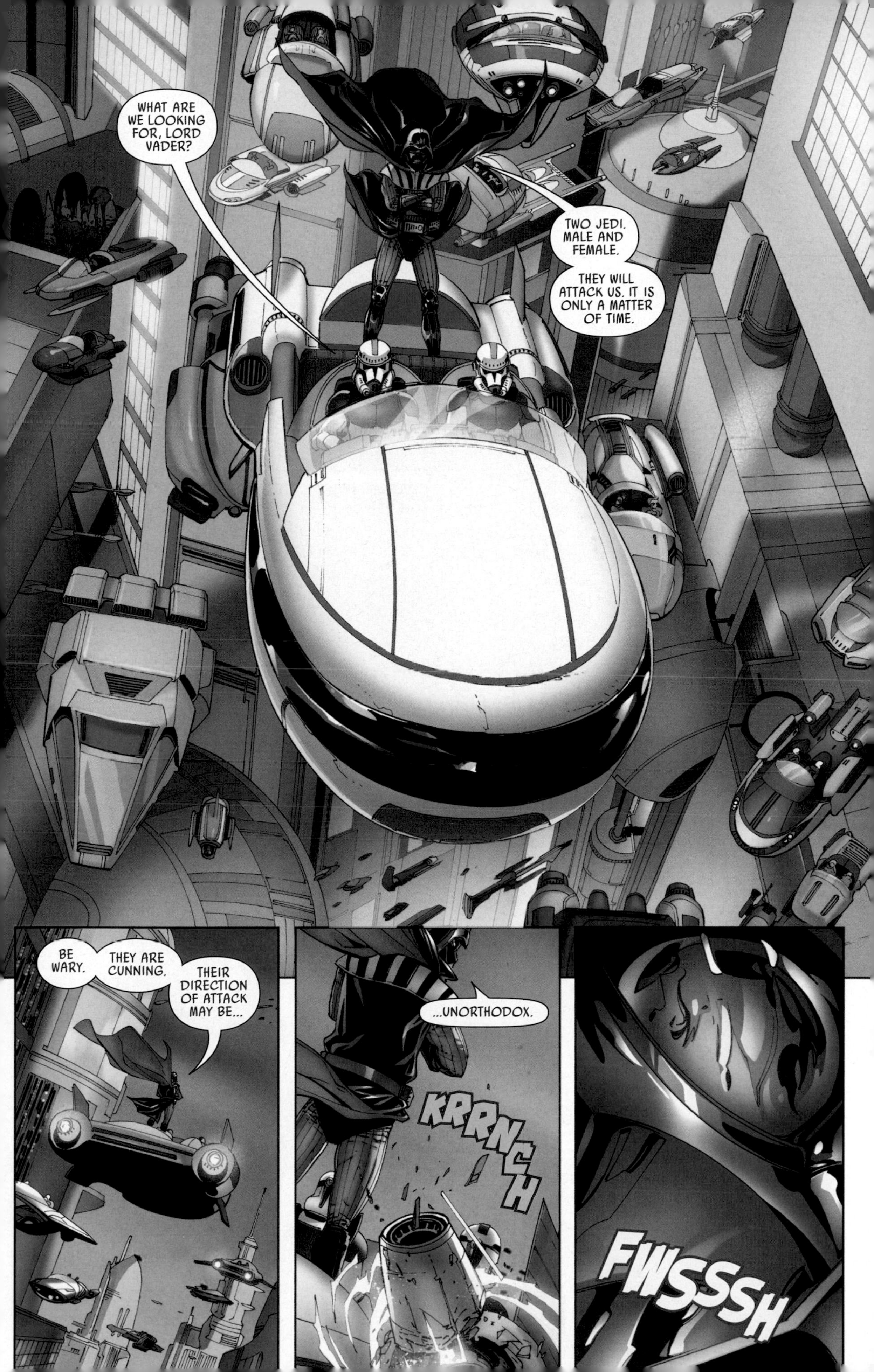
WHAT ARE WE LOOKING FOR, LORD VADER?
TWO JEDI. MALE AND FEMALE.
THEY WILL ATTACK US. IT IS ONLY A MATTER OF TIME.
BE WARY.
THEY ARE CUNNING.
THEIR DIRECTION OF ATTACK MAY BE...
...UNORTHODOX.
KRRNCH
FWSSSH

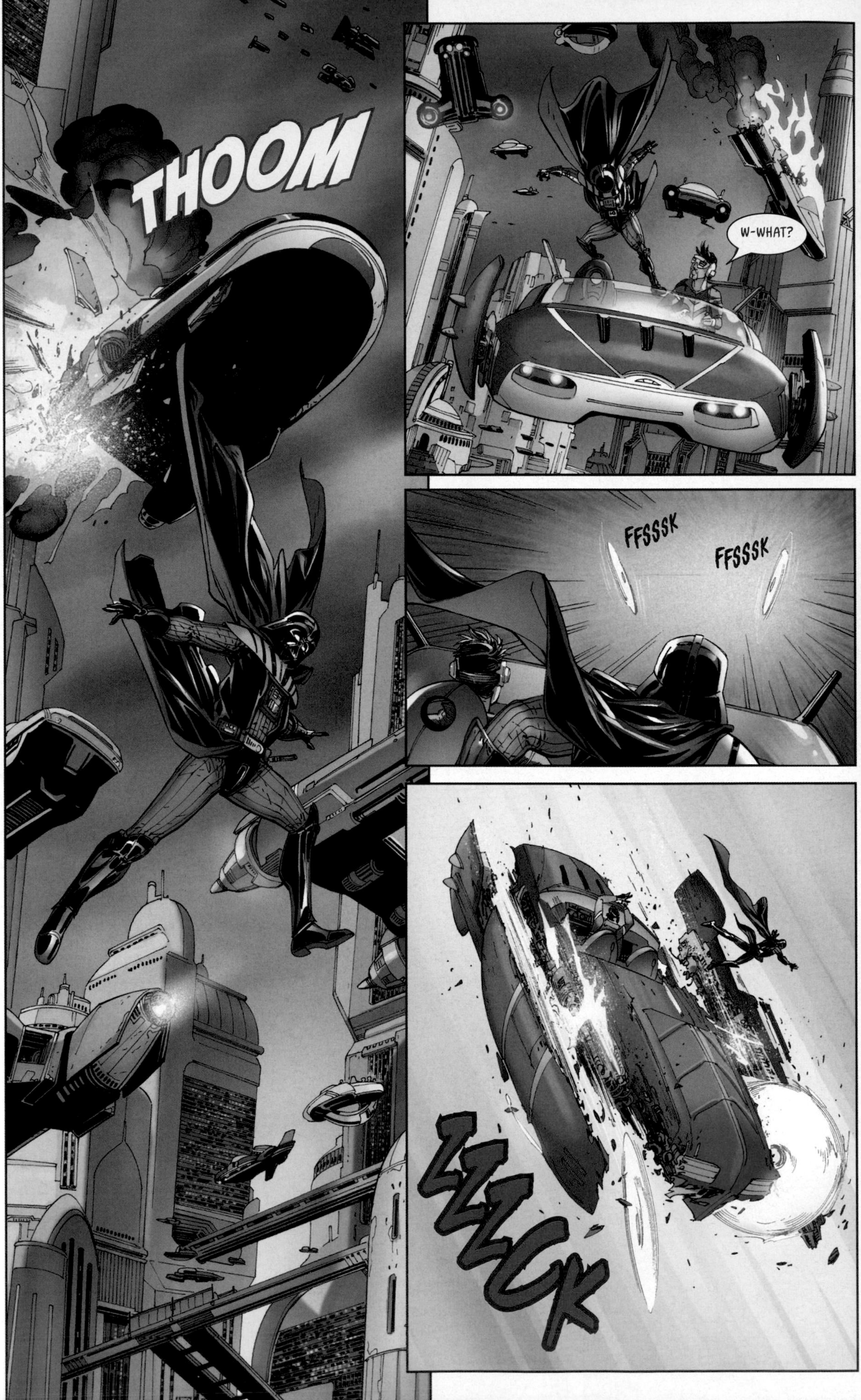
THOOM
W-WHAT?
FFSSSK
FFSSSK
ZZZCK

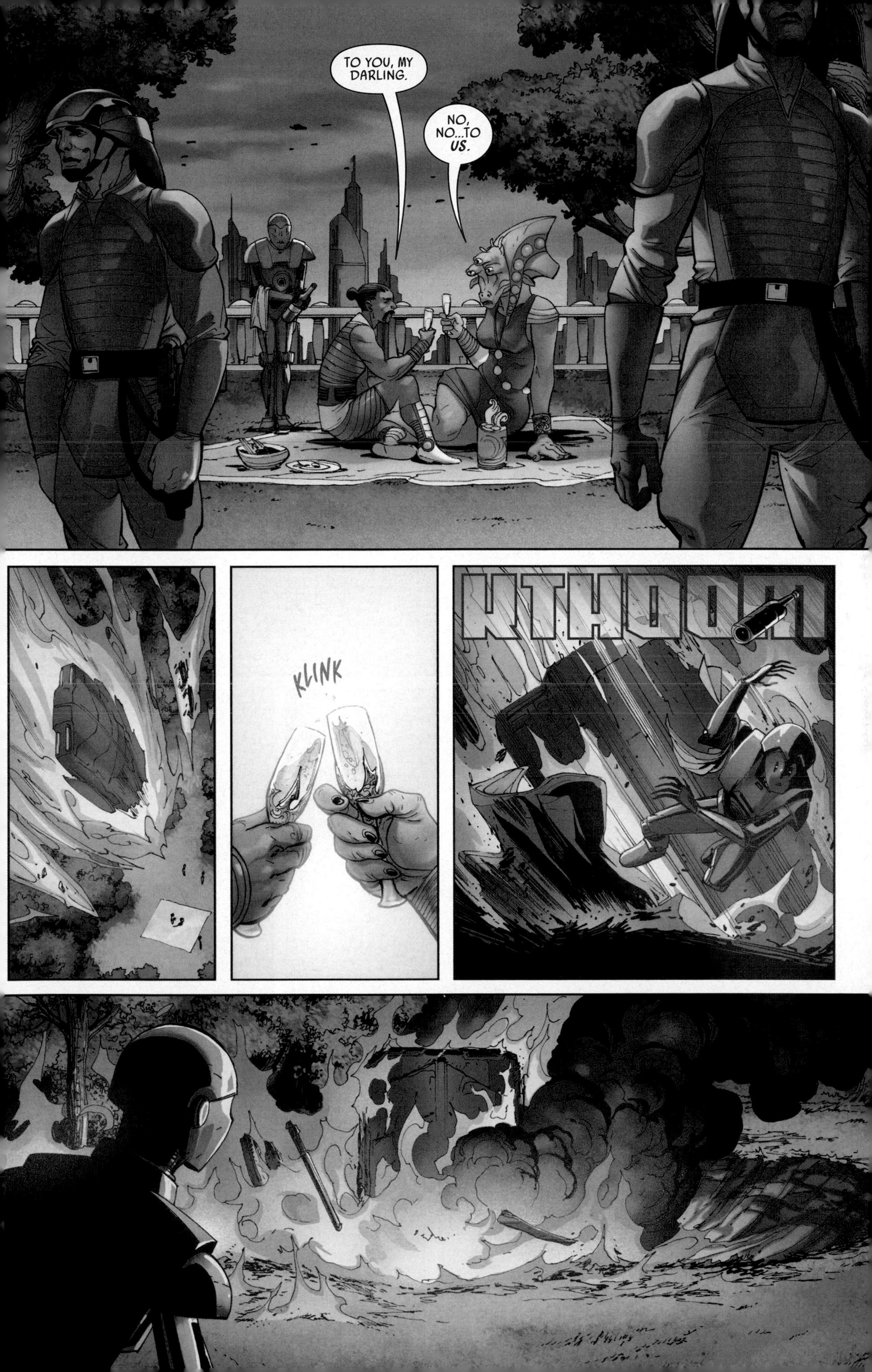
TO YOU, MY DARLING.
NO, NO...TO US.
KLINK
KTHOOM

FWOOSH

NOW!

HE...HE THREW IT BACK.

MOVE!

SSSZK

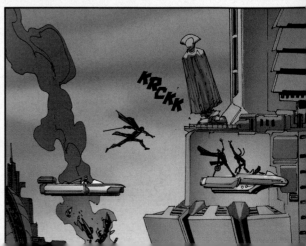

KRCKK

VADER'S STILL COMING!

JUST...FIGHT THE FEAR. FOCUS-- WE'LL DO THIS *TOGETHER*.

THAT SPEEDER... RIGHT AT HIM. FAST AS WE CAN.

READY...

HNH.

KRNCH

THOOM

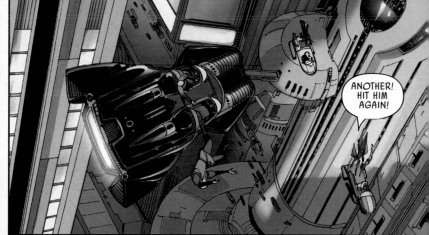

ANOTHER! HIT HIM AGAIN!

NNGH!

WHM

THD

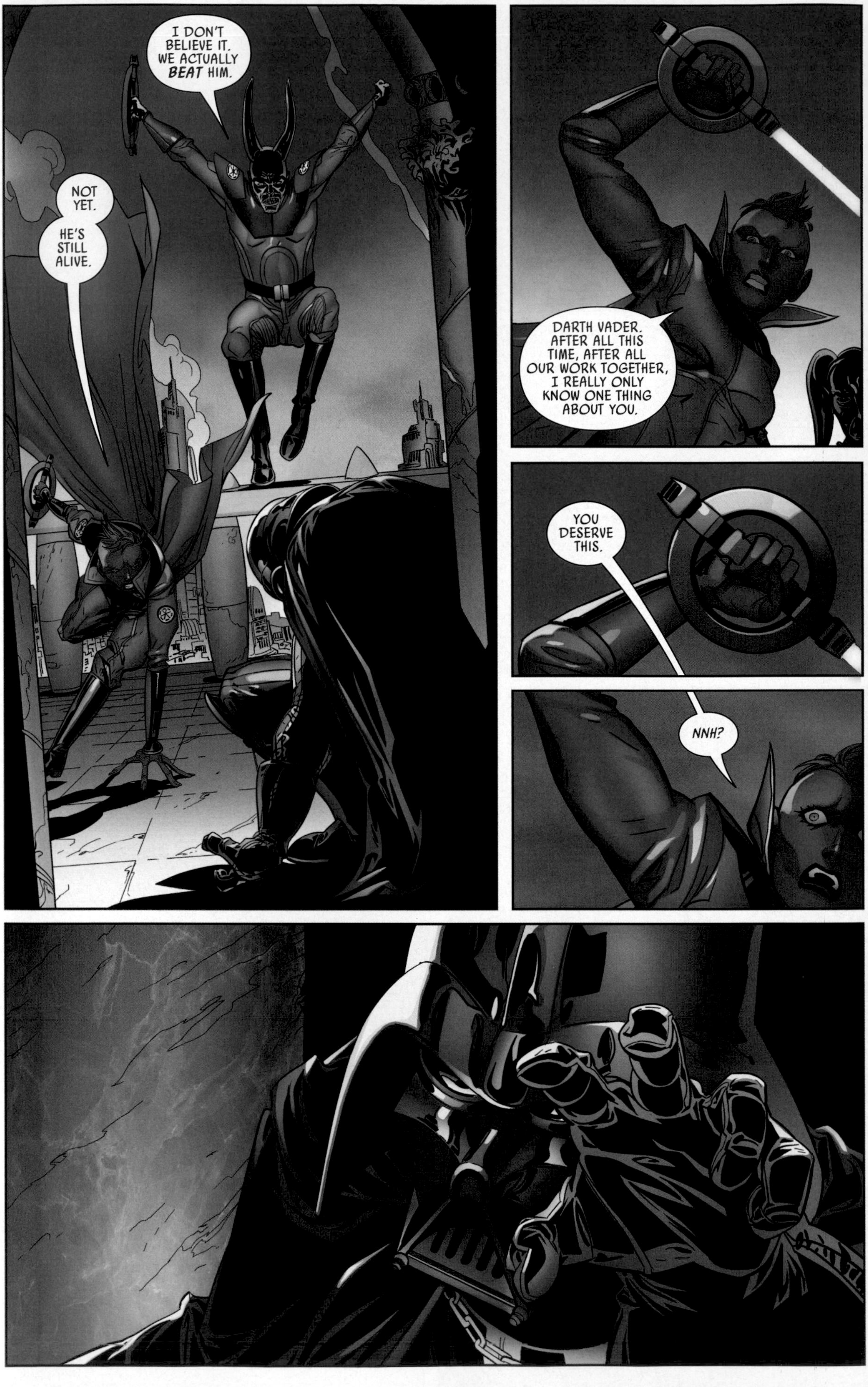
I DON'T BELIEVE IT. WE ACTUALLY BEAT HIM.
NOT YET.
HE'S STILL ALIVE.
DARTH VADER. AFTER ALL THIS TIME, AFTER ALL OUR WORK TOGETHER, I REALLY ONLY KNOW ONE THING ABOUT YOU.
YOU DESERVE THIS.
NNH?

NO... NO!

I'M SORRY.

IT'S ALL RIGHT. I DON'T THINK EITHER ONE OF US EXPECTED TO DIE IN BED. NOT AFTER THE CHOICES WE'VE MADE.

AND AT LEAST NOW WE'LL BE FR--

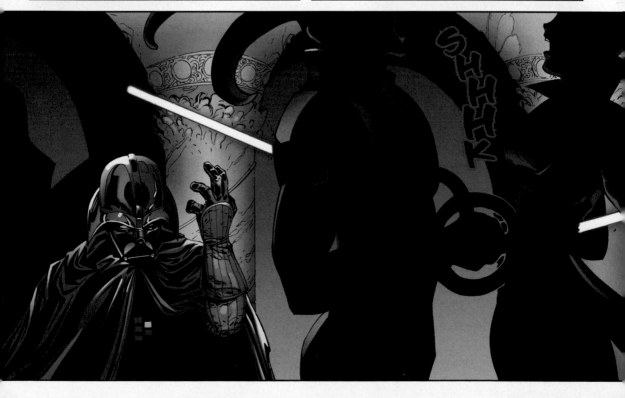

SHHK

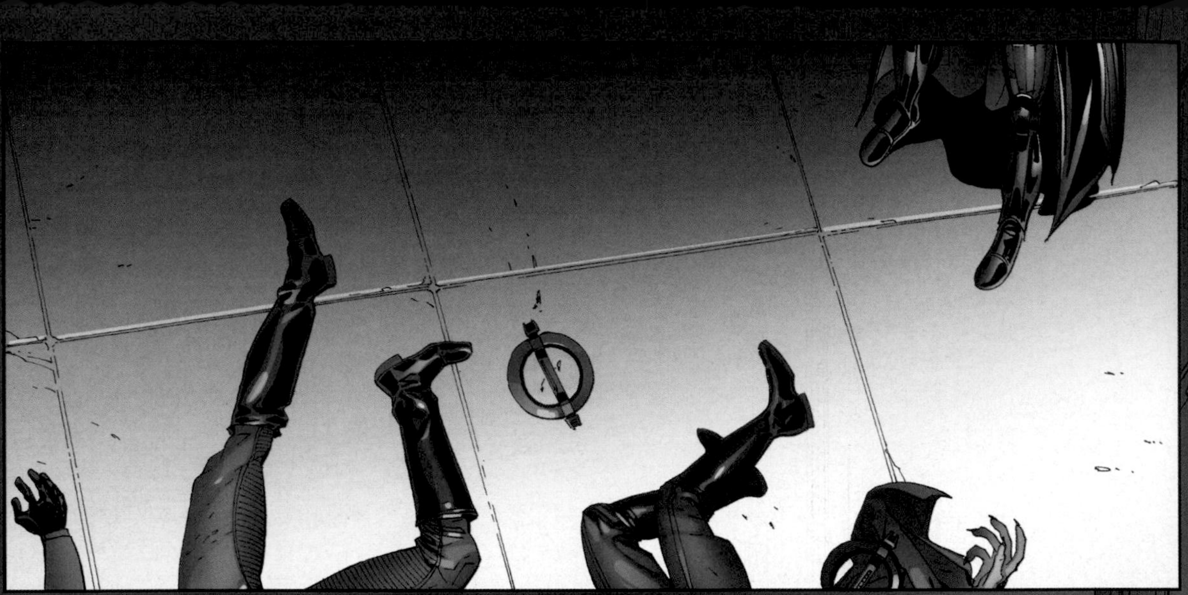
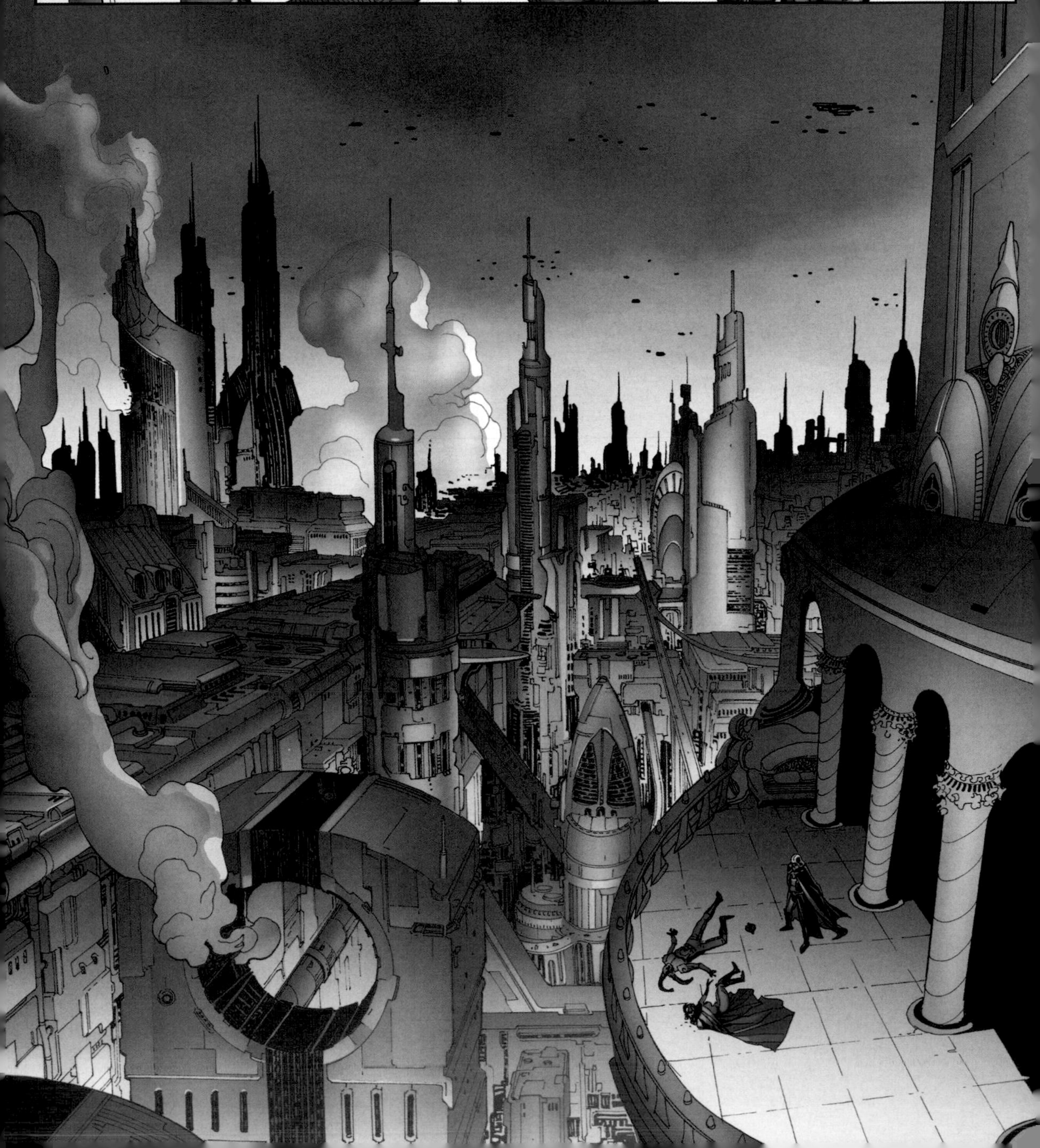

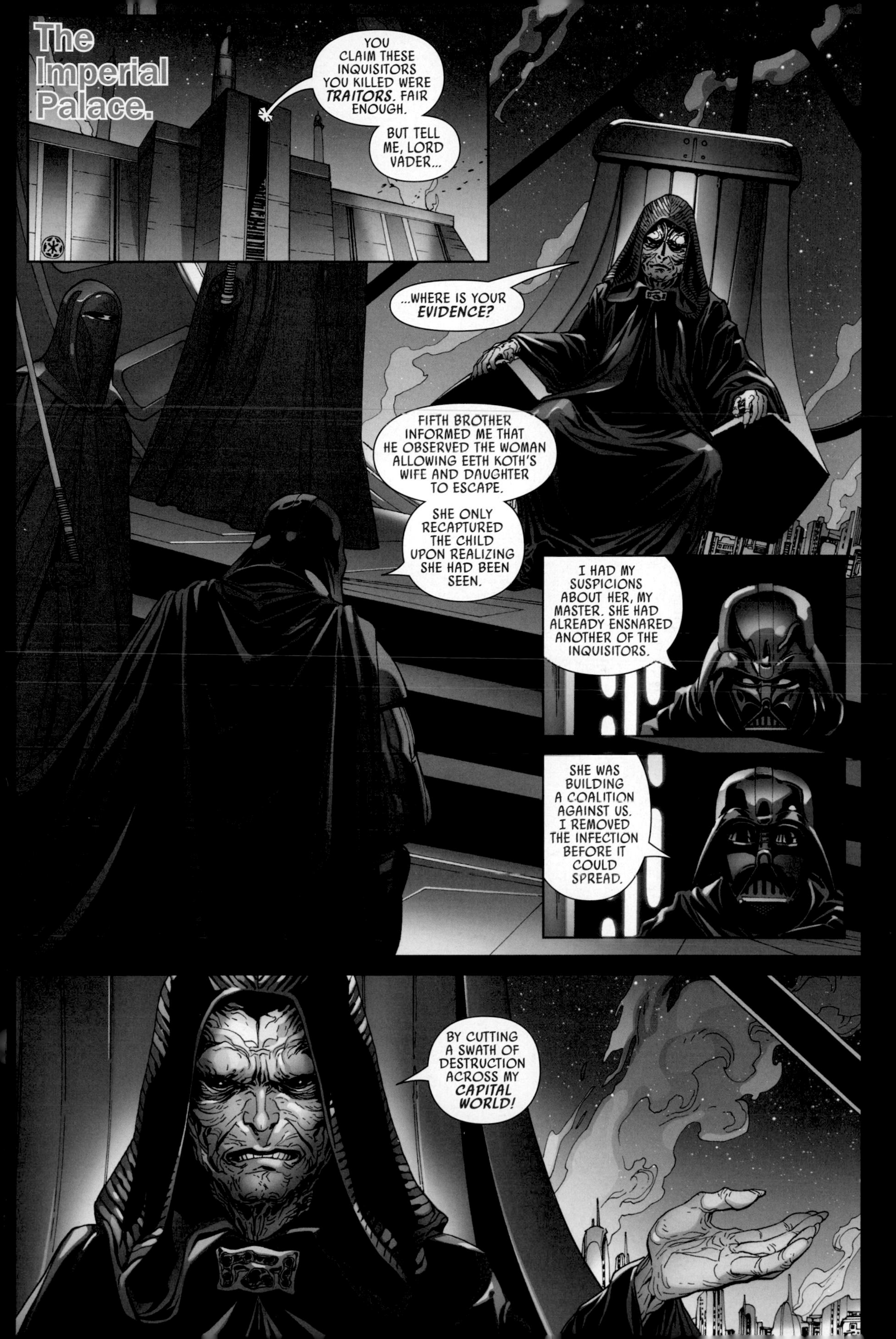
The Imperial Palace.
YOU CLAIM THESE INQUISITORS YOU KILLED WERE TRAITORS. FAIR ENOUGH.
BUT TELL ME, LORD VADER...
...WHERE IS YOUR EVIDENCE?
FIFTH BROTHER INFORMED ME THAT HE OBSERVED THE WOMAN ALLOWING EETH KOTH'S WIFE AND DAUGHTER TO ESCAPE.
SHE ONLY RECAPTURED THE CHILD UPON REALIZING SHE HAD BEEN SEEN.
I HAD MY SUSPICIONS ABOUT HER, MY MASTER. SHE HAD ALREADY ENSNARED ANOTHER OF THE INQUISITORS.
SHE WAS BUILDING A COALITION AGAINST US. I REMOVED THE INFECTION BEFORE IT COULD SPREAD.
BY CUTTING A SWATH OF DESTRUCTION ACROSS MY CAPITAL WORLD!

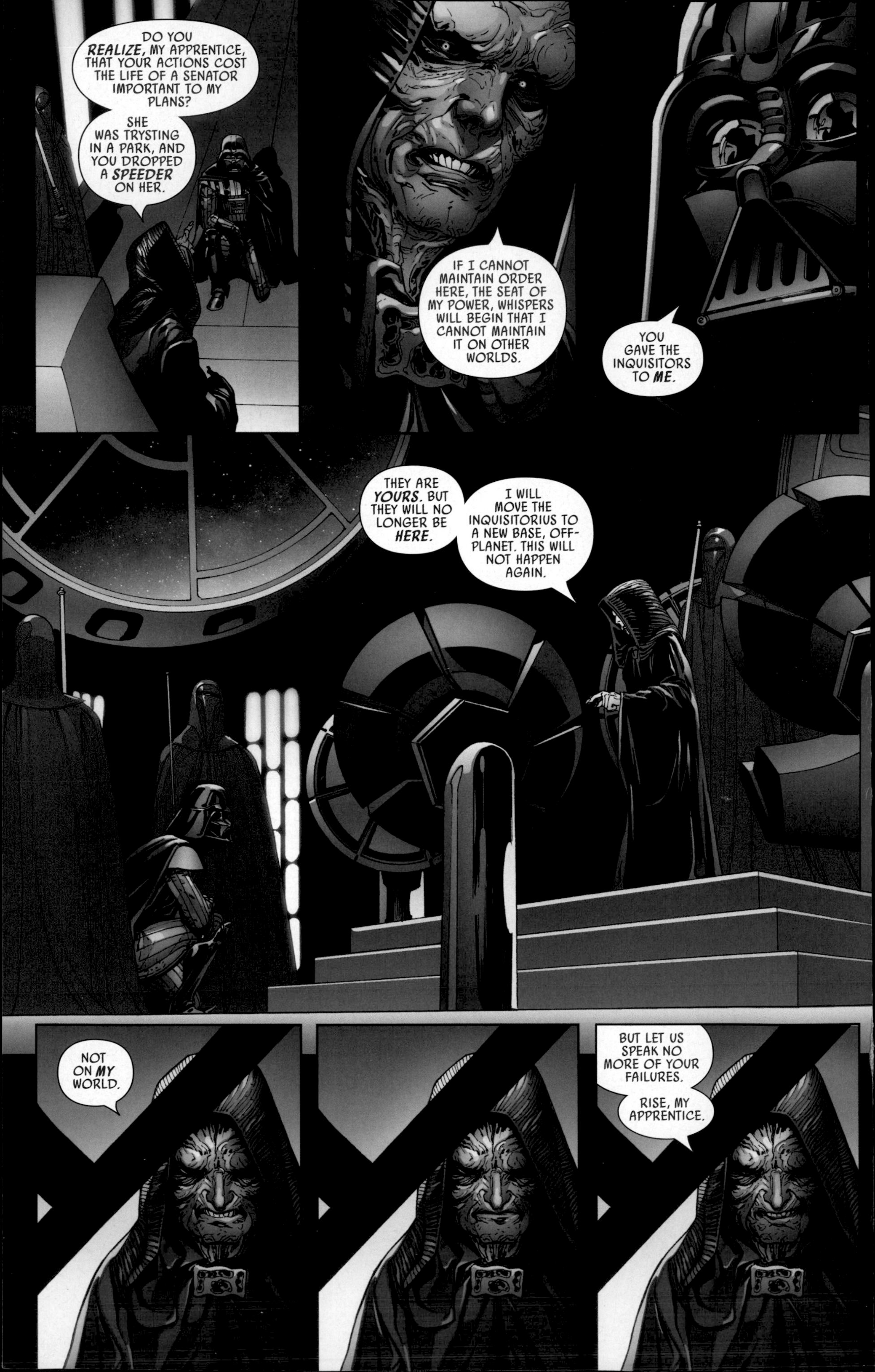
DO YOU REALIZE, MY APPRENTICE, THAT YOUR ACTIONS COST THE LIFE OF A SENATOR IMPORTANT TO MY PLANS?
SHE WAS TRYSTING IN A PARK, AND YOU DROPPED A SPEEDER ON HER.
IF I CANNOT MAINTAIN ORDER HERE, THE SEAT OF MY POWER, WHISPERS WILL BEGIN THAT I CANNOT MAINTAIN IT ON OTHER WORLDS.
YOU GAVE THE INQUISITORS TO ME.
THEY ARE YOURS. BUT THEY WILL NO LONGER BE HERE.
I WILL MOVE THE INQUISITORIUS TO A NEW BASE, OFF-PLANET. THIS WILL NOT HAPPEN AGAIN.
NOT ON MY WORLD.
BUT LET US SPEAK NO MORE OF YOUR FAILURES.
RISE, MY APPRENTICE.

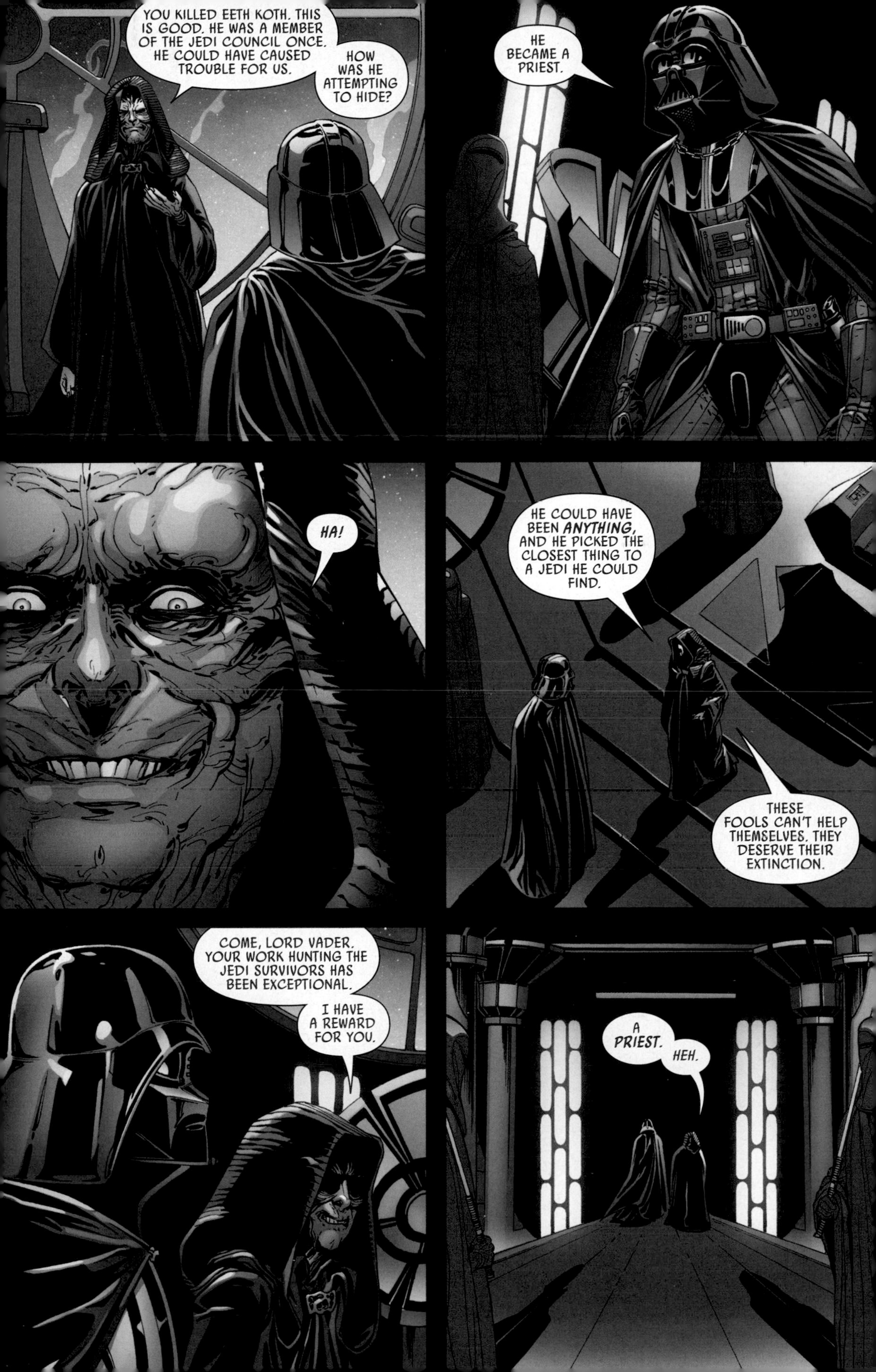
YOU KILLED EETH KOTH. THIS IS GOOD. HE WAS A MEMBER OF THE JEDI COUNCIL ONCE. HE COULD HAVE CAUSED TROUBLE FOR US.
HOW WAS HE ATTEMPTING TO HIDE?
HE BECAME A PRIEST.
HA!
HE COULD HAVE BEEN ANYTHING, AND HE PICKED THE CLOSEST THING TO A JEDI HE COULD FIND.
THESE FOOLS CAN'T HELP THEMSELVES. THEY DESERVE THEIR EXTINCTION.
COME, LORD VADER. YOUR WORK HUNTING THE JEDI SURVIVORS HAS BEEN EXCEPTIONAL.
I HAVE A REWARD FOR YOU.
A PRIEST.
HEH.

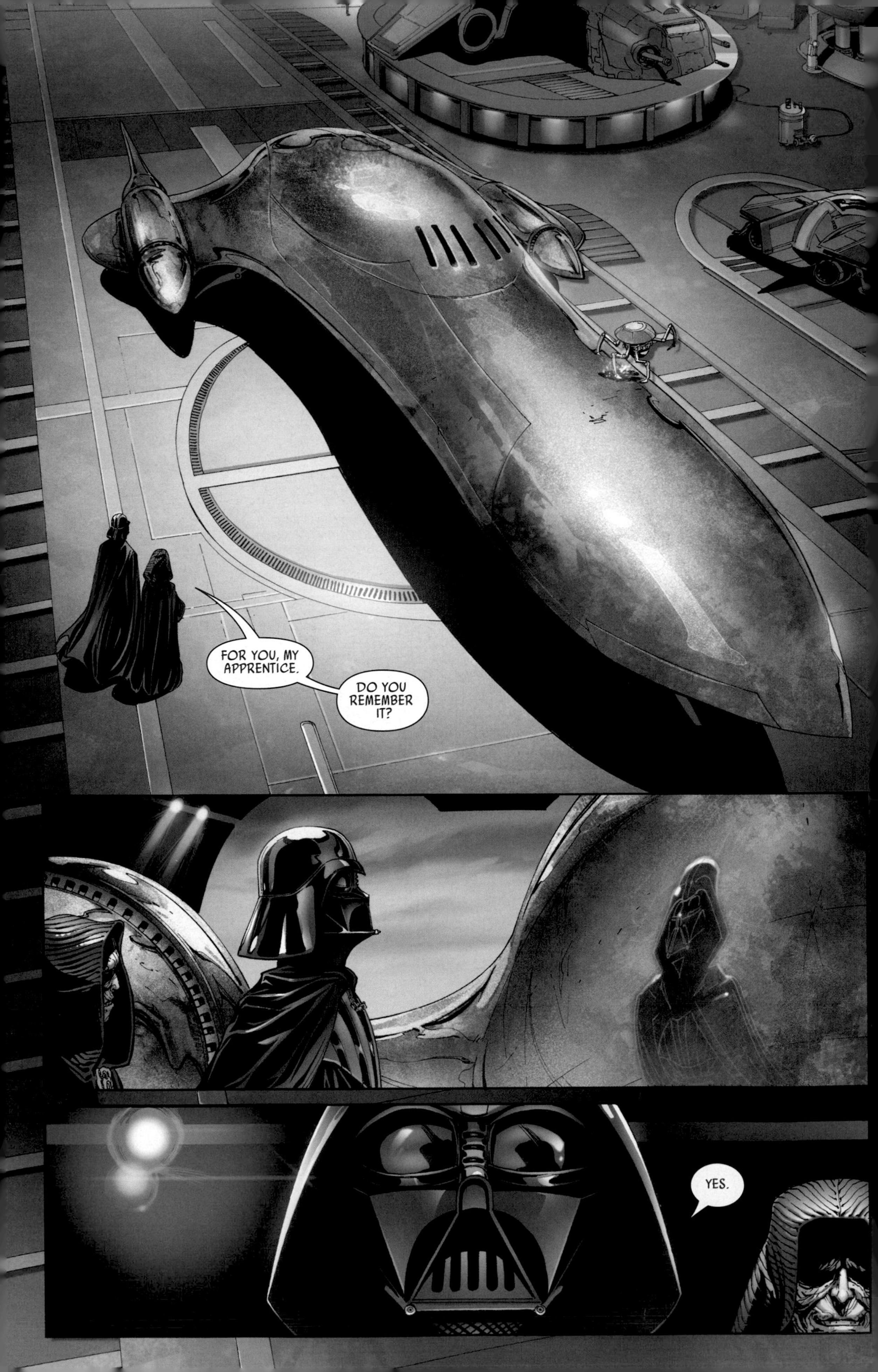
FOR YOU, MY APPRENTICE.
DO YOU REMEMBER IT?
YES.

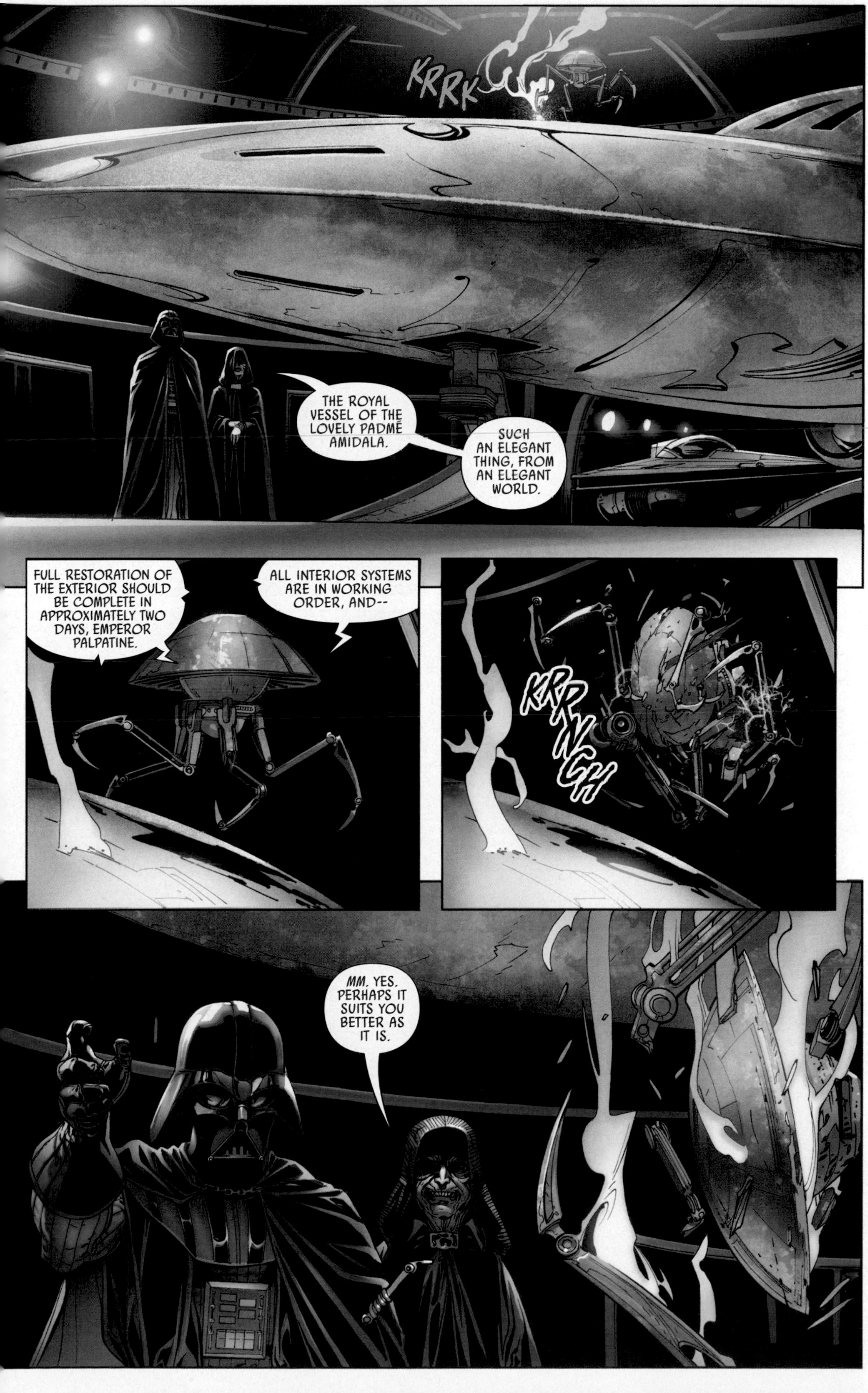
KRRK
THE ROYAL VESSEL OF THE LOVELY PADMÉ AMIDALA.
SUCH AN ELEGANT THING, FROM AN ELEGANT WORLD.
FULL RESTORATION OF THE EXTERIOR SHOULD BE COMPLETE IN APPROXIMATELY TWO DAYS, EMPEROR PALPATINE.
ALL INTERIOR SYSTEMS ARE IN WORKING ORDER, AND--
KRRNCH
MM. YES. PERHAPS IT SUITS YOU BETTER AS IT IS.

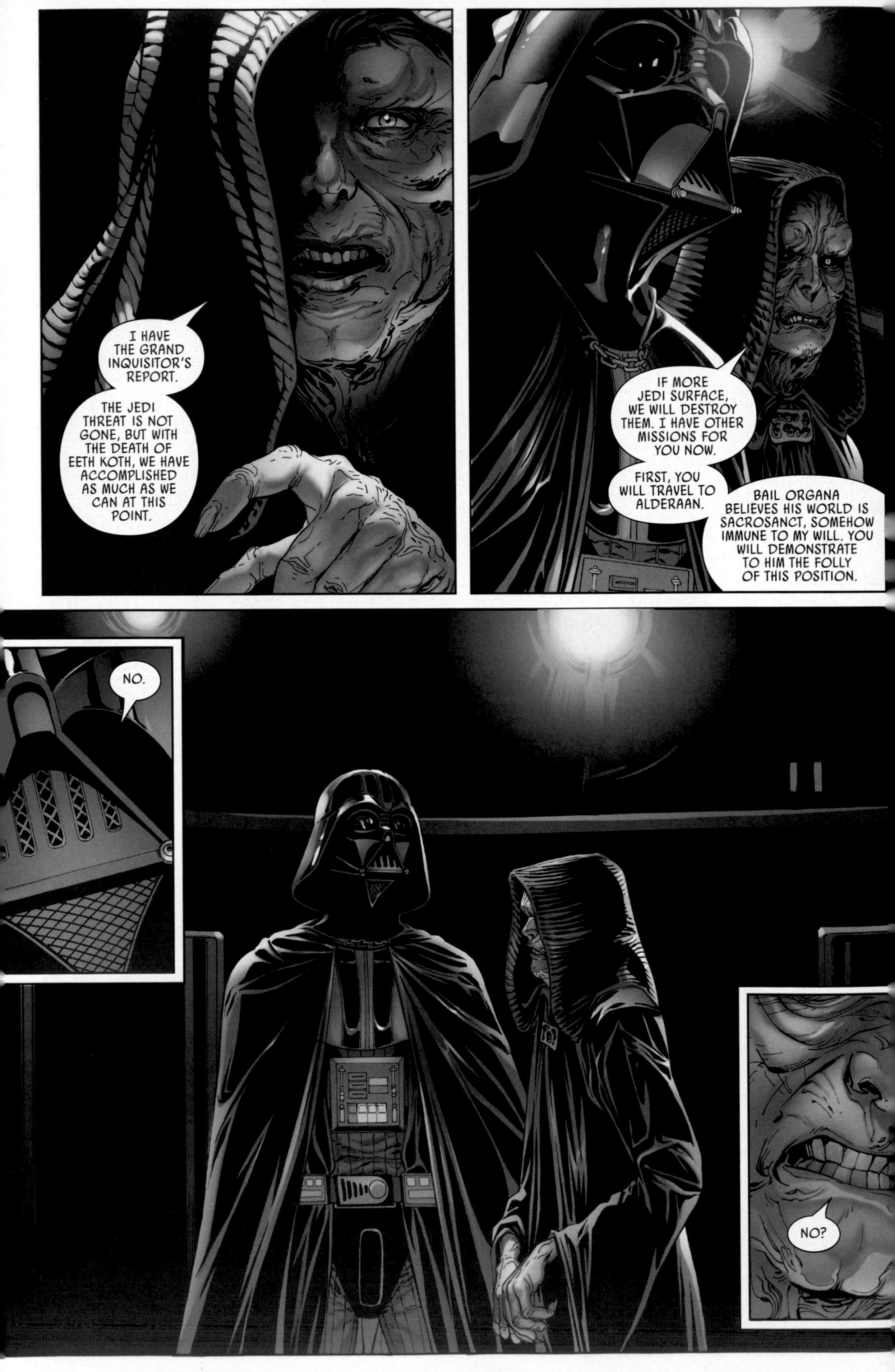
I HAVE THE GRAND INQUISITOR'S REPORT.
THE JEDI THREAT IS NOT GONE, BUT WITH THE DEATH OF EETH KOTH, WE HAVE ACCOMPLISHED AS MUCH AS WE CAN AT THIS POINT.
IF MORE JEDI SURFACE, WE WILL DESTROY THEM. I HAVE OTHER MISSIONS FOR YOU NOW.
FIRST, YOU WILL TRAVEL TO ALDERAAN.
BAIL ORGANA BELIEVES HIS WORLD IS SACROSANCT, SOMEHOW IMMUNE TO MY WILL. YOU WILL DEMONSTRATE TO HIM THE FOLLY OF THIS POSITION.
NO.
NO?

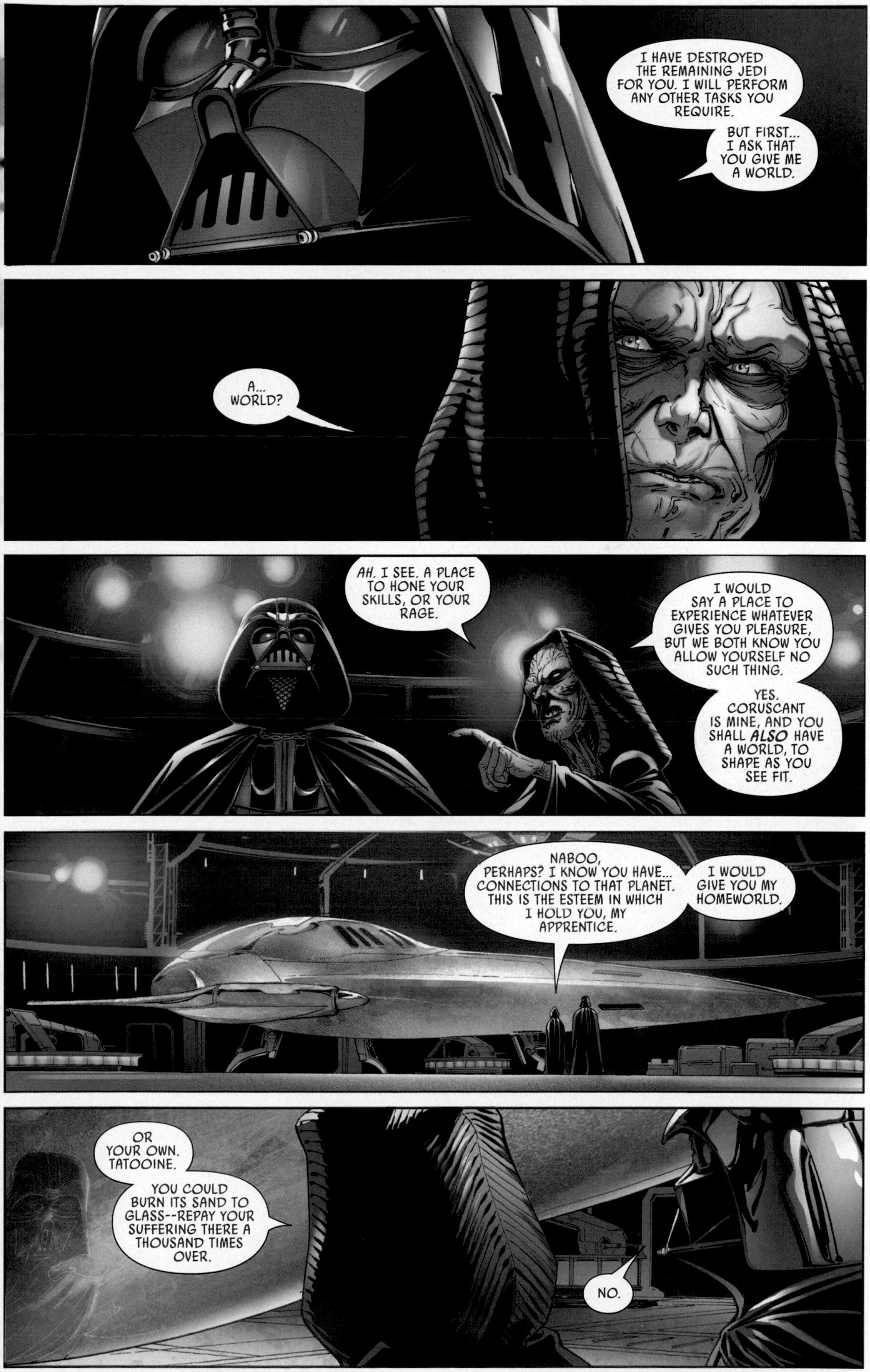
I HAVE DESTROYED THE REMAINING JEDI FOR YOU. I WILL PERFORM ANY OTHER TASKS YOU REQUIRE.
BUT FIRST... I ASK THAT YOU GIVE ME A WORLD.
A... WORLD?
AH. I SEE. A PLACE TO HONE YOUR SKILLS, OR YOUR RAGE.
I WOULD SAY A PLACE TO EXPERIENCE WHATEVER GIVES YOU PLEASURE, BUT WE BOTH KNOW YOU ALLOW YOURSELF NO SUCH THING.
YES. CORUSCANT IS MINE, AND YOU SHALL ALSO HAVE A WORLD, TO SHAPE AS YOU SEE FIT.
NABOO, PERHAPS? I KNOW YOU HAVE... CONNECTIONS TO THAT PLANET. THIS IS THE ESTEEM IN WHICH I HOLD YOU, MY APPRENTICE.
I WOULD GIVE YOU MY HOMEWORLD.
OR YOUR OWN. TATOOINE.
YOU COULD BURN ITS SAND TO GLASS--REPAY YOUR SUFFERING THERE A THOUSAND TIMES OVER.
NO.

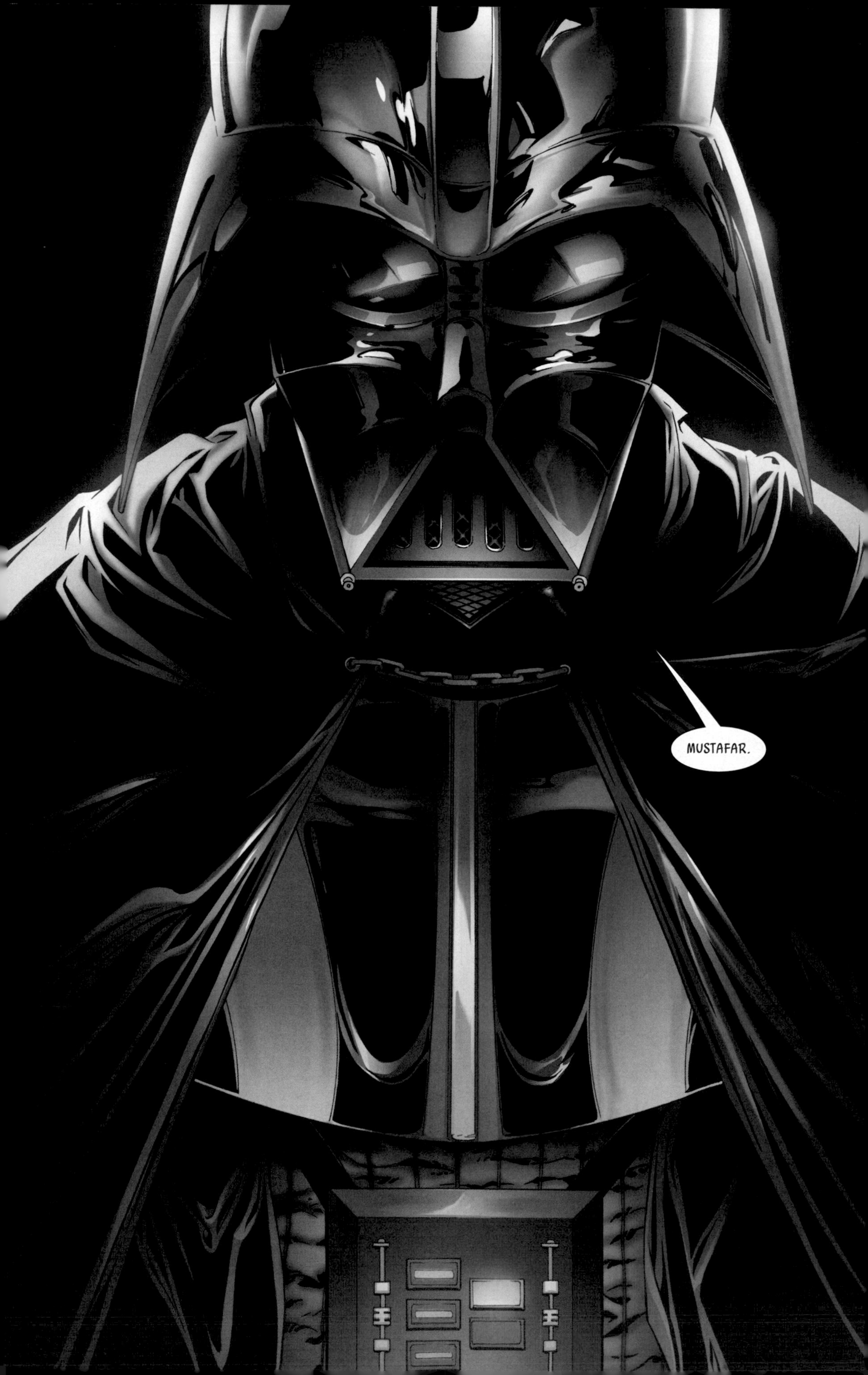
MUSTAFAR.

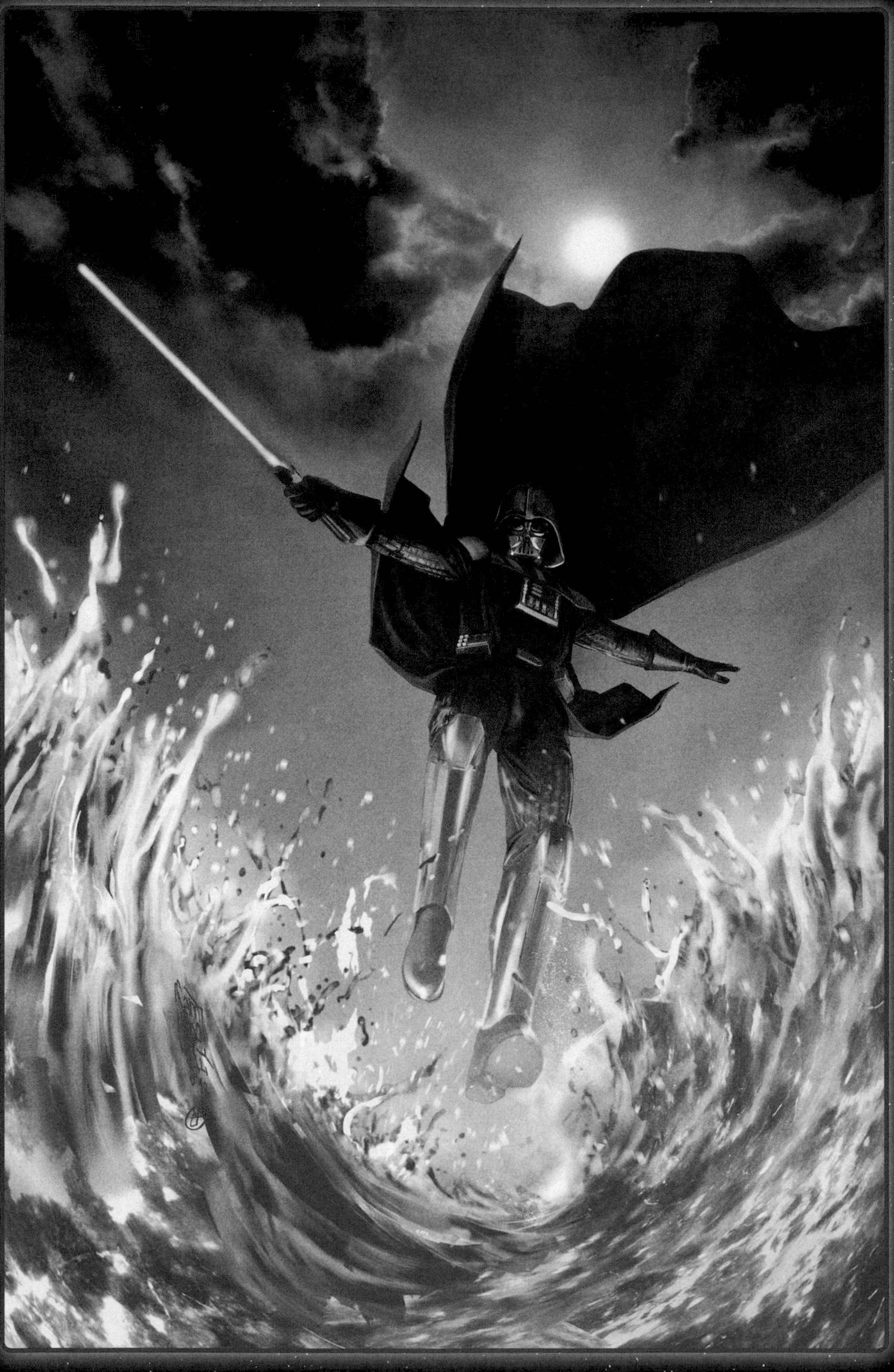

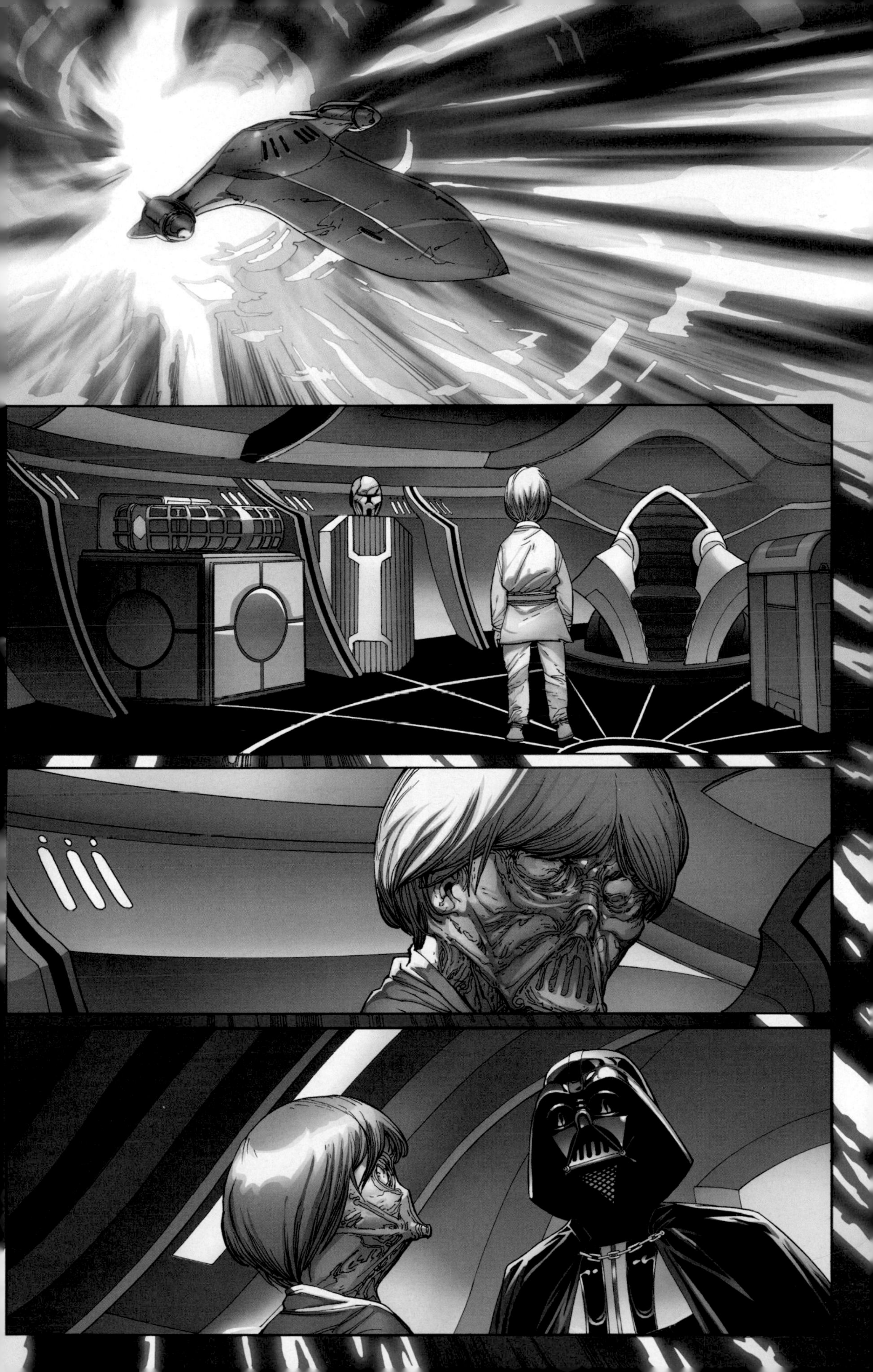

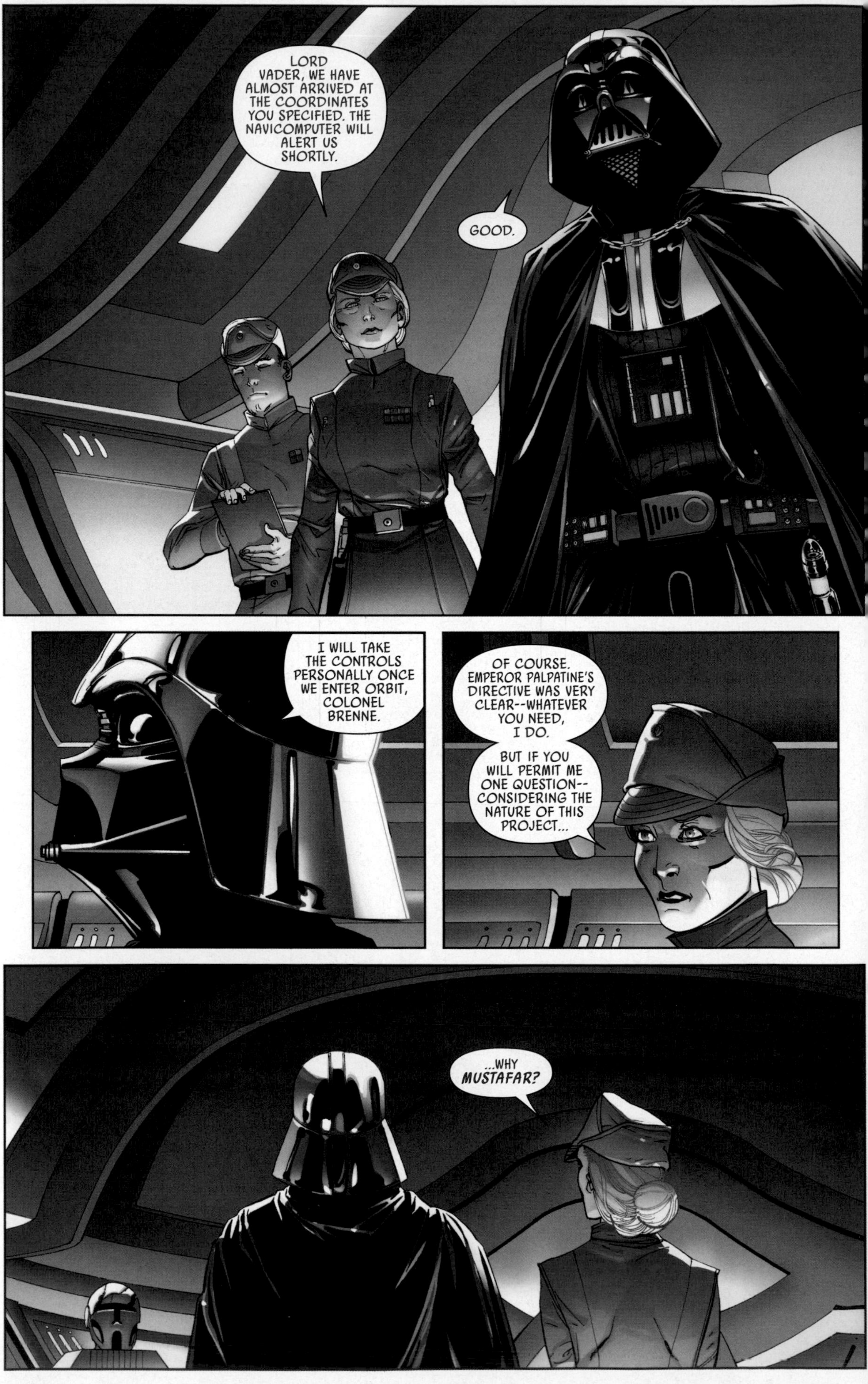
LORD VADER, WE HAVE ALMOST ARRIVED AT THE COORDINATES YOU SPECIFIED. THE NAVICOMPUTER WILL ALERT US SHORTLY.
GOOD.
I WILL TAKE THE CONTROLS PERSONALLY ONCE WE ENTER ORBIT, COLONEL BRENNE.
OF COURSE. EMPEROR PALPATINE'S DIRECTIVE WAS VERY CLEAR--WHATEVER YOU NEED, I DO.
BUT IF YOU WILL PERMIT ME ONE QUESTION--CONSIDERING THE NATURE OF THIS PROJECT...
...WHY *MUSTAFAR?*

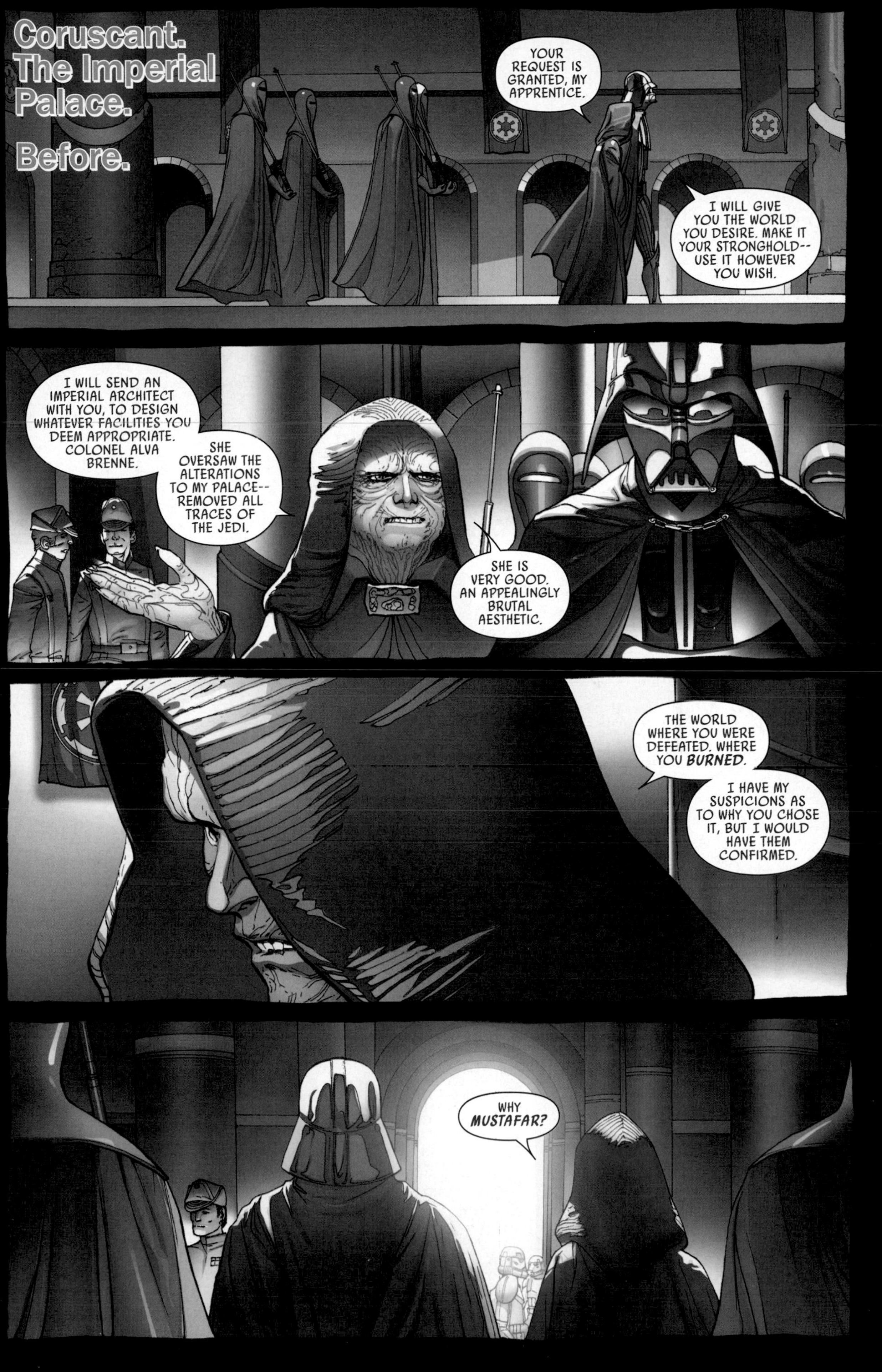
Coruscant. The Imperial Palace.
Before.
YOUR REQUEST IS GRANTED, MY APPRENTICE.
I WILL GIVE YOU THE WORLD YOU DESIRE. MAKE IT YOUR STRONGHOLD-- USE IT HOWEVER YOU WISH.
I WILL SEND AN IMPERIAL ARCHITECT WITH YOU, TO DESIGN WHATEVER FACILITIES YOU DEEM APPROPRIATE. COLONEL ALVA BRENNE.
SHE OVERSAW THE ALTERATIONS TO MY PALACE-- REMOVED ALL TRACES OF THE JEDI.
SHE IS VERY GOOD. AN APPEALINGLY BRUTAL AESTHETIC.
THE WORLD WHERE YOU WERE DEFEATED. WHERE YOU BURNED.
I HAVE MY SUSPICIONS AS TO WHY YOU CHOSE IT, BUT I WOULD HAVE THEM CONFIRMED.
WHY MUSTAFAR?

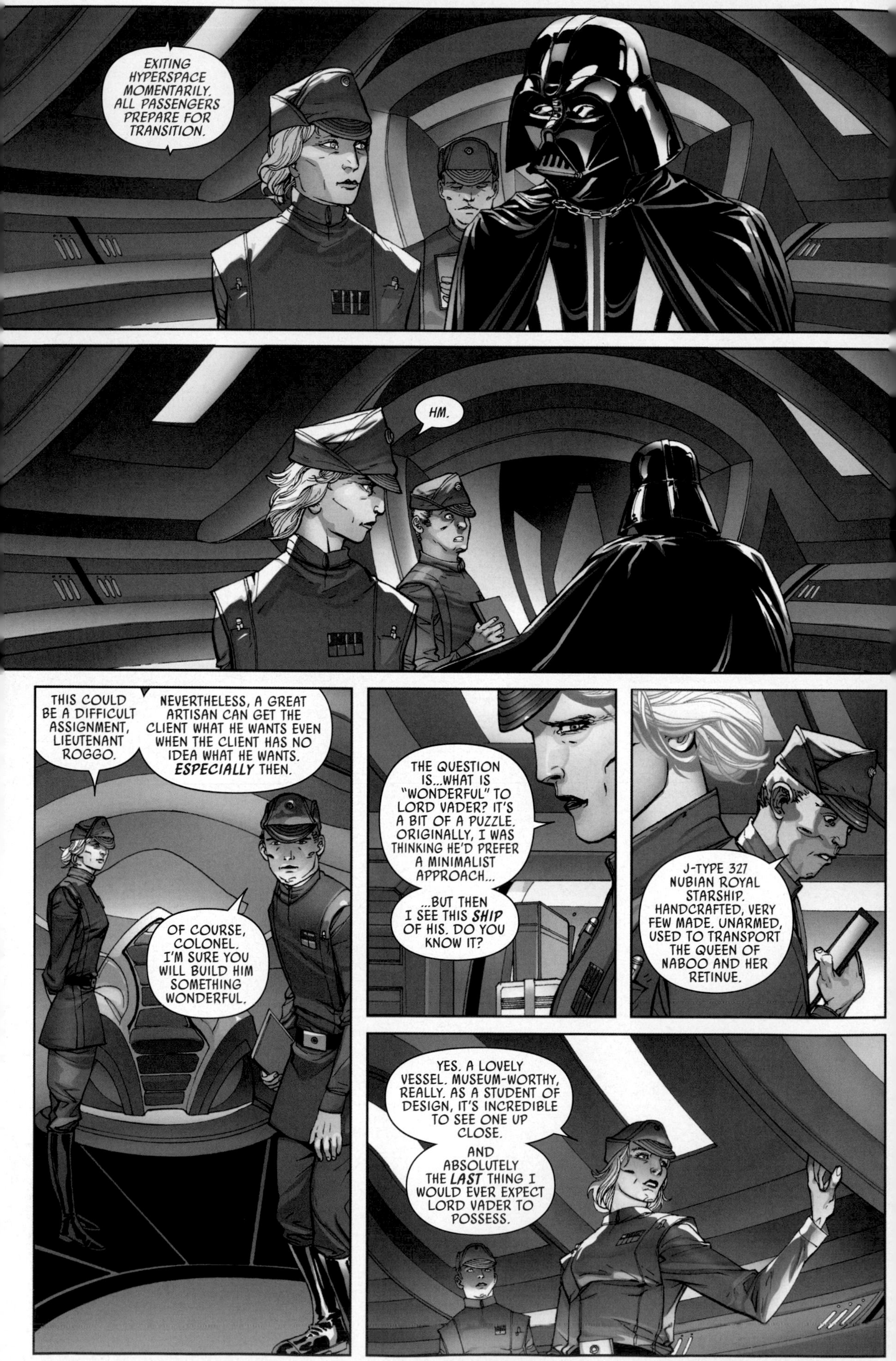
EXITING HYPERSPACE MOMENTARILY. ALL PASSENGERS PREPARE FOR TRANSITION.
HM.
THIS COULD BE A DIFFICULT ASSIGNMENT, LIEUTENANT ROGGO.
NEVERTHELESS, A GREAT ARTISAN CAN GET THE CLIENT WHAT HE WANTS EVEN WHEN THE CLIENT HAS NO IDEA WHAT HE WANTS. ESPECIALLY THEN.
OF COURSE, COLONEL. I'M SURE YOU WILL BUILD HIM SOMETHING WONDERFUL.
THE QUESTION IS...WHAT IS "WONDERFUL" TO LORD VADER? IT'S A BIT OF A PUZZLE. ORIGINALLY, I WAS THINKING HE'D PREFER A MINIMALIST APPROACH...
...BUT THEN I SEE THIS SHIP OF HIS. DO YOU KNOW IT?
J-TYPE 327 NUBIAN ROYAL STARSHIP. HANDCRAFTED, VERY FEW MADE. UNARMED, USED TO TRANSPORT THE QUEEN OF NABOO AND HER RETINUE.
YES. A LOVELY VESSEL. MUSEUM-WORTHY, REALLY. AS A STUDENT OF DESIGN, IT'S INCREDIBLE TO SEE ONE UP CLOSE.
AND ABSOLUTELY THE LAST THING I WOULD EVER EXPECT LORD VADER TO POSSESS.

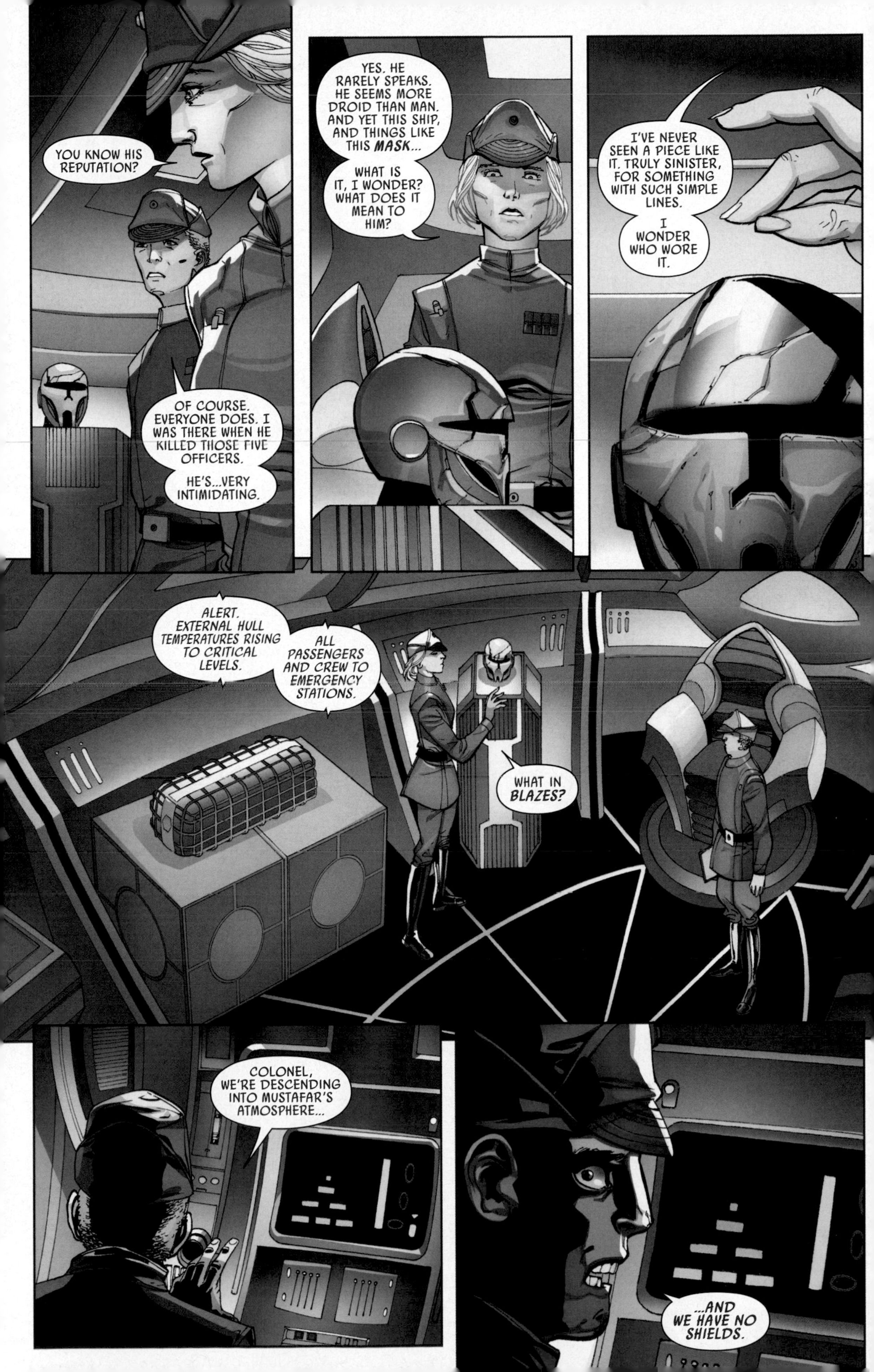
YOU KNOW HIS REPUTATION?
OF COURSE. EVERYONE DOES. I WAS THERE WHEN HE KILLED THOSE FIVE OFFICERS.
HE'S...VERY INTIMIDATING.
YES. HE RARELY SPEAKS. HE SEEMS MORE DROID THAN MAN. AND YET THIS SHIP, AND THINGS LIKE THIS MASK...
WHAT IS IT, I WONDER? WHAT DOES IT MEAN TO HIM?
I'VE NEVER SEEN A PIECE LIKE IT. TRULY SINISTER, FOR SOMETHING WITH SUCH SIMPLE LINES.
I WONDER WHO WORE IT.
ALERT. EXTERNAL HULL TEMPERATURES RISING TO CRITICAL LEVELS.
ALL PASSENGERS AND CREW TO EMERGENCY STATIONS.
WHAT IN BLAZES?
COLONEL, WE'RE DESCENDING INTO MUSTAFAR'S ATMOSPHERE...
...AND WE HAVE NO SHIELDS.

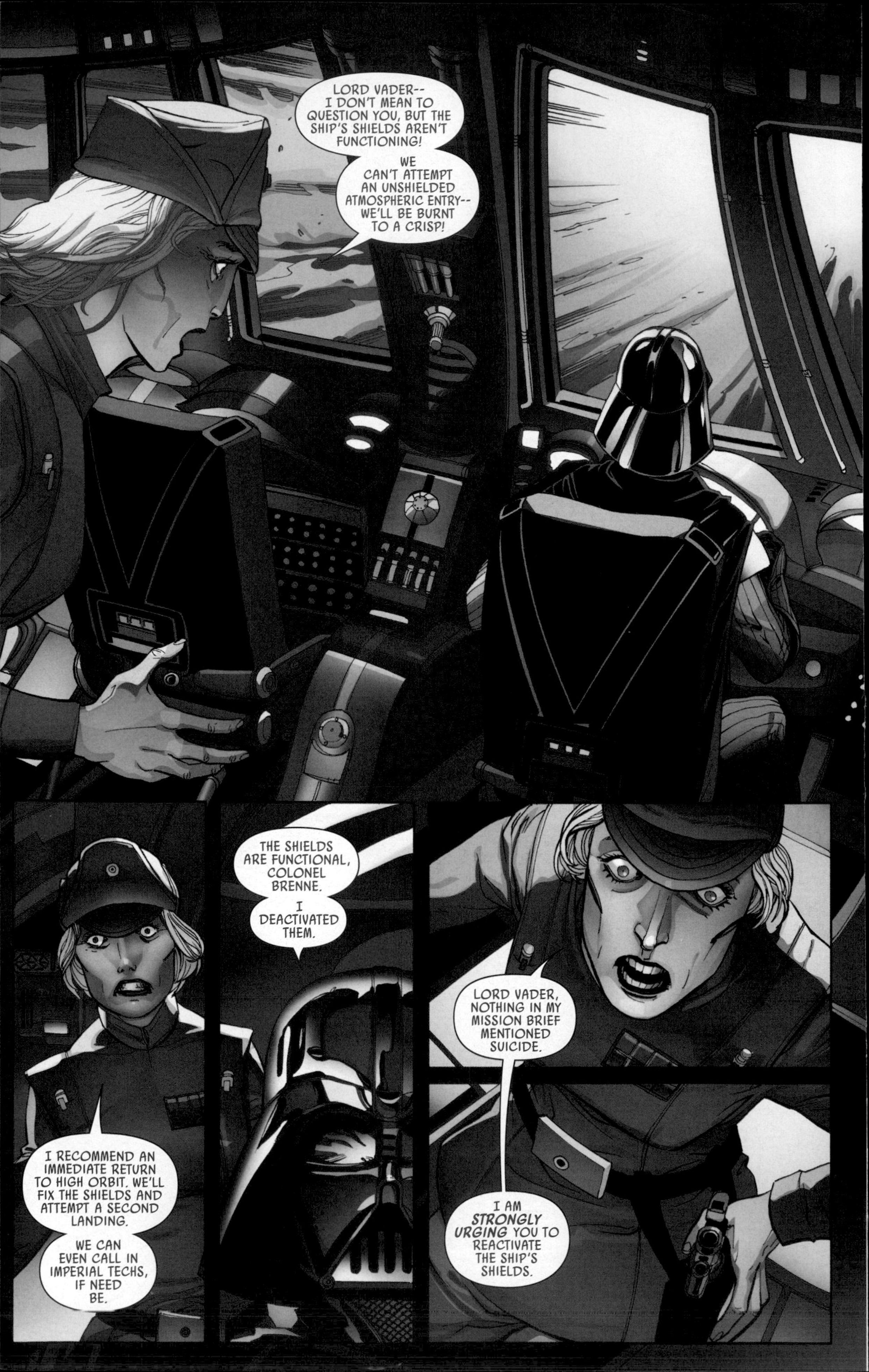
LORD VADER-- I DON'T MEAN TO QUESTION YOU, BUT THE SHIP'S SHIELDS AREN'T FUNCTIONING!
WE CAN'T ATTEMPT AN UNSHIELDED ATMOSPHERIC ENTRY-- WE'LL BE BURNT TO A CRISP!
I RECOMMEND AN IMMEDIATE RETURN TO HIGH ORBIT. WE'LL FIX THE SHIELDS AND ATTEMPT A SECOND LANDING.
WE CAN EVEN CALL IN IMPERIAL TECHS, IF NEED BE.
THE SHIELDS ARE FUNCTIONAL, COLONEL BRENNE.
I DEACTIVATED THEM.
LORD VADER, NOTHING IN MY MISSION BRIEF MENTIONED SUICIDE.
I AM ***STRONGLY URGING*** YOU TO REACTIVATE THE SHIP'S SHIELDS.

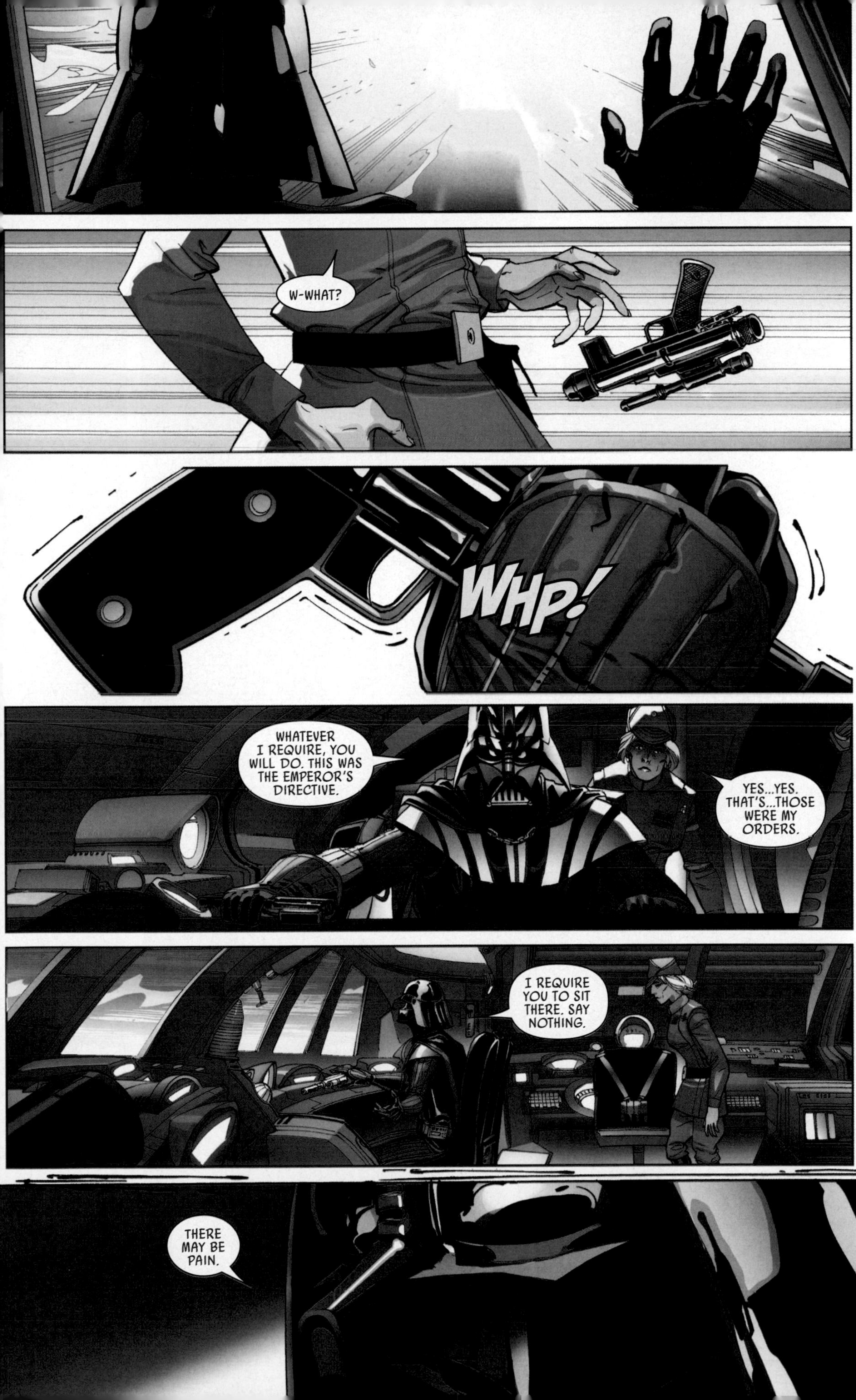
W-WHAT?
WHP!
WHATEVER I REQUIRE, YOU WILL DO. THIS WAS THE EMPEROR'S DIRECTIVE.
YES...YES. THAT'S...THOSE WERE MY ORDERS.
I REQUIRE YOU TO SIT THERE. SAY NOTHING.
THERE MAY BE PAIN.

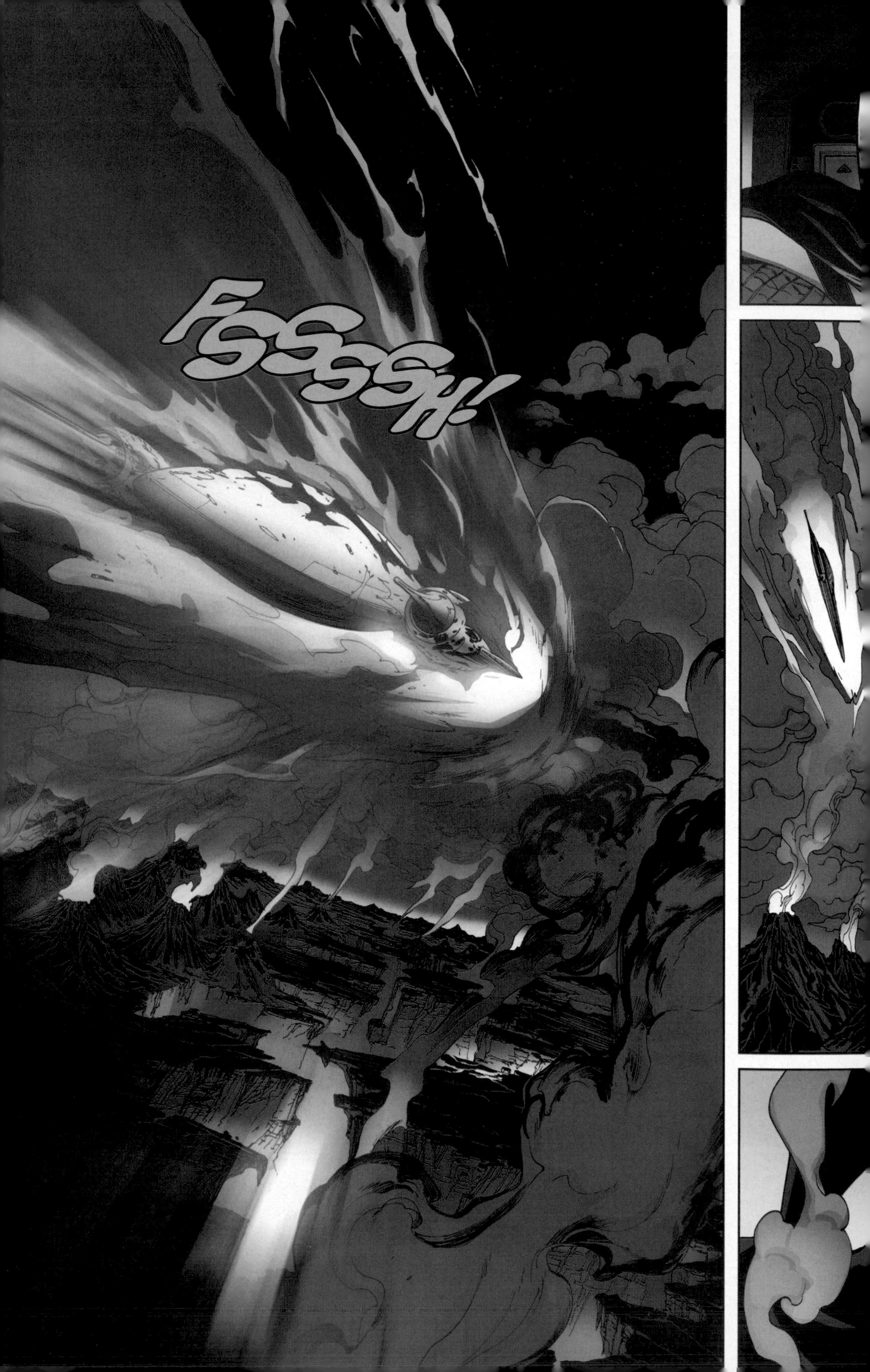
FSSSSH!

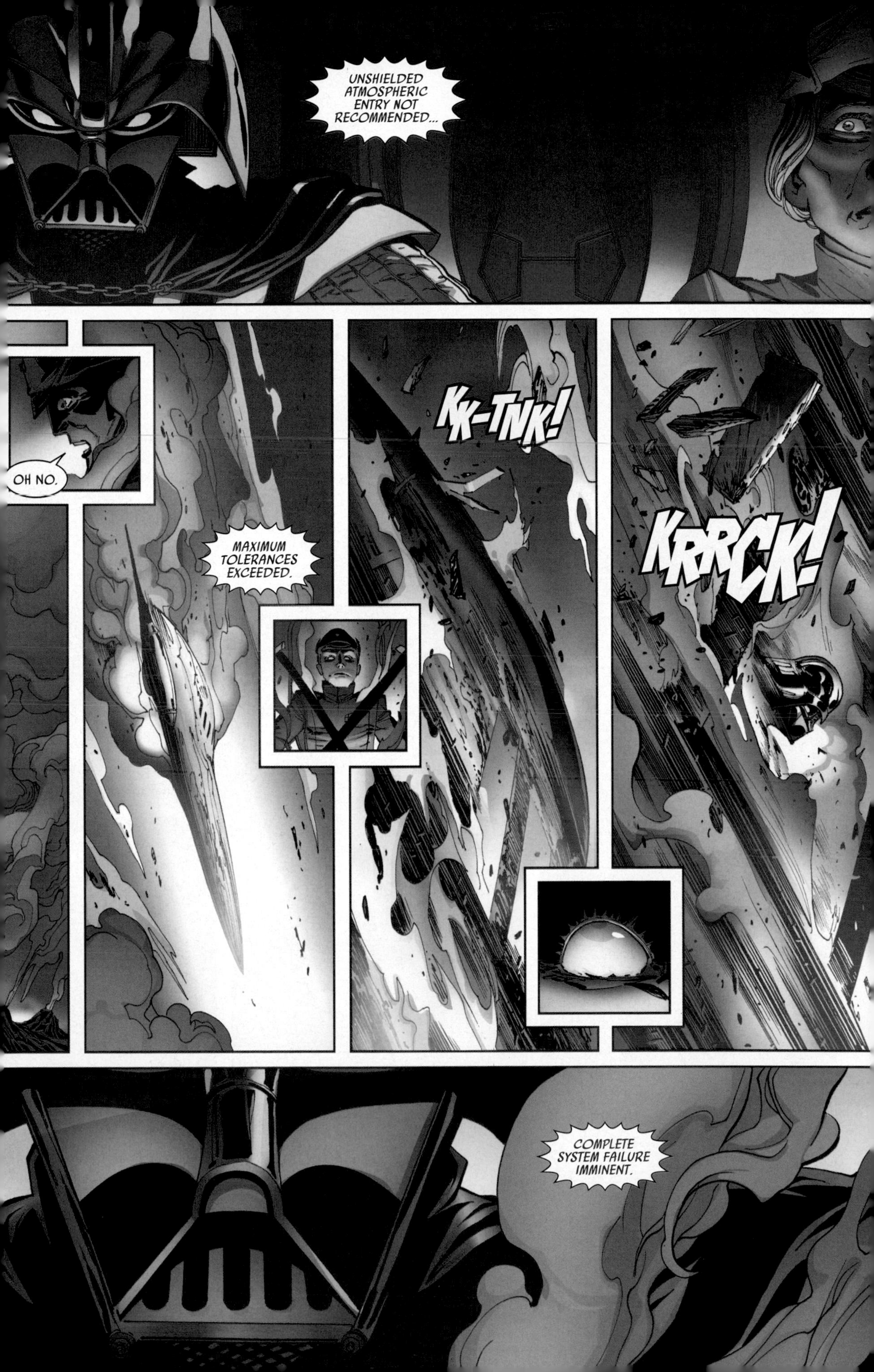
UNSHIELDED ATMOSPHERIC ENTRY NOT RECOMMENDED...
OH NO.
MAXIMUM TOLERANCES EXCEEDED.
KK-TNK!
KRRCK!
COMPLETE SYSTEM FAILURE IMMINENT.

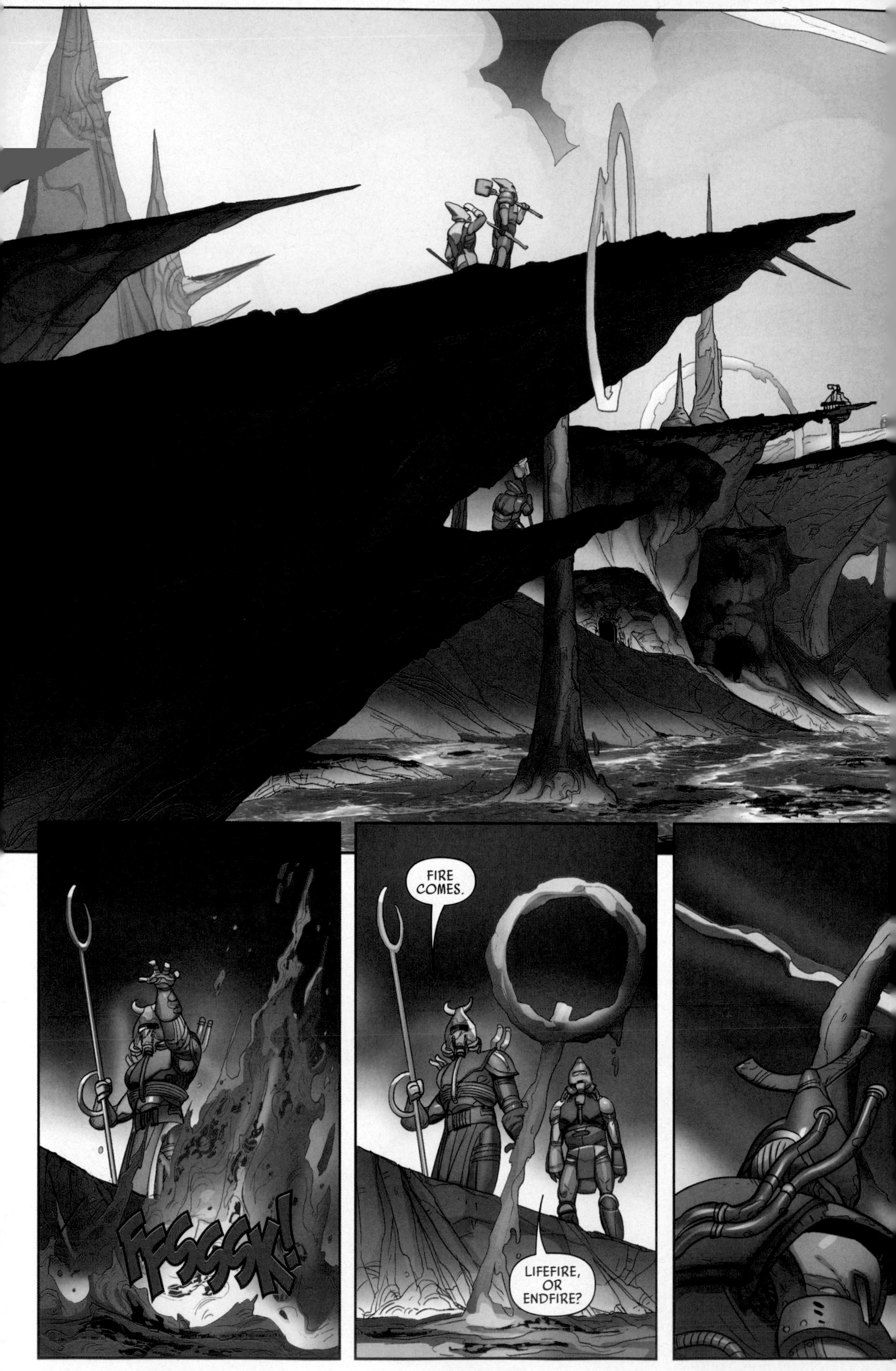
FFSSSK!
FIRE COMES.
LIFEFIRE, OR ENDFIRE?

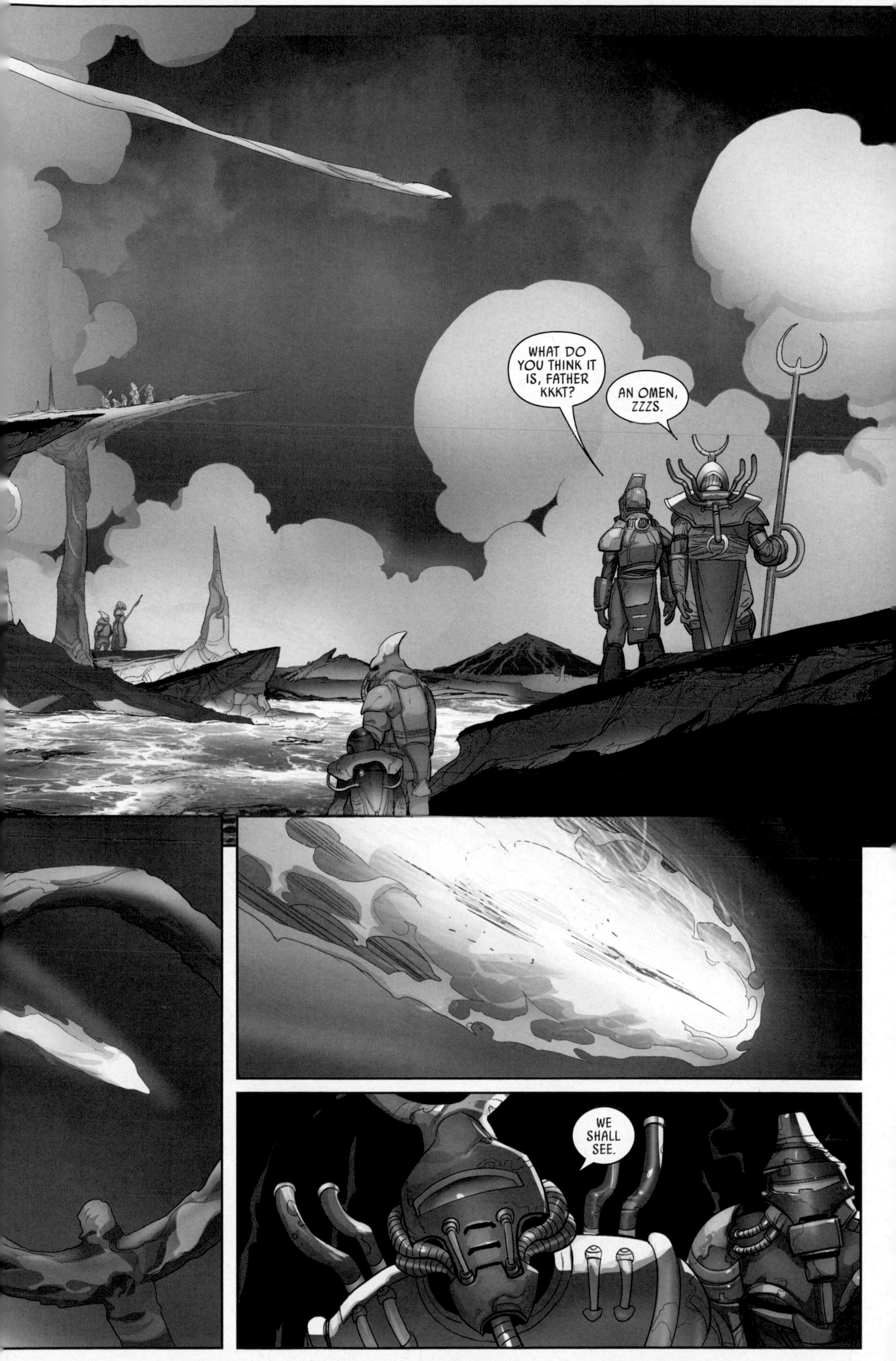
WHAT DO YOU THINK IT IS, FATHER KKKT?
AN OMEN, ZZZS.
WE SHALL SEE.

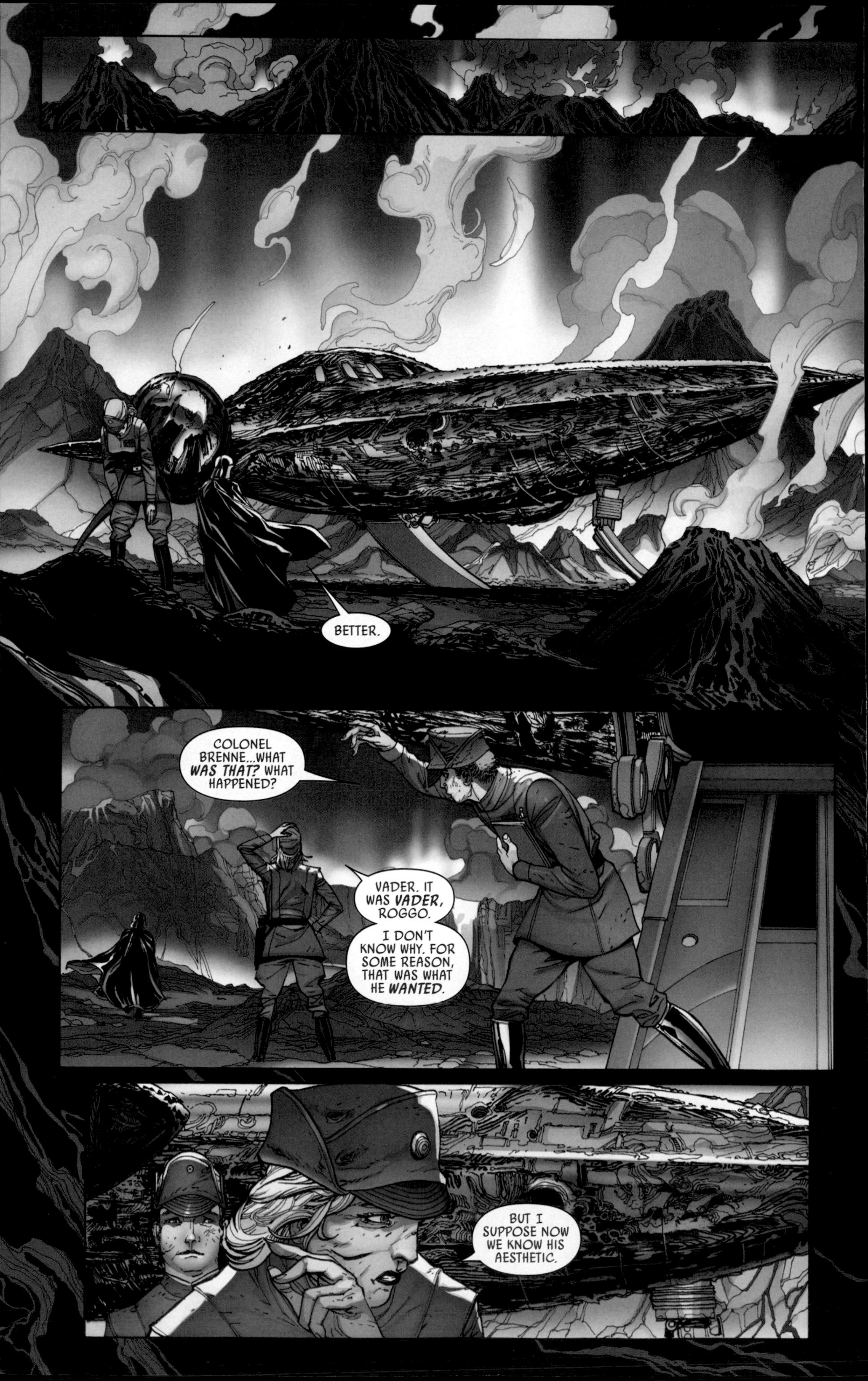
BETTER.
COLONEL BRENNE...WHAT WAS THAT? WHAT HAPPENED?
VADER. IT WAS VADER, ROGGO.
I DON'T KNOW WHY. FOR SOME REASON, THAT WAS WHAT HE WANTED.
BUT I SUPPOSE NOW WE KNOW HIS AESTHETIC.

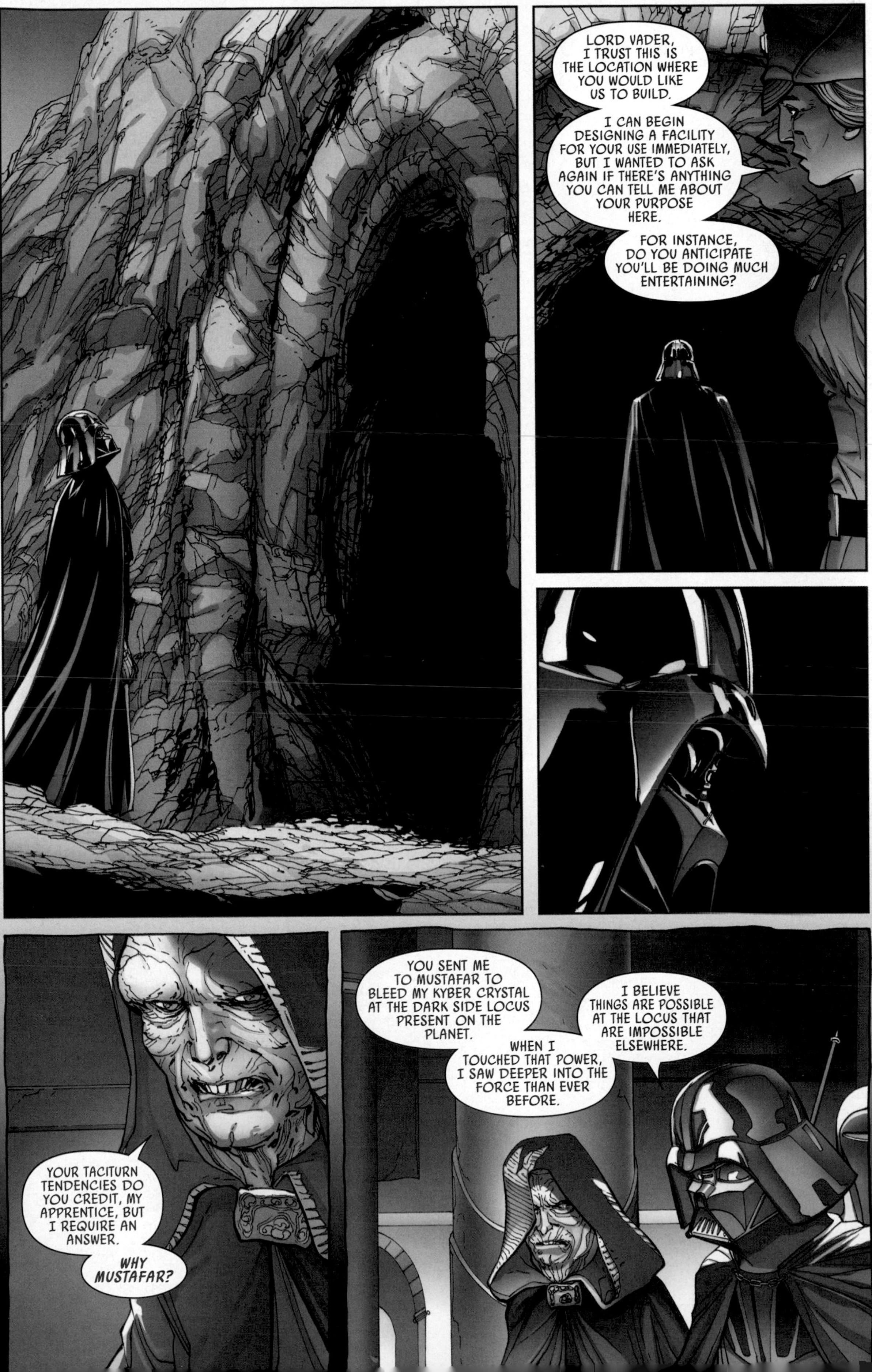

LORD VADER, I TRUST THIS IS THE LOCATION WHERE YOU WOULD LIKE US TO BUILD.
I CAN BEGIN DESIGNING A FACILITY FOR YOUR USE IMMEDIATELY, BUT I WANTED TO ASK AGAIN IF THERE'S ANYTHING YOU CAN TELL ME ABOUT YOUR PURPOSE HERE.
FOR INSTANCE, DO YOU ANTICIPATE YOU'LL BE DOING MUCH ENTERTAINING?
YOUR TACITURN TENDENCIES DO YOU CREDIT, MY APPRENTICE, BUT I REQUIRE AN ANSWER.
WHY MUSTAFAR?
YOU SENT ME TO MUSTAFAR TO BLEED MY KYBER CRYSTAL AT THE DARK SIDE LOCUS PRESENT ON THE PLANET.
WHEN I TOUCHED THAT POWER, I SAW DEEPER INTO THE FORCE THAN EVER BEFORE.
I BELIEVE THINGS ARE POSSIBLE AT THE LOCUS THAT ARE IMPOSSIBLE ELSEWHERE.

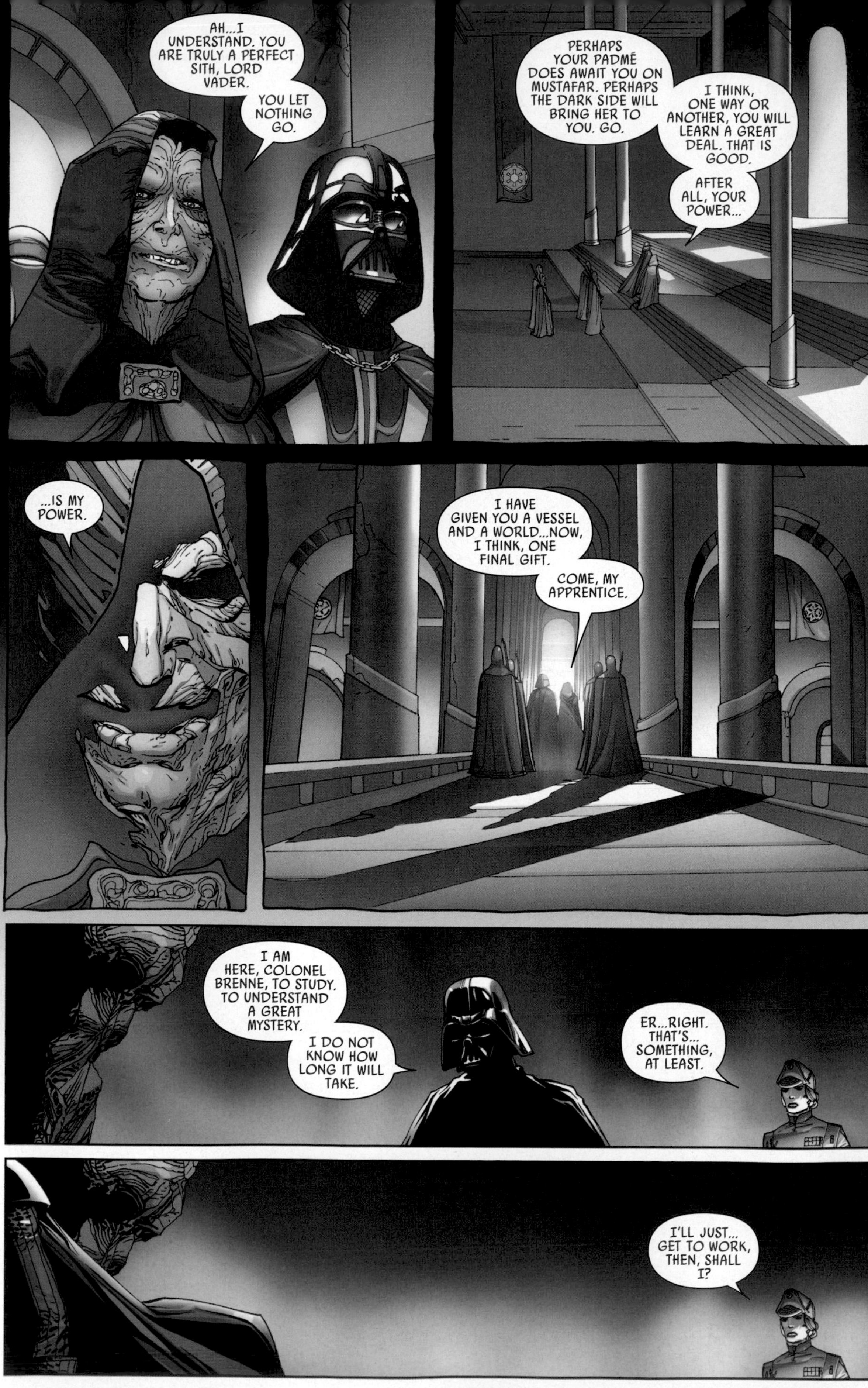
AH...I UNDERSTAND. YOU ARE TRULY A PERFECT SITH, LORD VADER.
YOU LET NOTHING GO.
PERHAPS YOUR PADMÉ DOES AWAIT YOU ON MUSTAFAR. PERHAPS THE DARK SIDE WILL BRING HER TO YOU. GO.
I THINK, ONE WAY OR ANOTHER, YOU WILL LEARN A GREAT DEAL. THAT IS GOOD.
AFTER ALL, YOUR POWER...
...IS MY POWER.
I HAVE GIVEN YOU A VESSEL AND A WORLD...NOW, I THINK, ONE FINAL GIFT.
COME, MY APPRENTICE.
I AM HERE, COLONEL BRENNE, TO STUDY. TO UNDERSTAND A GREAT MYSTERY.
I DO NOT KNOW HOW LONG IT WILL TAKE.
ER...RIGHT. THAT'S... SOMETHING, AT LEAST.
I'LL JUST... GET TO WORK, THEN, SHALL I?

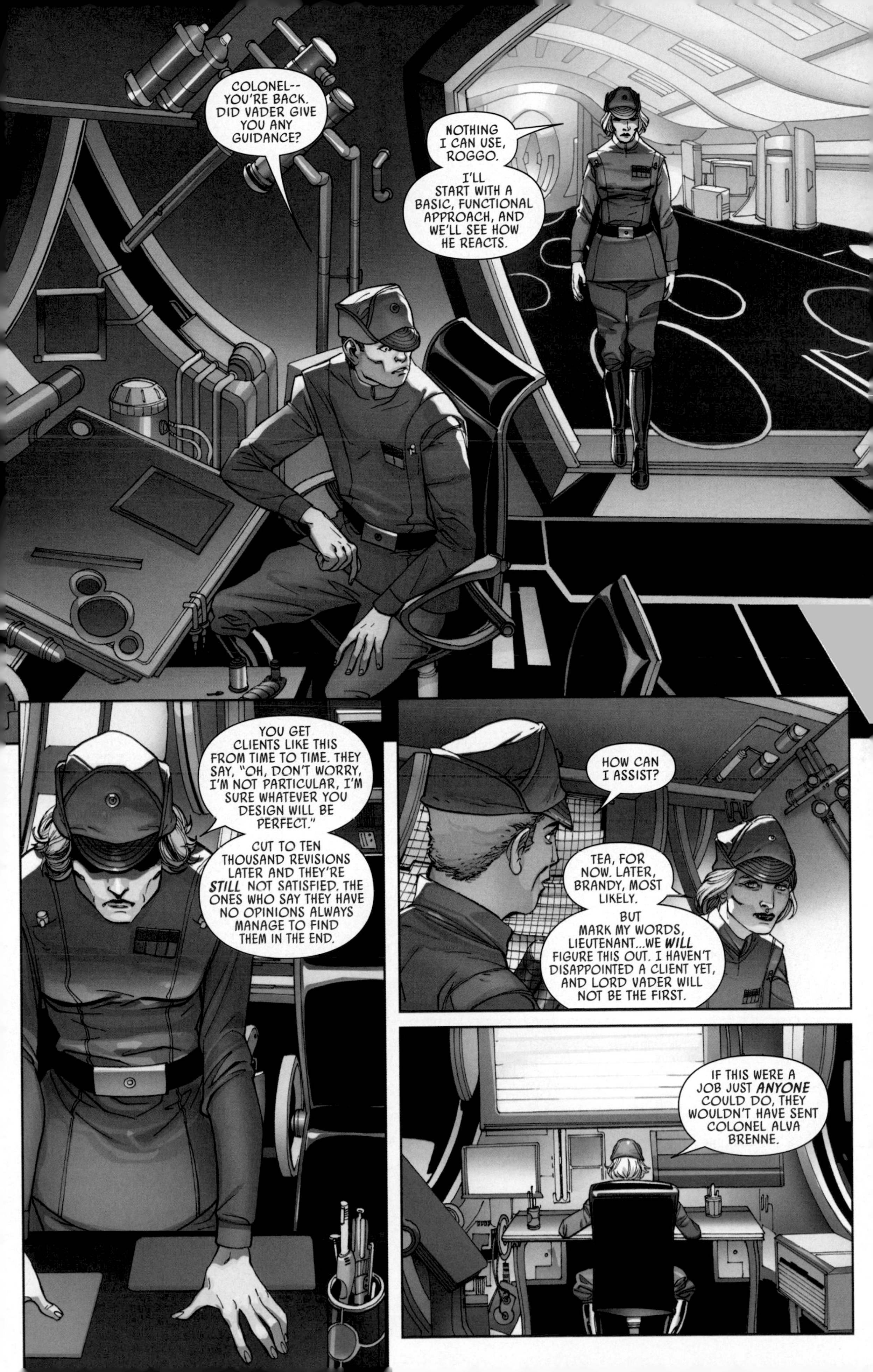
COLONEL-- YOU'RE BACK. DID VADER GIVE YOU ANY GUIDANCE?
NOTHING I CAN USE, ROGGO.
I'LL START WITH A BASIC, FUNCTIONAL APPROACH, AND WE'LL SEE HOW HE REACTS.
YOU GET CLIENTS LIKE THIS FROM TIME TO TIME. THEY SAY, "OH, DON'T WORRY, I'M NOT PARTICULAR, I'M SURE WHATEVER YOU DESIGN WILL BE PERFECT."
CUT TO TEN THOUSAND REVISIONS LATER AND THEY'RE STILL NOT SATISFIED. THE ONES WHO SAY THEY HAVE NO OPINIONS ALWAYS MANAGE TO FIND THEM IN THE END.
HOW CAN I ASSIST?
TEA, FOR NOW. LATER, BRANDY, MOST LIKELY.
BUT MARK MY WORDS, LIEUTENANT...WE WILL FIGURE THIS OUT. I HAVEN'T DISAPPOINTED A CLIENT YET, AND LORD VADER WILL NOT BE THE FIRST.
IF THIS WERE A JOB JUST ANYONE COULD DO, THEY WOULDN'T HAVE SENT COLONEL ALVA BRENNE.

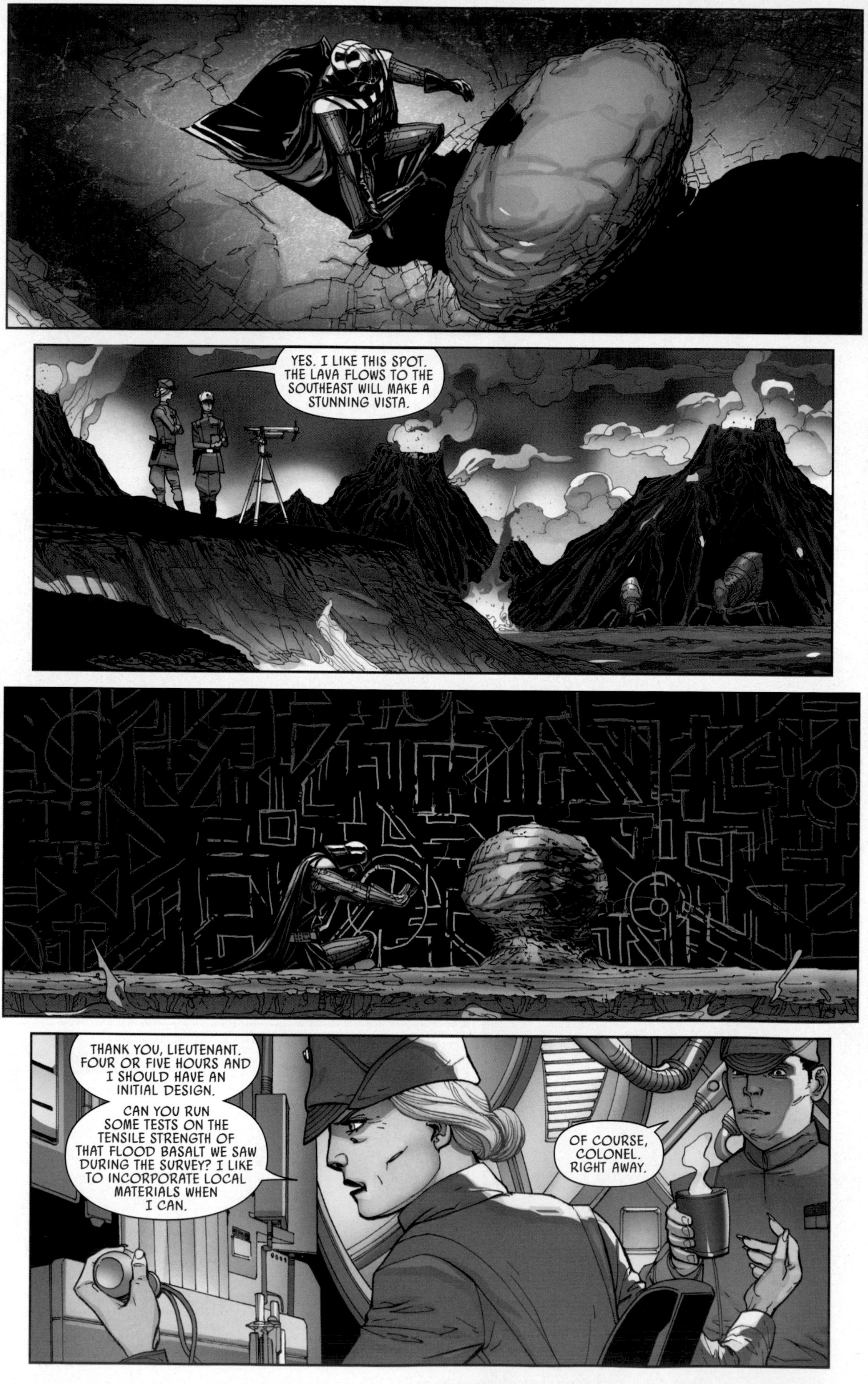

YES. I LIKE THIS SPOT. THE LAVA FLOWS TO THE SOUTHEAST WILL MAKE A STUNNING VISTA.
THANK YOU, LIEUTENANT. FOUR OR FIVE HOURS AND I SHOULD HAVE AN INITIAL DESIGN.
CAN YOU RUN SOME TESTS ON THE TENSILE STRENGTH OF THAT FLOOD BASALT WE SAW DURING THE SURVEY? I LIKE TO INCORPORATE LOCAL MATERIALS WHEN I CAN.
OF COURSE, COLONEL. RIGHT AWAY.

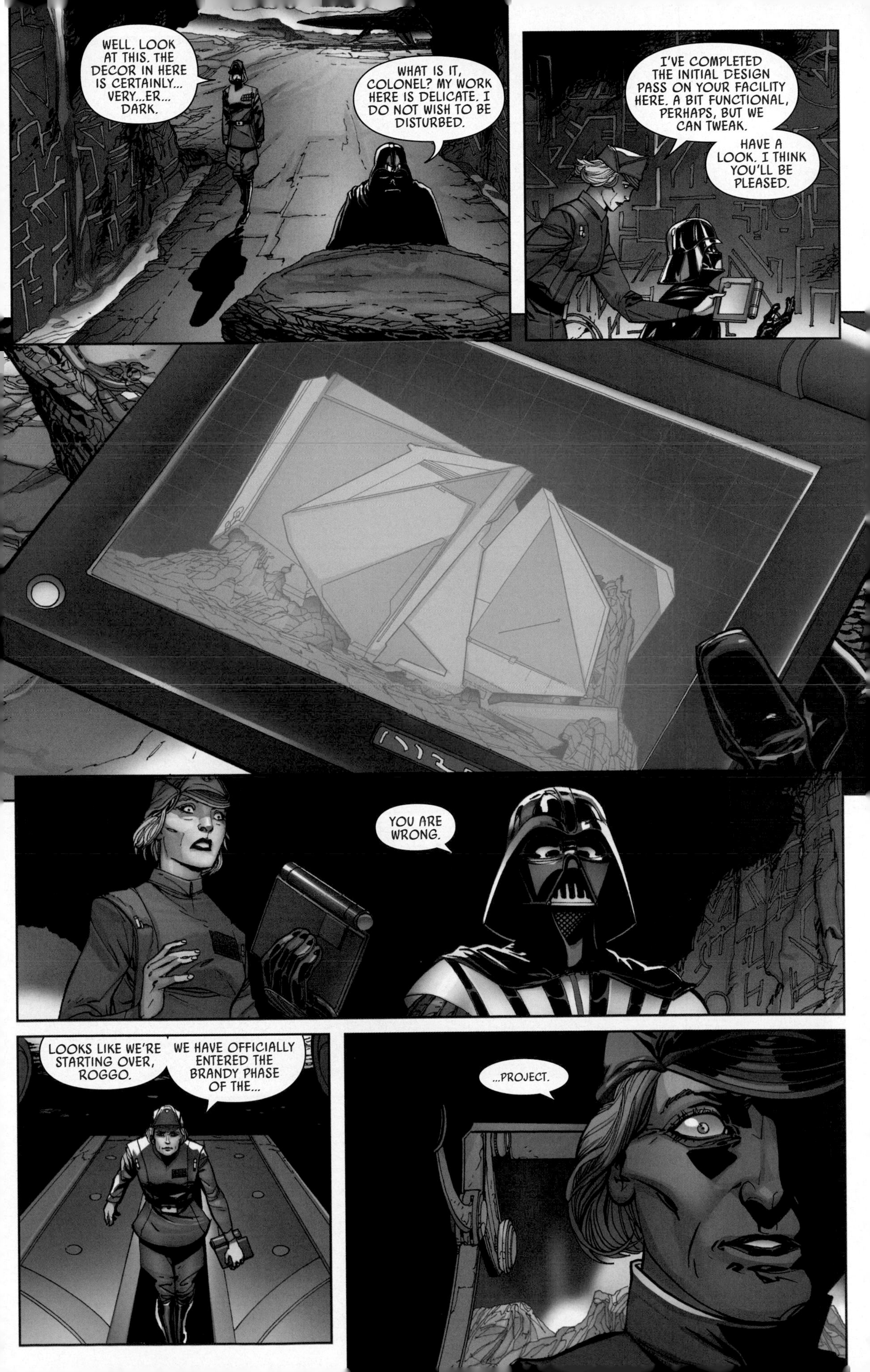
WELL. LOOK AT THIS. THE DECOR IN HERE IS CERTAINLY... VERY...ER... DARK.
WHAT IS IT, COLONEL? MY WORK HERE IS DELICATE. I DO NOT WISH TO BE DISTURBED.
I'VE COMPLETED THE INITIAL DESIGN PASS ON YOUR FACILITY HERE. A BIT FUNCTIONAL, PERHAPS, BUT WE CAN TWEAK.
HAVE A LOOK. I THINK YOU'LL BE PLEASED.
YOU ARE WRONG.
LOOKS LIKE WE'RE STARTING OVER, ROGGO.
WE HAVE OFFICIALLY ENTERED THE BRANDY PHASE OF THE...
...PROJECT.

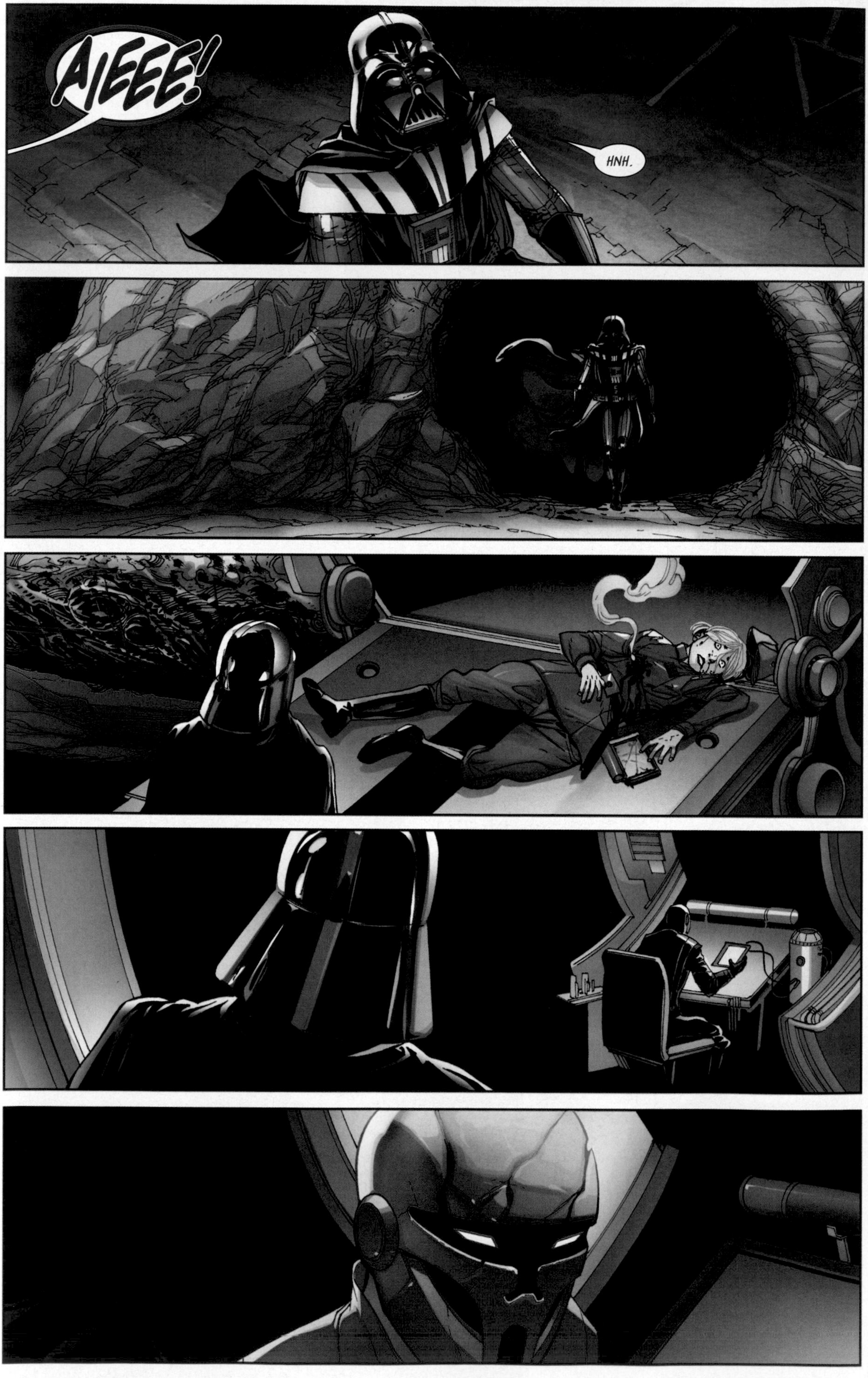
AIEEE!
HNH.

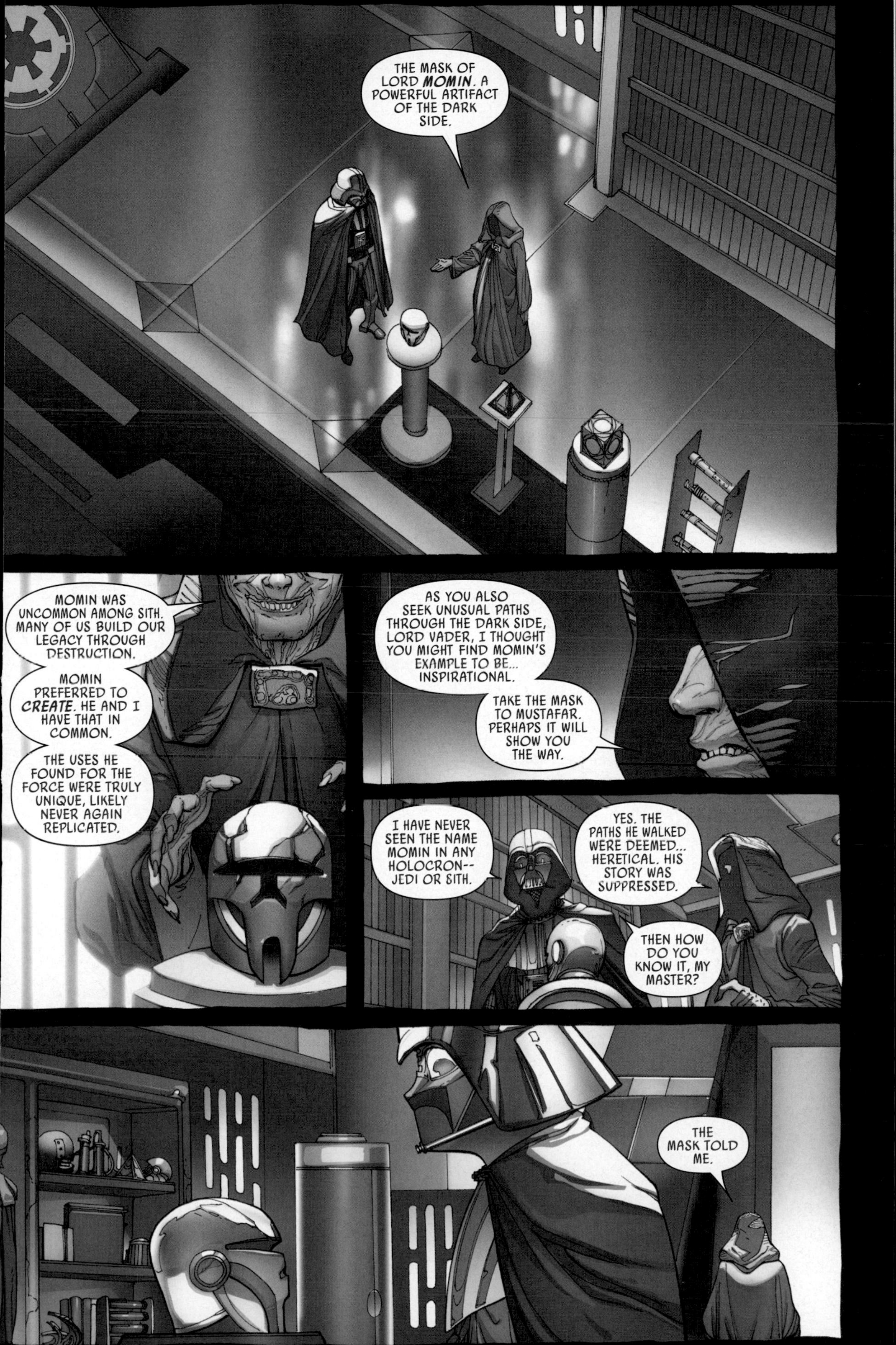
THE MASK OF LORD MOMIN. A POWERFUL ARTIFACT OF THE DARK SIDE.
MOMIN WAS UNCOMMON AMONG SITH. MANY OF US BUILD OUR LEGACY THROUGH DESTRUCTION.
MOMIN PREFERRED TO CREATE. HE AND I HAVE THAT IN COMMON.
THE USES HE FOUND FOR THE FORCE WERE TRULY UNIQUE, LIKELY NEVER AGAIN REPLICATED.
AS YOU ALSO SEEK UNUSUAL PATHS THROUGH THE DARK SIDE, LORD VADER, I THOUGHT YOU MIGHT FIND MOMIN'S EXAMPLE TO BE... INSPIRATIONAL.
TAKE THE MASK TO MUSTAFAR. PERHAPS IT WILL SHOW YOU THE WAY.
I HAVE NEVER SEEN THE NAME MOMIN IN ANY HOLOCRON-- JEDI OR SITH.
YES. THE PATHS HE WALKED WERE DEEMED... HERETICAL. HIS STORY WAS SUPPRESSED.
THEN HOW DO YOU KNOW IT, MY MASTER?
THE MASK TOLD ME.

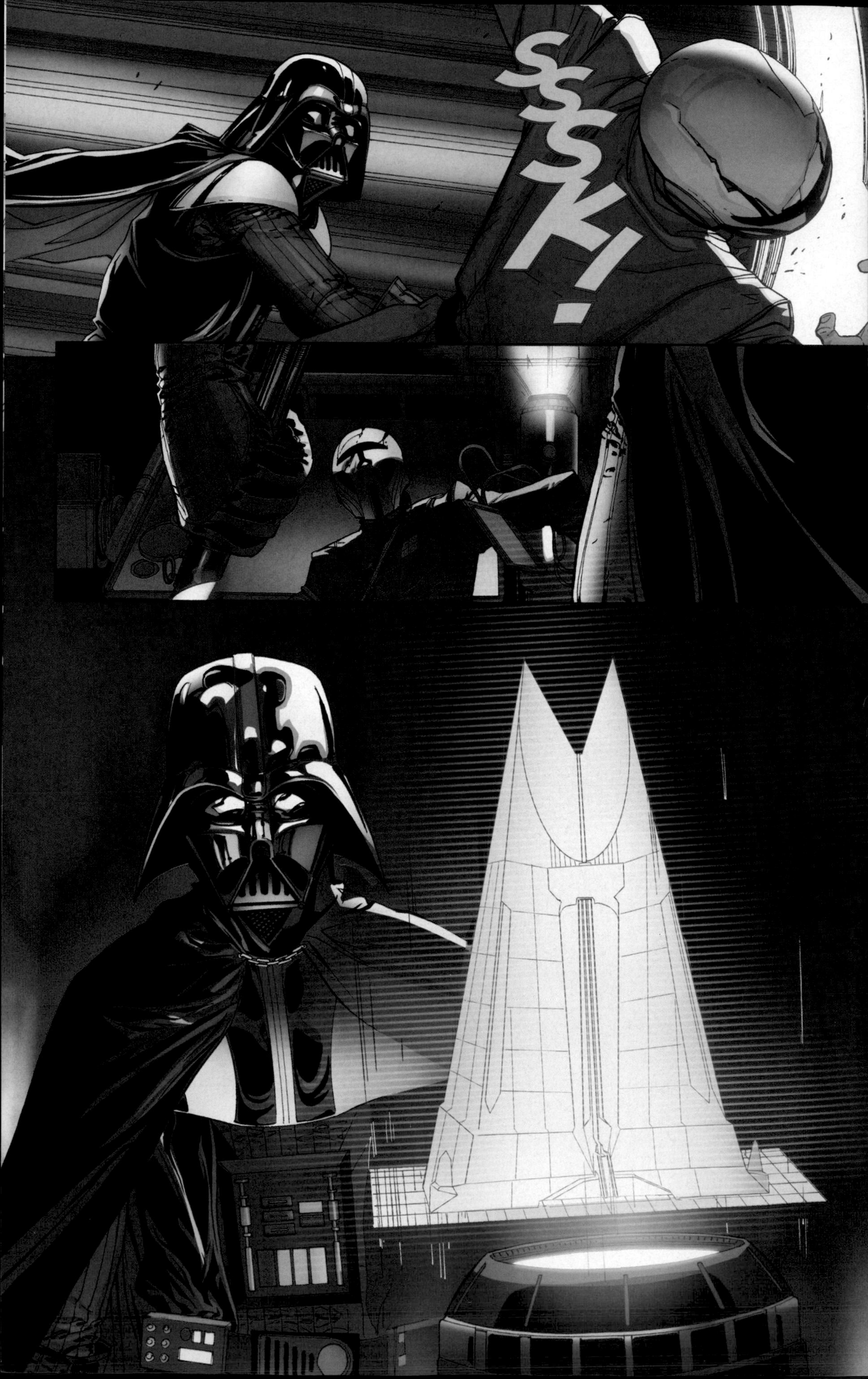
SSSK!

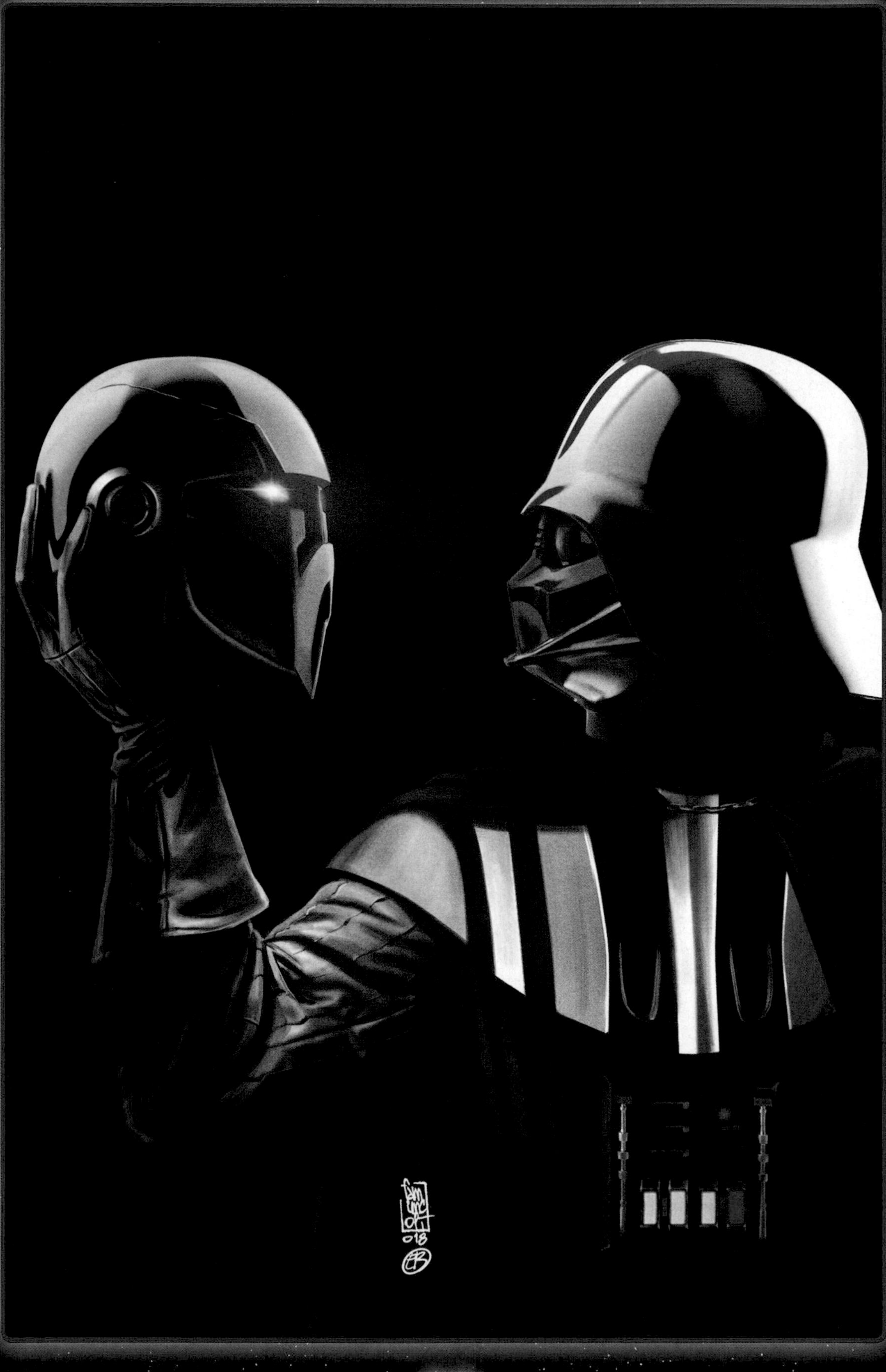

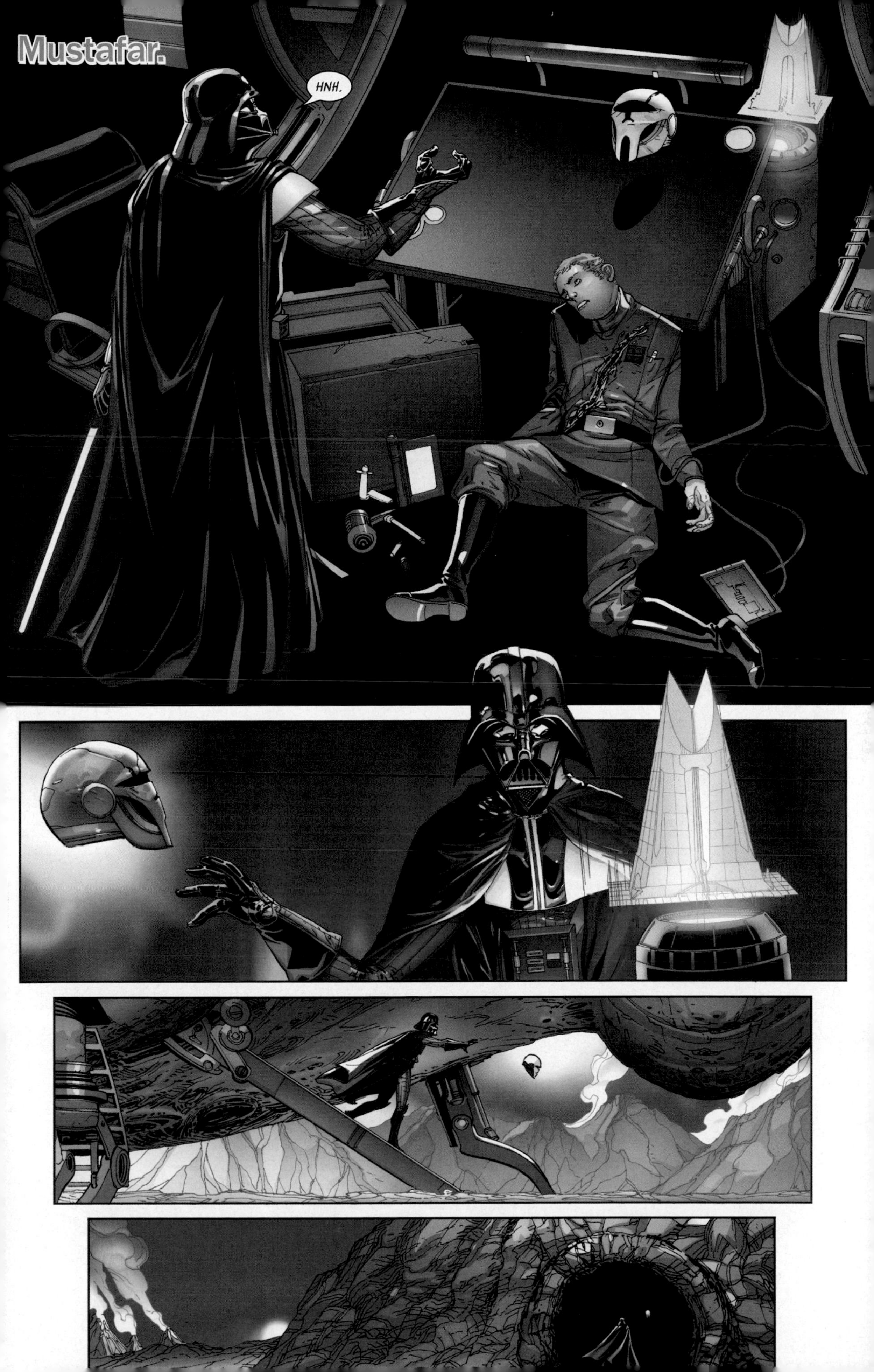
Mustafar.
HNH.

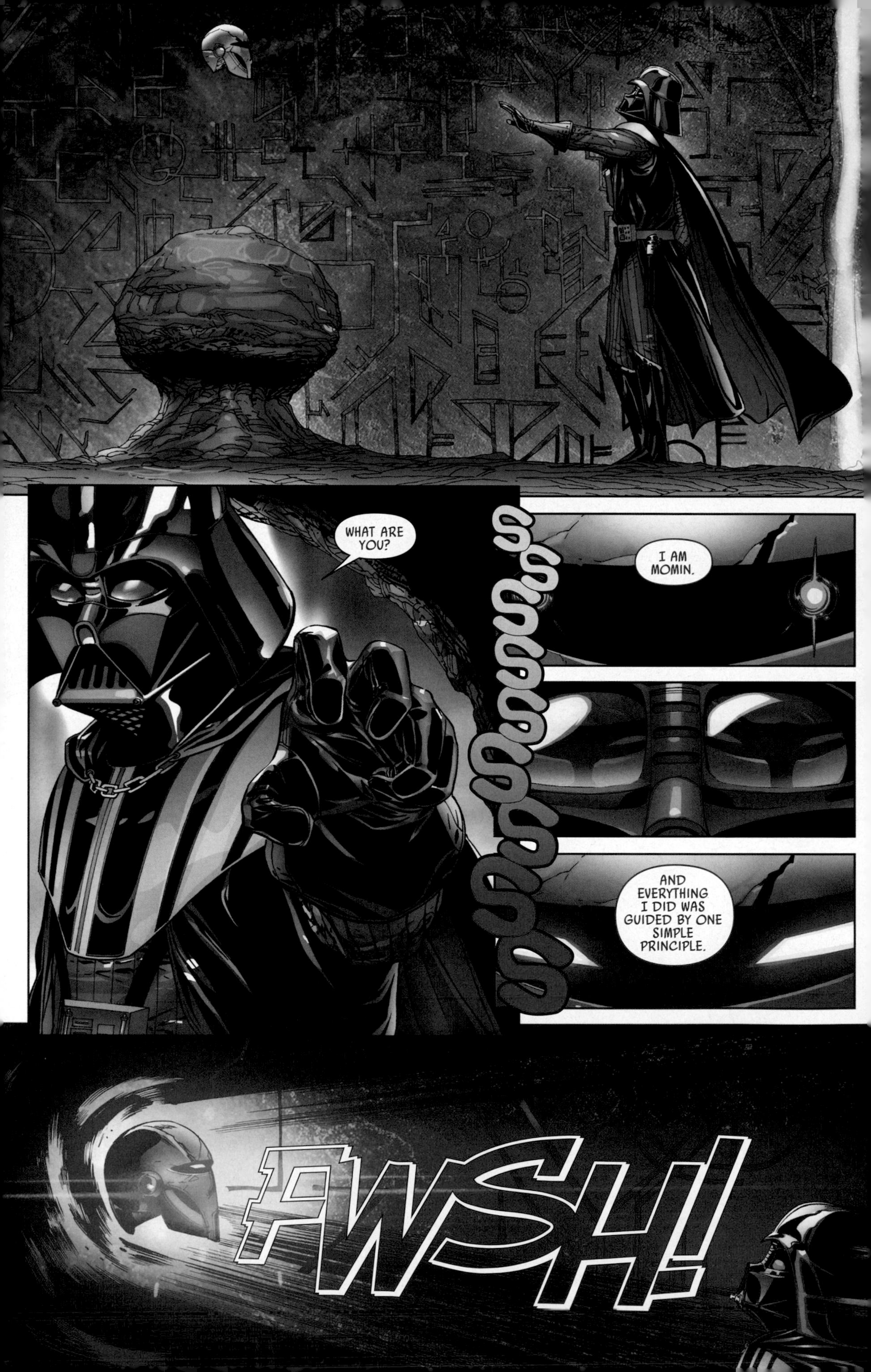
WHAT ARE YOU?
SSSSSSSSSSSSSSS
I AM MOMIN.
AND EVERYTHING I DID WAS GUIDED BY ONE SIMPLE PRINCIPLE.
FWSH!

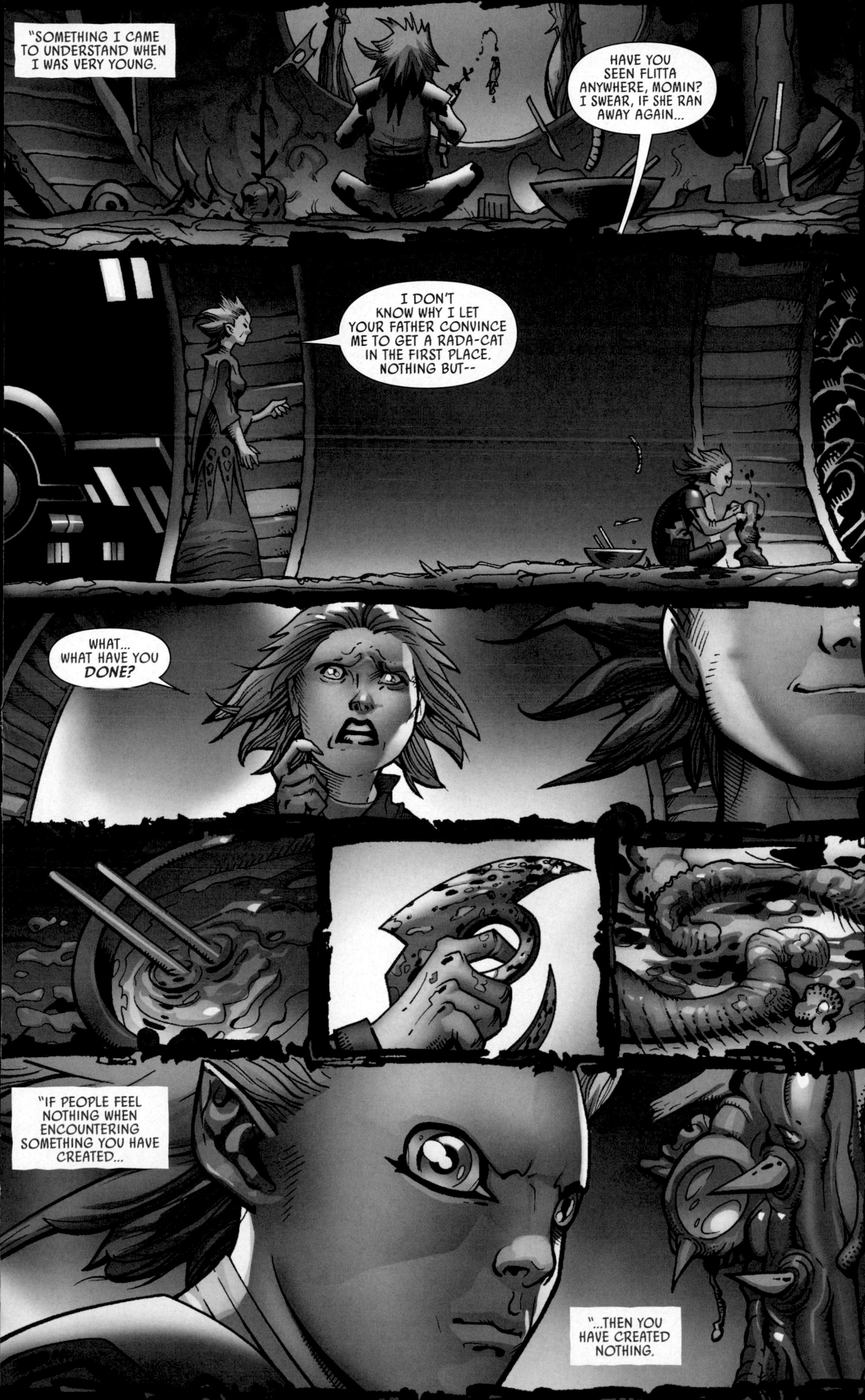

"SOMETHING I CAME TO UNDERSTAND WHEN I WAS VERY YOUNG.
HAVE YOU SEEN FLITTA ANYWHERE, MOMIN? I SWEAR, IF SHE RAN AWAY AGAIN...
I DON'T KNOW WHY I LET YOUR FATHER CONVINCE ME TO GET A RADA-CAT IN THE FIRST PLACE. NOTHING BUT--
WHAT... WHAT HAVE YOU *DONE?*
"IF PEOPLE FEEL NOTHING WHEN ENCOUNTERING SOMETHING YOU HAVE CREATED...
"...THEN YOU HAVE CREATED NOTHING.

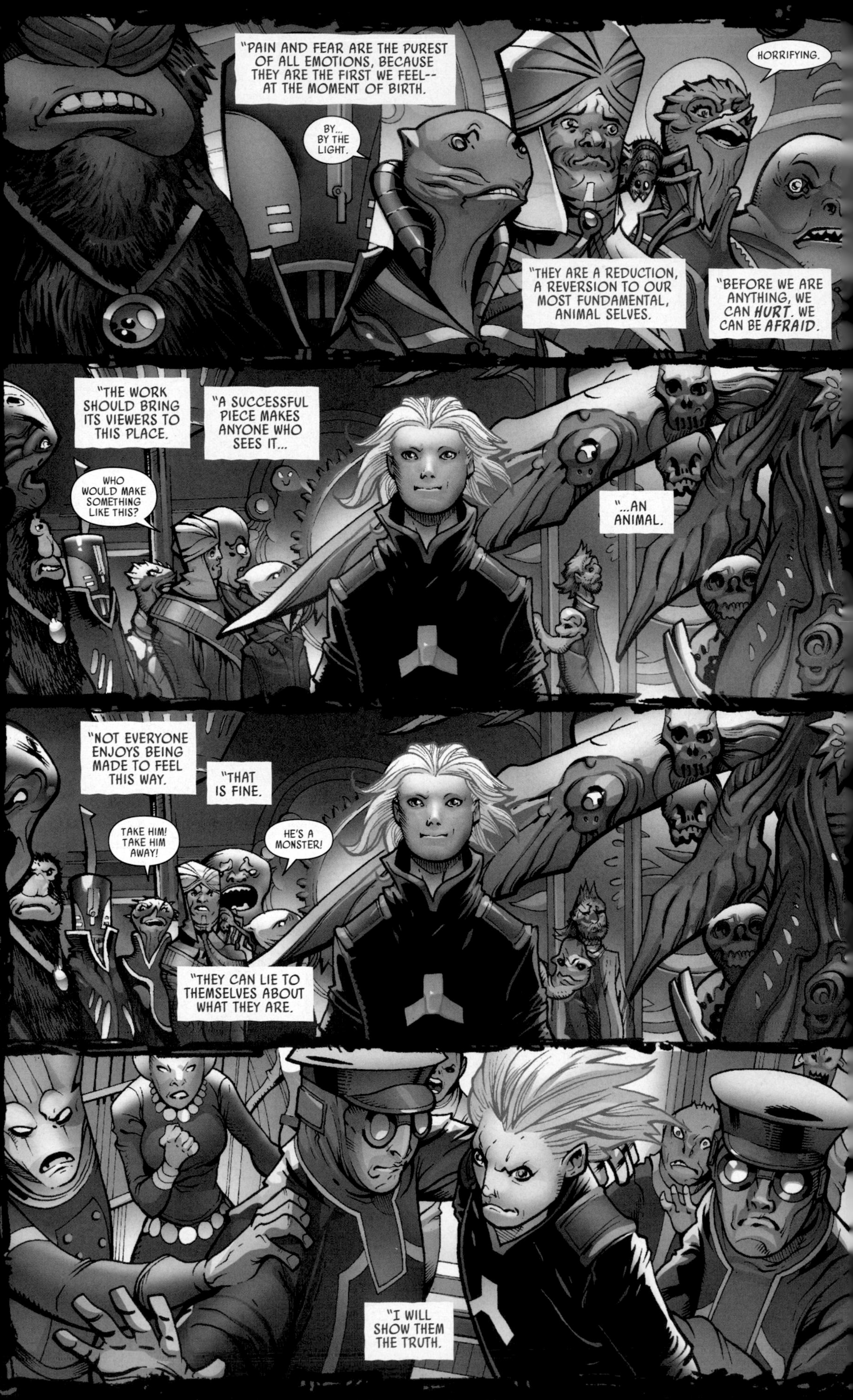
"PAIN AND FEAR ARE THE PUREST OF ALL EMOTIONS, BECAUSE THEY ARE THE FIRST WE FEEL-- AT THE MOMENT OF BIRTH.
BY... BY THE LIGHT.
HORRIFYING.
"THEY ARE A REDUCTION, A REVERSION TO OUR MOST FUNDAMENTAL, ANIMAL SELVES.
"BEFORE WE ARE ANYTHING, WE CAN HURT. WE CAN BE AFRAID.
"THE WORK SHOULD BRING ITS VIEWERS TO THIS PLACE.
"A SUCCESSFUL PIECE MAKES ANYONE WHO SEES IT...
WHO WOULD MAKE SOMETHING LIKE THIS?
"...AN ANIMAL.
"NOT EVERYONE ENJOYS BEING MADE TO FEEL THIS WAY.
"THAT IS FINE.
TAKE HIM! TAKE HIM AWAY!
HE'S A MONSTER!
"THEY CAN LIE TO THEMSELVES ABOUT WHAT THEY ARE.
"I WILL SHOW THEM THE TRUTH.

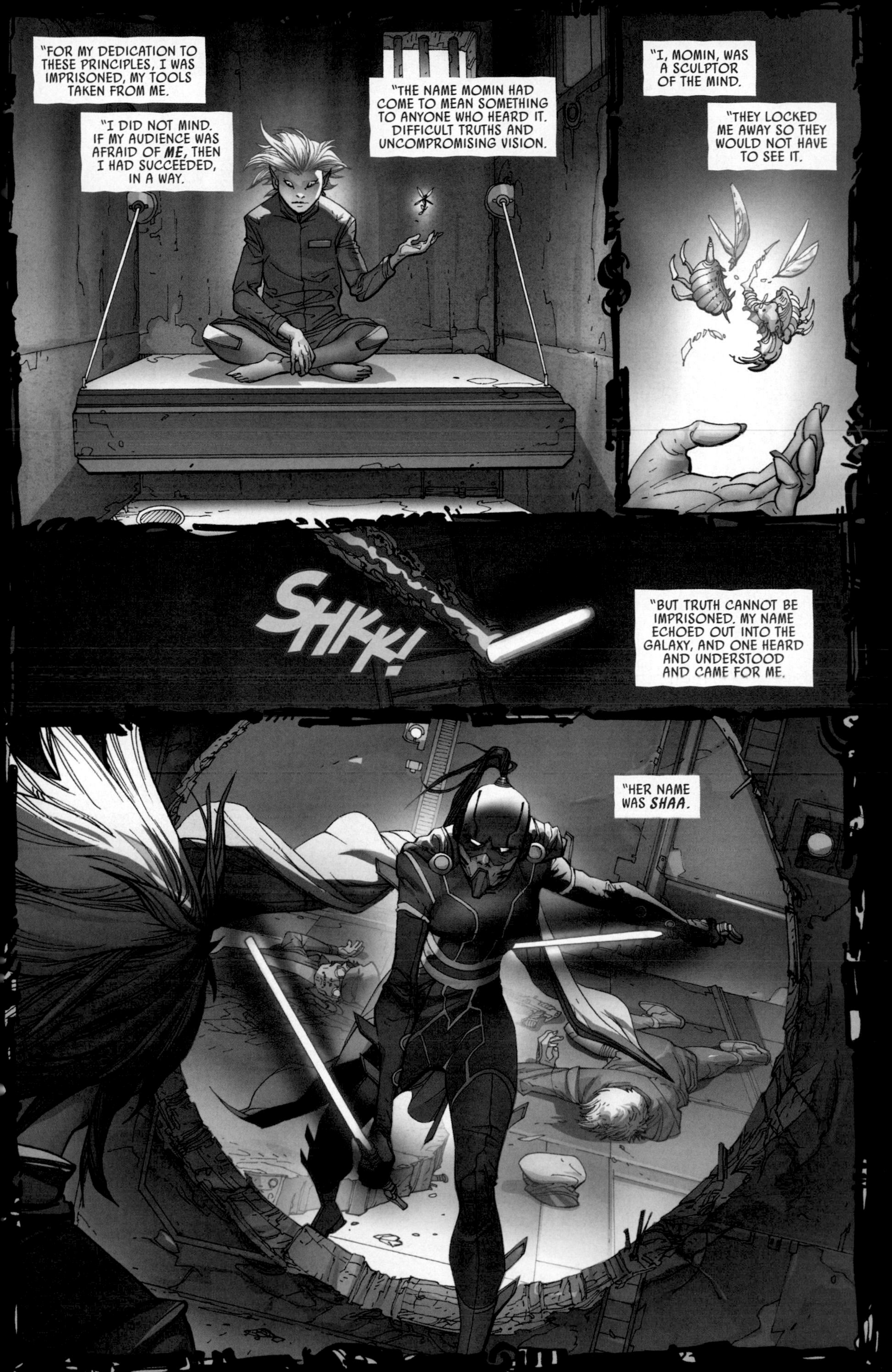
"FOR MY DEDICATION TO THESE PRINCIPLES, I WAS IMPRISONED, MY TOOLS TAKEN FROM ME.
"I DID NOT MIND. IF MY AUDIENCE WAS AFRAID OF ME, THEN I HAD SUCCEEDED, IN A WAY.
"THE NAME MOMIN HAD COME TO MEAN SOMETHING TO ANYONE WHO HEARD IT. DIFFICULT TRUTHS AND UNCOMPROMISING VISION.
"I, MOMIN, WAS A SCULPTOR OF THE MIND.
"THEY LOCKED ME AWAY SO THEY WOULD NOT HAVE TO SEE IT.
SHKK!
"BUT TRUTH CANNOT BE IMPRISONED. MY NAME ECHOED OUT INTO THE GALAXY, AND ONE HEARD AND UNDERSTOOD AND CAME FOR ME.
"HER NAME WAS SHAA.

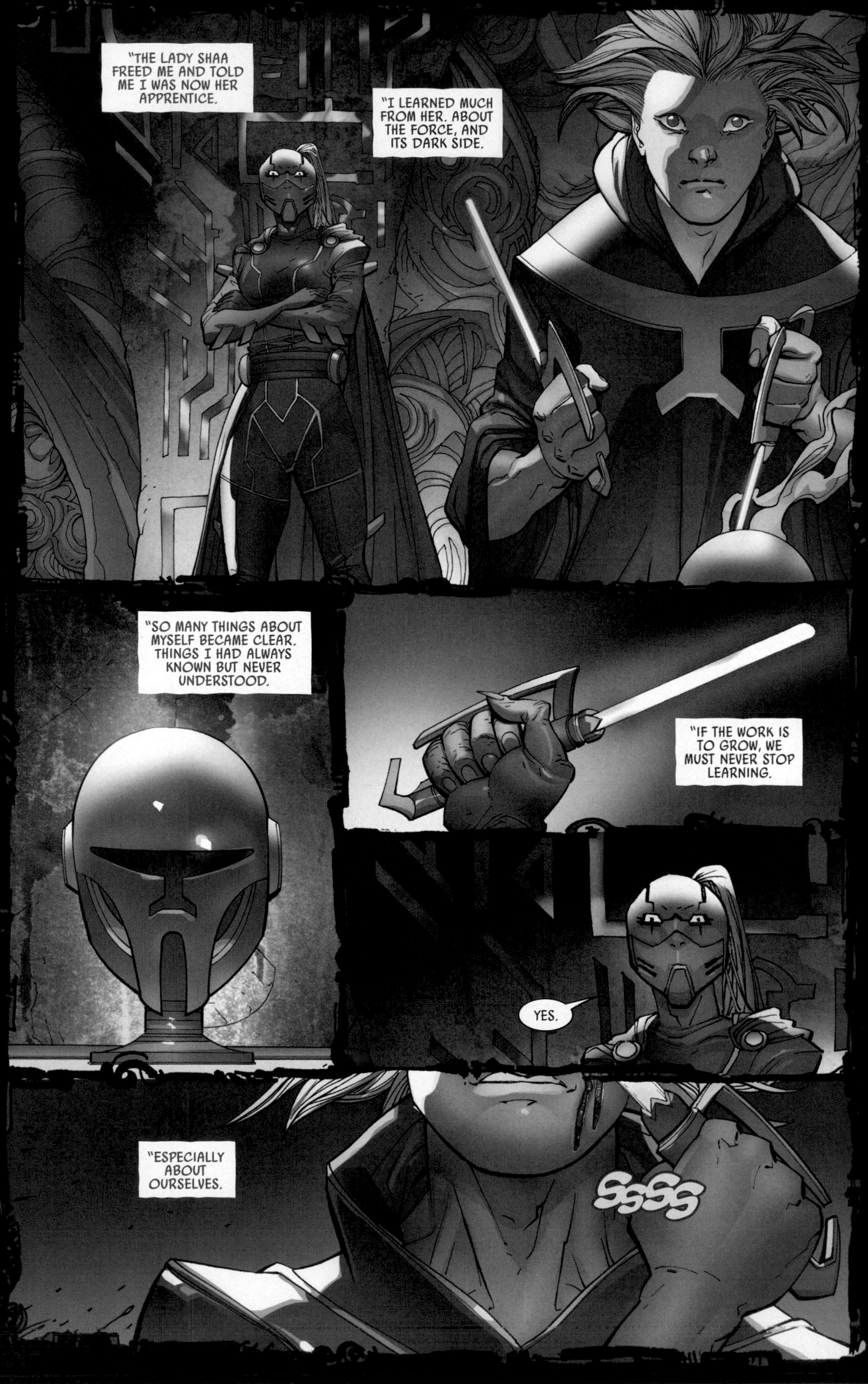
"THE LADY SHAA FREED ME AND TOLD ME I WAS NOW HER APPRENTICE.
"I LEARNED MUCH FROM HER. ABOUT THE FORCE, AND ITS DARK SIDE.
"SO MANY THINGS ABOUT MYSELF BECAME CLEAR. THINGS I HAD ALWAYS KNOWN BUT NEVER UNDERSTOOD.
"IF THE WORK IS TO GROW, WE MUST NEVER STOP LEARNING.
YES.
"ESPECIALLY ABOUT OURSELVES.
SSSS

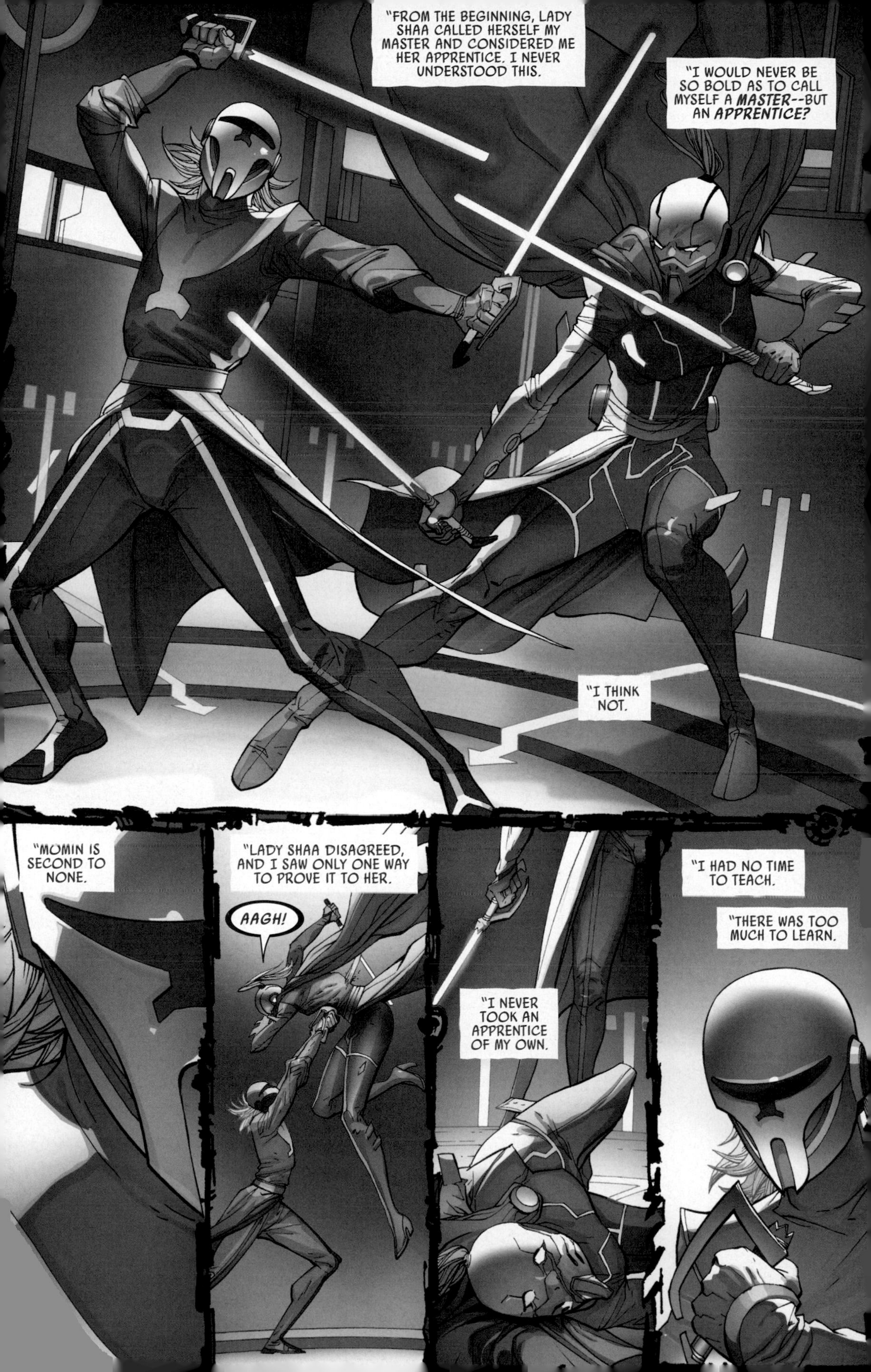
"FROM THE BEGINNING, LADY SHAA CALLED HERSELF MY MASTER AND CONSIDERED ME HER APPRENTICE. I NEVER UNDERSTOOD THIS.
"I WOULD NEVER BE SO BOLD AS TO CALL MYSELF A MASTER--BUT AN APPRENTICE?
"I THINK NOT.
"MOMIN IS SECOND TO NONE.
"LADY SHAA DISAGREED, AND I SAW ONLY ONE WAY TO PROVE IT TO HER.
AAGH!
"I NEVER TOOK AN APPRENTICE OF MY OWN.
"I HAD NO TIME TO TEACH.
"THERE WAS TOO MUCH TO LEARN.

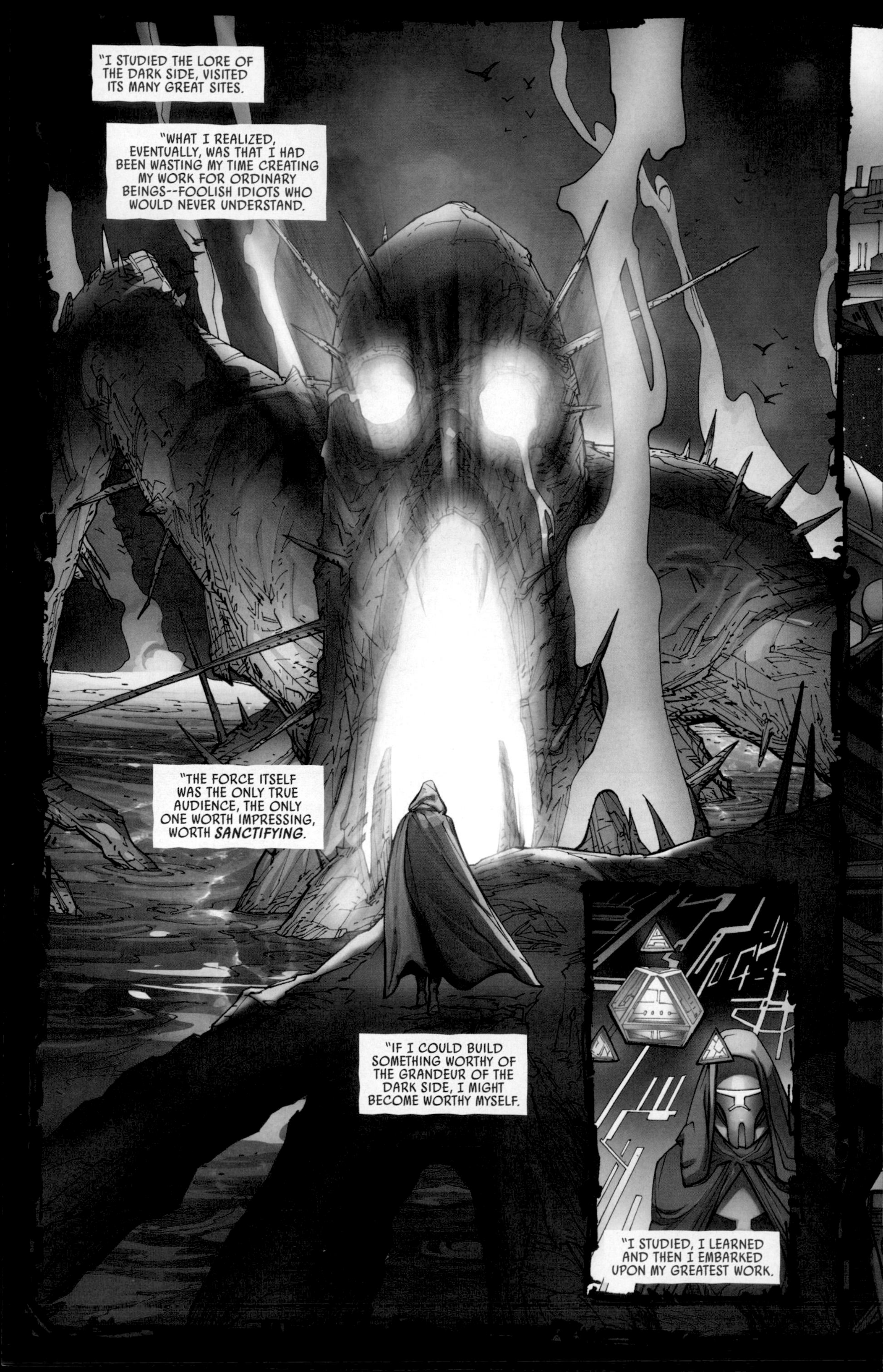
"I STUDIED THE LORE OF THE DARK SIDE, VISITED ITS MANY GREAT SITES.
"WHAT I REALIZED, EVENTUALLY, WAS THAT I HAD BEEN WASTING MY TIME CREATING MY WORK FOR ORDINARY BEINGS--FOOLISH IDIOTS WHO WOULD NEVER UNDERSTAND.
"THE FORCE ITSELF WAS THE ONLY TRUE AUDIENCE, THE ONLY ONE WORTH IMPRESSING, WORTH *SANCTIFYING*.
"IF I COULD BUILD SOMETHING WORTHY OF THE GRANDEUR OF THE DARK SIDE, I MIGHT BECOME WORTHY MYSELF.
"I STUDIED, I LEARNED AND THEN I EMBARKED UPON MY GREATEST WORK.

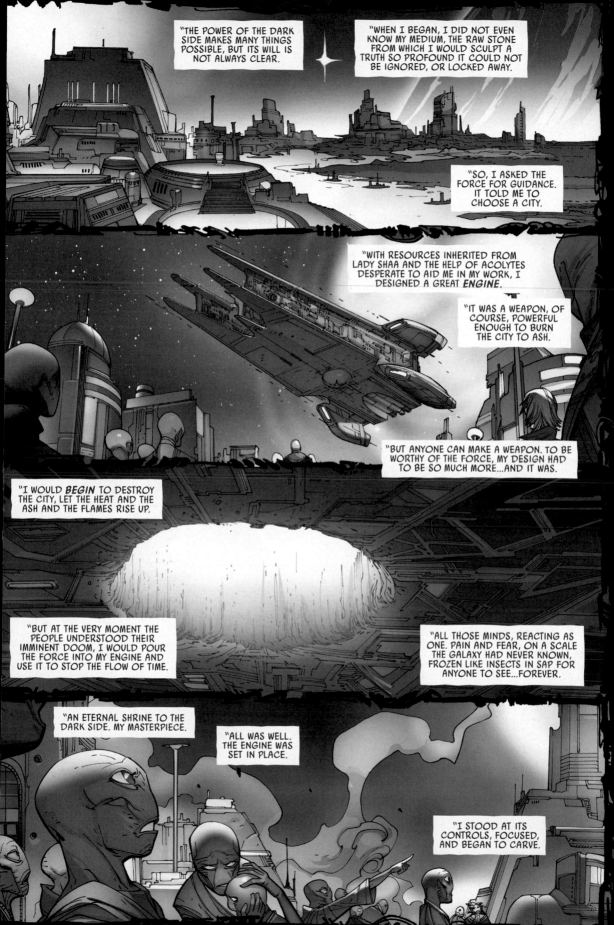

"THE POWER OF THE DARK SIDE MAKES MANY THINGS POSSIBLE, BUT ITS WILL IS NOT ALWAYS CLEAR.

"WHEN I BEGAN, I DID NOT EVEN KNOW MY MEDIUM, THE RAW STONE FROM WHICH I WOULD SCULPT A TRUTH SO PROFOUND IT COULD NOT BE IGNORED, OR LOCKED AWAY.

"SO, I ASKED THE FORCE FOR GUIDANCE. IT TOLD ME TO CHOOSE A CITY.

"WITH RESOURCES INHERITED FROM LADY SHAA AND THE HELP OF ACOLYTES DESPERATE TO AID ME IN MY WORK, I DESIGNED A GREAT *ENGINE*.

"IT WAS A WEAPON, OF COURSE, POWERFUL ENOUGH TO BURN THE CITY TO ASH.

"BUT ANYONE CAN MAKE A WEAPON. TO BE WORTHY OF THE FORCE, MY DESIGN HAD TO BE SO MUCH MORE...AND IT WAS.

"I WOULD *BEGIN* TO DESTROY THE CITY, LET THE HEAT AND THE ASH AND THE FLAMES RISE UP.

"BUT AT THE VERY MOMENT THE PEOPLE UNDERSTOOD THEIR IMMINENT DOOM, I WOULD POUR THE FORCE INTO MY ENGINE AND USE IT TO STOP THE FLOW OF TIME.

"ALL THOSE MINDS, REACTING AS ONE. PAIN AND FEAR, ON A SCALE THE GALAXY HAD NEVER KNOWN, FROZEN LIKE INSECTS IN SAP FOR ANYONE TO SEE...FOREVER.

"AN ETERNAL SHRINE TO THE DARK SIDE. MY MASTERPIECE.

"ALL WAS WELL. THE ENGINE WAS SET IN PLACE.

"I STOOD AT ITS CONTROLS, FOCUSED, AND BEGAN TO CARVE.

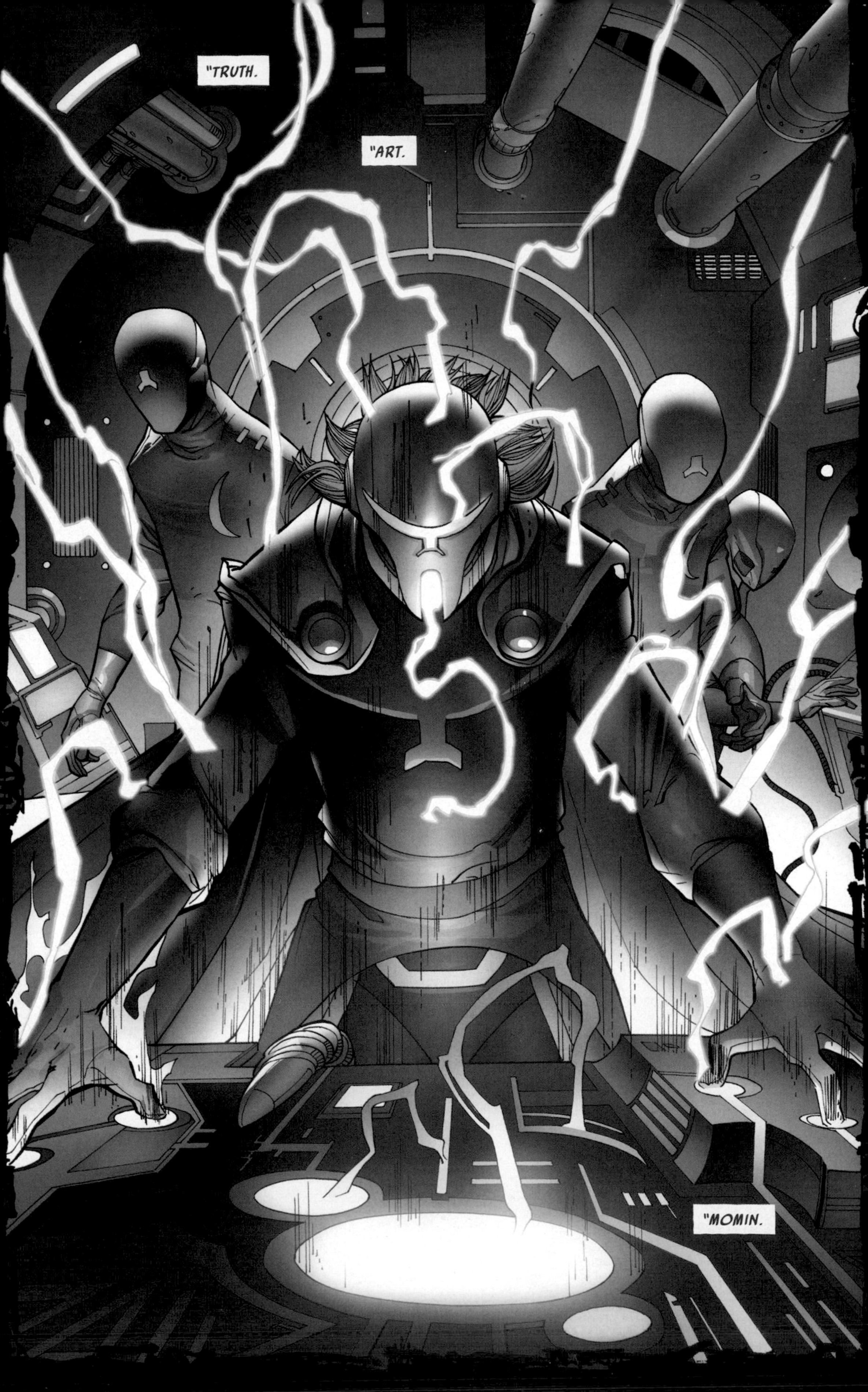
"TRUTH.
"ART.
"MOMIN.

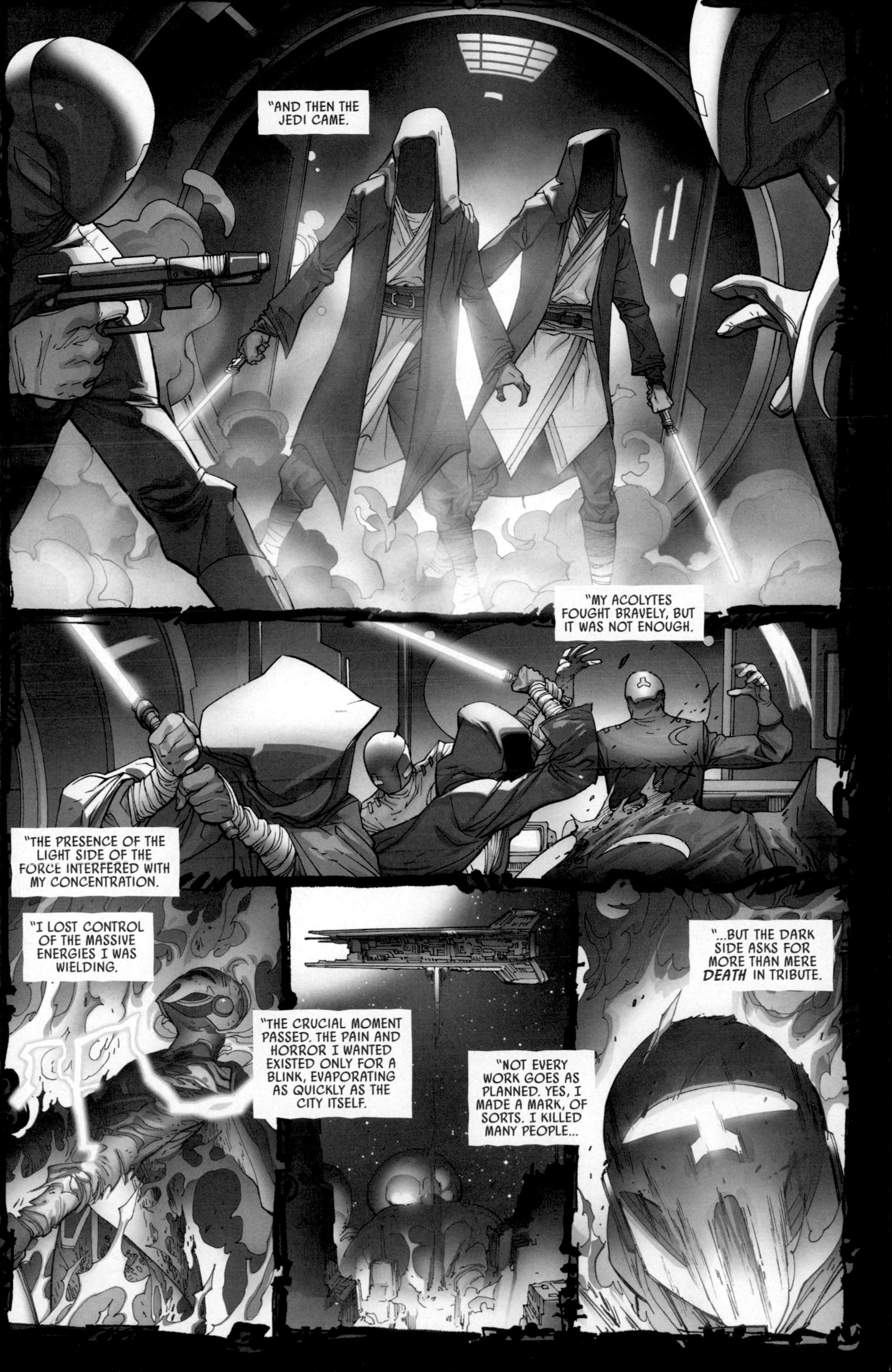
"AND THEN THE JEDI CAME.
"MY ACOLYTES FOUGHT BRAVELY, BUT IT WAS NOT ENOUGH.
"THE PRESENCE OF THE LIGHT SIDE OF THE FORCE INTERFERED WITH MY CONCENTRATION.
"I LOST CONTROL OF THE MASSIVE ENERGIES I WAS WIELDING.
"THE CRUCIAL MOMENT PASSED. THE PAIN AND HORROR I WANTED EXISTED ONLY FOR A BLINK, EVAPORATING AS QUICKLY AS THE CITY ITSELF.
"NOT EVERY WORK GOES AS PLANNED. YES, I MADE A MARK, OF SORTS. I KILLED MANY PEOPLE...
"...BUT THE DARK SIDE ASKS FOR MORE THAN MERE *DEATH* IN TRIBUTE.

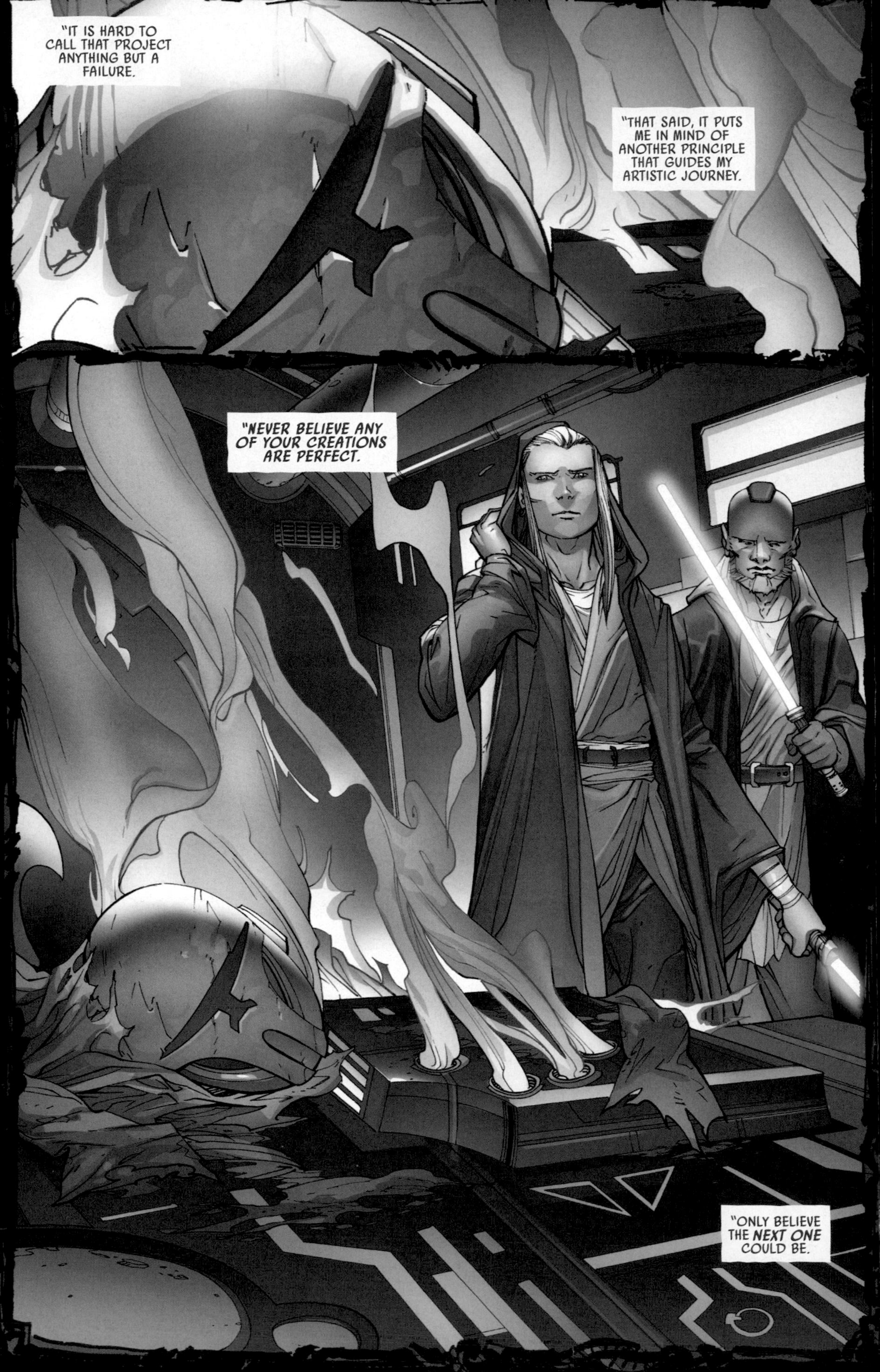
"IT IS HARD TO CALL THAT PROJECT ANYTHING BUT A FAILURE.
"THAT SAID, IT PUTS ME IN MIND OF ANOTHER PRINCIPLE THAT GUIDES MY ARTISTIC JOURNEY.
"*NEVER BELIEVE ANY OF YOUR CREATIONS ARE PERFECT.*
"ONLY BELIEVE THE ***NEXT ONE*** COULD BE.

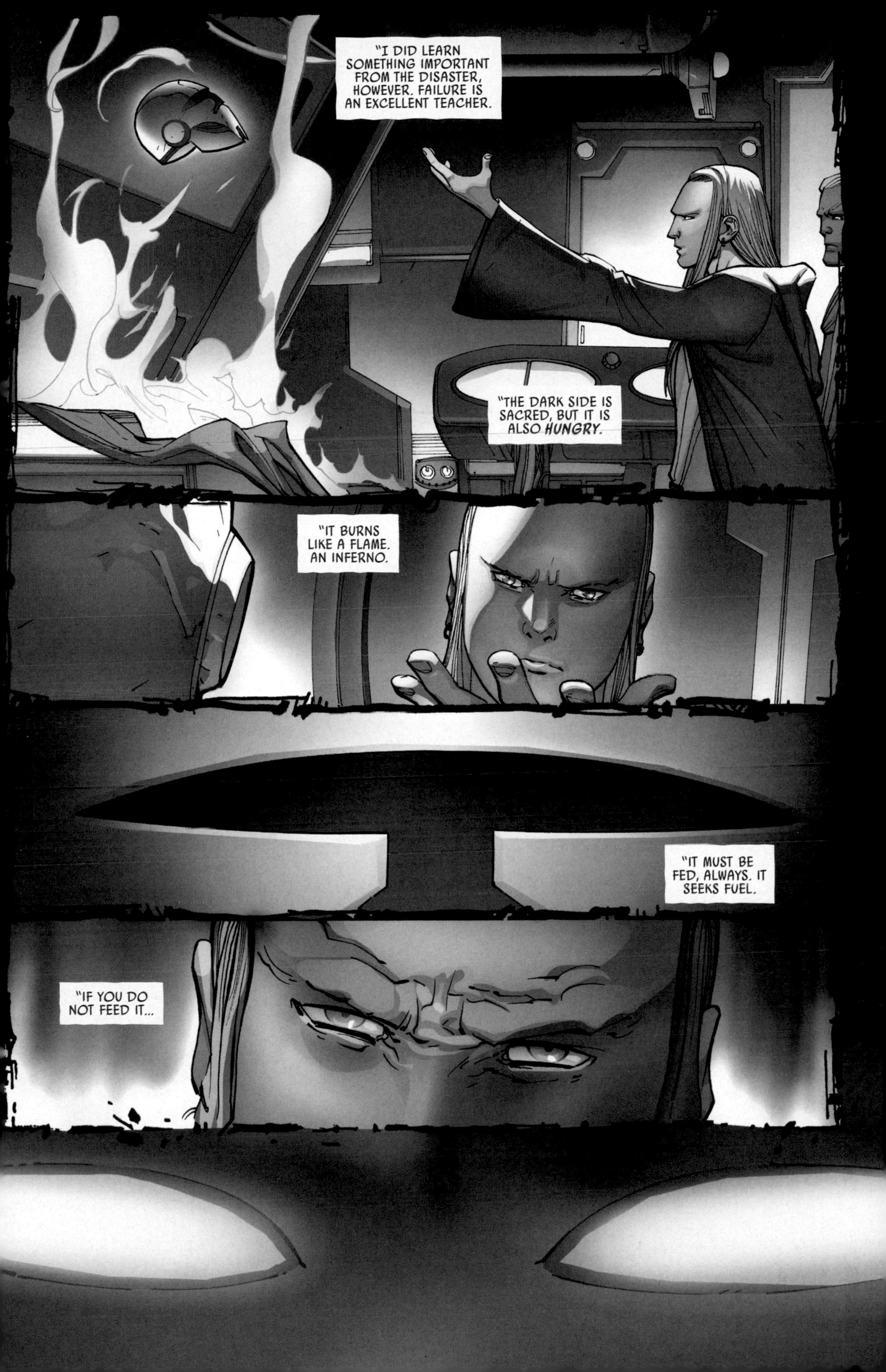
"I DID LEARN SOMETHING IMPORTANT FROM THE DISASTER, HOWEVER. FAILURE IS AN EXCELLENT TEACHER.
"THE DARK SIDE IS SACRED, BUT IT IS ALSO HUNGRY.
"IT BURNS LIKE A FLAME. AN INFERNO.
"IT MUST BE FED, ALWAYS. IT SEEKS FUEL.
"IF YOU DO NOT FEED IT...

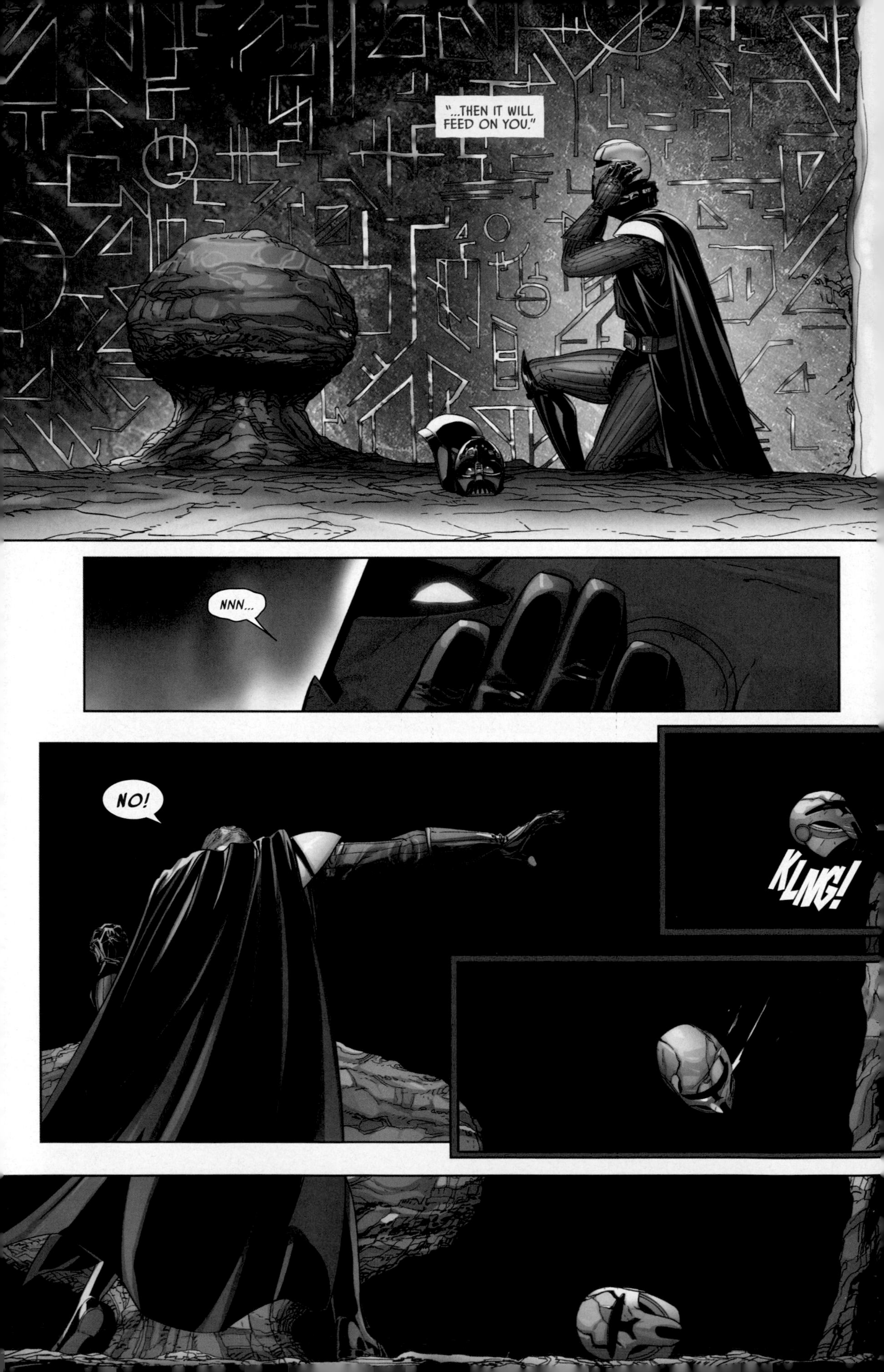
"...THEN IT WILL FEED ON YOU."
NNN...
NO!
KLNG!

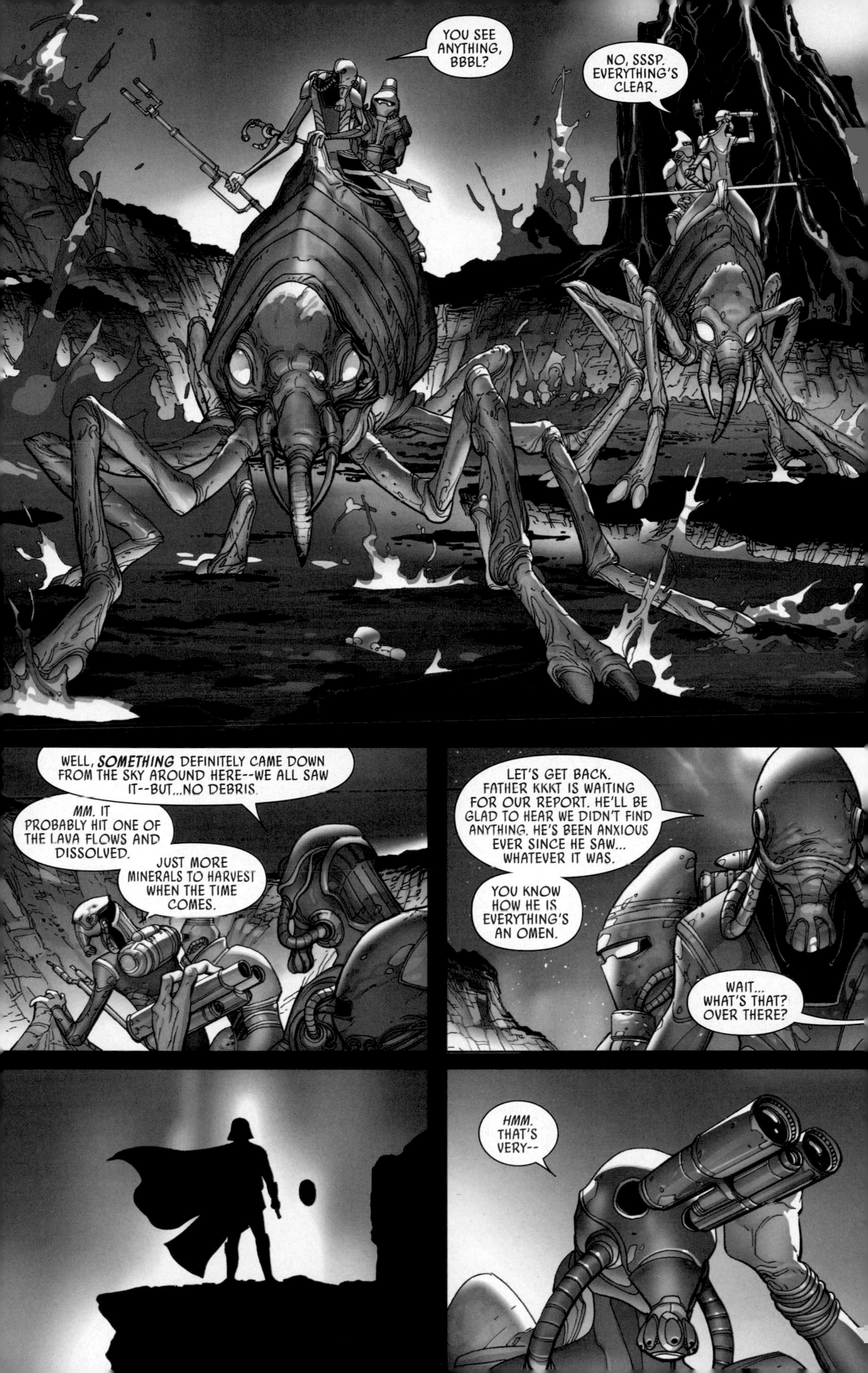
YOU SEE ANYTHING, BBBL?
NO, SSSP. EVERYTHING'S CLEAR.
WELL, *SOMETHING* DEFINITELY CAME DOWN FROM THE SKY AROUND HERE--WE ALL SAW IT--BUT...NO DEBRIS.
MM. IT PROBABLY HIT ONE OF THE LAVA FLOWS AND DISSOLVED.
JUST MORE MINERALS TO HARVEST WHEN THE TIME COMES.
LET'S GET BACK. FATHER KKKT IS WAITING FOR OUR REPORT. HE'LL BE GLAD TO HEAR WE DIDN'T FIND ANYTHING. HE'S BEEN ANXIOUS EVER SINCE HE SAW... WHATEVER IT WAS.
YOU KNOW HOW HE IS EVERYTHING'S AN OMEN.
WAIT... WHAT'S THAT? OVER THERE?
HMM. THAT'S VERY--

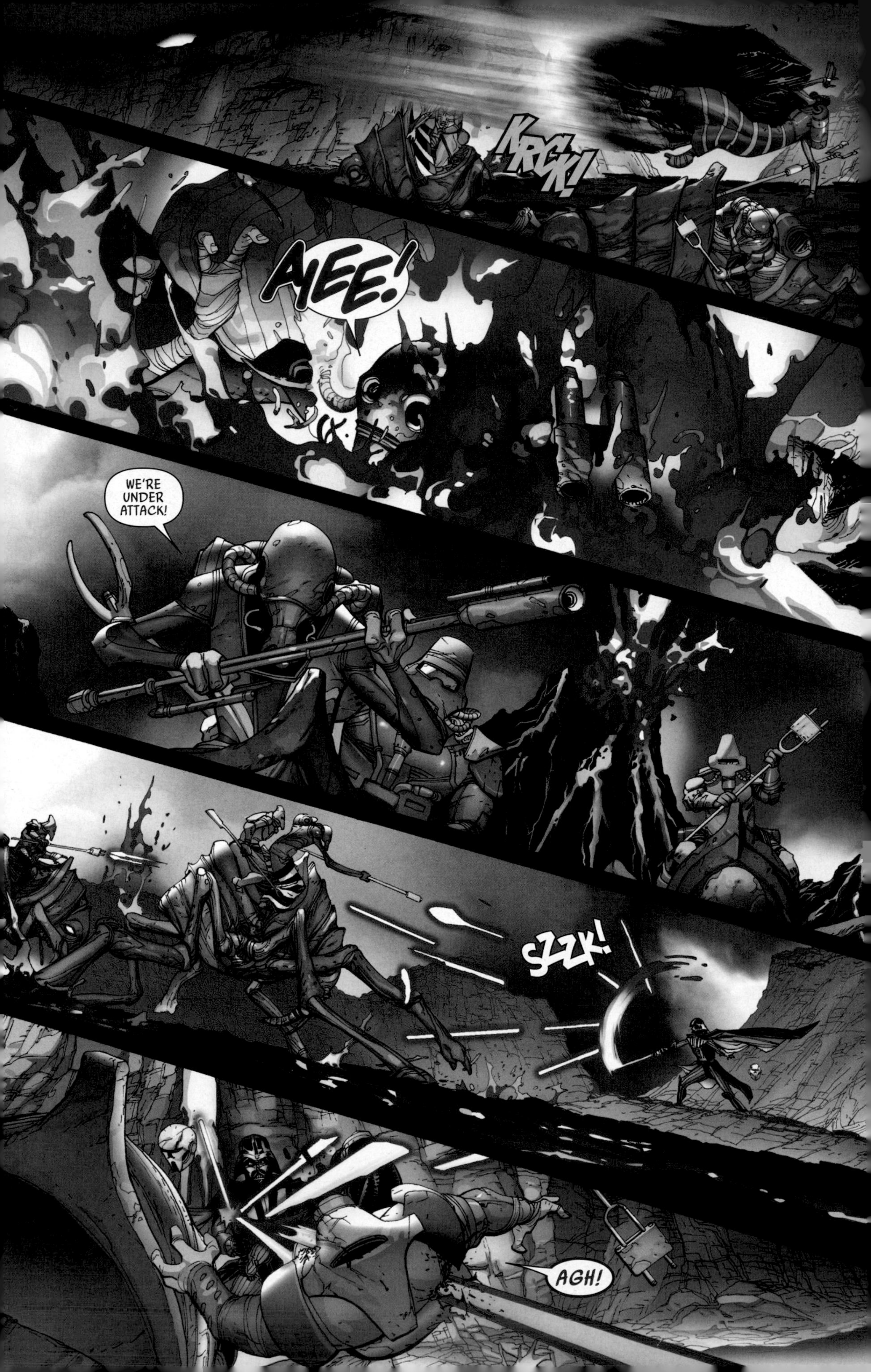
KRCK!
AIEE!
WE'RE UNDER ATTACK!
SZZK!
AGH!

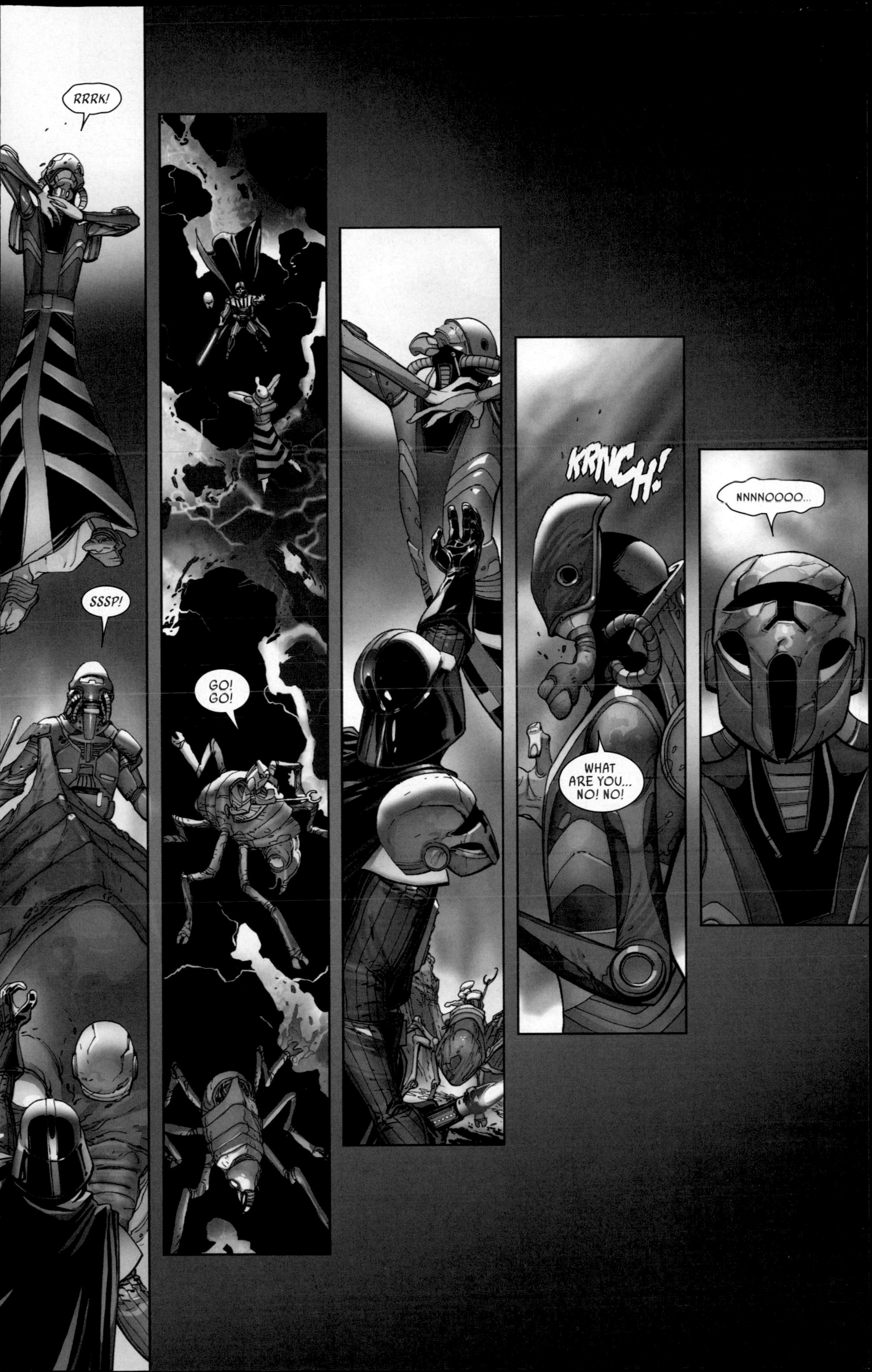
RRRK!
SSSP!
GO! GO!
KRNCH!
WHAT ARE YOU... NO! NO!
NNNNOOOO...

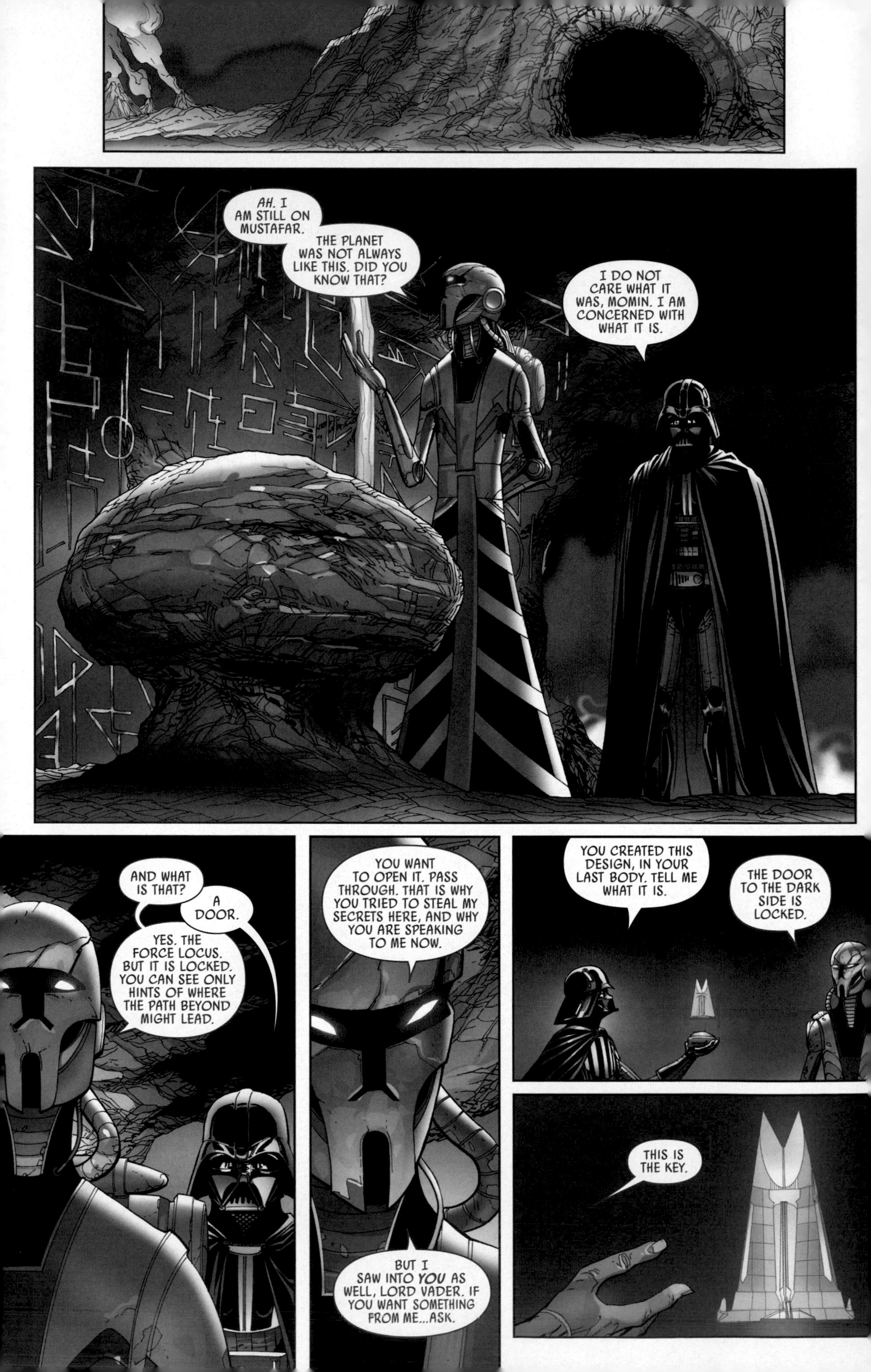
AH. I AM STILL ON MUSTAFAR.
THE PLANET WAS NOT ALWAYS LIKE THIS. DID YOU KNOW THAT?
I DO NOT CARE WHAT IT WAS, MOMIN. I AM CONCERNED WITH WHAT IT IS.
AND WHAT IS THAT?
A DOOR.
YES. THE FORCE LOCUS. BUT IT IS LOCKED. YOU CAN SEE ONLY HINTS OF WHERE THE PATH BEYOND MIGHT LEAD.
YOU WANT TO OPEN IT. PASS THROUGH. THAT IS WHY YOU TRIED TO STEAL MY SECRETS HERE, AND WHY YOU ARE SPEAKING TO ME NOW.
BUT I SAW INTO *YOU* AS WELL, LORD VADER. IF YOU WANT SOMETHING FROM ME...ASK.
YOU CREATED THIS DESIGN, IN YOUR LAST BODY. TELL ME WHAT IT IS.
THE DOOR TO THE DARK SIDE IS LOCKED.
THIS IS THE KEY.

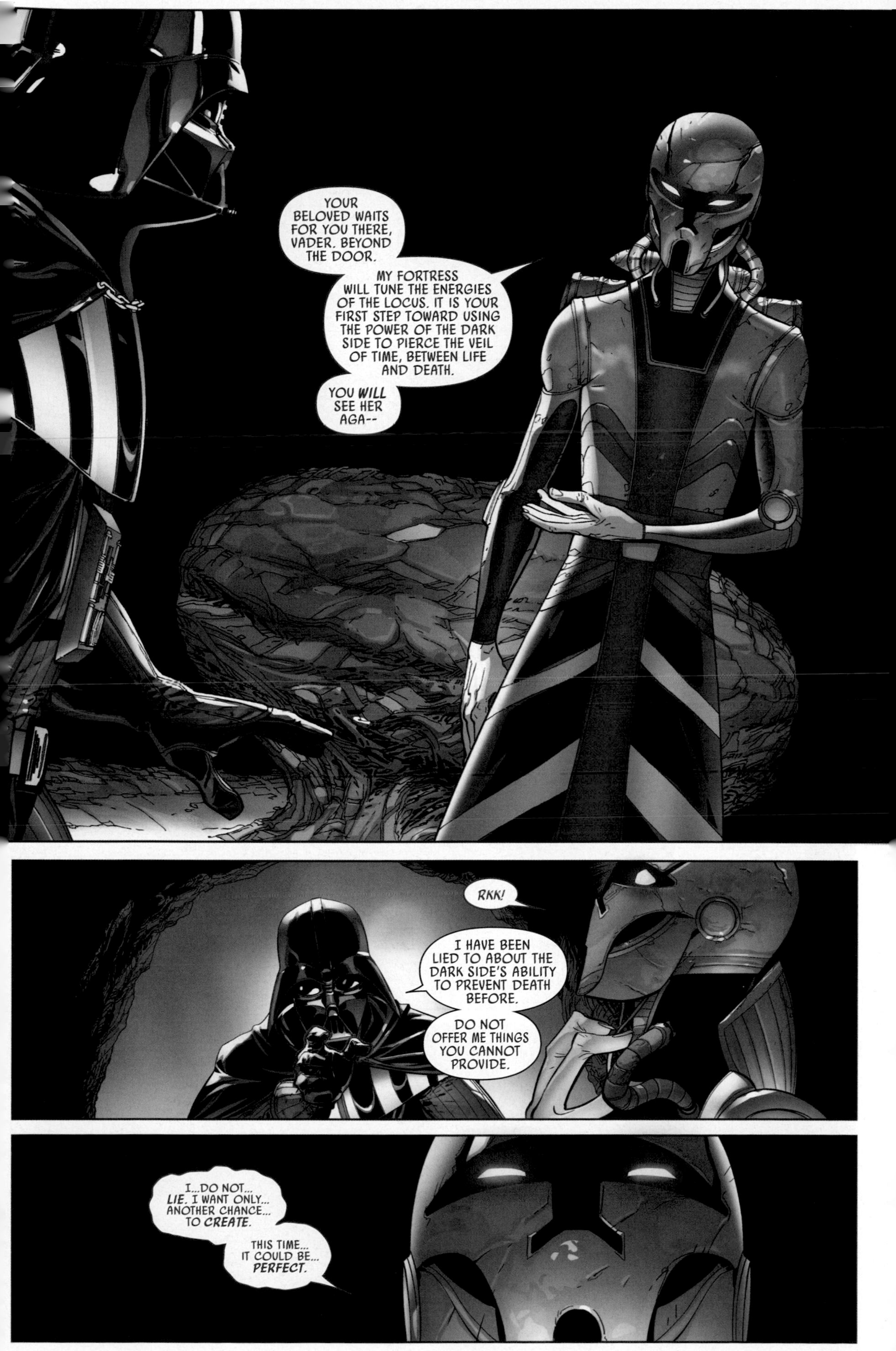
YOUR BELOVED WAITS FOR YOU THERE, VADER. BEYOND THE DOOR.
MY FORTRESS WILL TUNE THE ENERGIES OF THE LOCUS. IT IS YOUR FIRST STEP TOWARD USING THE POWER OF THE DARK SIDE TO PIERCE THE VEIL OF TIME, BETWEEN LIFE AND DEATH.
YOU WILL SEE HER AGA--
RKK!
I HAVE BEEN LIED TO ABOUT THE DARK SIDE'S ABILITY TO PREVENT DEATH BEFORE.
DO NOT OFFER ME THINGS YOU CANNOT PROVIDE.
I...DO NOT... LIE. I WANT ONLY... ANOTHER CHANCE... TO CREATE.
THIS TIME... IT COULD BE... PERFECT.

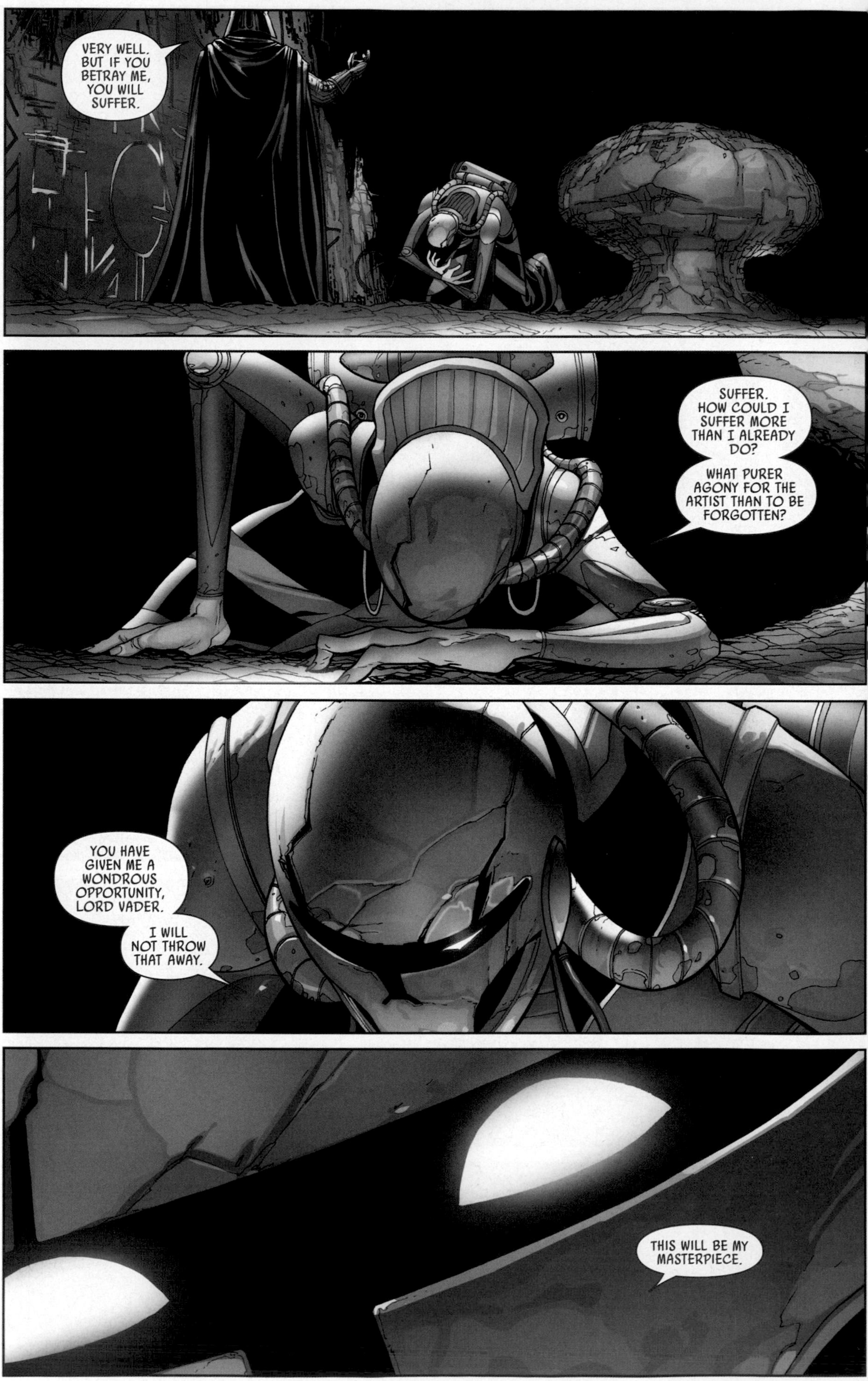
VERY WELL. BUT IF YOU BETRAY ME, YOU WILL SUFFER.
SUFFER. HOW COULD I SUFFER MORE THAN I ALREADY DO?
WHAT PURER AGONY FOR THE ARTIST THAN TO BE FORGOTTEN?
YOU HAVE GIVEN ME A WONDROUS OPPORTUNITY, LORD VADER.
I WILL NOT THROW THAT AWAY.
THIS WILL BE MY MASTERPIECE.

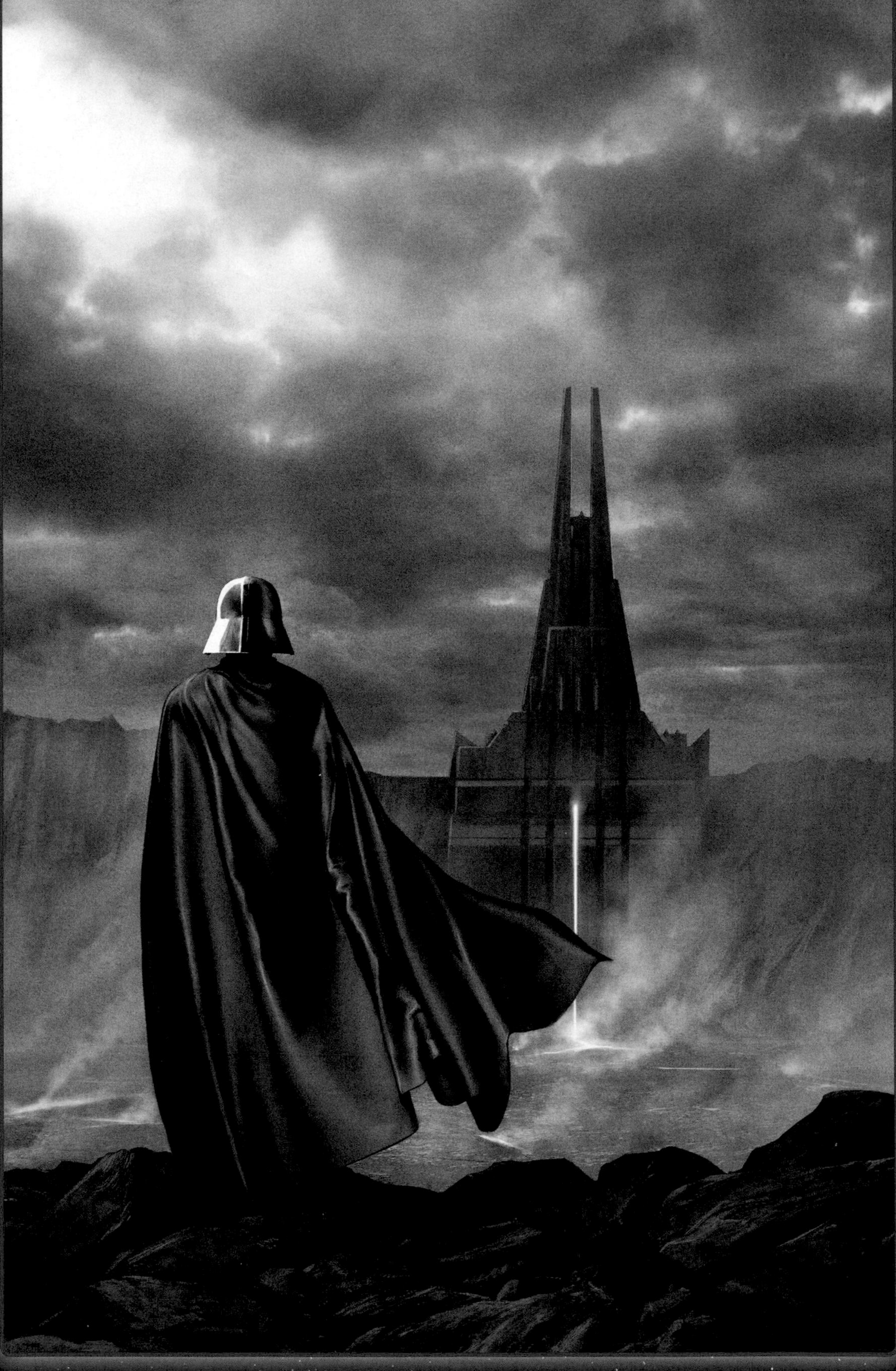

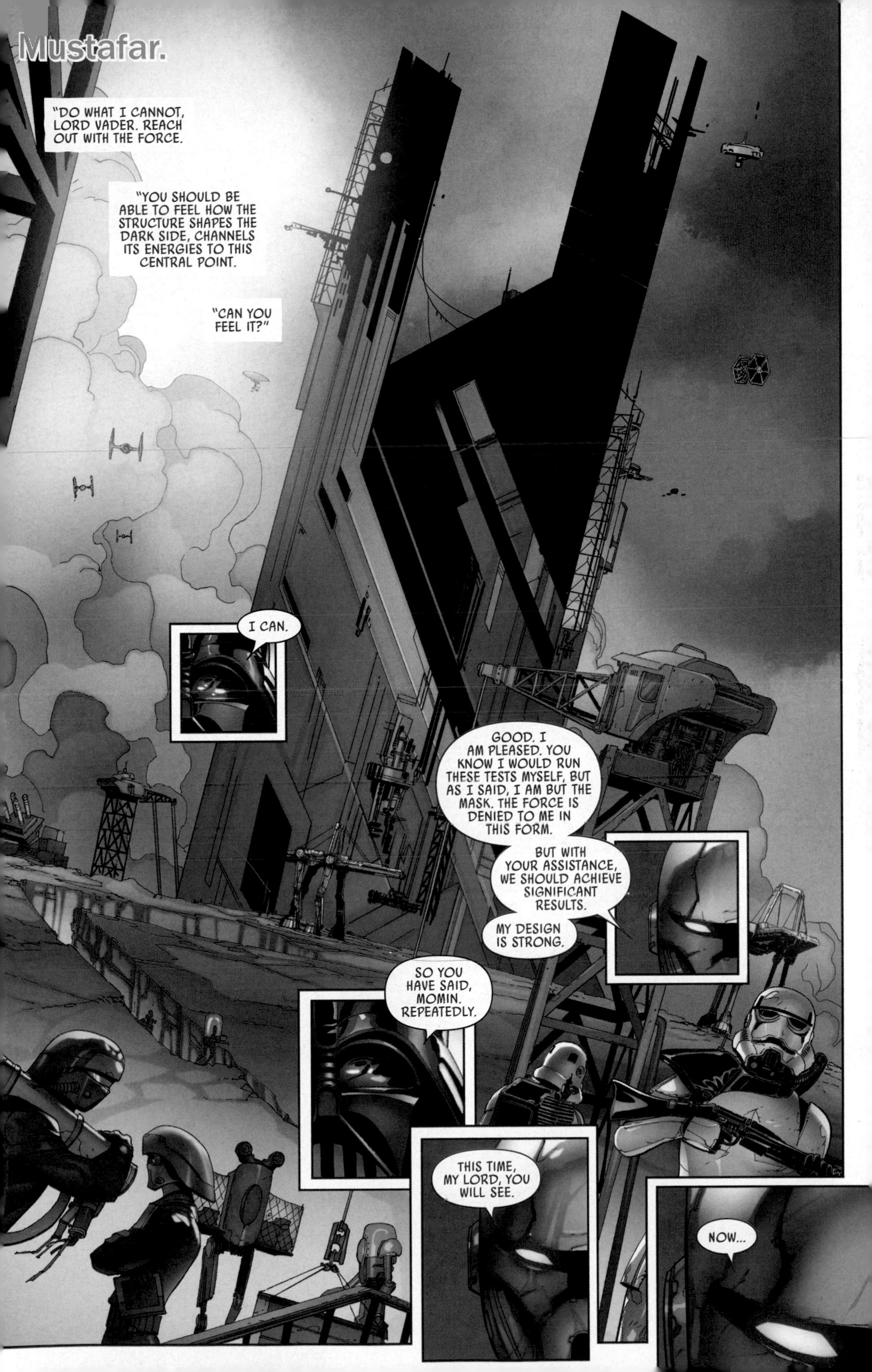
Mustafar.
"DO WHAT I CANNOT, LORD VADER. REACH OUT WITH THE FORCE.
"YOU SHOULD BE ABLE TO FEEL HOW THE STRUCTURE SHAPES THE DARK SIDE, CHANNELS ITS ENERGIES TO THIS CENTRAL POINT.
"CAN YOU FEEL IT?"
I CAN.
GOOD. I AM PLEASED. YOU KNOW I WOULD RUN THESE TESTS MYSELF, BUT AS I SAID, I AM BUT THE MASK. THE FORCE IS DENIED TO ME IN THIS FORM.
BUT WITH YOUR ASSISTANCE, WE SHOULD ACHIEVE SIGNIFICANT RESULTS.
MY DESIGN IS STRONG.
SO YOU HAVE SAID, MOMIN. REPEATEDLY.
THIS TIME, MY LORD, YOU WILL SEE.
NOW...

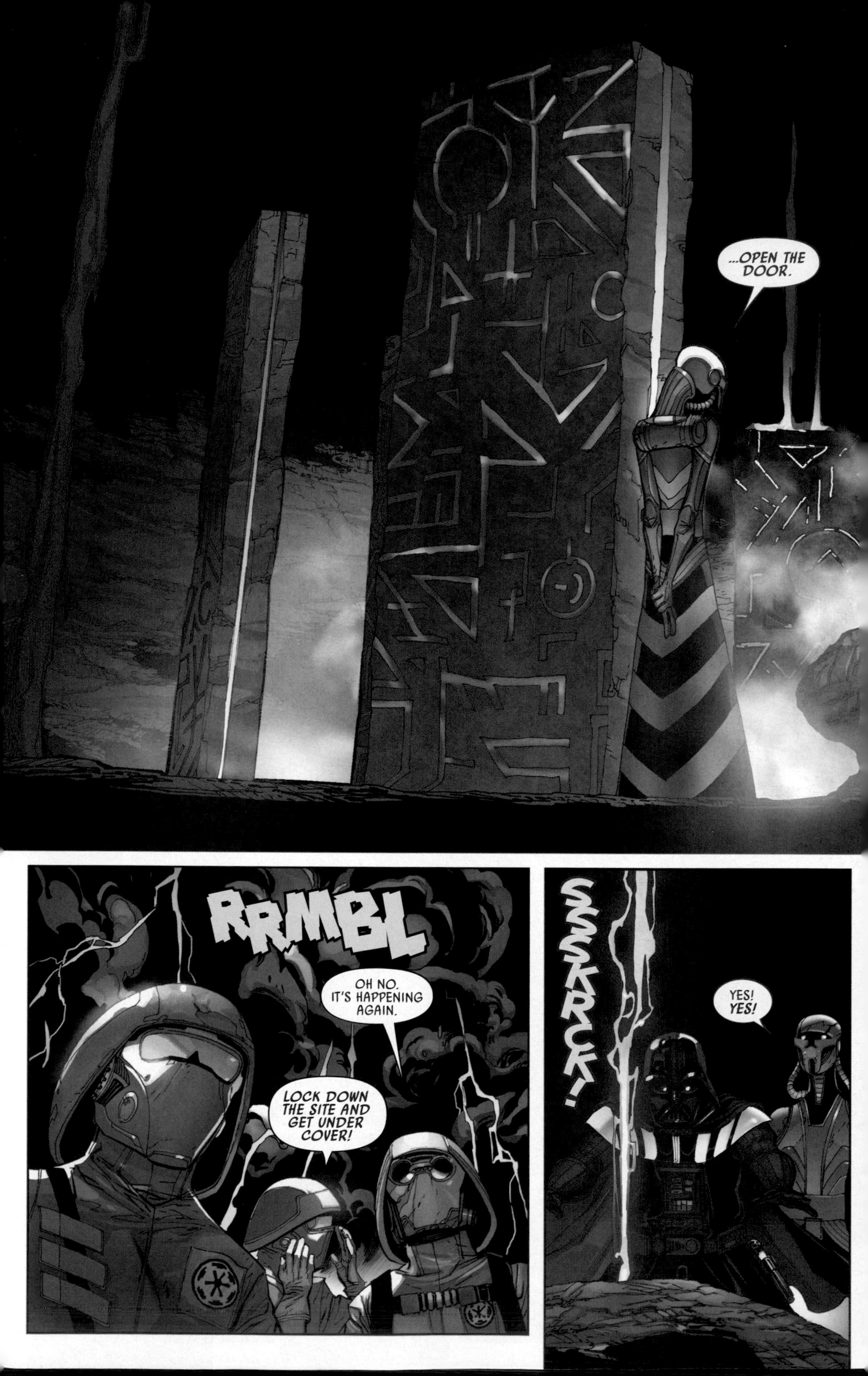
...OPEN THE DOOR.
RRMBL
OH NO. IT'S HAPPENING AGAIN.
LOCK DOWN THE SITE AND GET UNDER COVER!
SSSKRCK!
YES! YES!

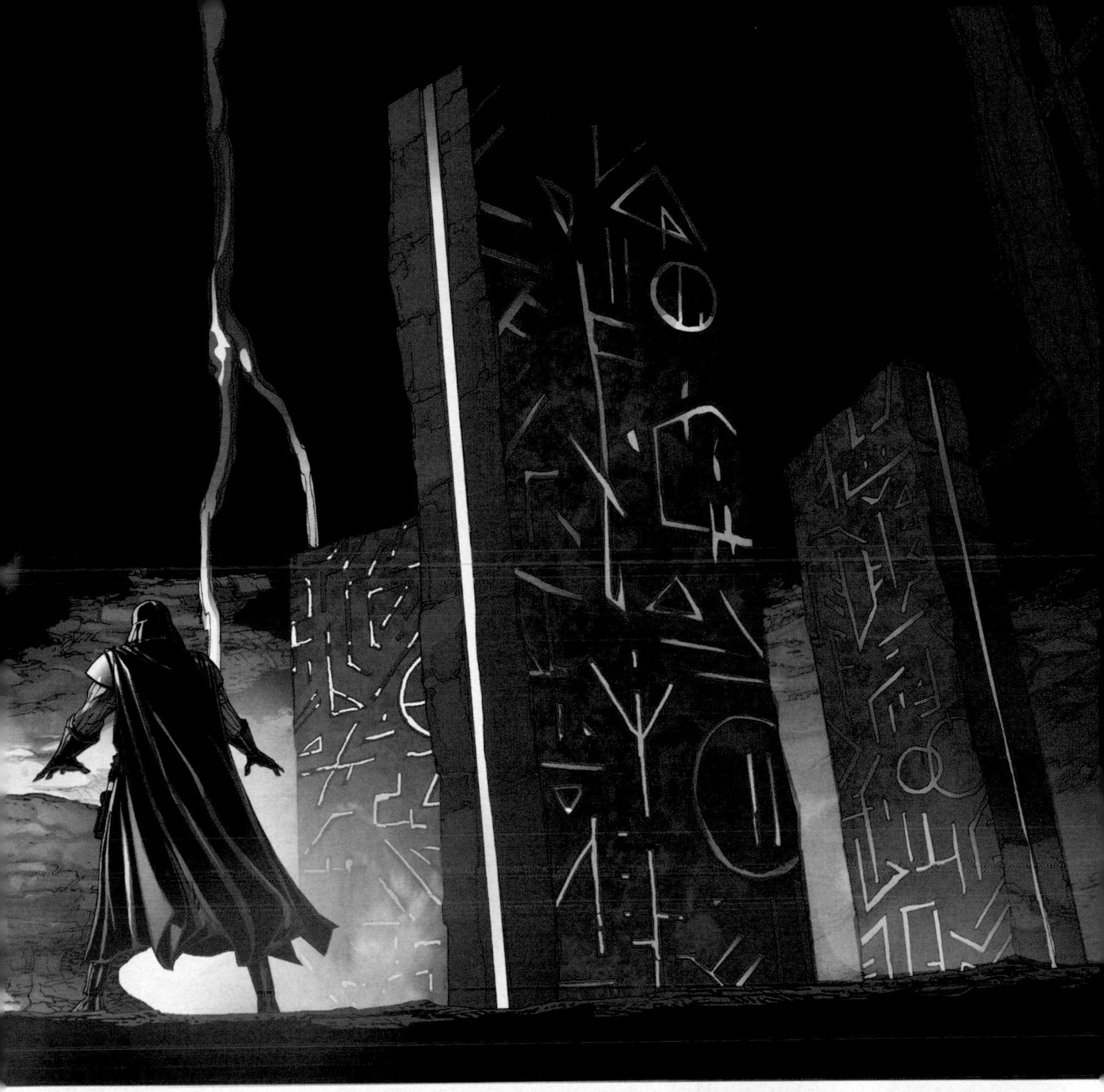

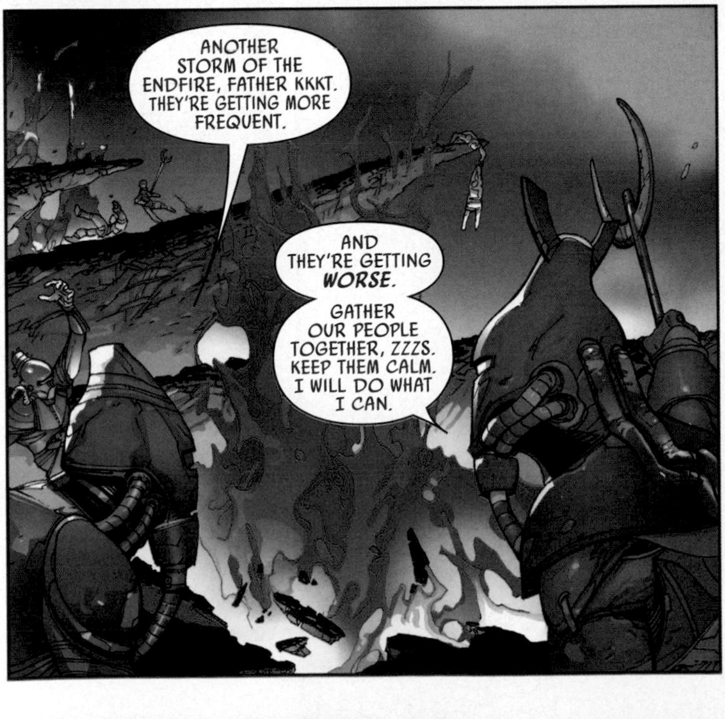
ANOTHER STORM OF THE ENDFIRE, FATHER KKKT. THEY'RE GETTING MORE FREQUENT.
AND THEY'RE GETTING **WORSE**.
GATHER OUR PEOPLE TOGETHER, ZZZS. KEEP THEM CALM. I WILL DO WHAT I CAN.

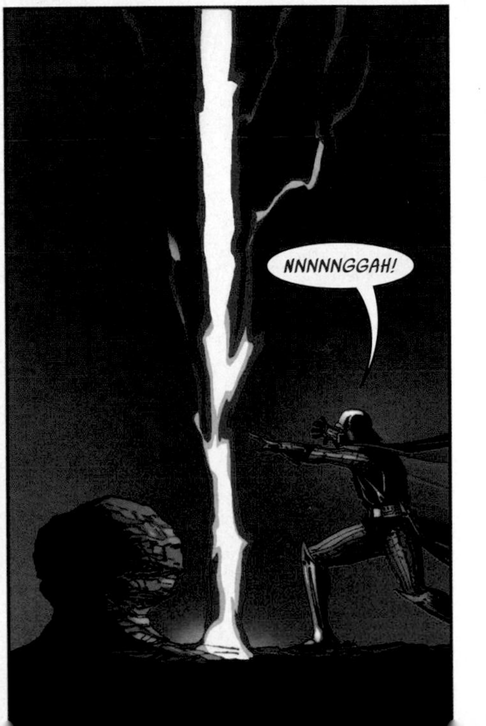
NNNNNGGAH!

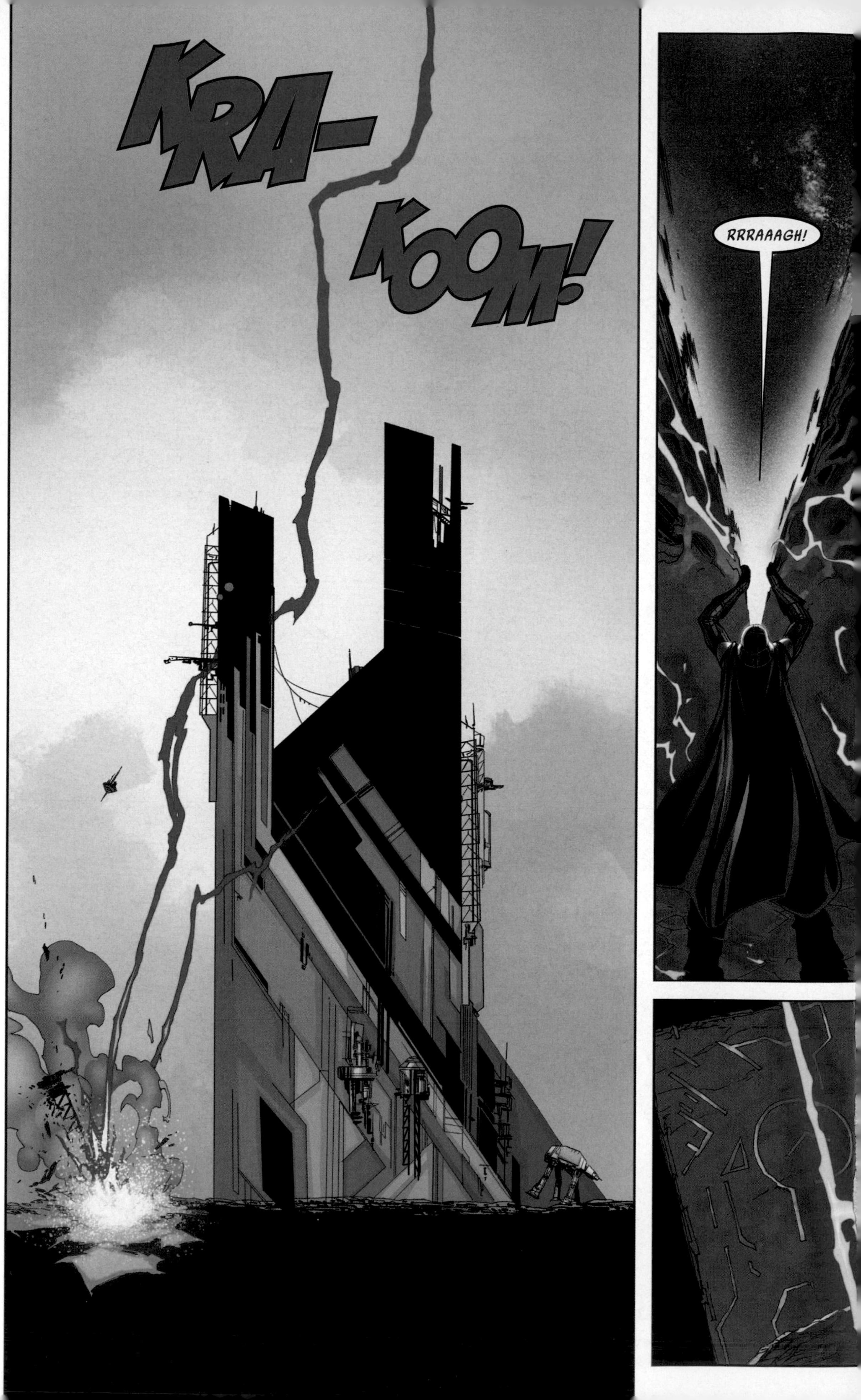
KRA-
KOOM!
RRRAAAGH!

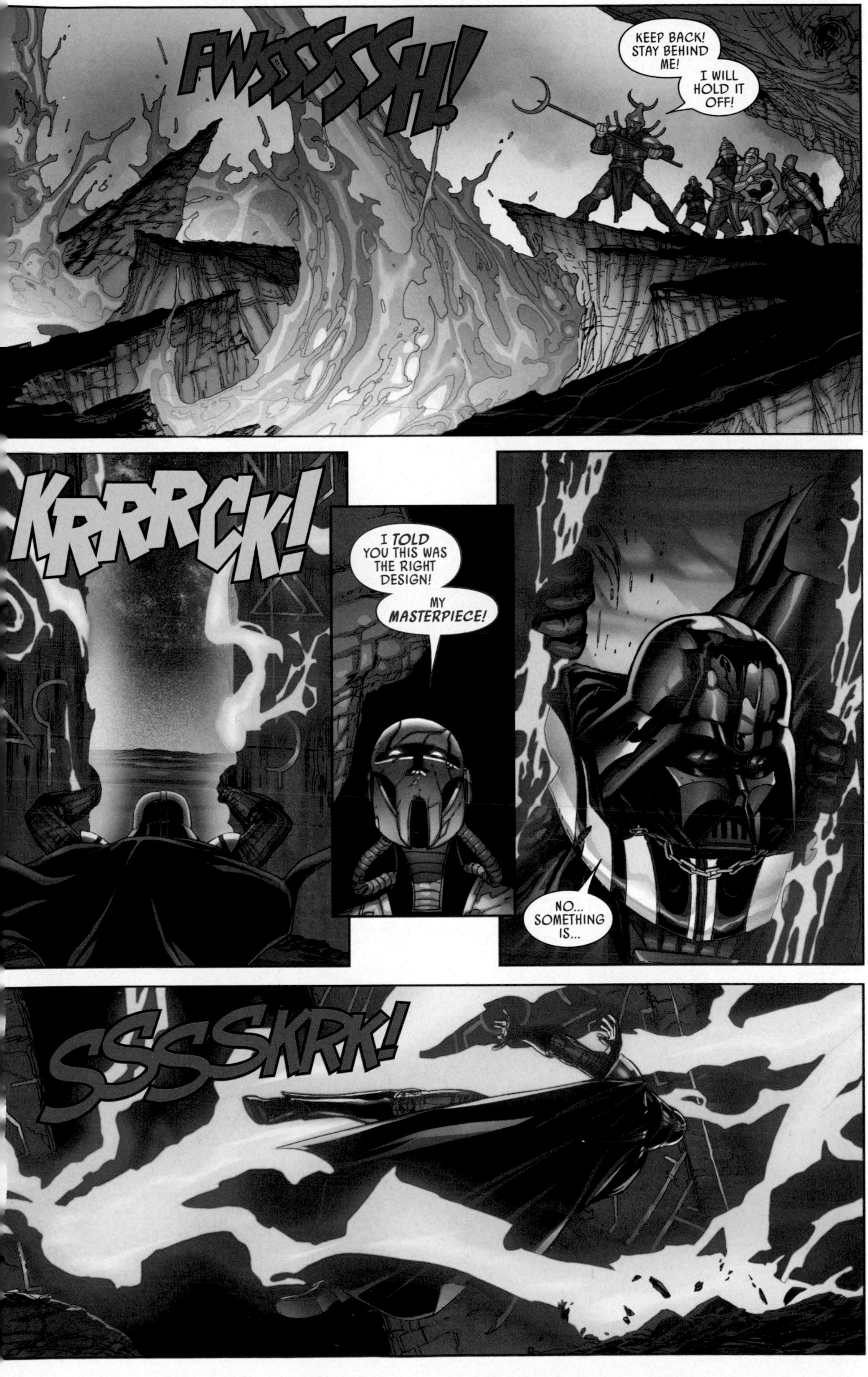
FWSSSSSH!
KEEP BACK! STAY BEHIND ME!
I WILL HOLD IT OFF!
KRRRCK!
I TOLD YOU THIS WAS THE RIGHT DESIGN!
MY MASTERPIECE!
NO... SOMETHING IS...
SSSSKRK!

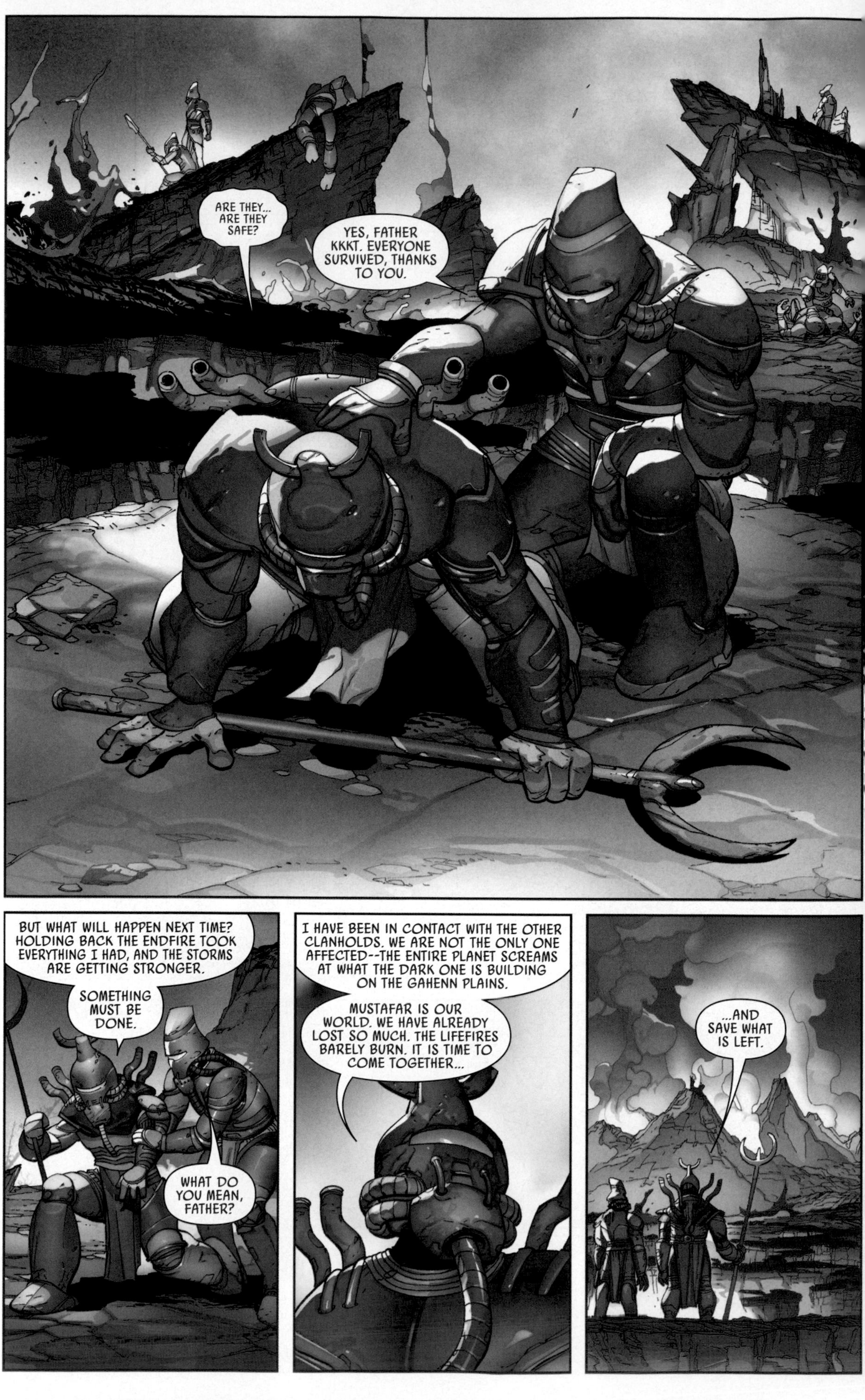
ARE THEY... ARE THEY SAFE?
YES, FATHER KKKT. EVERYONE SURVIVED, THANKS TO YOU.
BUT WHAT WILL HAPPEN NEXT TIME? HOLDING BACK THE ENDFIRE TOOK EVERYTHING I HAD, AND THE STORMS ARE GETTING STRONGER.
SOMETHING MUST BE DONE.
WHAT DO YOU MEAN, FATHER?
I HAVE BEEN IN CONTACT WITH THE OTHER CLANHOLDS. WE ARE NOT THE ONLY ONE AFFECTED--THE ENTIRE PLANET SCREAMS AT WHAT THE DARK ONE IS BUILDING ON THE GAHENN PLAINS.
MUSTAFAR IS OUR WORLD. WE HAVE ALREADY LOST SO MUCH. THE LIFEFIRES BARELY BURN. IT IS TIME TO COME TOGETHER...
...AND SAVE WHAT IS LEFT.

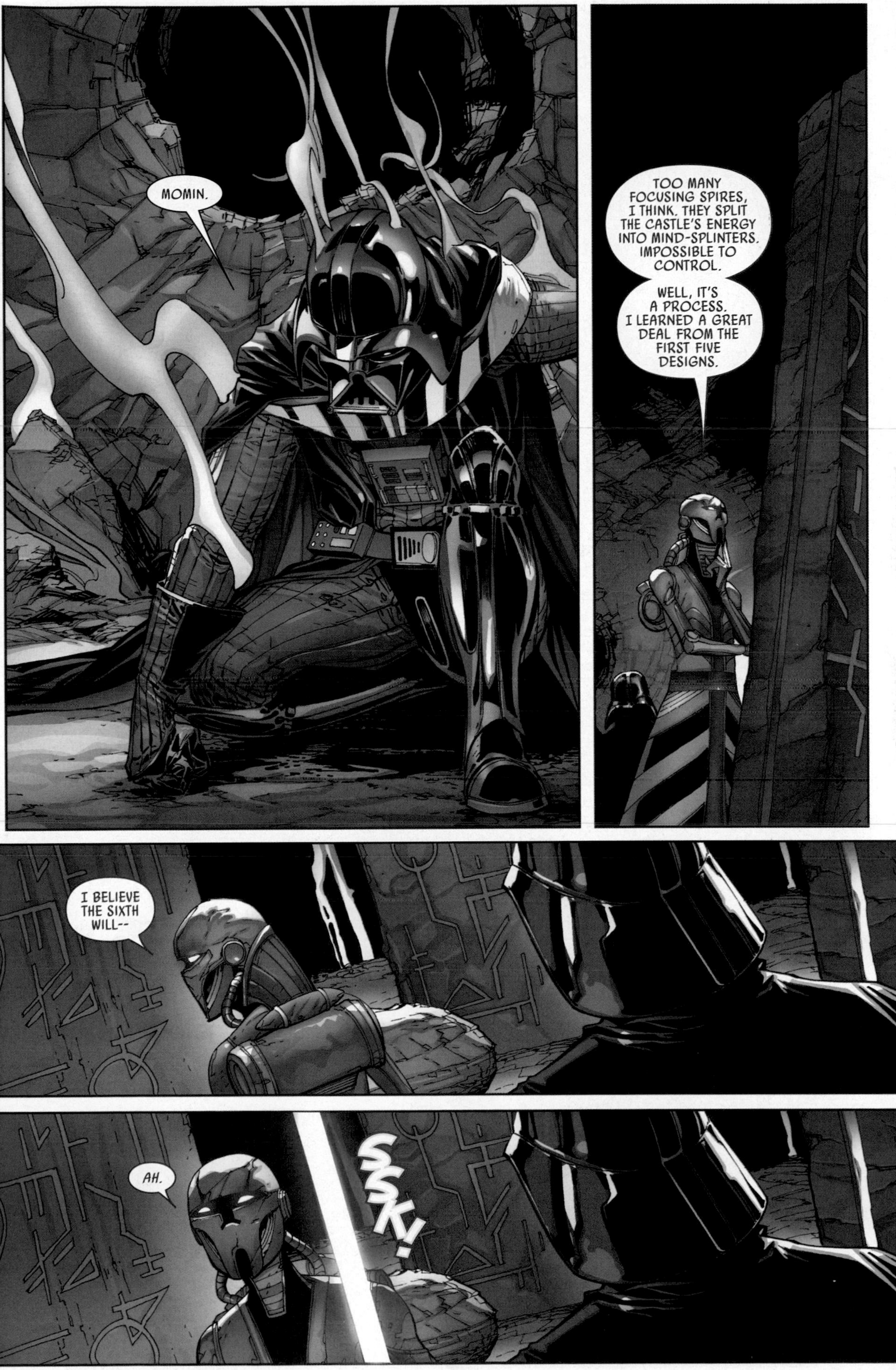
MOMIN.
TOO MANY FOCUSING SPIRES, I THINK. THEY SPLIT THE CASTLE'S ENERGY INTO MIND-SPLINTERS. IMPOSSIBLE TO CONTROL.
WELL, IT'S A PROCESS. I LEARNED A GREAT DEAL FROM THE FIRST FIVE DESIGNS.
I BELIEVE THE SIXTH WILL--
AH.
SSK!

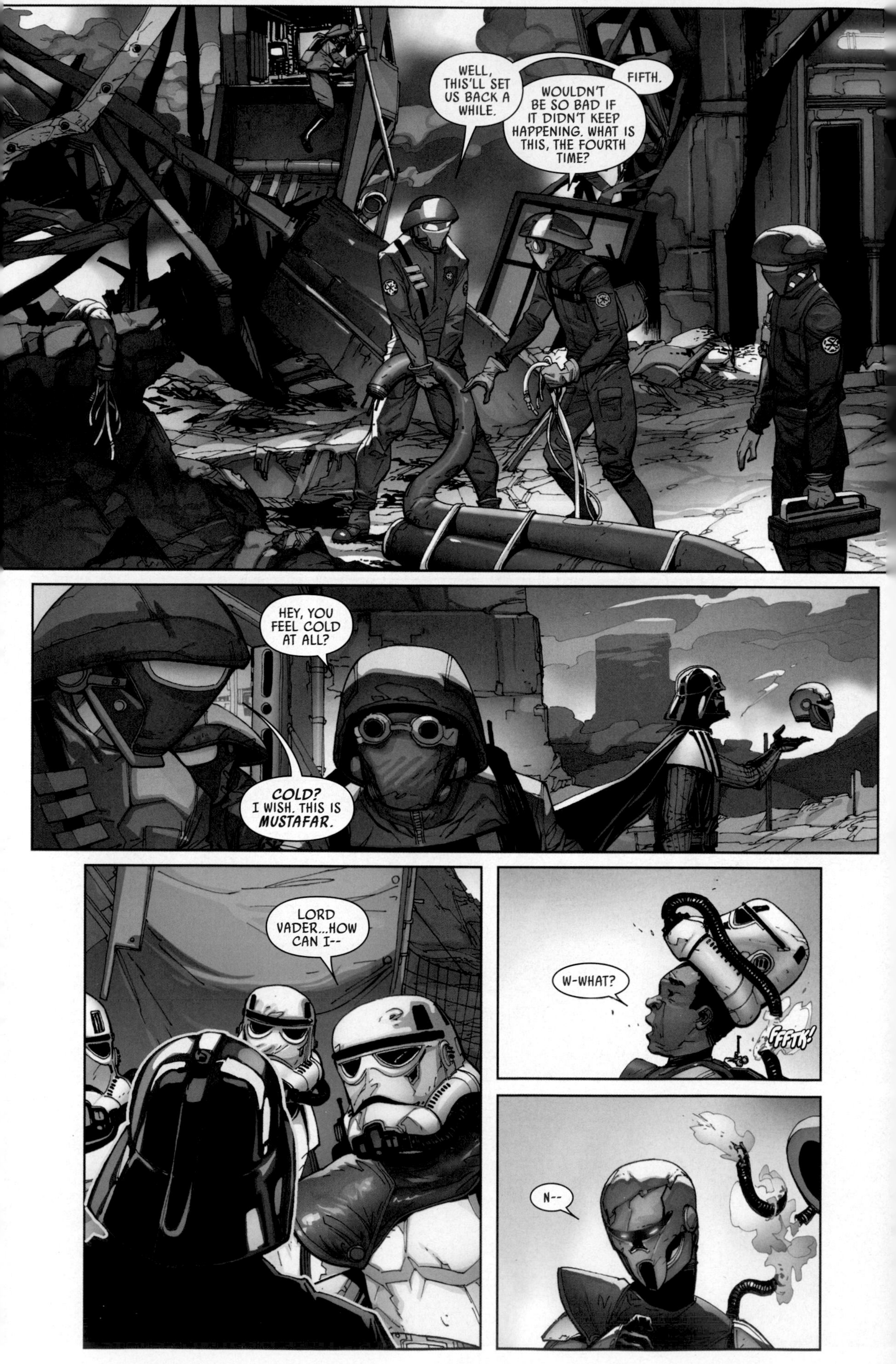
WELL, THIS'LL SET US BACK A WHILE.
WOULDN'T BE SO BAD IF IT DIDN'T KEEP HAPPENING. WHAT IS THIS, THE FOURTH TIME?
FIFTH.
HEY, YOU FEEL COLD AT ALL?
COLD? I WISH. THIS IS MUSTAFAR.
LORD VADER...HOW CAN I--
W-WHAT?
FFFTK!
N--

WHAT WAS I-- OH YES.

THE SIXTH DESIGN--THAT WILL BE THE ONE.

I WILL HAVE A NEW SET OF PLANS READY VERY SHORTLY, LORD VADER.

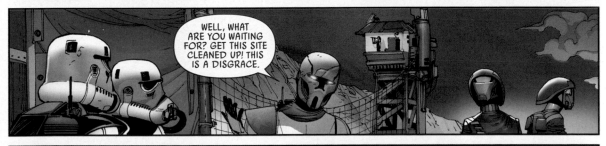

WELL, WHAT ARE YOU WAITING FOR? GET THIS SITE CLEANED UP! THIS IS A DISGRACE.

INCOMING! WE'VE GOT INCOMING!

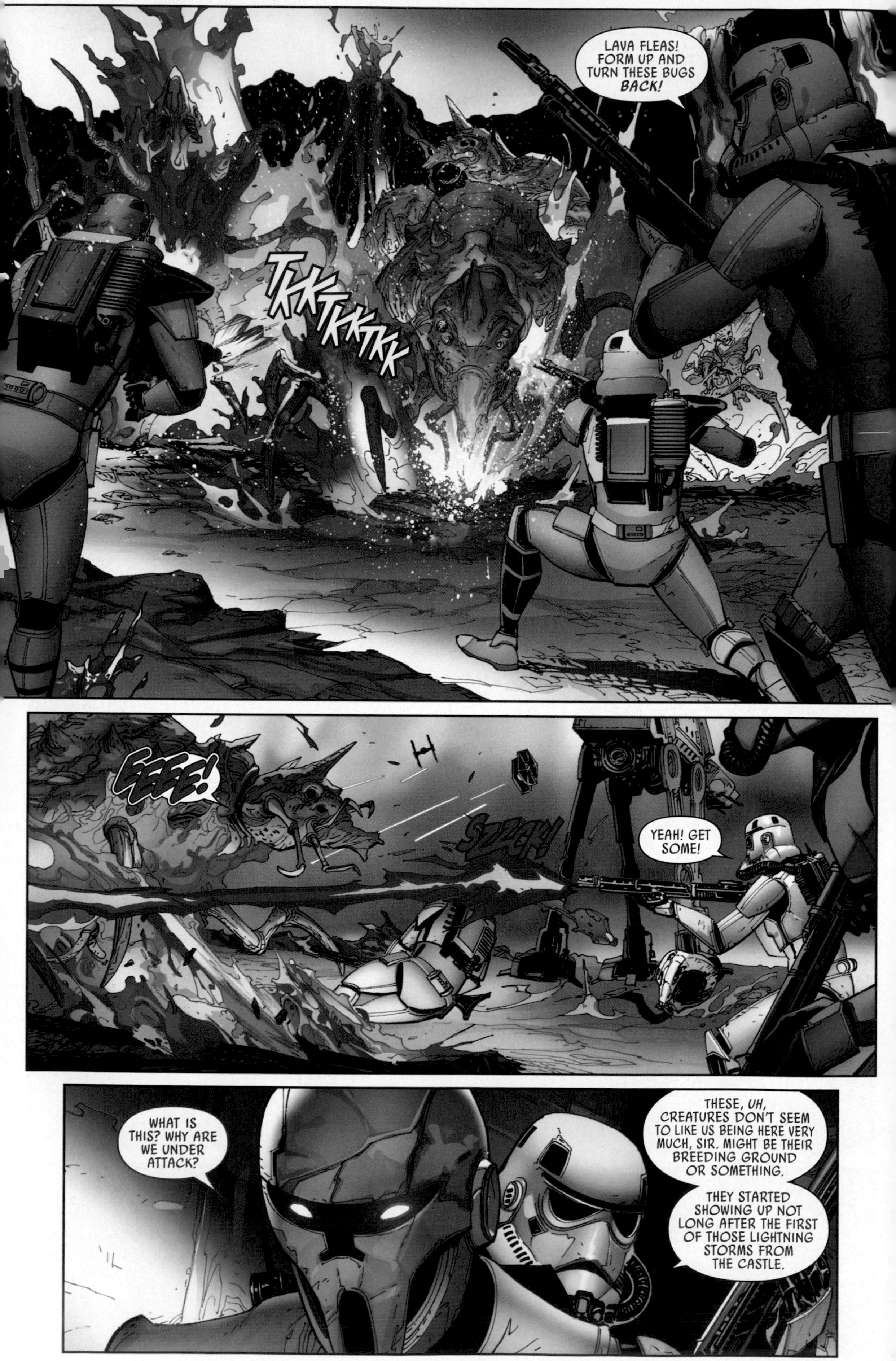

LAVA FLEAS! FORM UP AND TURN THESE BUGS *BACK!*
EEEE!
YEAH! GET SOME!
WHAT IS THIS? WHY ARE WE UNDER ATTACK?
THESE, *UH,* CREATURES DON'T SEEM TO LIKE US BEING HERE VERY MUCH, SIR. MIGHT BE THEIR BREEDING GROUND OR SOMETHING.
THEY STARTED SHOWING UP NOT LONG AFTER THE FIRST OF THOSE LIGHTNING STORMS FROM THE CASTLE.

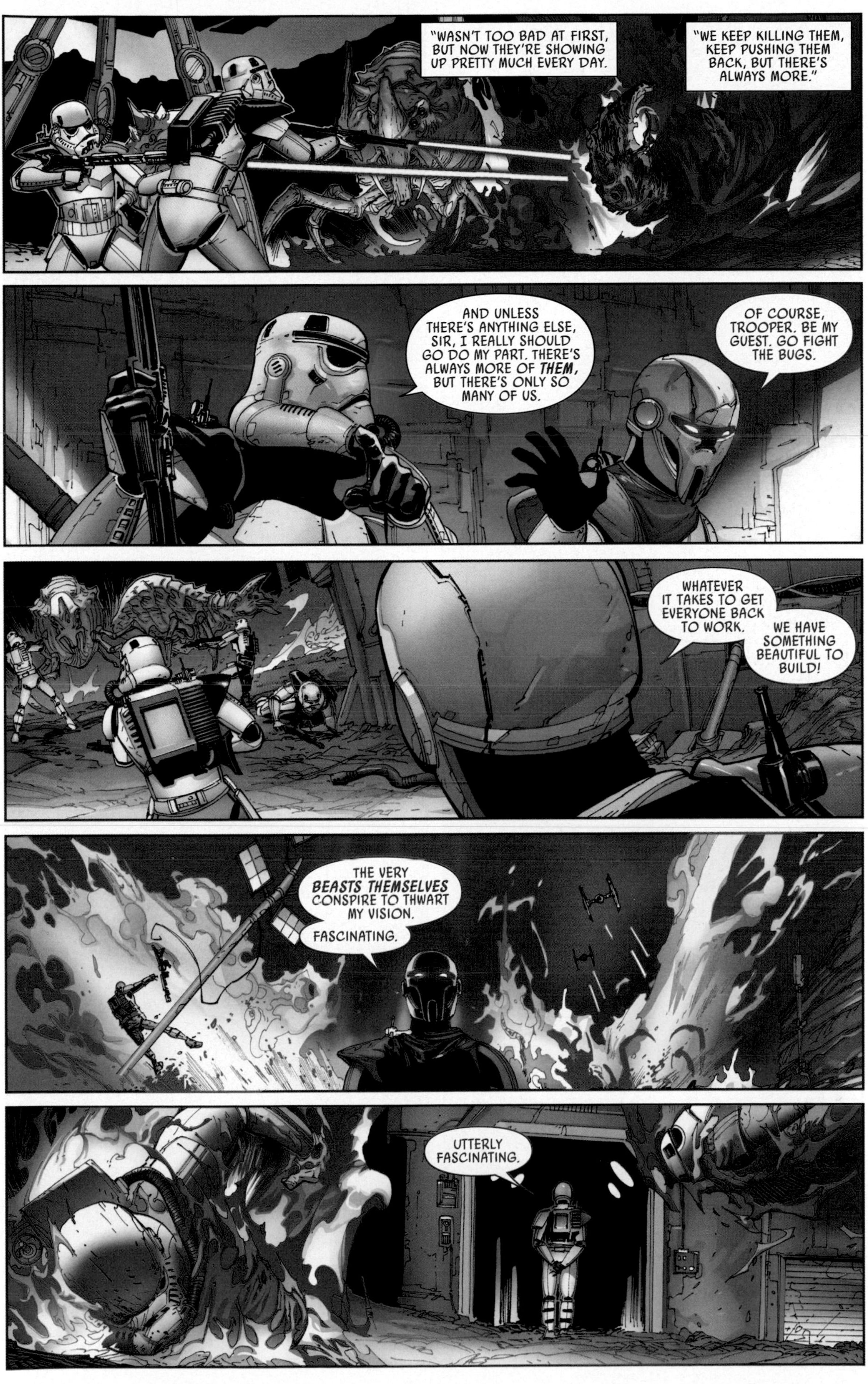
"WASN'T TOO BAD AT FIRST, BUT NOW THEY'RE SHOWING UP PRETTY MUCH EVERY DAY.
"WE KEEP KILLING THEM, KEEP PUSHING THEM BACK, BUT THERE'S ALWAYS MORE."
AND UNLESS THERE'S ANYTHING ELSE, SIR, I REALLY SHOULD GO DO MY PART. THERE'S ALWAYS MORE OF *THEM,* BUT THERE'S ONLY SO MANY OF US.
OF COURSE, TROOPER. BE MY GUEST. GO FIGHT THE BUGS.
WHATEVER IT TAKES TO GET EVERYONE BACK TO WORK.
WE HAVE SOMETHING BEAUTIFUL TO BUILD!
THE VERY ***BEASTS THEMSELVES*** CONSPIRE TO THWART MY VISION.
FASCINATING.
UTTERLY FASCINATING.

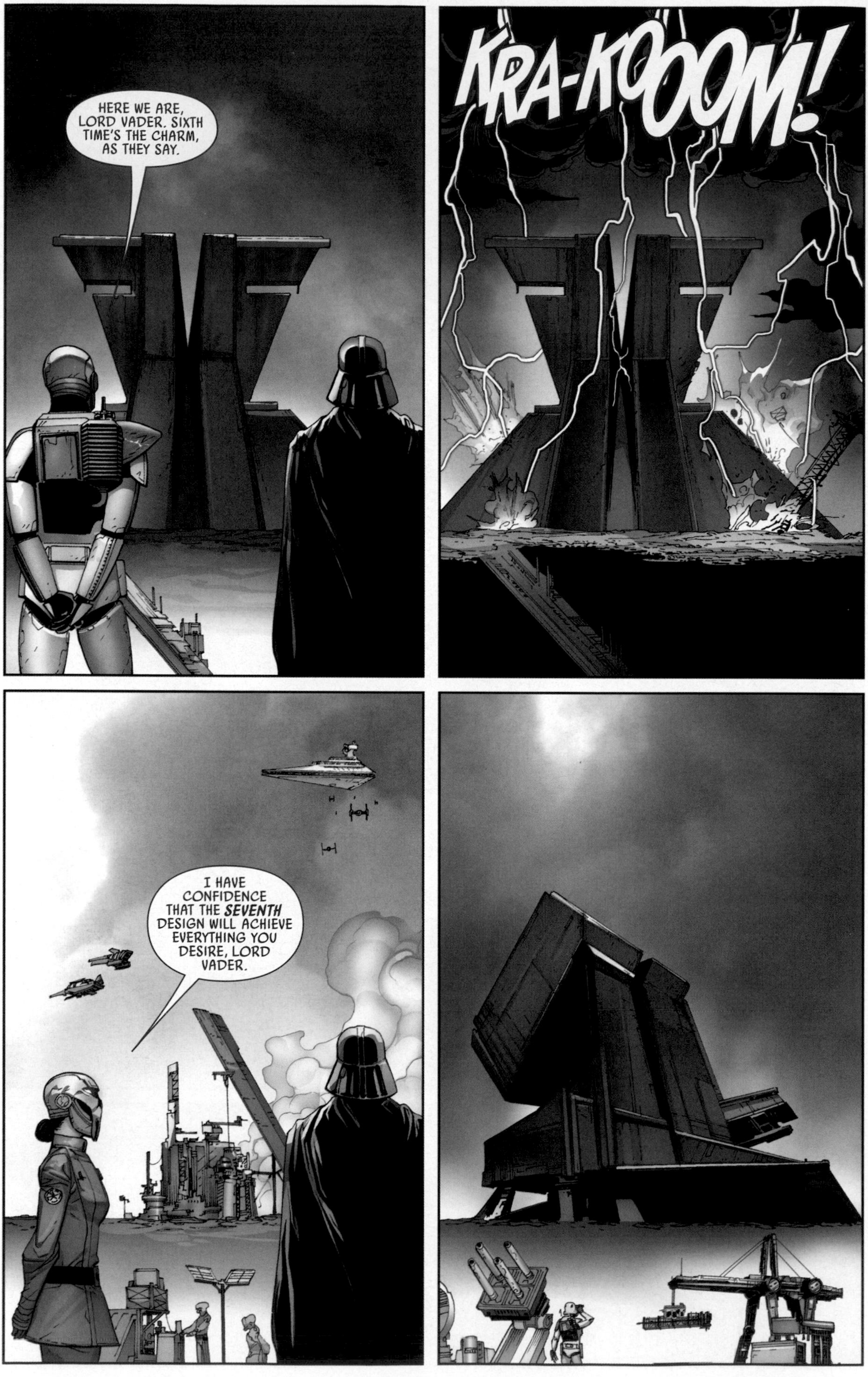
HERE WE ARE, LORD VADER. SIXTH TIME'S THE CHARM, AS THEY SAY.
KRA-KOOOOM!
I HAVE CONFIDENCE THAT THE *SEVENTH* DESIGN WILL ACHIEVE EVERYTHING YOU DESIRE, LORD VADER.

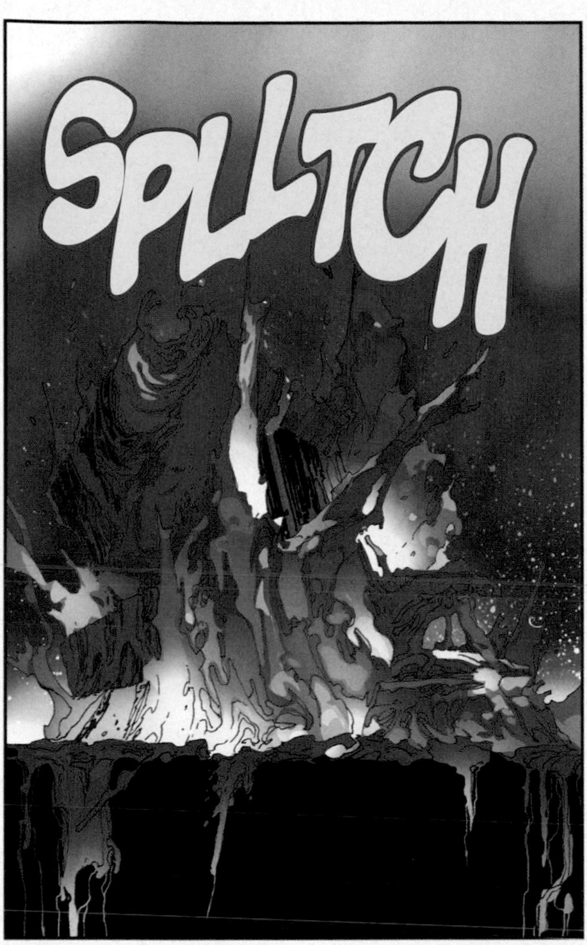
SPLLTCH

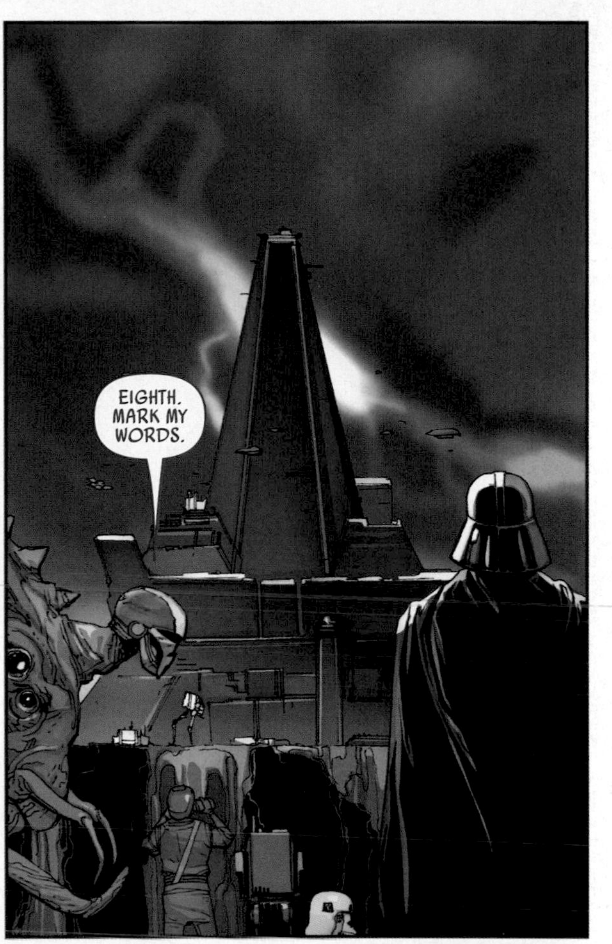
EIGHTH. MARK MY WORDS.

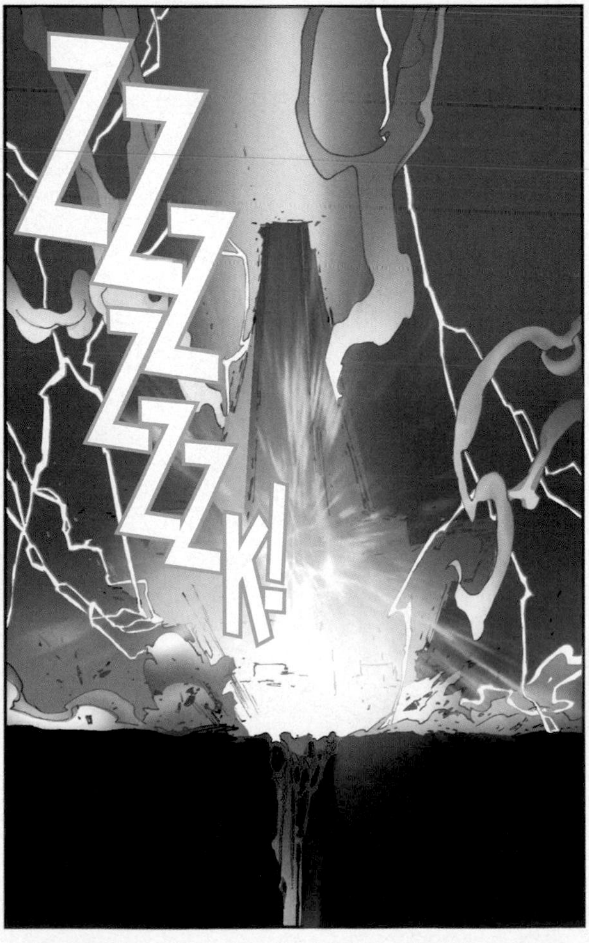
ZZZZZZK!

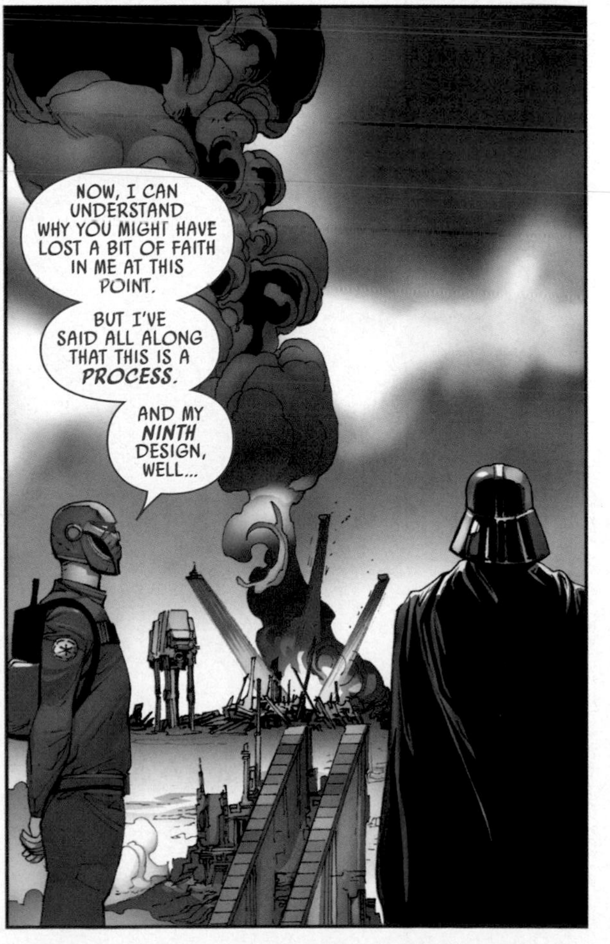
NOW, I CAN UNDERSTAND WHY YOU MIGHT HAVE LOST A BIT OF FAITH IN ME AT THIS POINT.
BUT I'VE SAID ALL ALONG THAT THIS IS A *PROCESS.*
AND MY *NINTH* DESIGN, WELL...

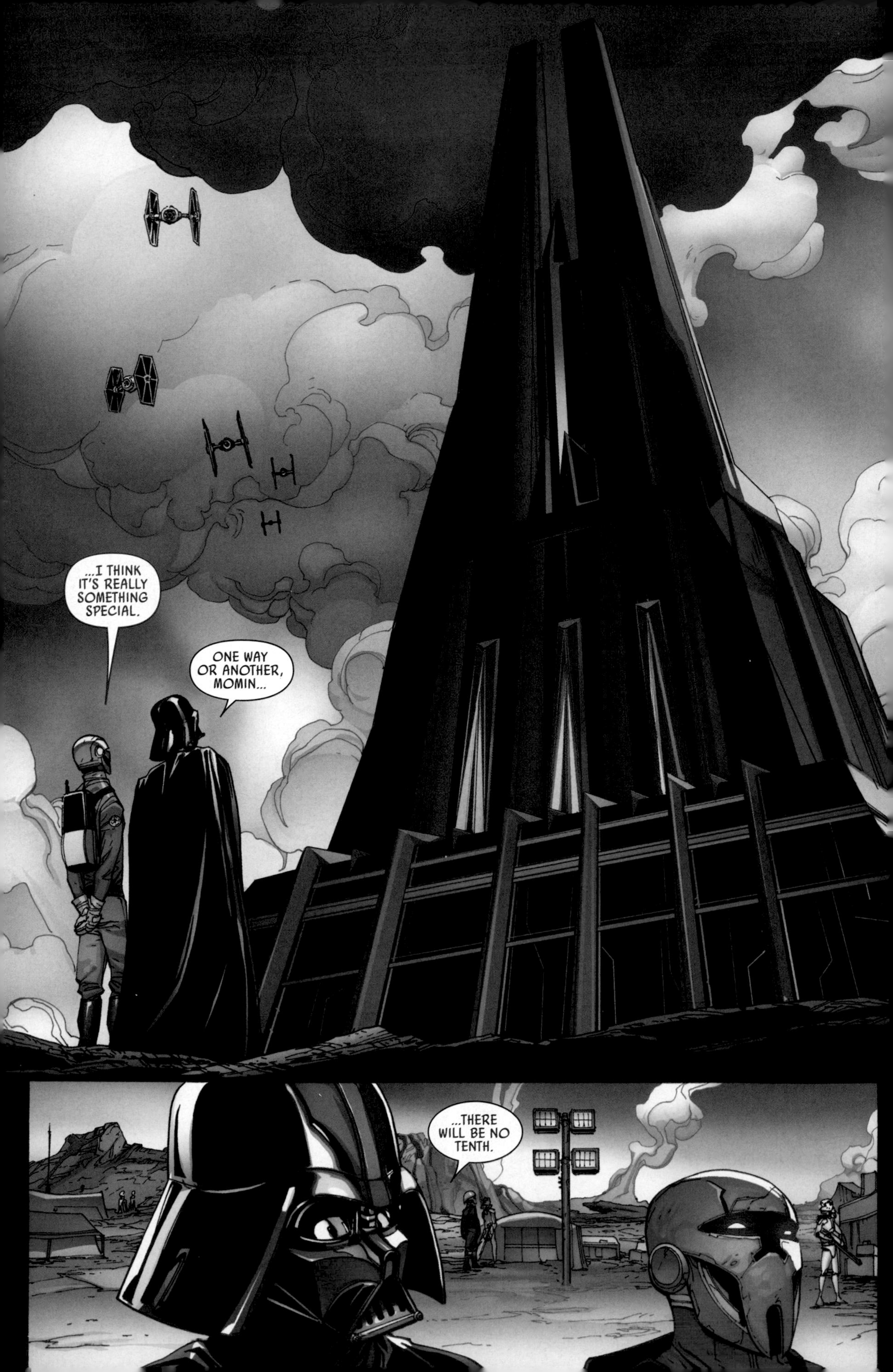
...I THINK IT'S REALLY SOMETHING SPECIAL.
ONE WAY OR ANOTHER, MOMIN...
...THERE WILL BE NO TENTH.

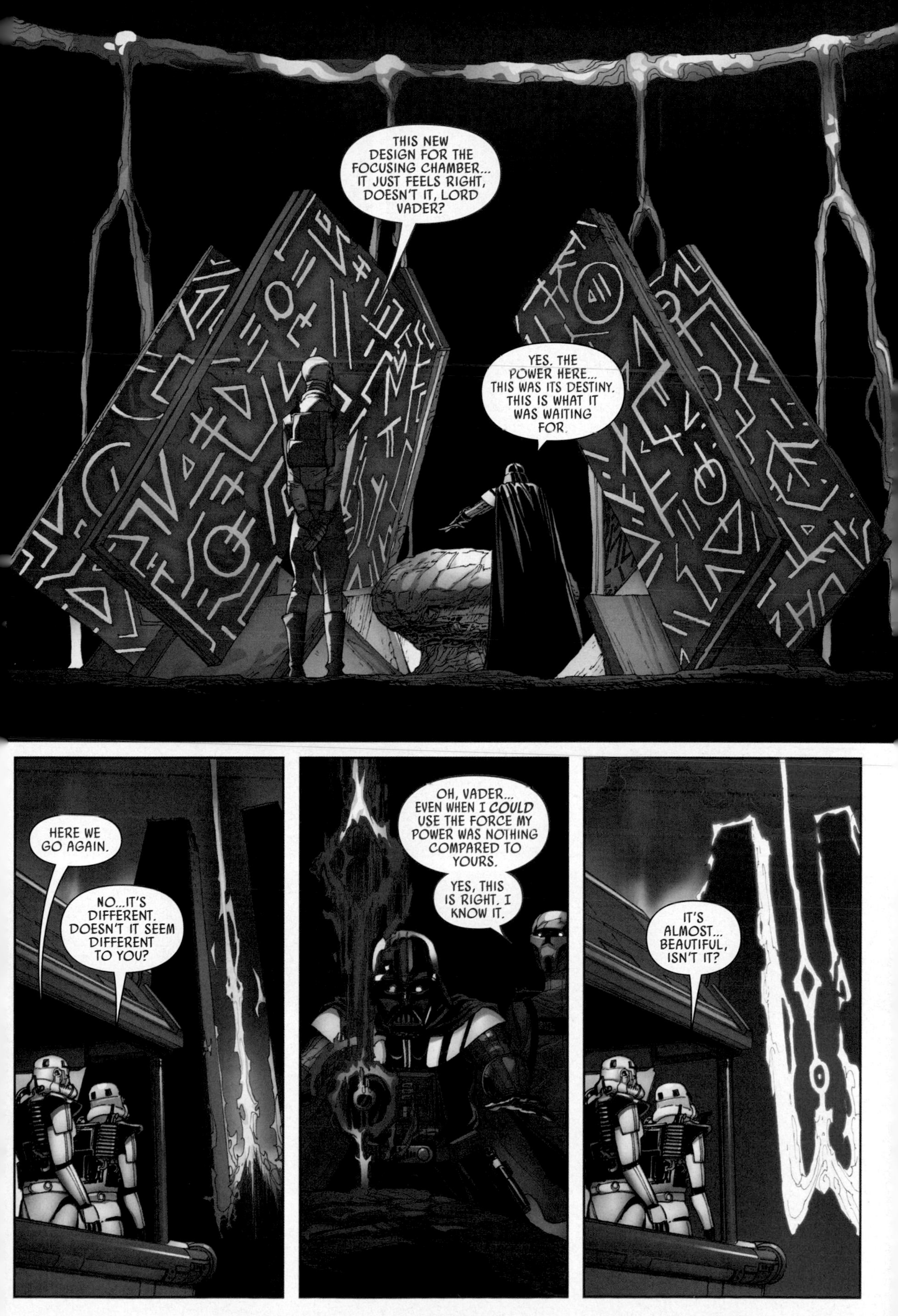
THIS NEW DESIGN FOR THE FOCUSING CHAMBER... IT JUST FEELS RIGHT, DOESN'T IT, LORD VADER?
YES. THE POWER HERE... THIS WAS ITS DESTINY. THIS IS WHAT IT WAS WAITING FOR.
HERE WE GO AGAIN.
NO...IT'S DIFFERENT. DOESN'T IT SEEM DIFFERENT TO YOU?
OH, VADER... EVEN WHEN I COULD USE THE FORCE MY POWER WAS NOTHING COMPARED TO YOURS.
YES, THIS IS RIGHT. I KNOW IT.
IT'S ALMOST... BEAUTIFUL, ISN'T IT?

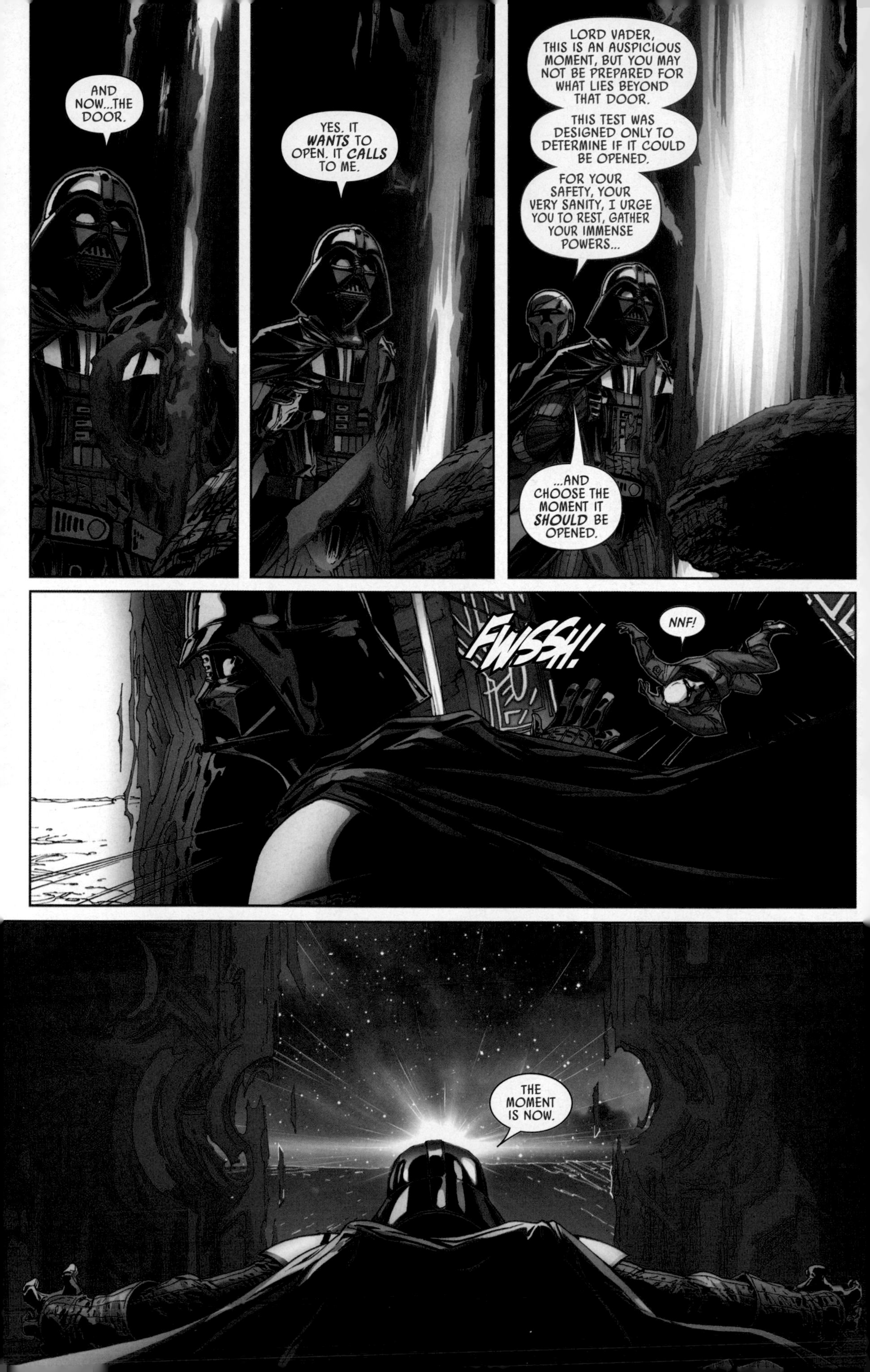
AND NOW...THE DOOR.
YES. IT *WANTS* TO OPEN. IT *CALLS* TO ME.
LORD VADER, THIS IS AN AUSPICIOUS MOMENT, BUT YOU MAY NOT BE PREPARED FOR WHAT LIES BEYOND THAT DOOR.
THIS TEST WAS DESIGNED ONLY TO DETERMINE IF IT COULD BE OPENED.
FOR YOUR SAFETY, YOUR VERY SANITY, I URGE YOU TO REST, GATHER YOUR IMMENSE POWERS...
...AND CHOOSE THE MOMENT IT *SHOULD* BE OPENED.
FWSSH!
NNF!
THE MOMENT IS NOW.

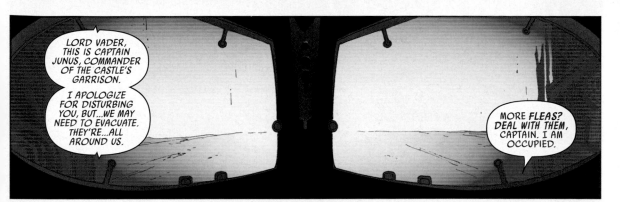

LORD VADER, THIS IS CAPTAIN JUNUS, COMMANDER OF THE CASTLE'S GARRISON.

I APOLOGIZE FOR DISTURBING YOU, BUT...WE MAY NEED TO EVACUATE. THEY'RE...ALL AROUND US.

MORE *FLEAS?* DEAL WITH THEM, CAPTAIN. I AM OCCUPIED.

MY LORD, I BELIEVE WE ARE FACING A SERIOUS THREAT. PERHAPS YOU SHOULD JUST COME SEE FOR YOURSELF.

I...

BAH!

YOU WILL DO *NOTHING* UNTIL I RETURN.

WHAT WOULD I POSSIBLY WANT TO DO? MY WORK HERE IS COMPLETE.

HNH.

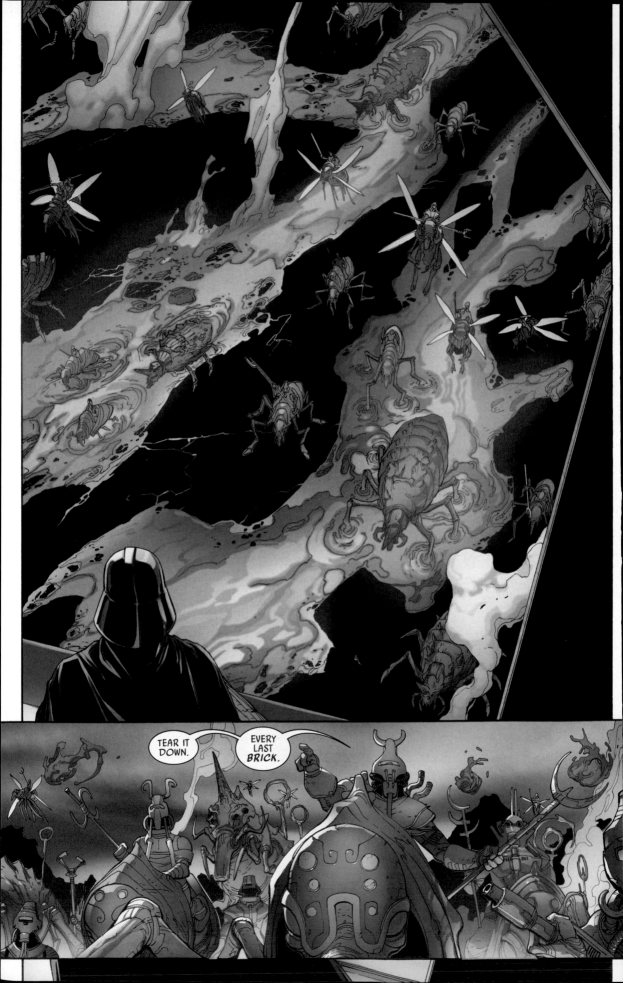

TEAR IT DOWN.

EVERY LAST BRICK.

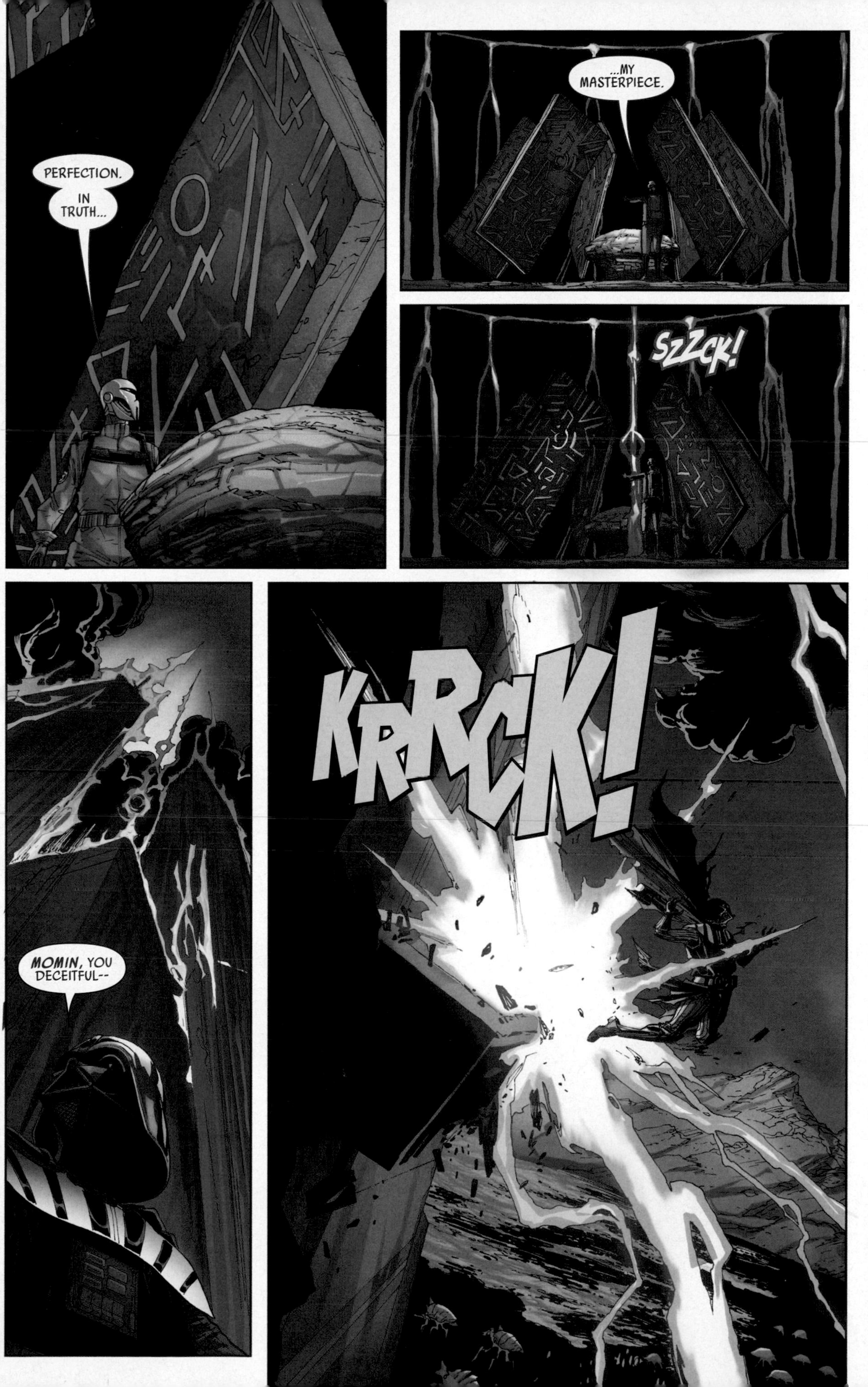
PERFECTION.
IN TRUTH...
...MY MASTERPIECE.
SZZCK!
MOMIN, YOU DECEITFUL--
KRRCK!

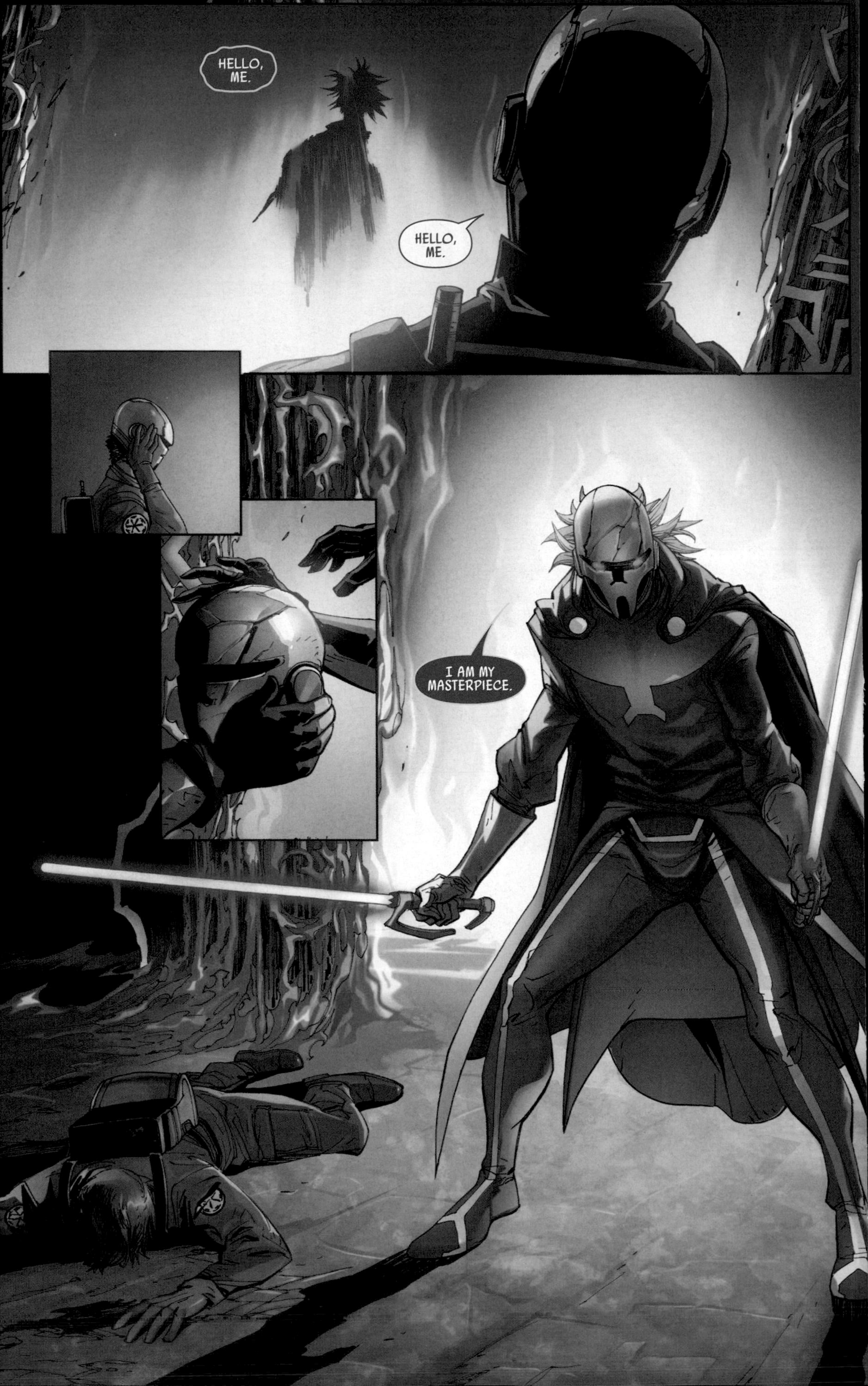
HELLO, ME.
HELLO, ME.
I AM MY MASTERPIECE.

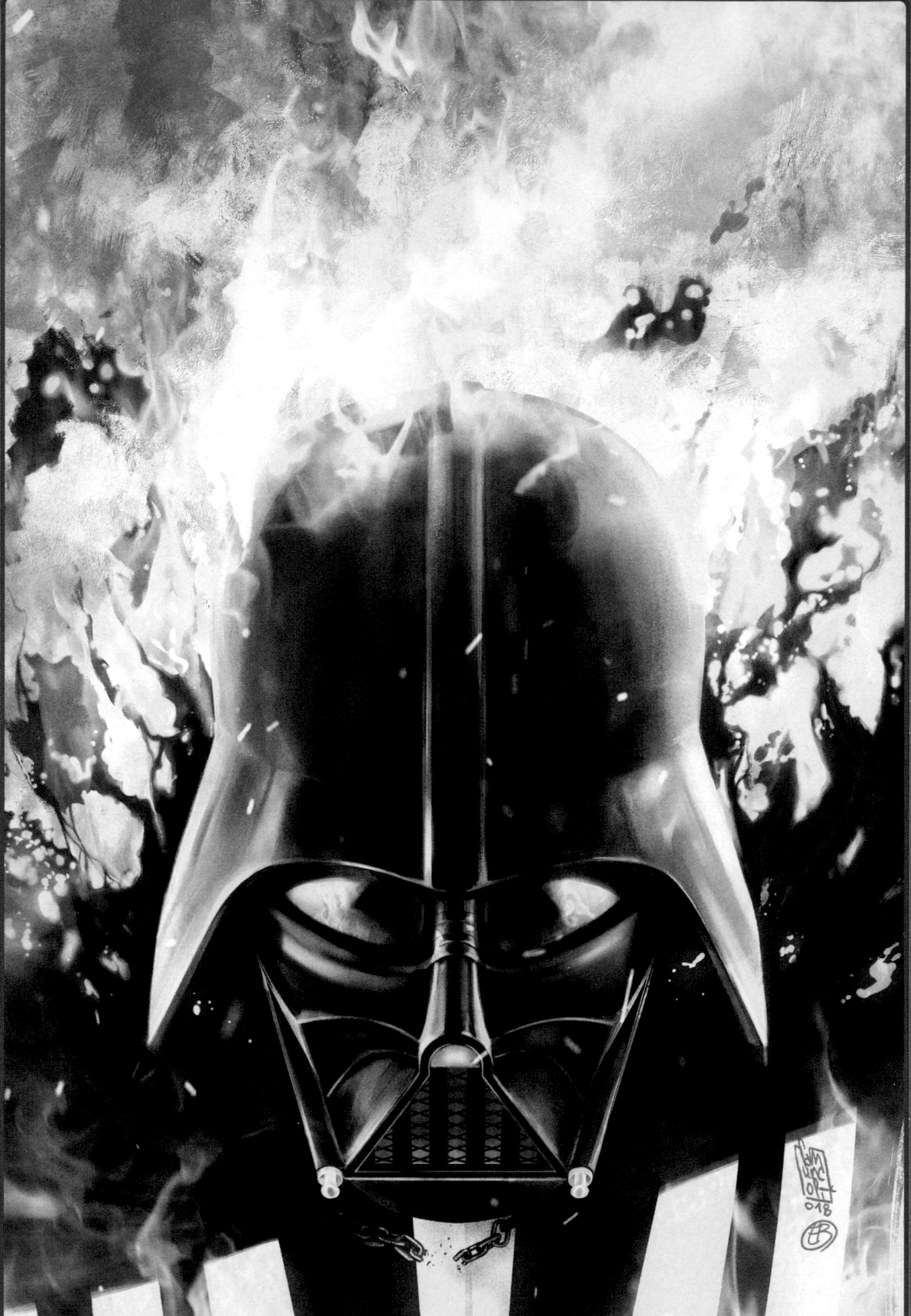

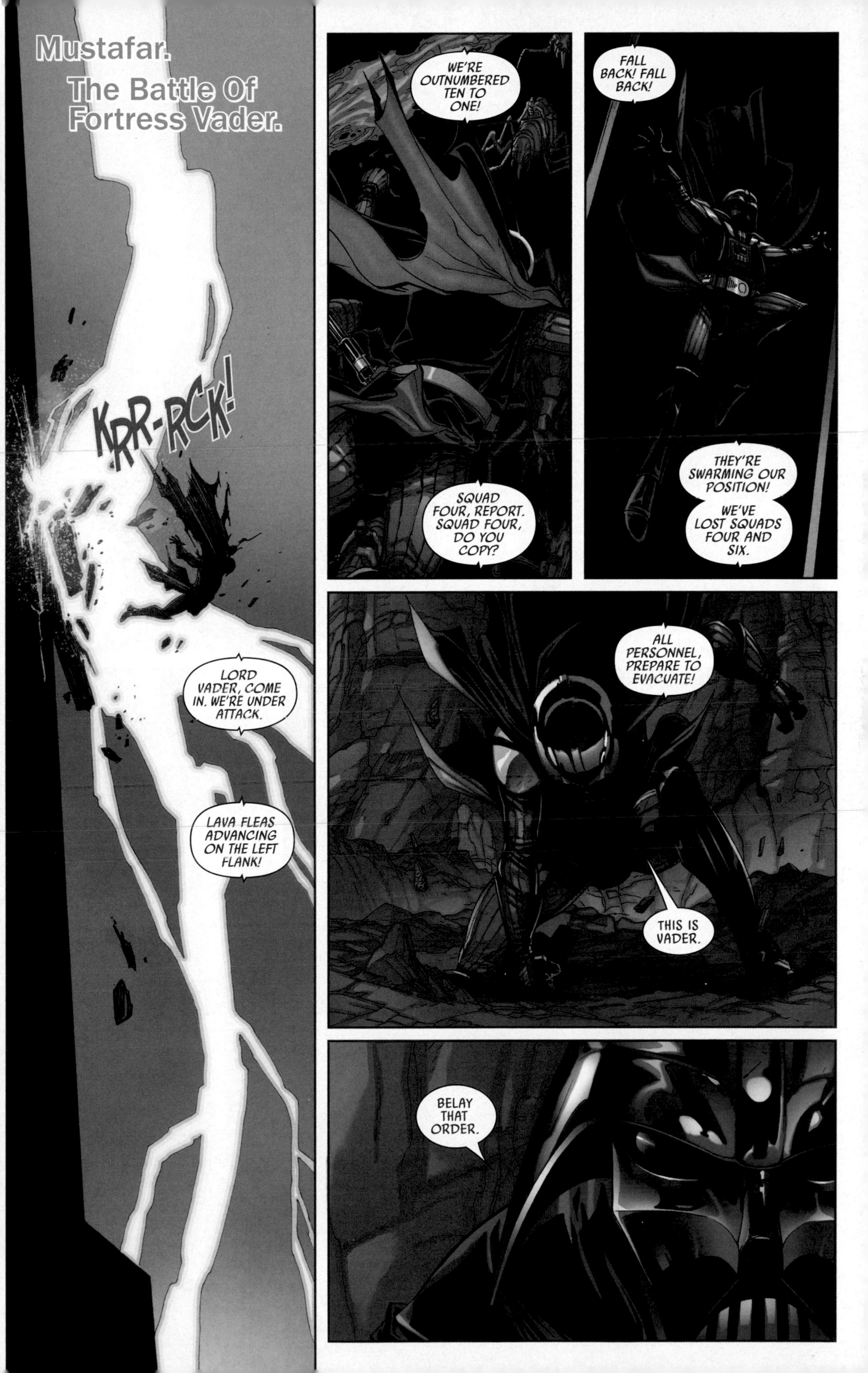
Mustafar.
The Battle Of Fortress Vader.
KRR-RCK!
LORD VADER, COME IN. WE'RE UNDER ATTACK.
LAVA FLEAS ADVANCING ON THE LEFT FLANK!
WE'RE OUTNUMBERED TEN TO ONE!
SQUAD FOUR, REPORT. SQUAD FOUR, DO YOU COPY?
FALL BACK! FALL BACK!
THEY'RE SWARMING OUR POSITION!
WE'VE LOST SQUADS FOUR AND SIX.
ALL PERSONNEL, PREPARE TO EVACUATE!
THIS IS VADER.
BELAY THAT ORDER.

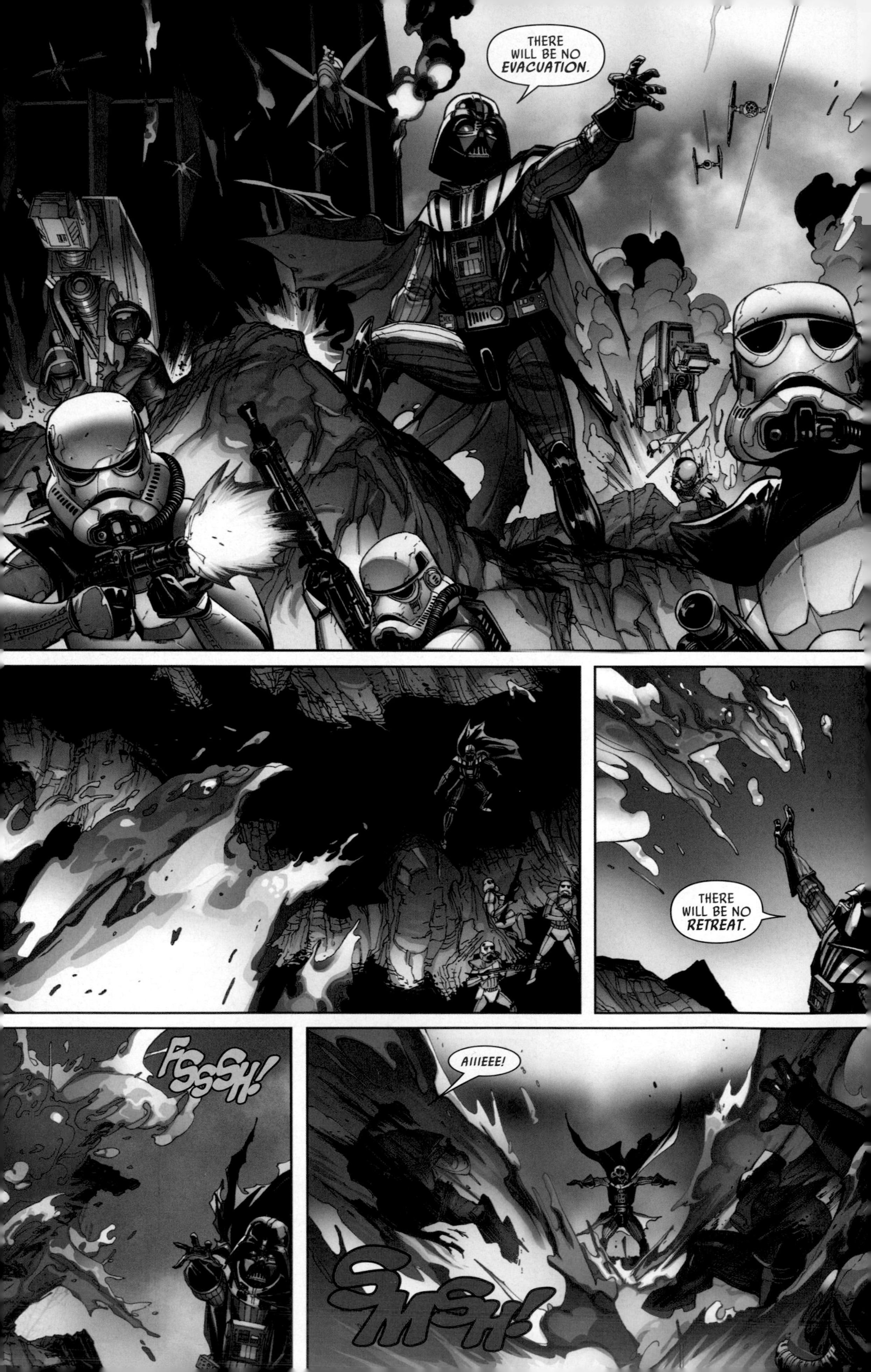
THERE WILL BE NO EVACUATION.
THERE WILL BE NO RETREAT.
FSSSH!
AIIIEEE!
SMSH!

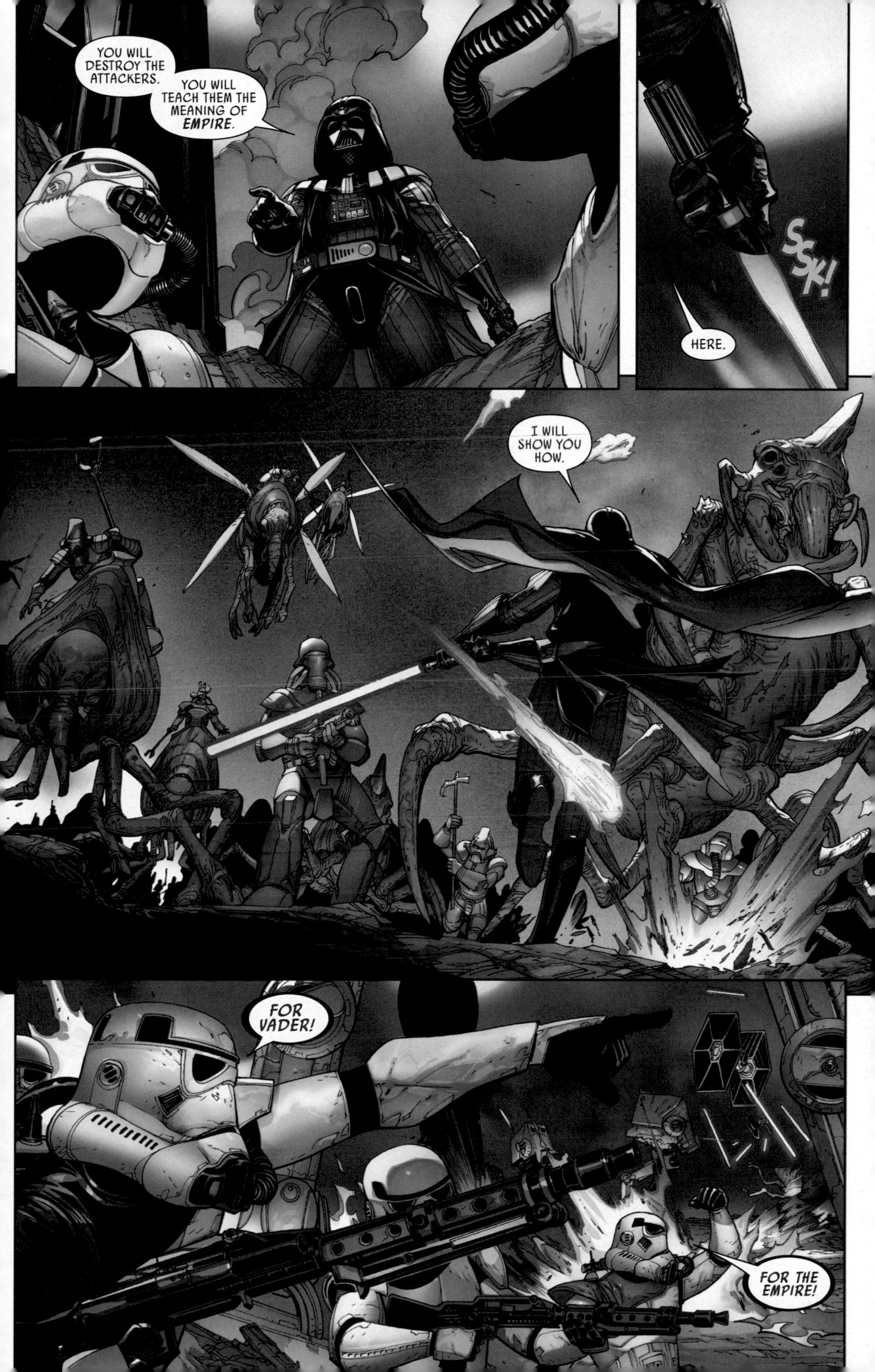
YOU WILL DESTROY THE ATTACKERS.
YOU WILL TEACH THEM THE MEANING OF EMPIRE.
SSK!
HERE.
I WILL SHOW YOU HOW.
FOR VADER!
FOR THE EMPIRE!

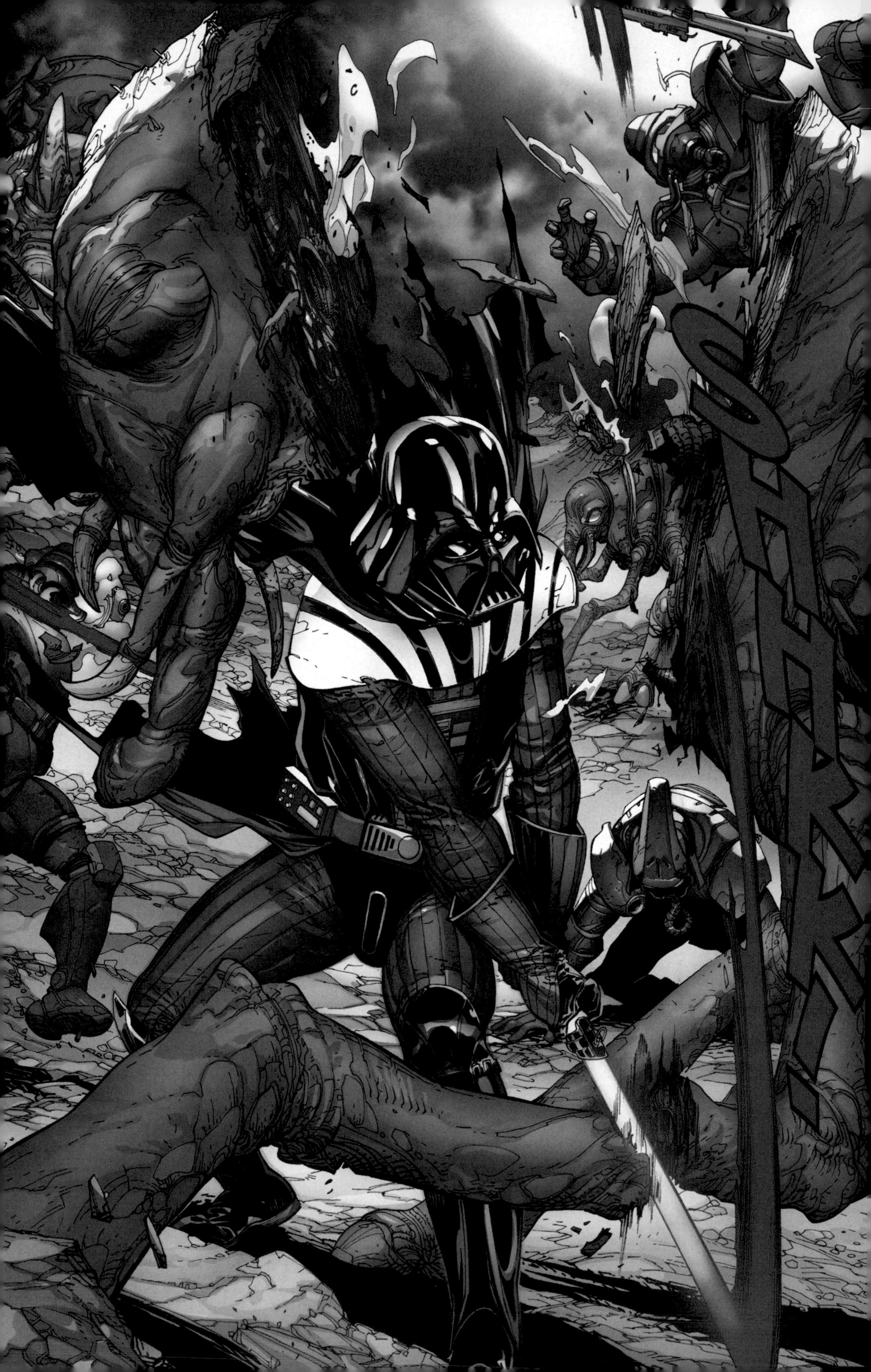

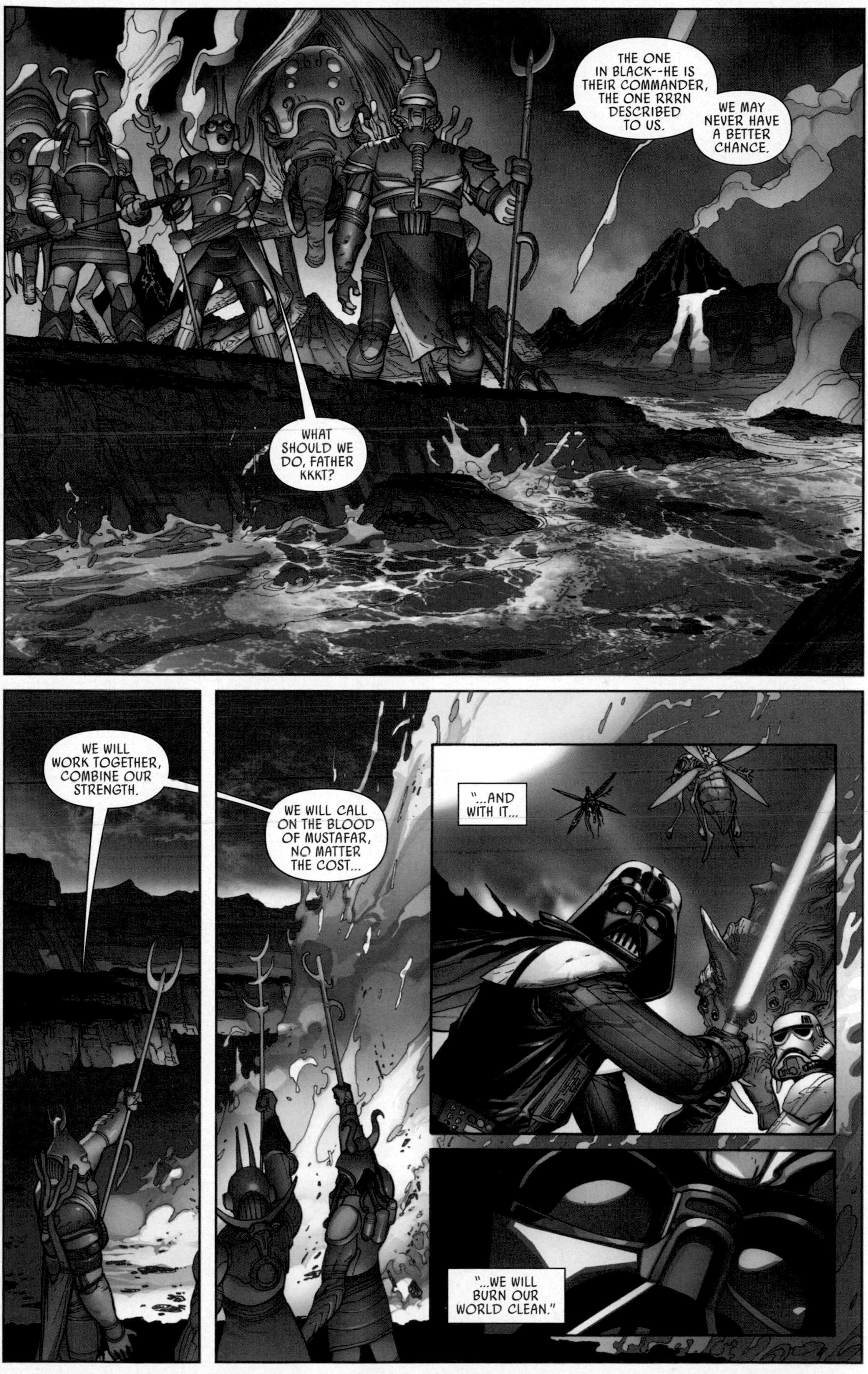
THE ONE IN BLACK--HE IS THEIR COMMANDER, THE ONE RRRN DESCRIBED TO US.
WE MAY NEVER HAVE A BETTER CHANCE.
WHAT SHOULD WE DO, FATHER KKKT?
WE WILL WORK TOGETHER, COMBINE OUR STRENGTH.
WE WILL CALL ON THE BLOOD OF MUSTAFAR, NO MATTER THE COST...
"...AND WITH IT...
"...WE WILL BURN OUR WORLD CLEAN."

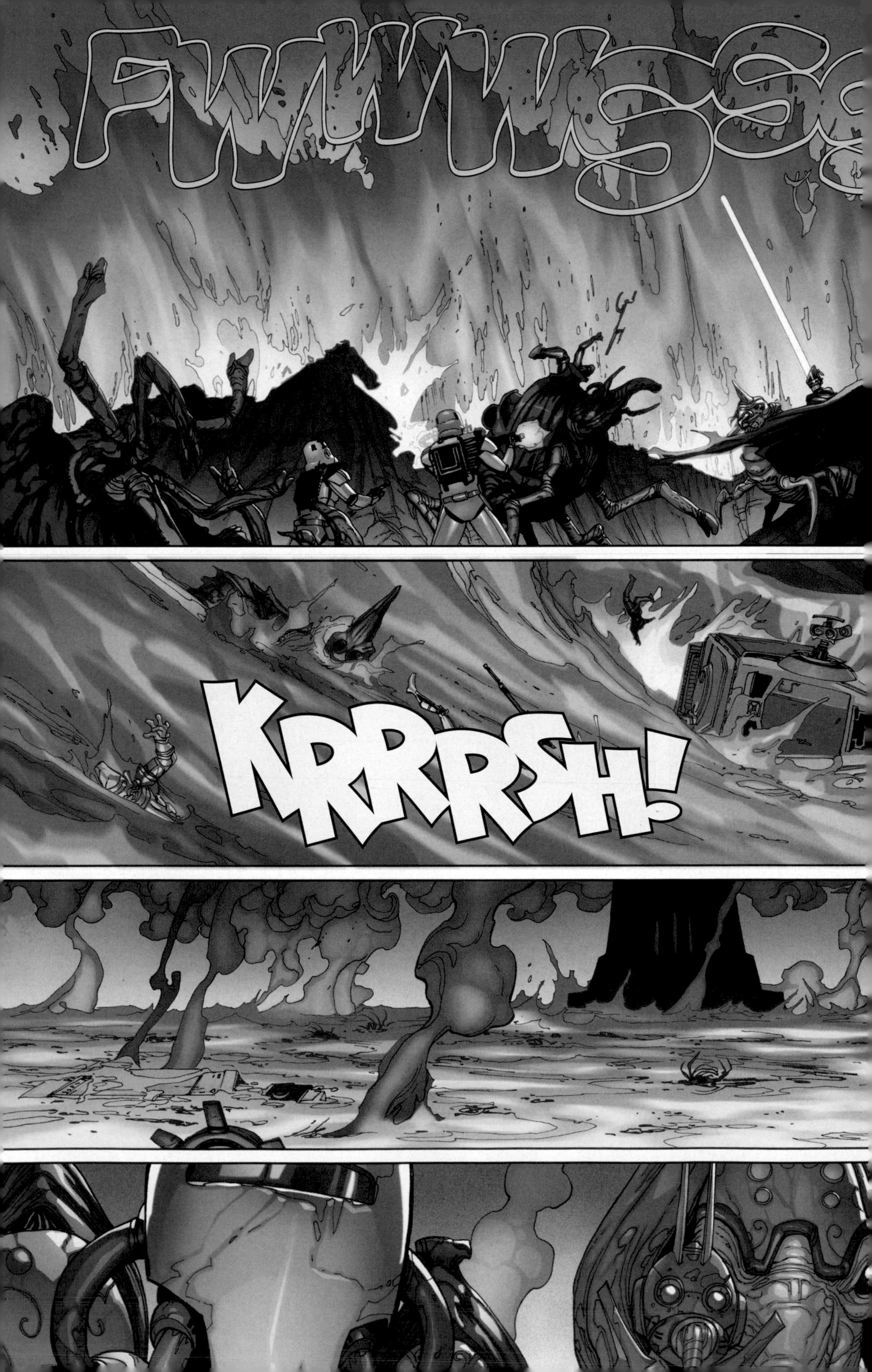
FWWWSSS
KRRRSH!

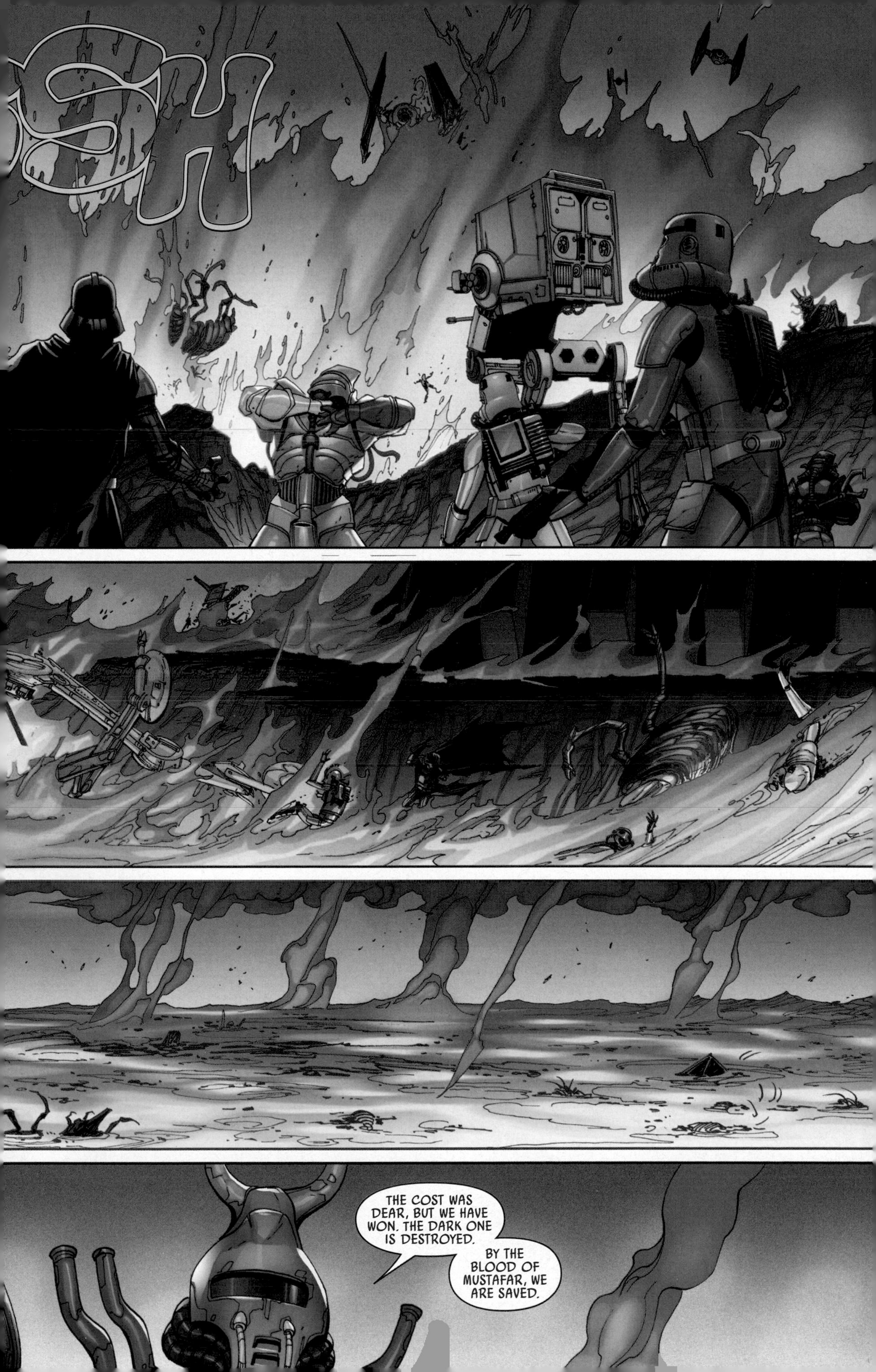
SH
THE COST WAS DEAR, BUT WE HAVE WON. THE DARK ONE IS DESTROYED.
BY THE BLOOD OF MUSTAFAR, WE ARE SAVED.

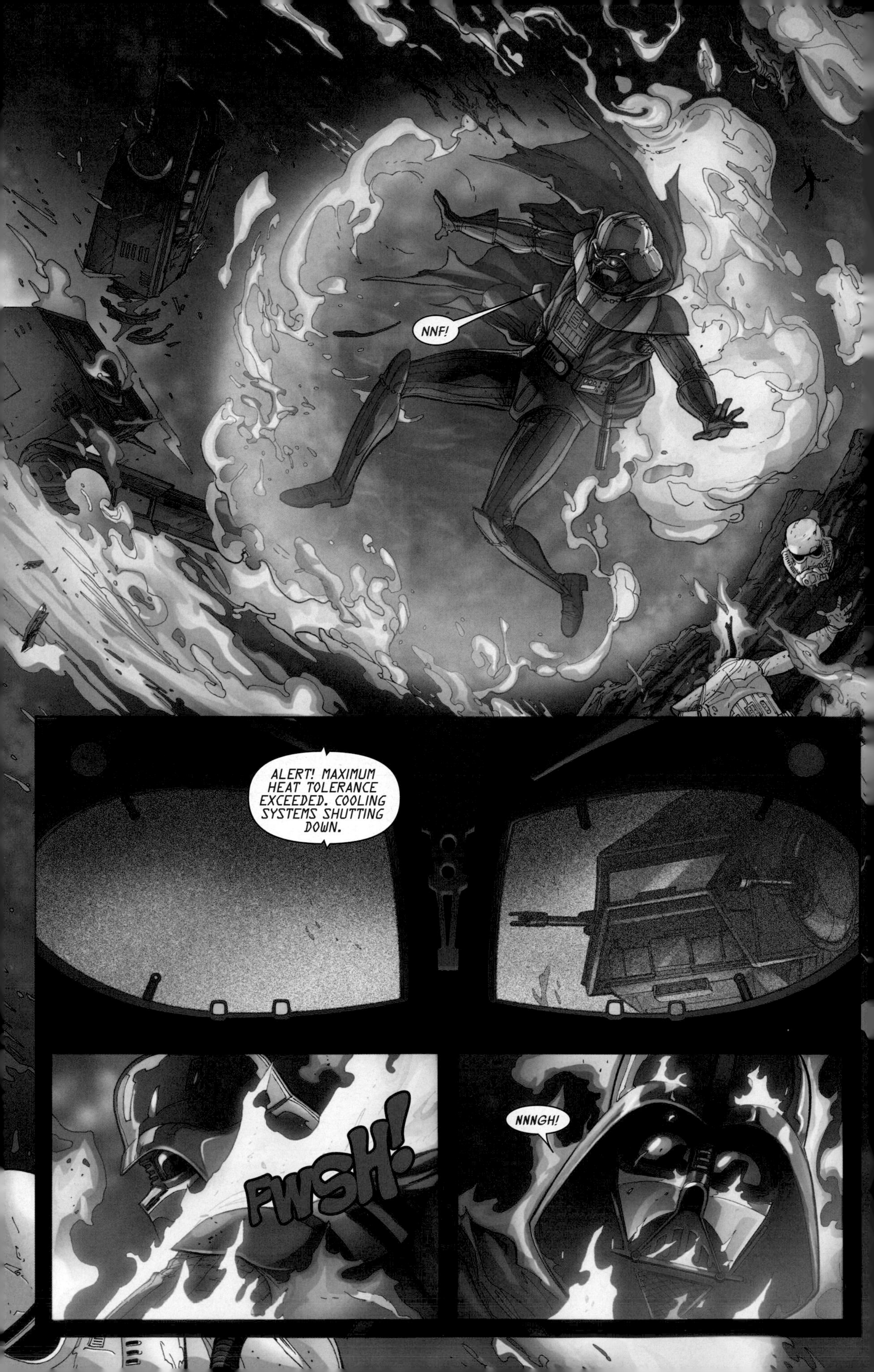
NNF!
ALERT! MAXIMUM HEAT TOLERANCE EXCEEDED. COOLING SYSTEMS SHUTTING DOWN.
FWSH!
NNNGH!

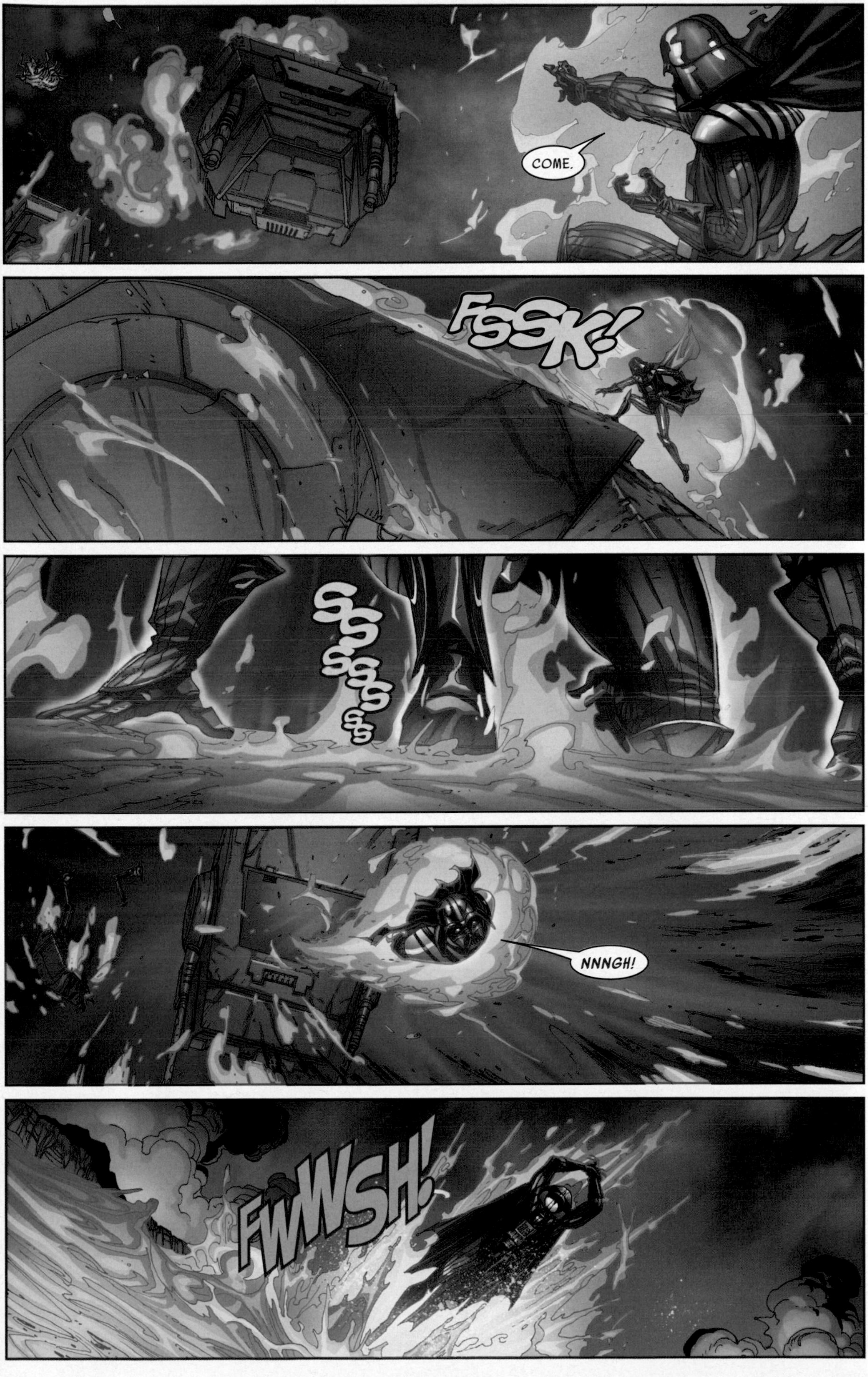
COME.
FSSK!
SSSSSS
NNNGH!
FWWSH!

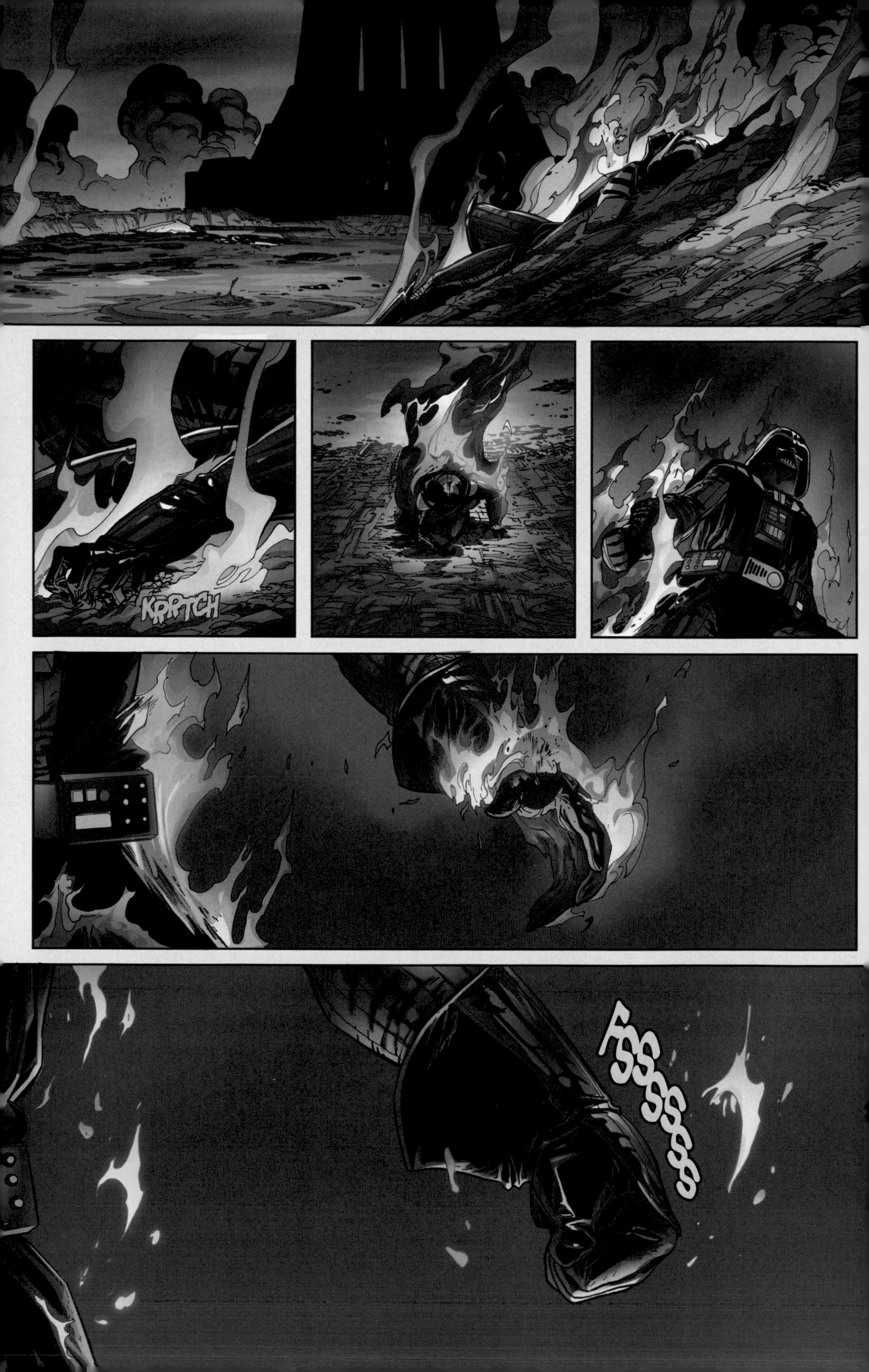
KRRTCH
FSSSSSS

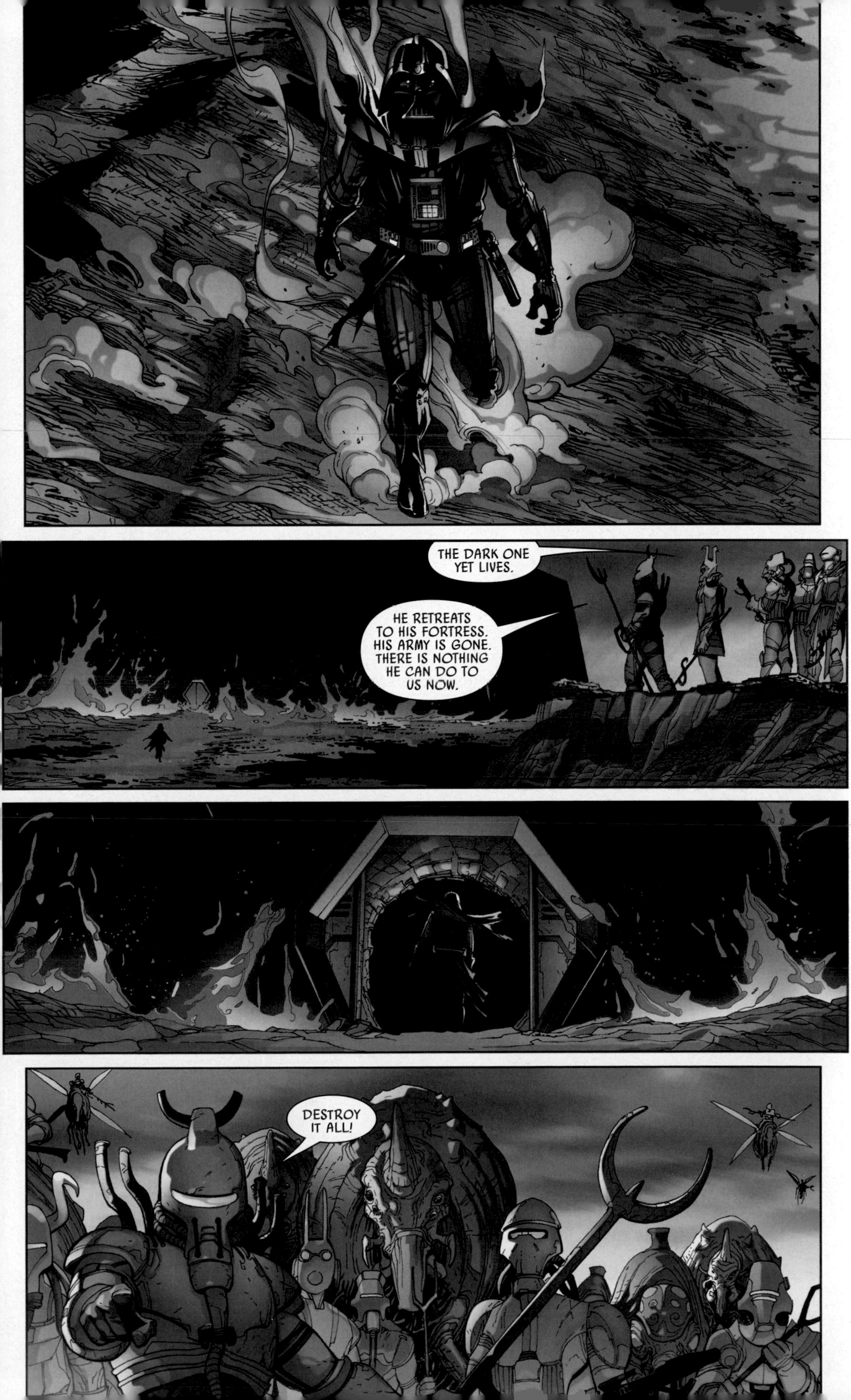
THE DARK ONE YET LIVES.
HE RETREATS TO HIS FORTRESS. HIS ARMY IS GONE. THERE IS NOTHING HE CAN DO TO US NOW.
DESTROY IT ALL!

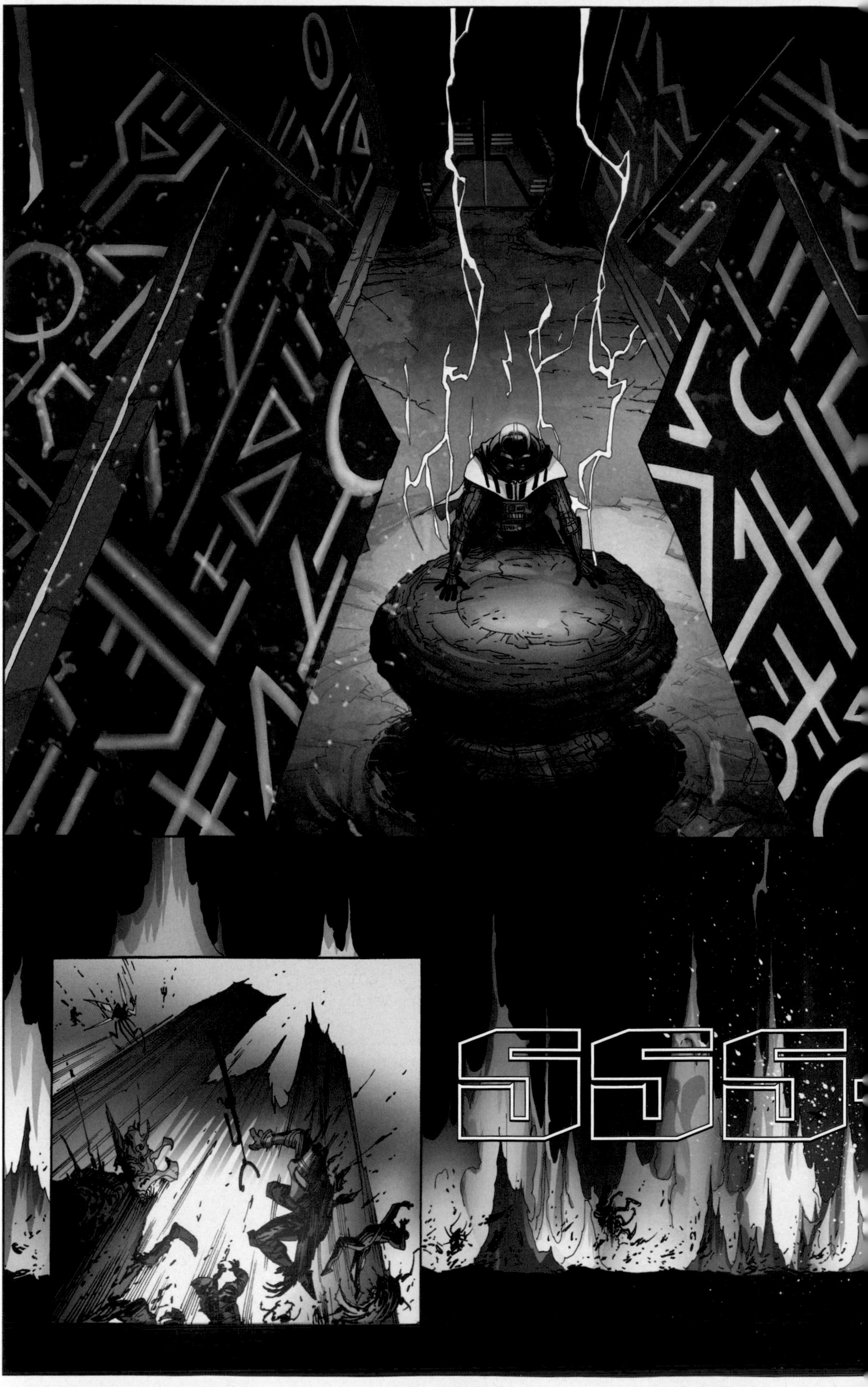
SSS-

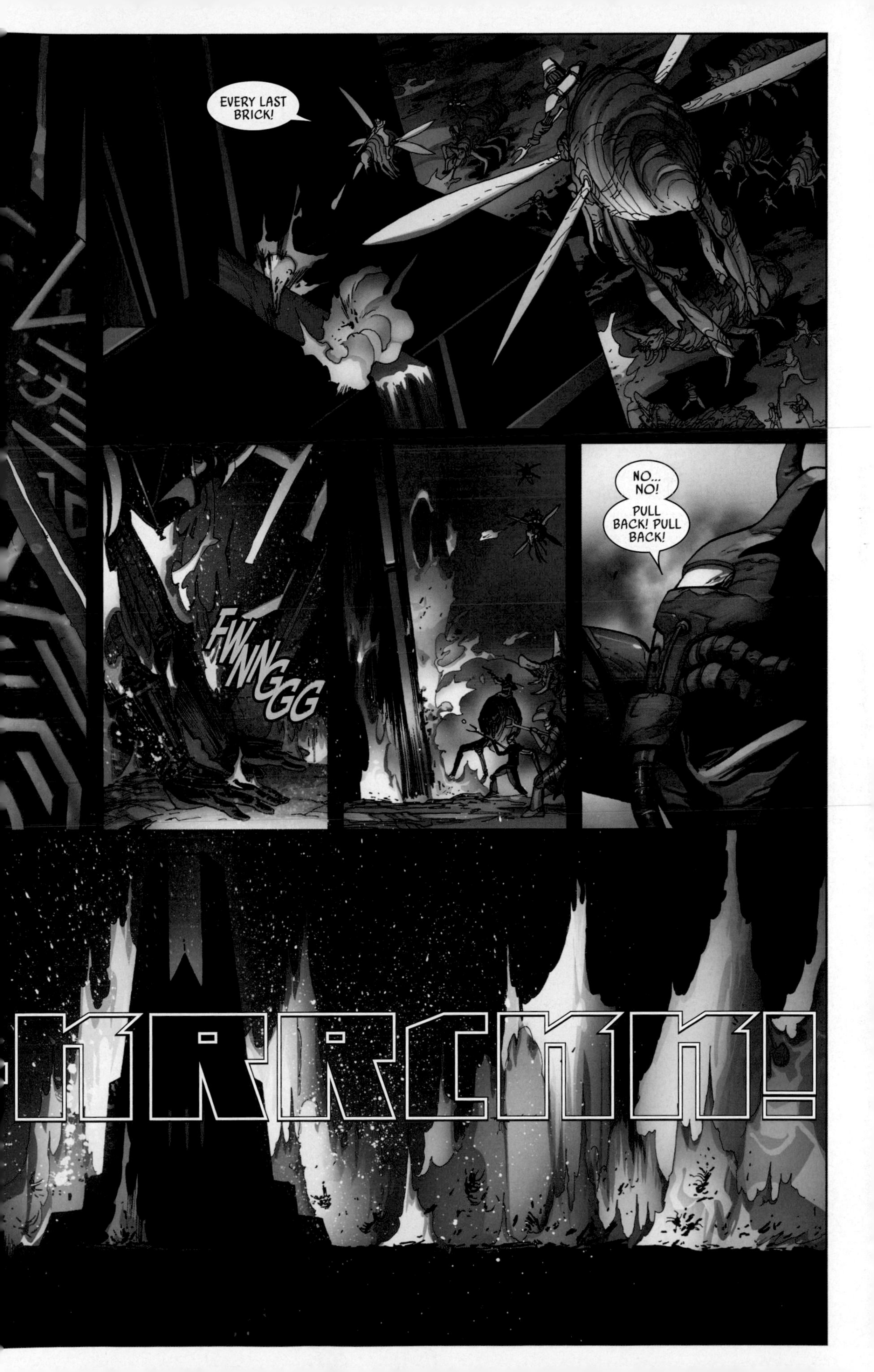
EVERY LAST BRICK!
FWNNGGG
NO... NO!
PULL BACK! PULL BACK!
KRRCKKK!

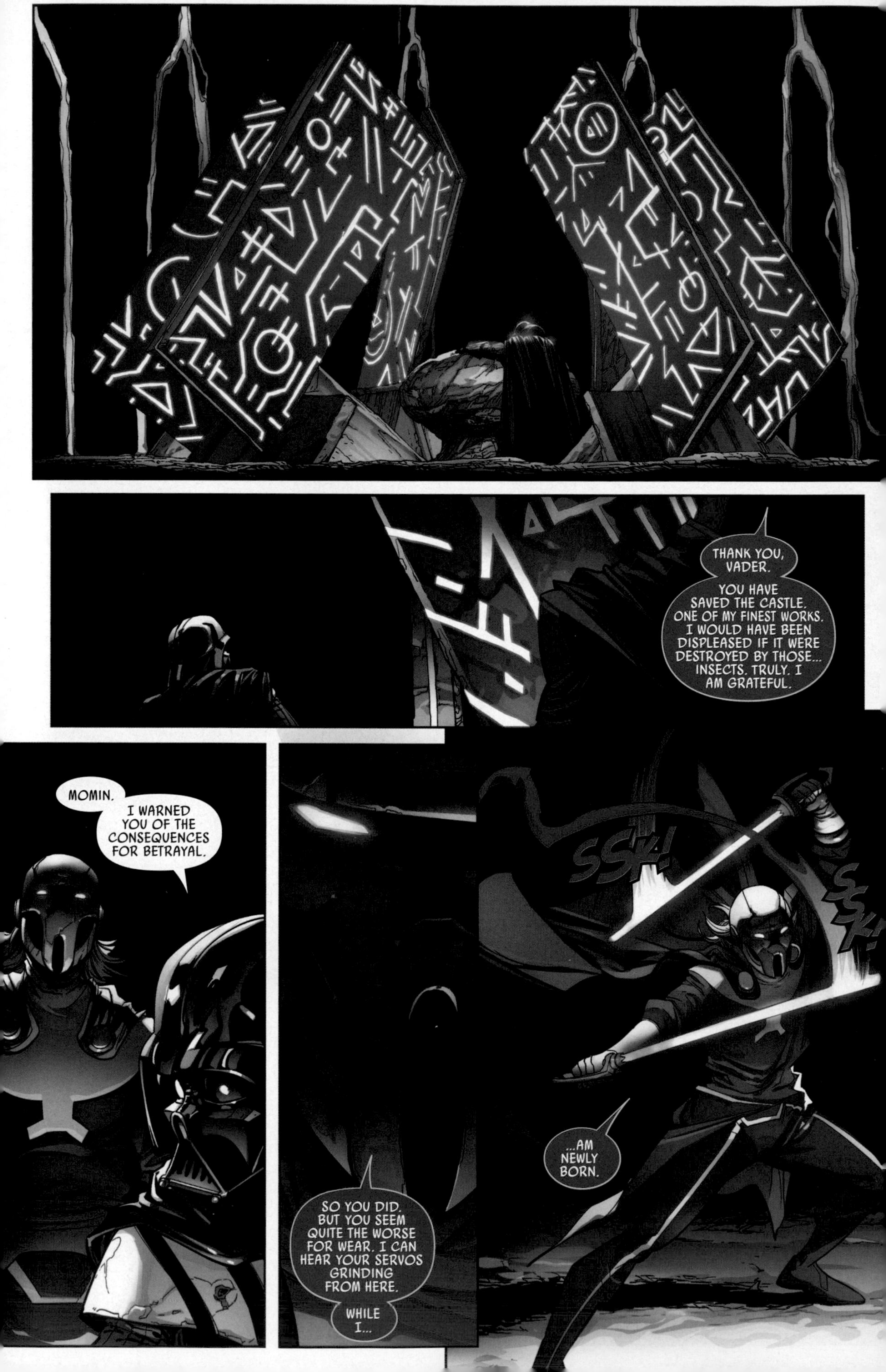
THANK YOU, VADER.
YOU HAVE SAVED THE CASTLE. ONE OF MY FINEST WORKS. I WOULD HAVE BEEN DISPLEASED IF IT WERE DESTROYED BY THOSE... INSECTS. TRULY. I AM GRATEFUL.
MOMIN.
I WARNED YOU OF THE CONSEQUENCES FOR BETRAYAL.
SO YOU DID, BUT YOU SEEM QUITE THE WORSE FOR WEAR. I CAN HEAR YOUR SERVOS GRINDING FROM HERE.
WHILE I...
SSKK!
SSKK!
...AM NEWLY BORN.

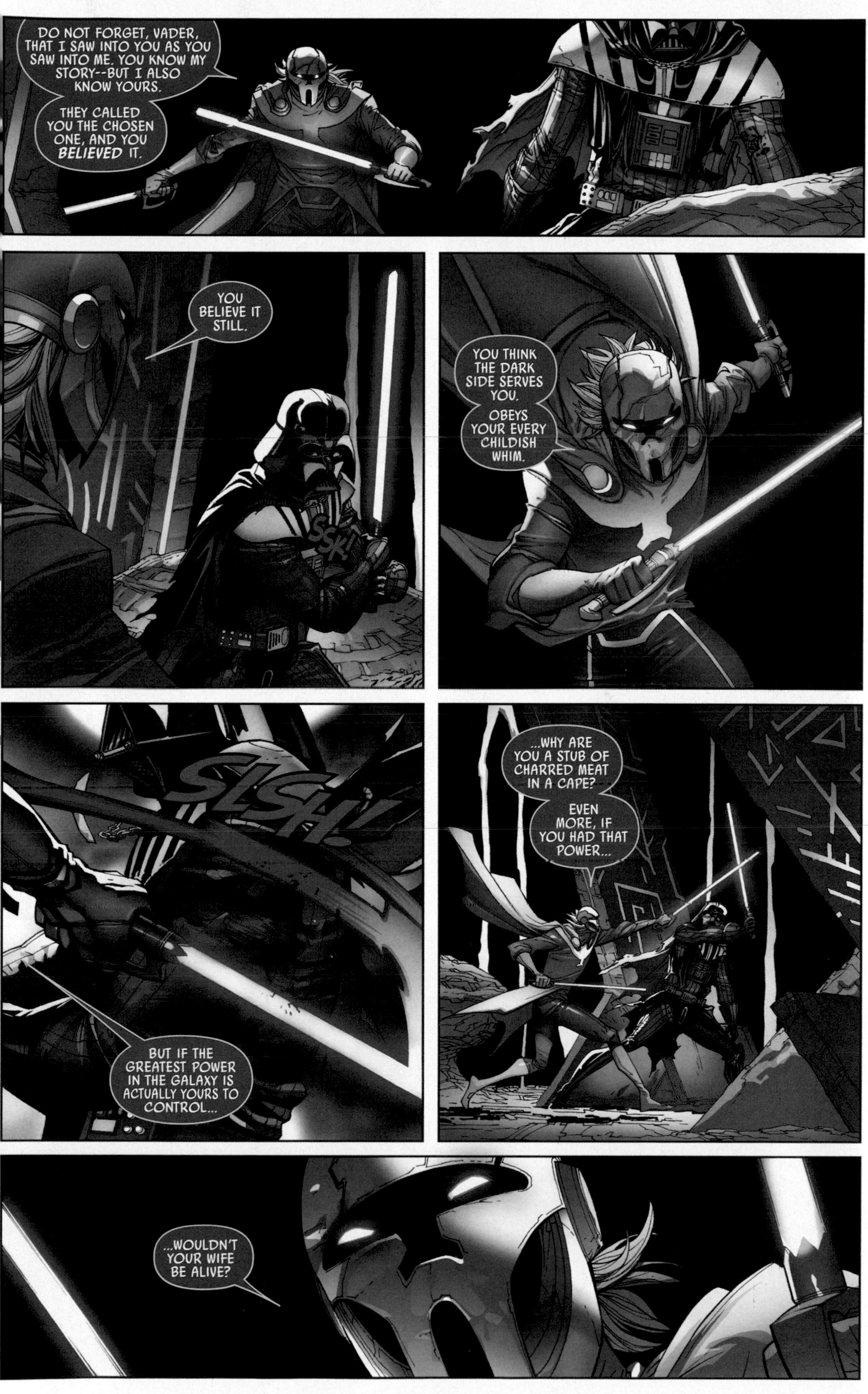
DO NOT FORGET, VADER, THAT I SAW INTO YOU AS YOU SAW INTO ME. YOU KNOW MY STORY--BUT I ALSO KNOW YOURS.
THEY CALLED YOU THE CHOSEN ONE, AND YOU *BELIEVED* IT.
YOU BELIEVE IT STILL.
SSK!
YOU THINK THE DARK SIDE SERVES YOU.
OBEYS YOUR EVERY CHILDISH WHIM.
SLSH!
BUT IF THE GREATEST POWER IN THE GALAXY IS ACTUALLY YOURS TO CONTROL...
...WHY ARE YOU A STUB OF CHARRED MEAT IN A CAPE?
EVEN MORE, IF YOU HAD THAT POWER...
...WOULDN'T YOUR WIFE BE ALIVE?

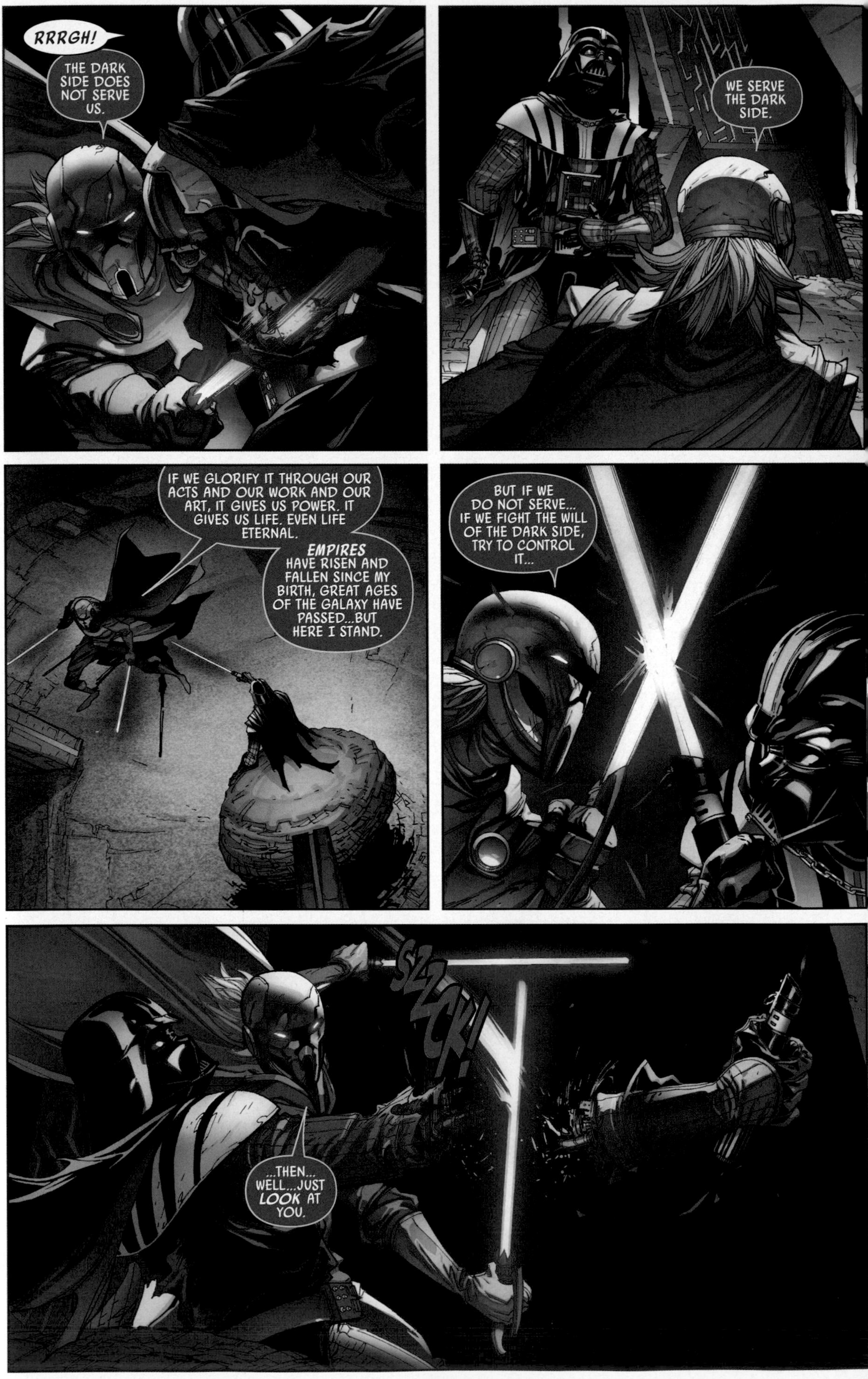

RRRGH!
THE DARK SIDE DOES NOT SERVE US.
WE SERVE THE DARK SIDE.
IF WE GLORIFY IT THROUGH OUR ACTS AND OUR WORK AND OUR ART, IT GIVES US POWER. IT GIVES US LIFE. EVEN LIFE ETERNAL.
EMPIRES HAVE RISEN AND FALLEN SINCE MY BIRTH, GREAT AGES OF THE GALAXY HAVE PASSED...BUT HERE I STAND.
BUT IF WE DO NOT SERVE... IF WE FIGHT THE WILL OF THE DARK SIDE, TRY TO CONTROL IT...
SZZZCK!
...THEN... WELL...JUST LOOK AT YOU.

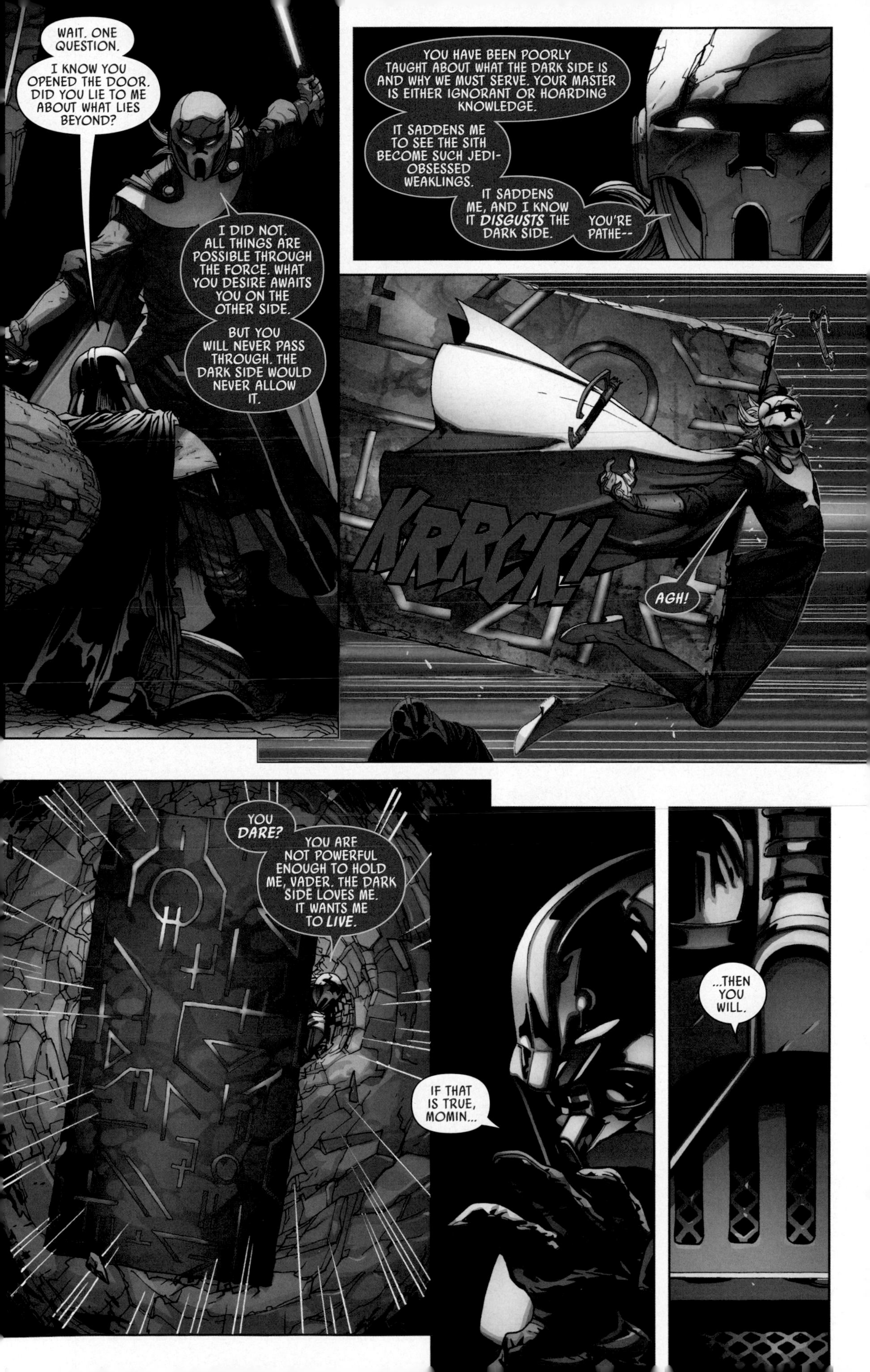
WAIT. ONE QUESTION.
I KNOW YOU OPENED THE DOOR. DID YOU LIE TO ME ABOUT WHAT LIES BEYOND?
I DID NOT. ALL THINGS ARE POSSIBLE THROUGH THE FORCE. WHAT YOU DESIRE AWAITS YOU ON THE OTHER SIDE.
BUT YOU WILL NEVER PASS THROUGH. THE DARK SIDE WOULD NEVER ALLOW IT.
YOU HAVE BEEN POORLY TAUGHT ABOUT WHAT THE DARK SIDE IS AND WHY WE MUST SERVE. YOUR MASTER IS EITHER IGNORANT OR HOARDING KNOWLEDGE.
IT SADDENS ME TO SEE THE SITH BECOME SUCH JEDI-OBSESSED WEAKLINGS.
IT SADDENS ME, AND I KNOW IT DISGUSTS THE DARK SIDE.
YOU'RE PATHE--
KRRCK!
AGH!
YOU DARE?
YOU ARE NOT POWERFUL ENOUGH TO HOLD ME, VADER. THE DARK SIDE LOVES ME. IT WANTS ME TO LIVE.
IF THAT IS TRUE, MOMIN...
...THEN YOU WILL.

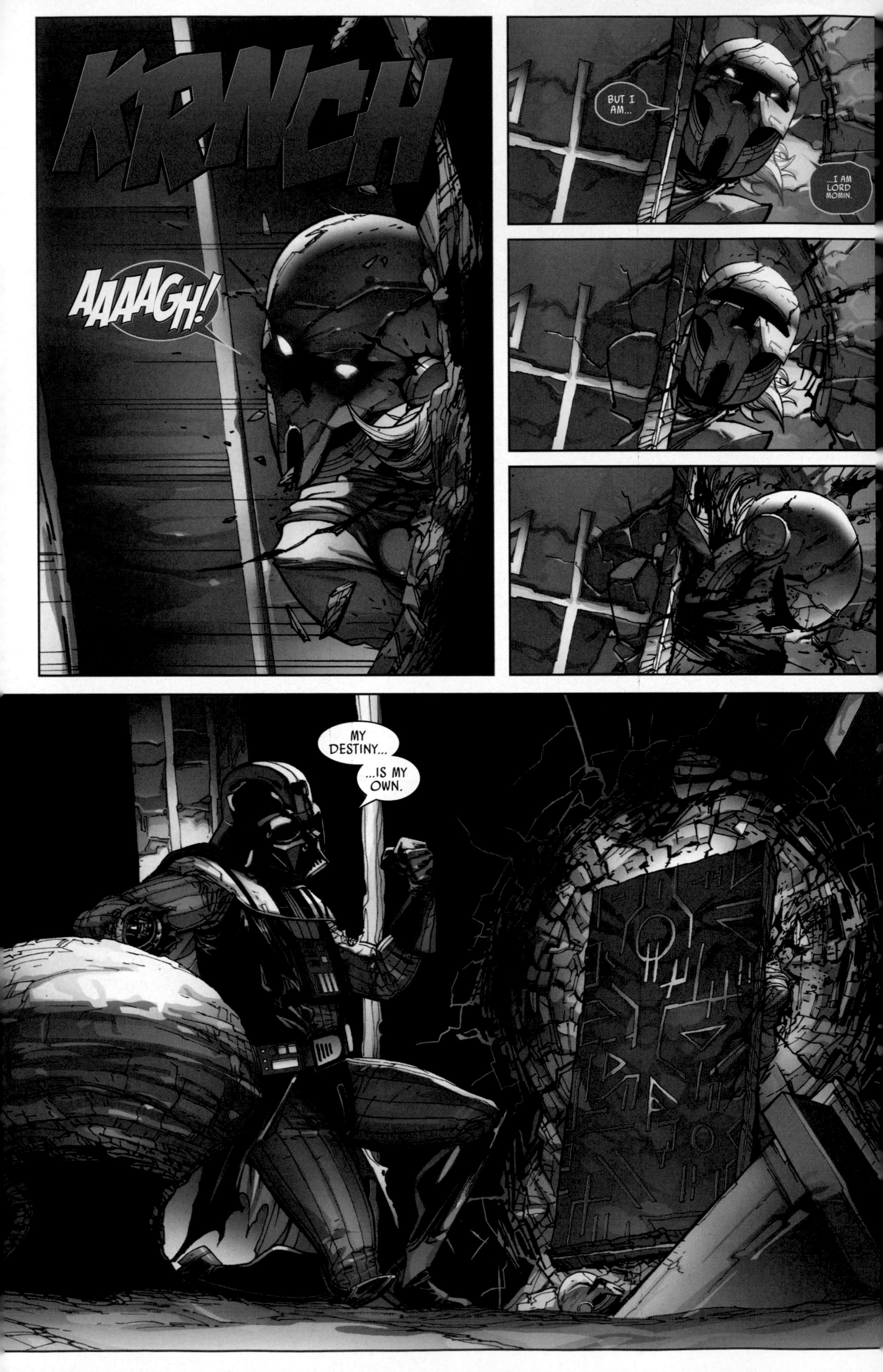
KRNCH
AAAAGH!
BUT I AM...
...I AM LORD MOMIN.
MY DESTINY...
...IS MY OWN.

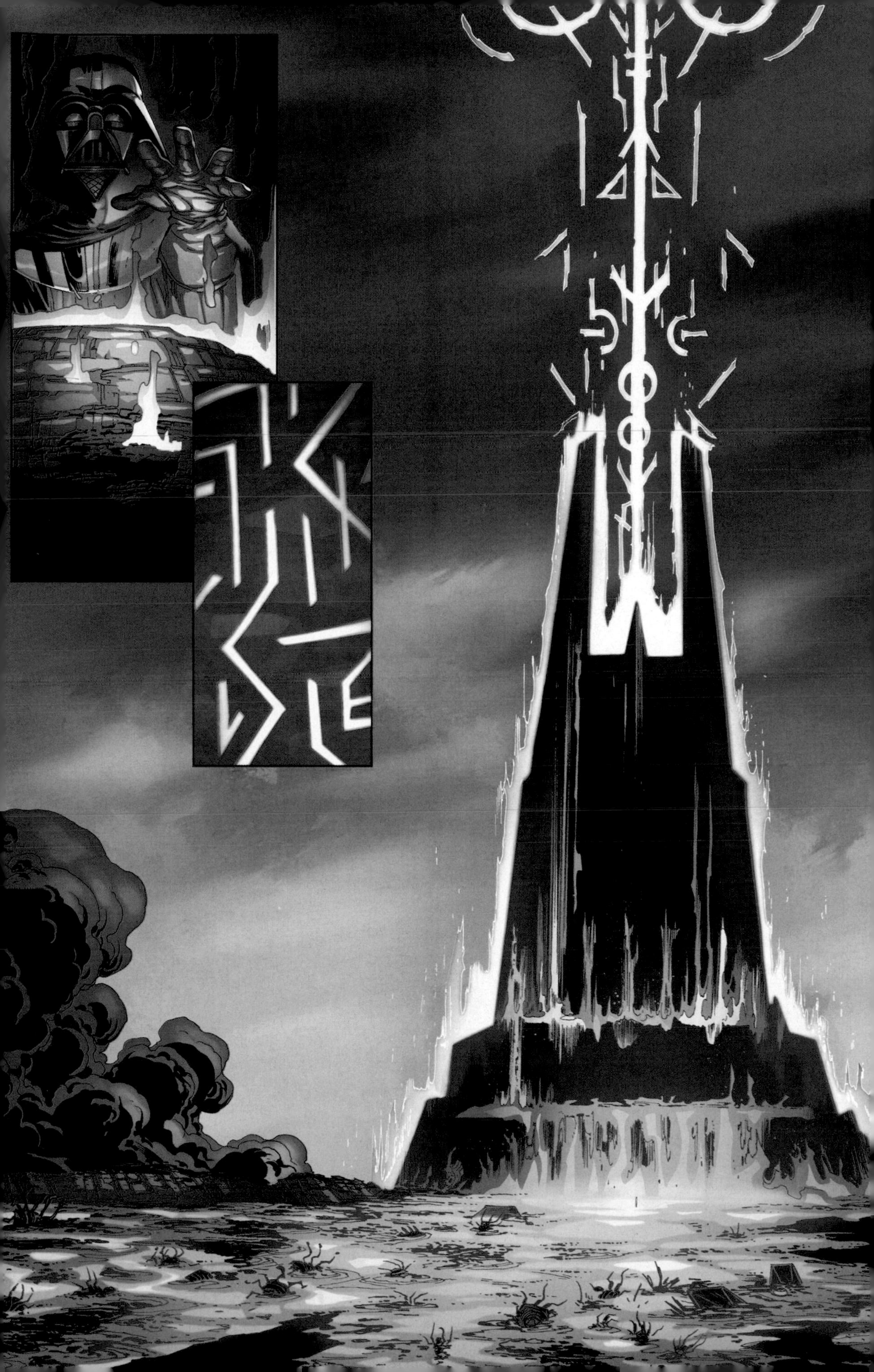

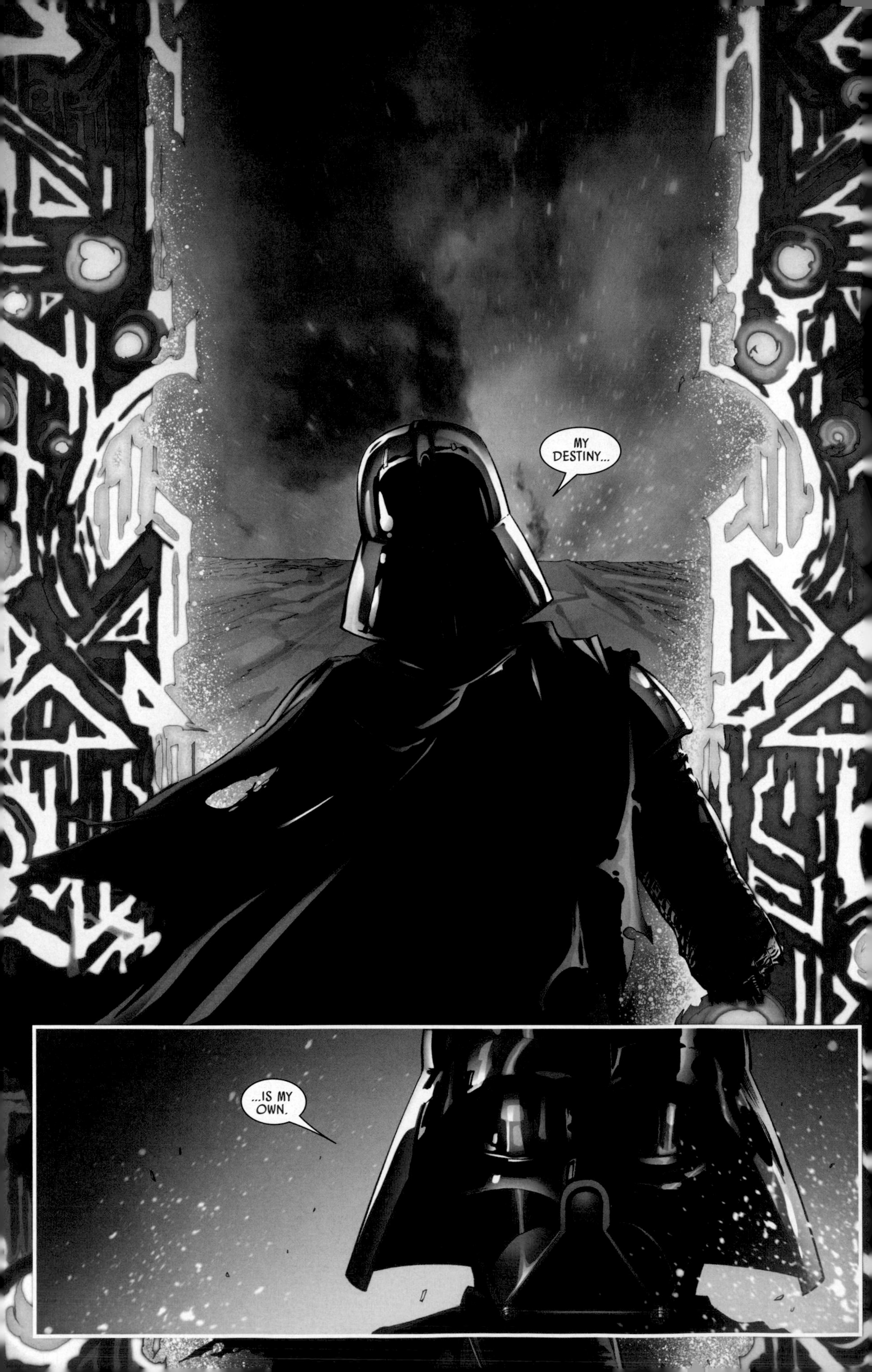
MY DESTINY...
...IS MY OWN.

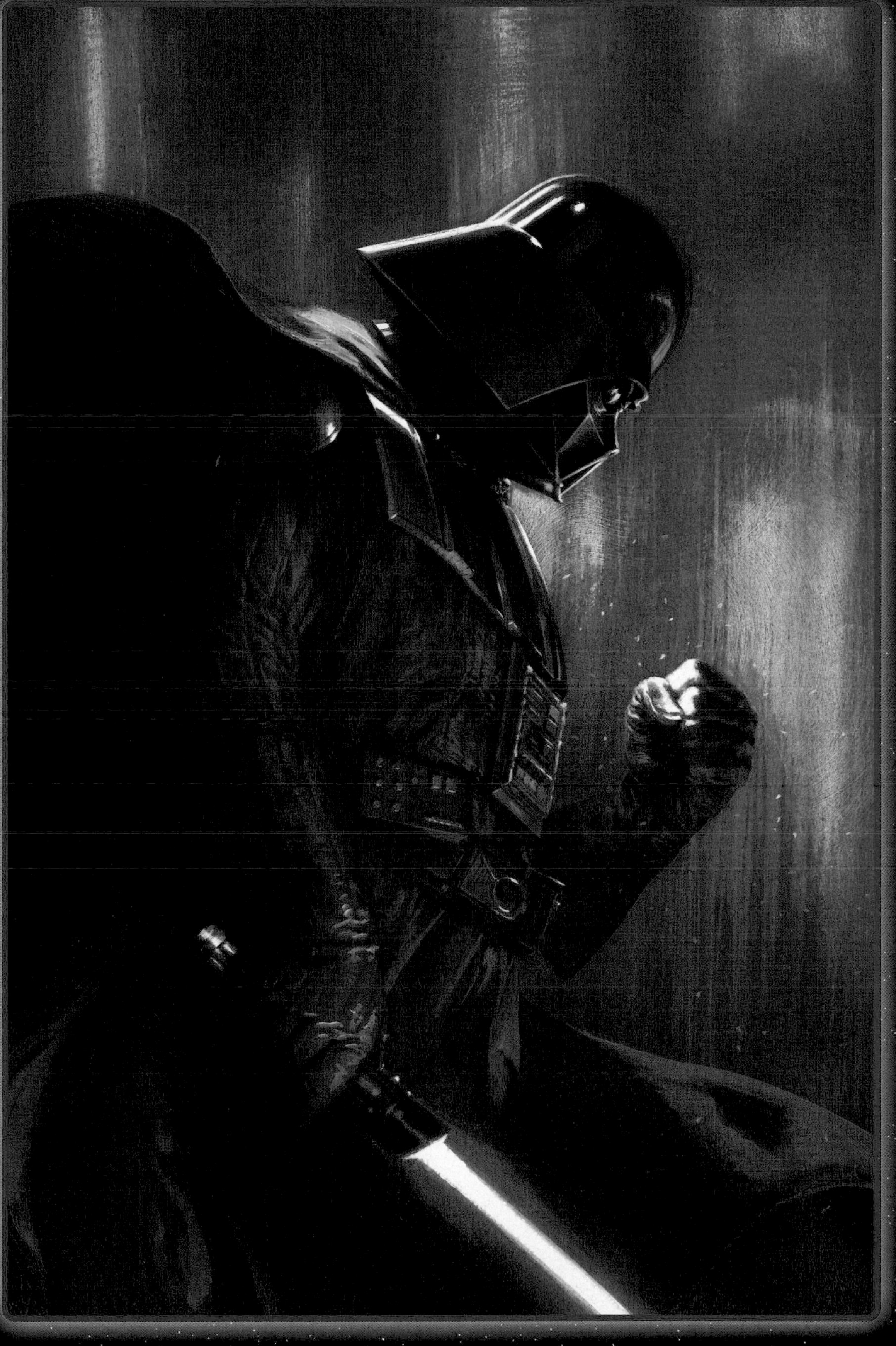

STAR WARS: DARTH VADER — DARK LORD OF THE SITH 25 Variant by

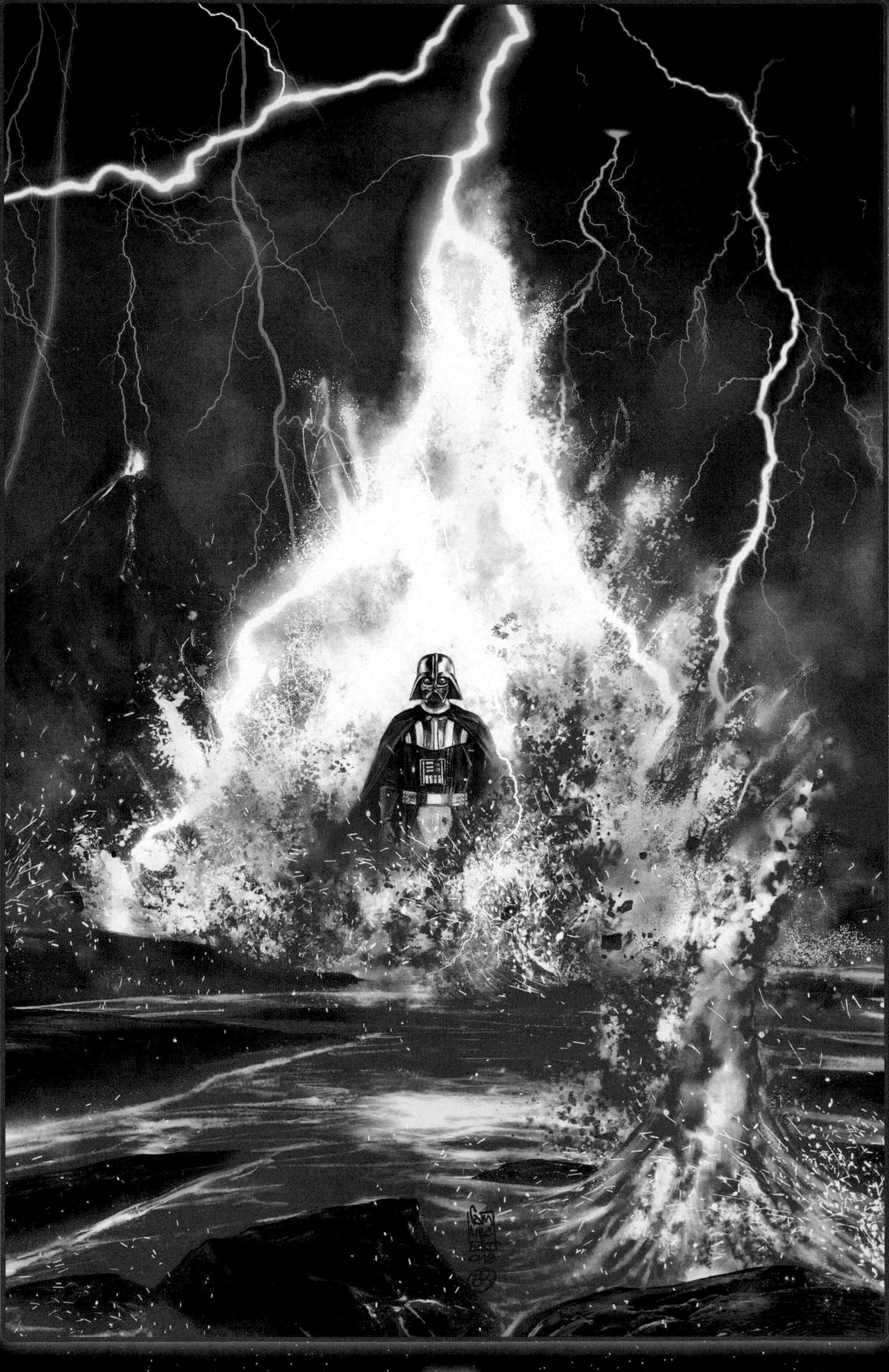

25

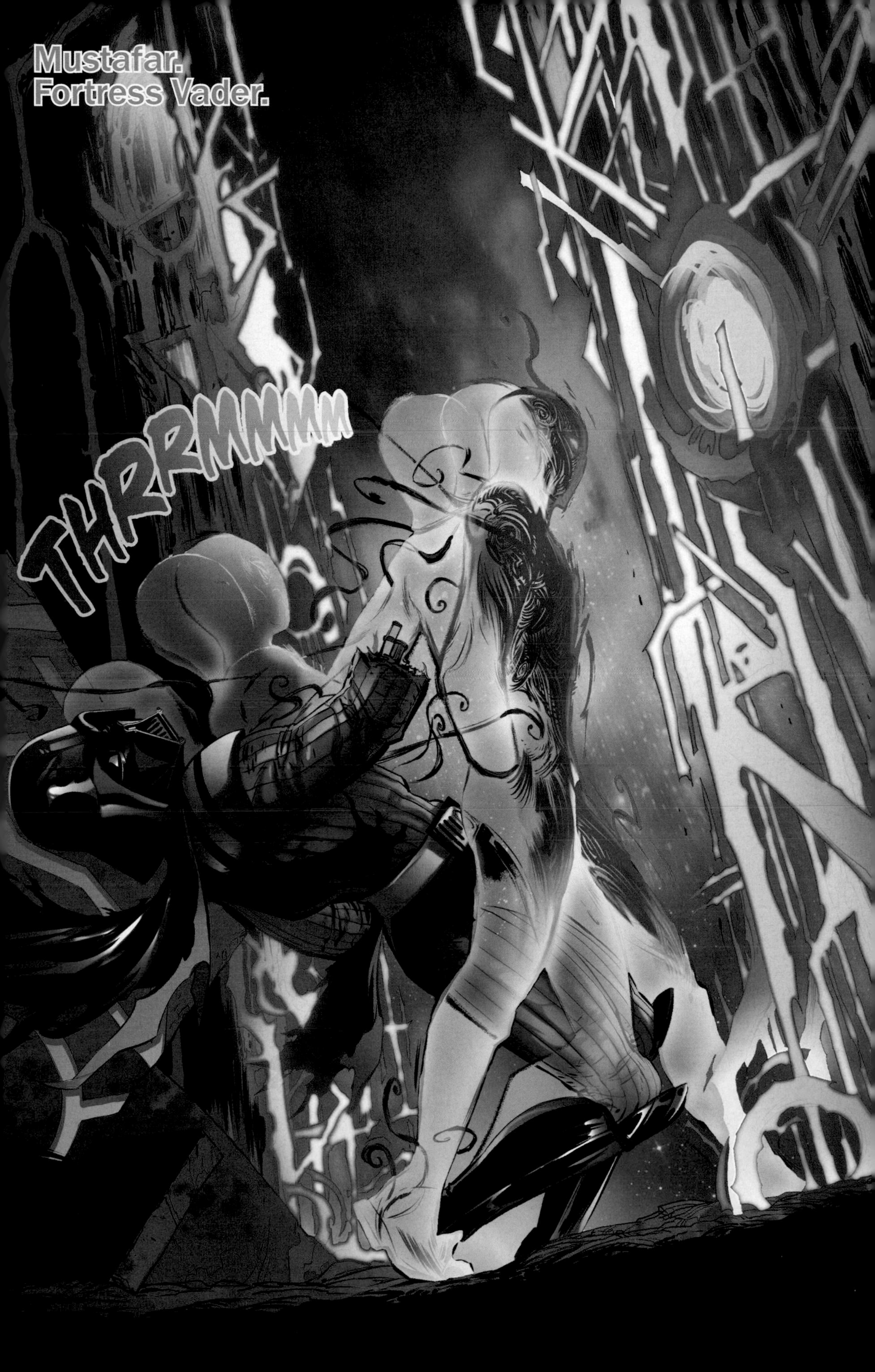
Mustafar.
Fortress Vader.
THRRMMMMM

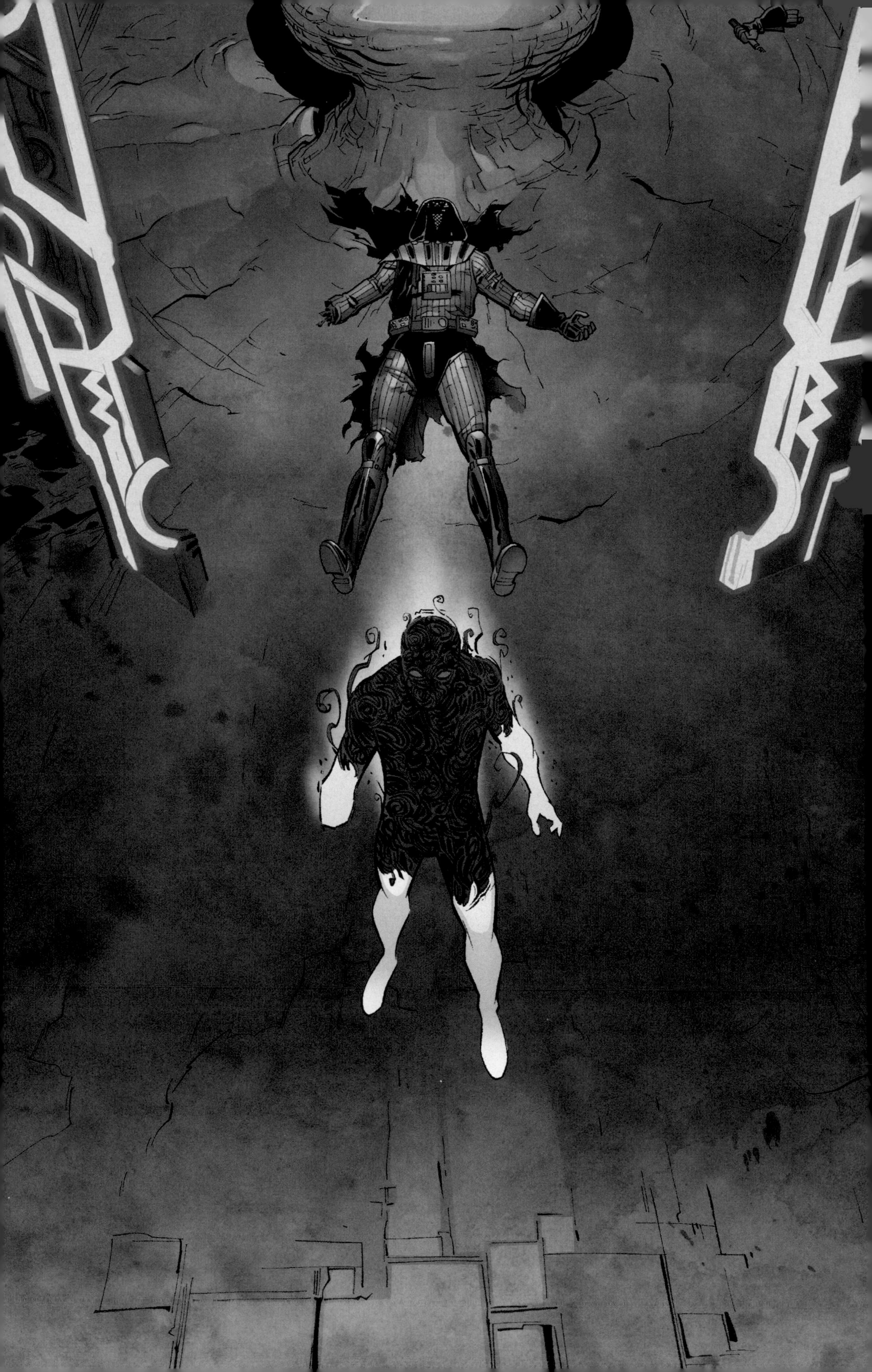

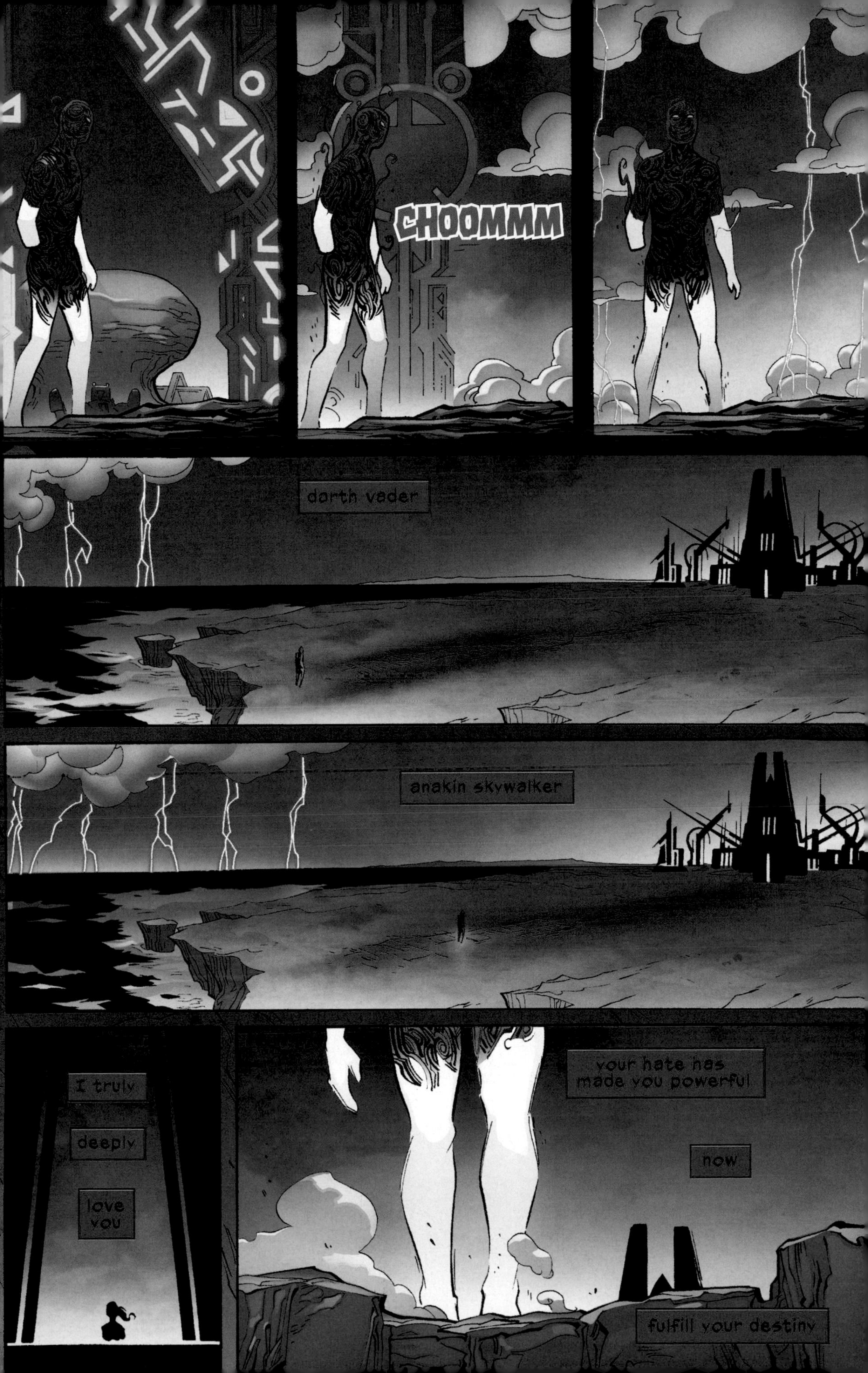
CHOOMMM
darth vader
anakin skywalker
I truly
deeply
love you
your hate has made you powerful
now
fulfill your destiny

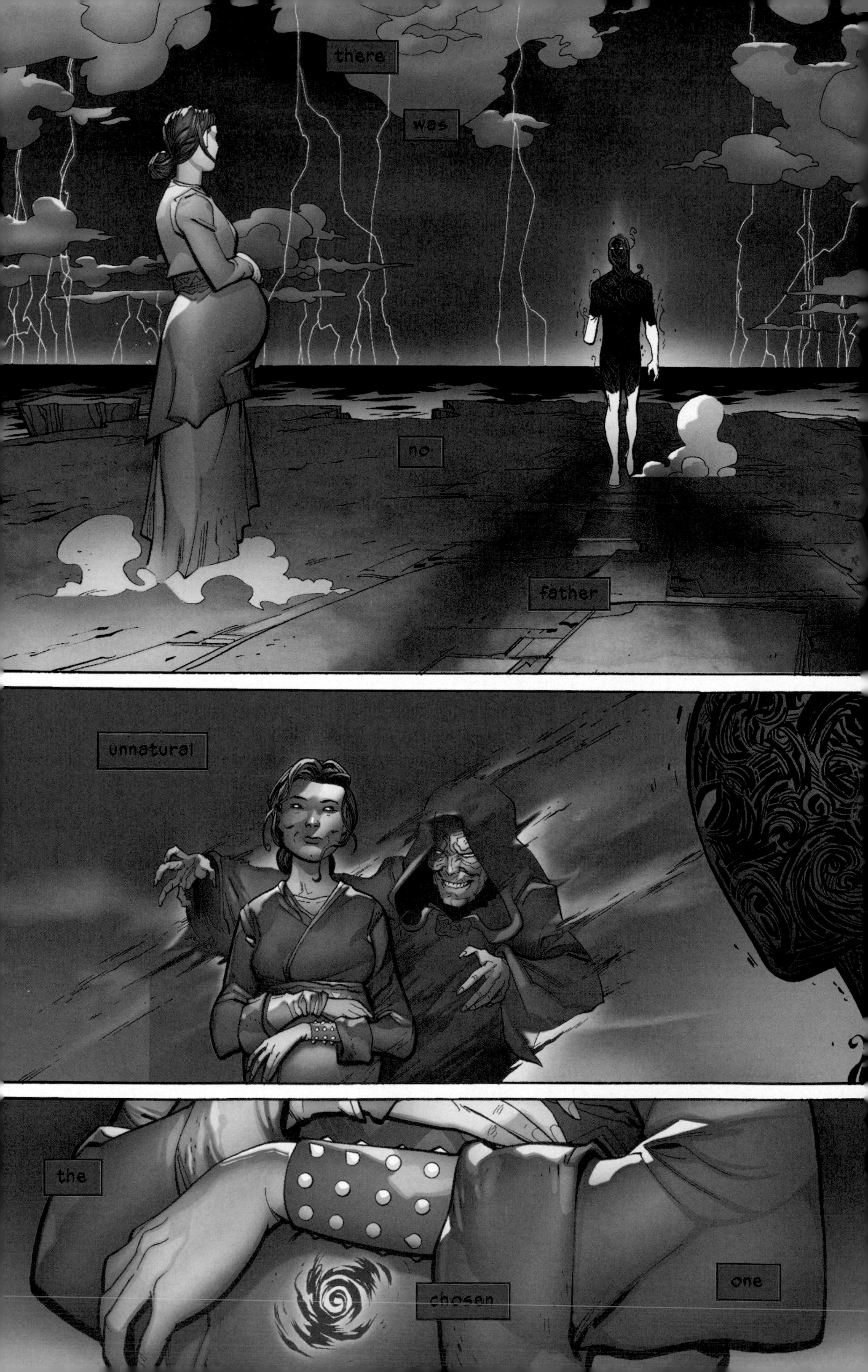
there
was
no
father
unnatural
the
chosen
one

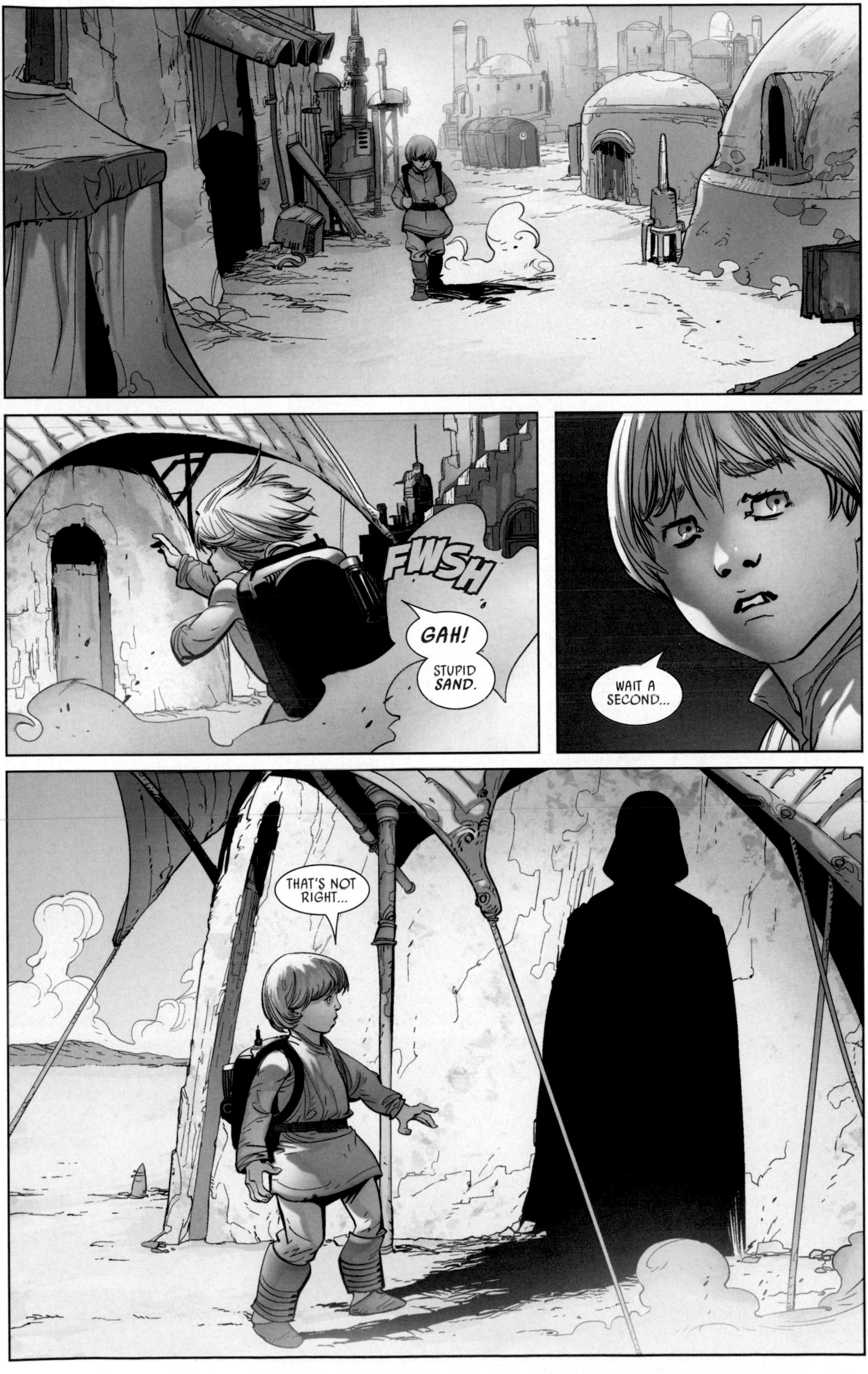
FWSH
GAH!
STUPID SAND.
WAIT A SECOND...
THAT'S NOT RIGHT...

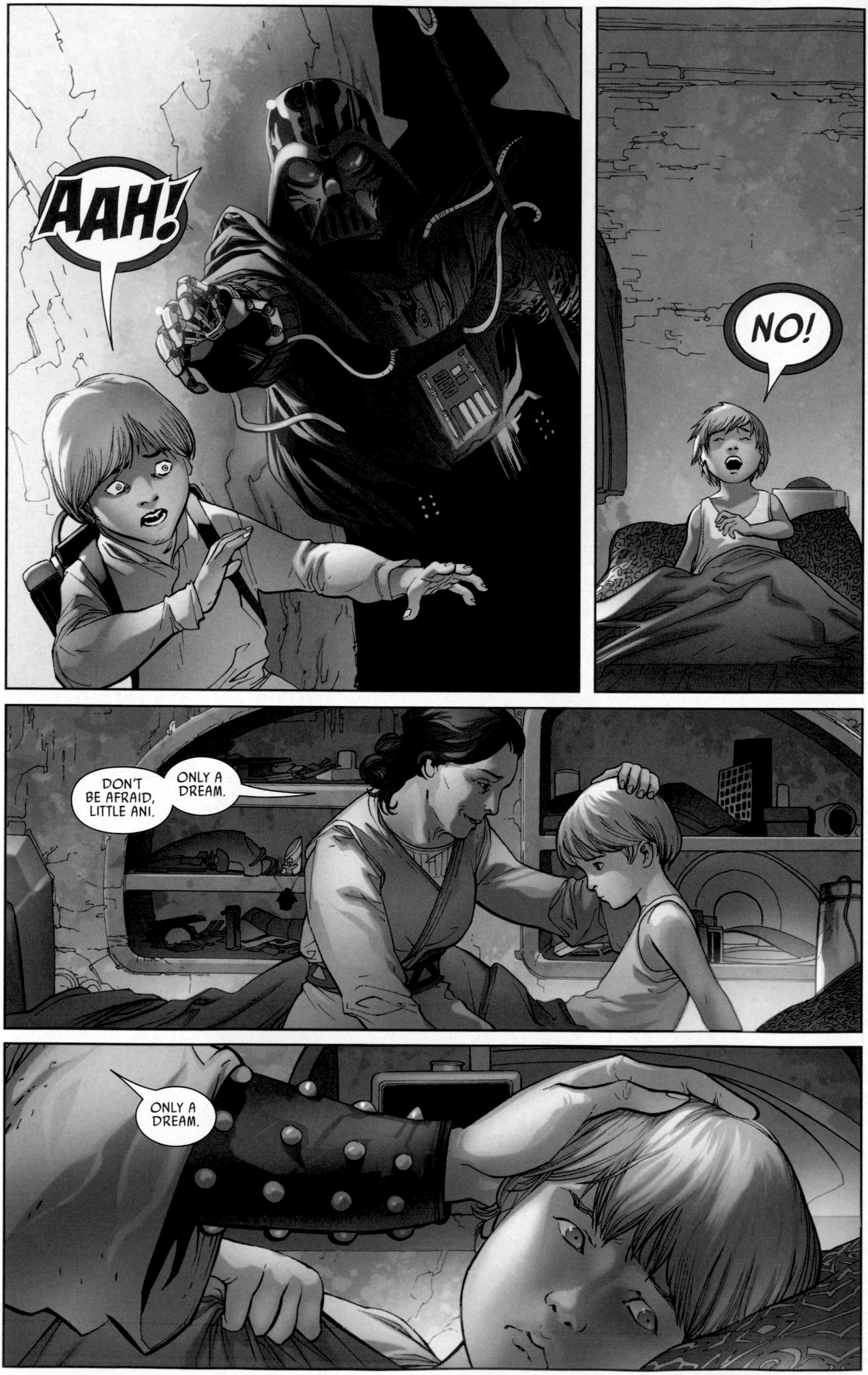
AAH!
NO!
DON'T BE AFRAID, LITTLE ANI.
ONLY A DREAM.
ONLY A DREAM.

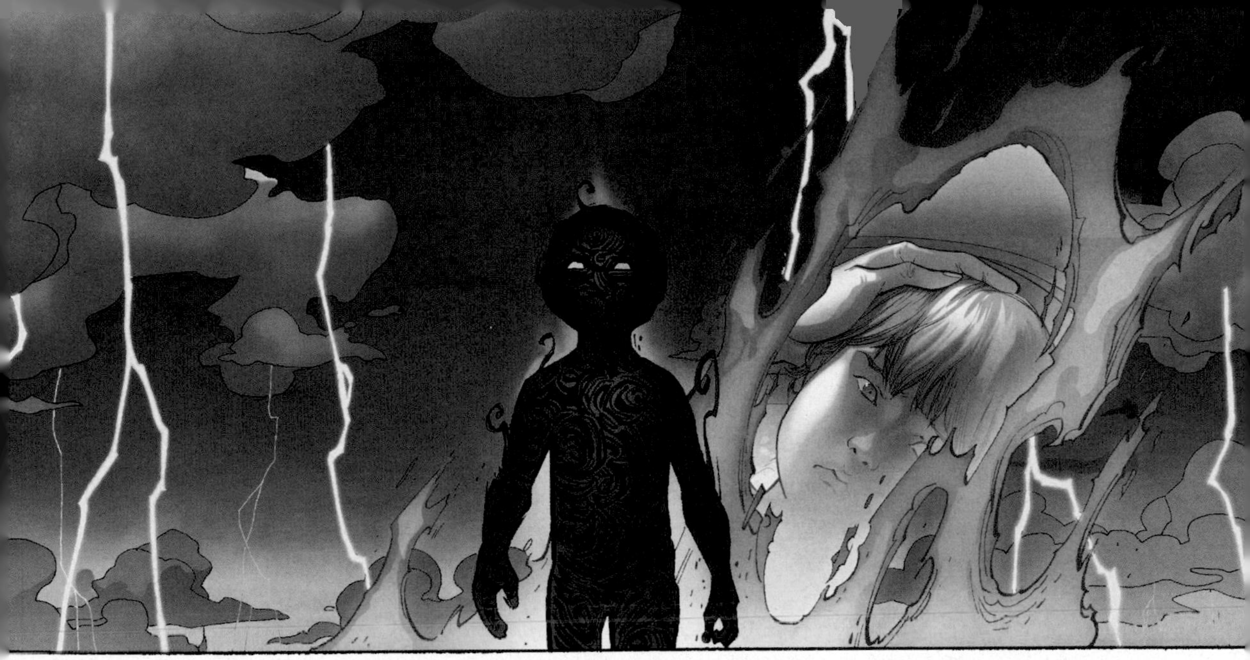

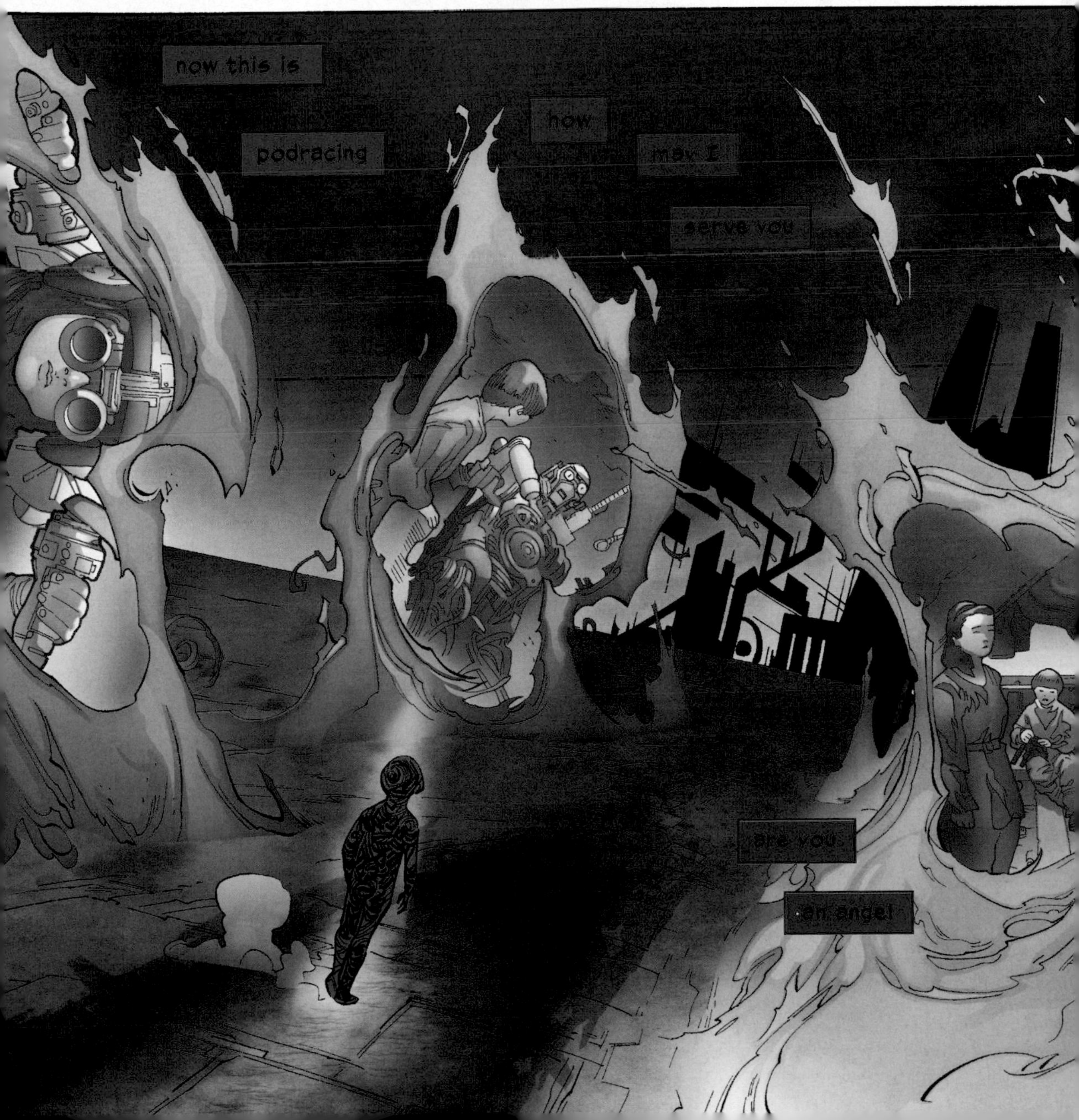
now this is
podracing
how
may I
serve you
are you
an angel

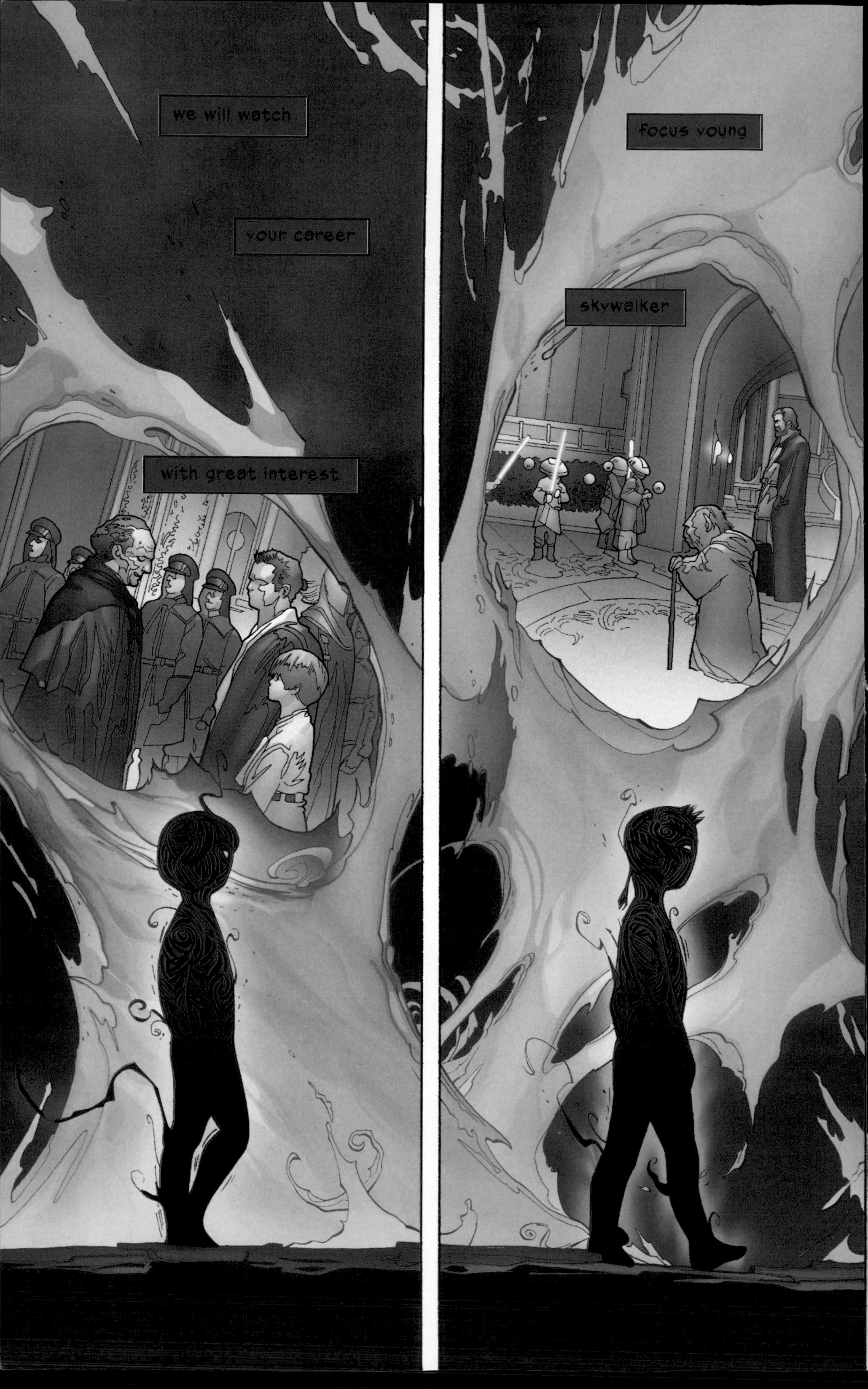
we will watch
your career
with great interest
focus young
skywalker

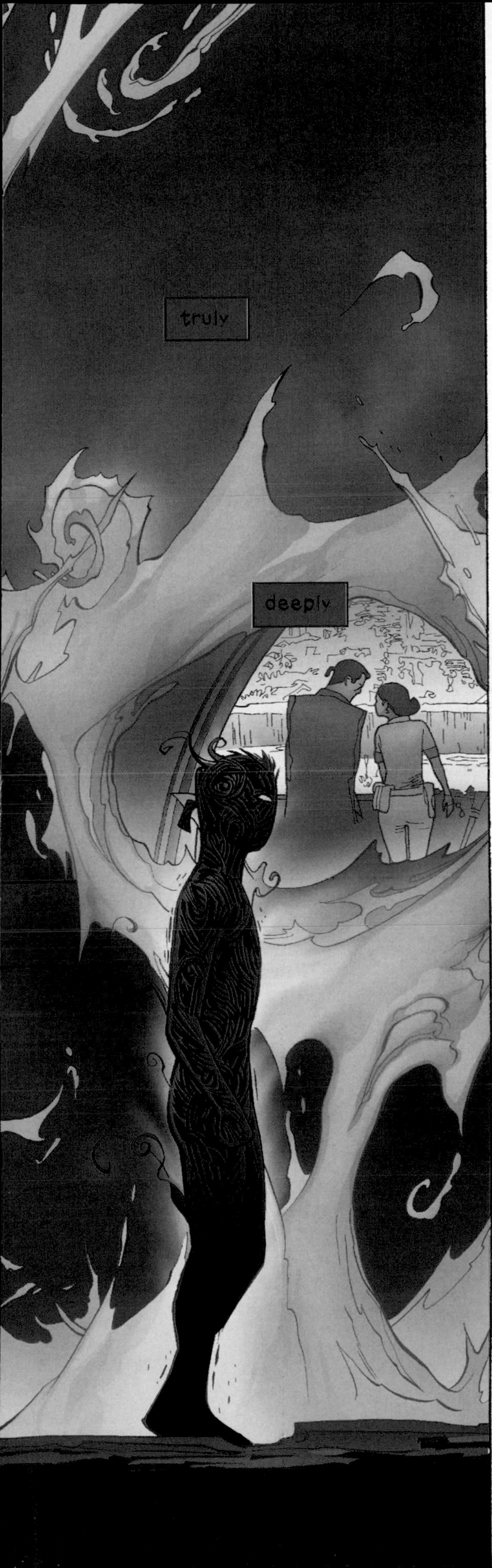
truly
deeply

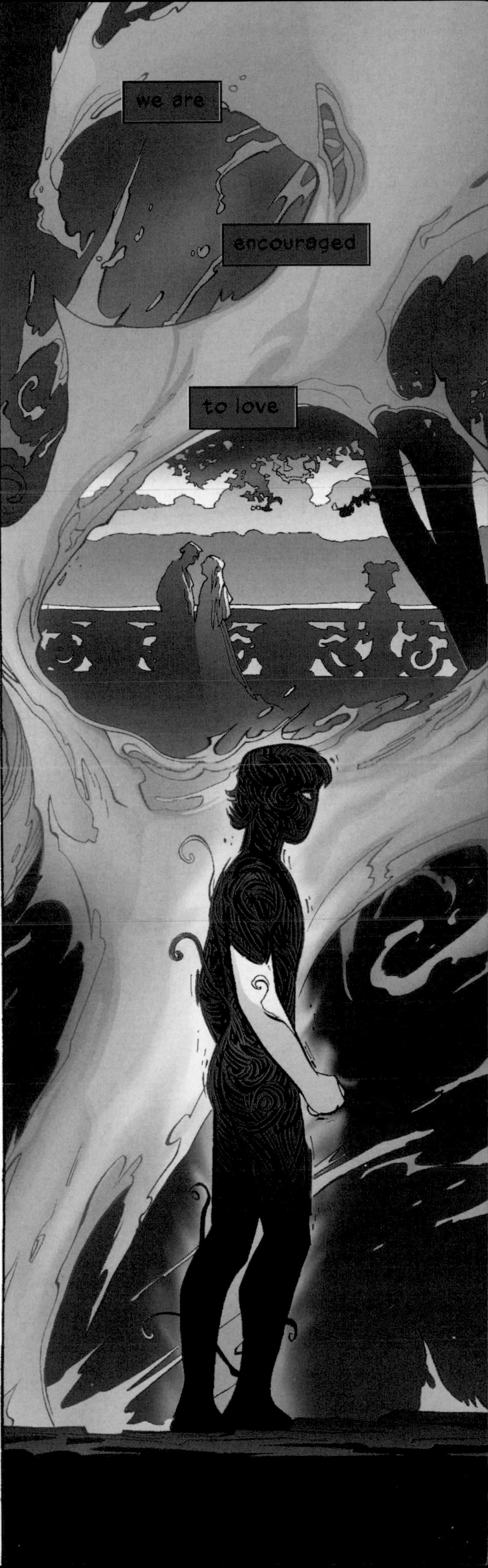
we are
encouraged
to love

it was foretold that you would

be here

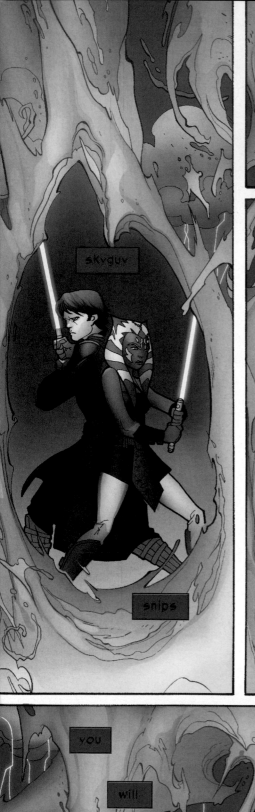

skyguy

snips

I

am

no

jedi

you

will

die

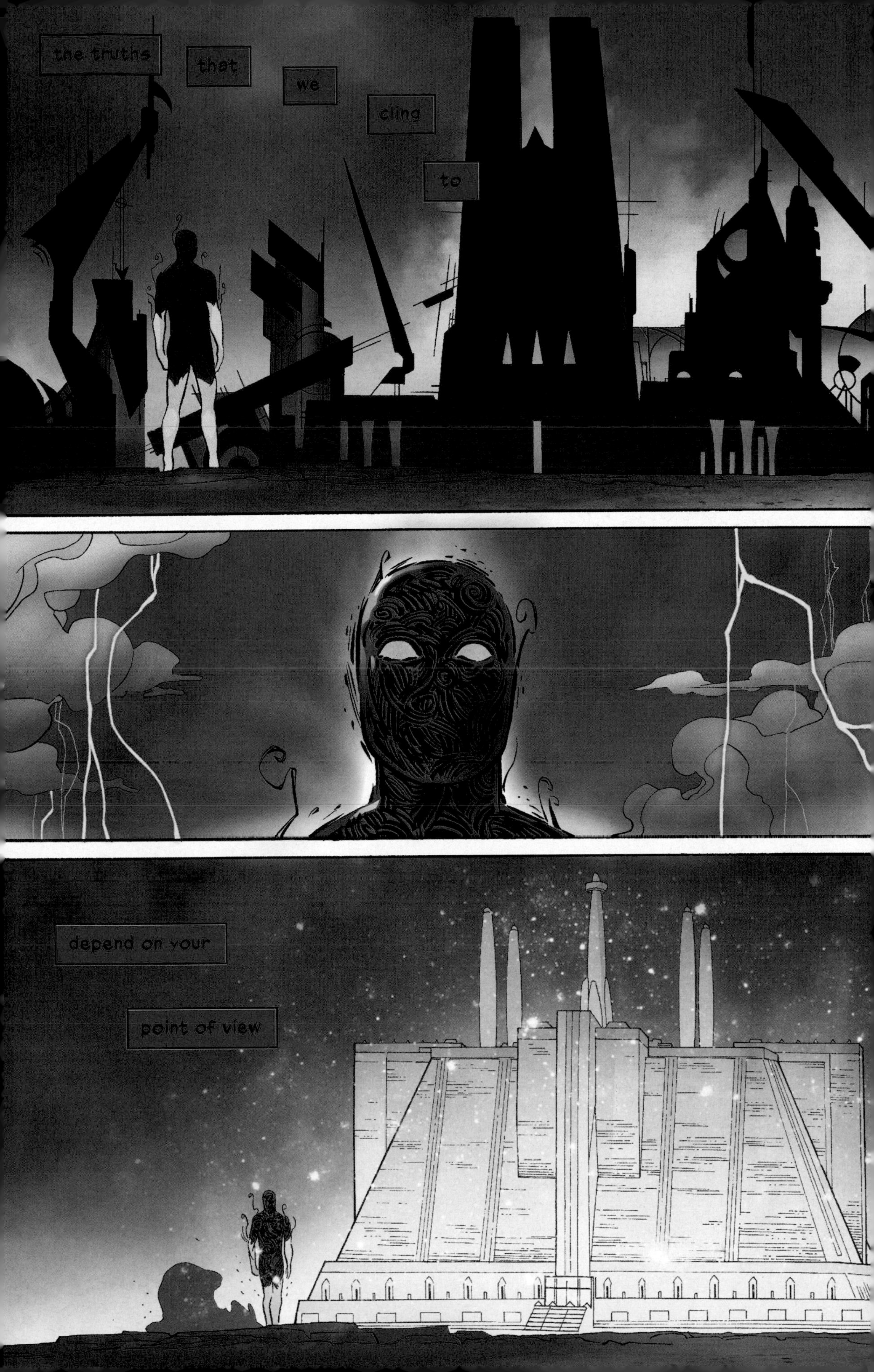
the truths
that
we
cling
to
depend on your
point of view

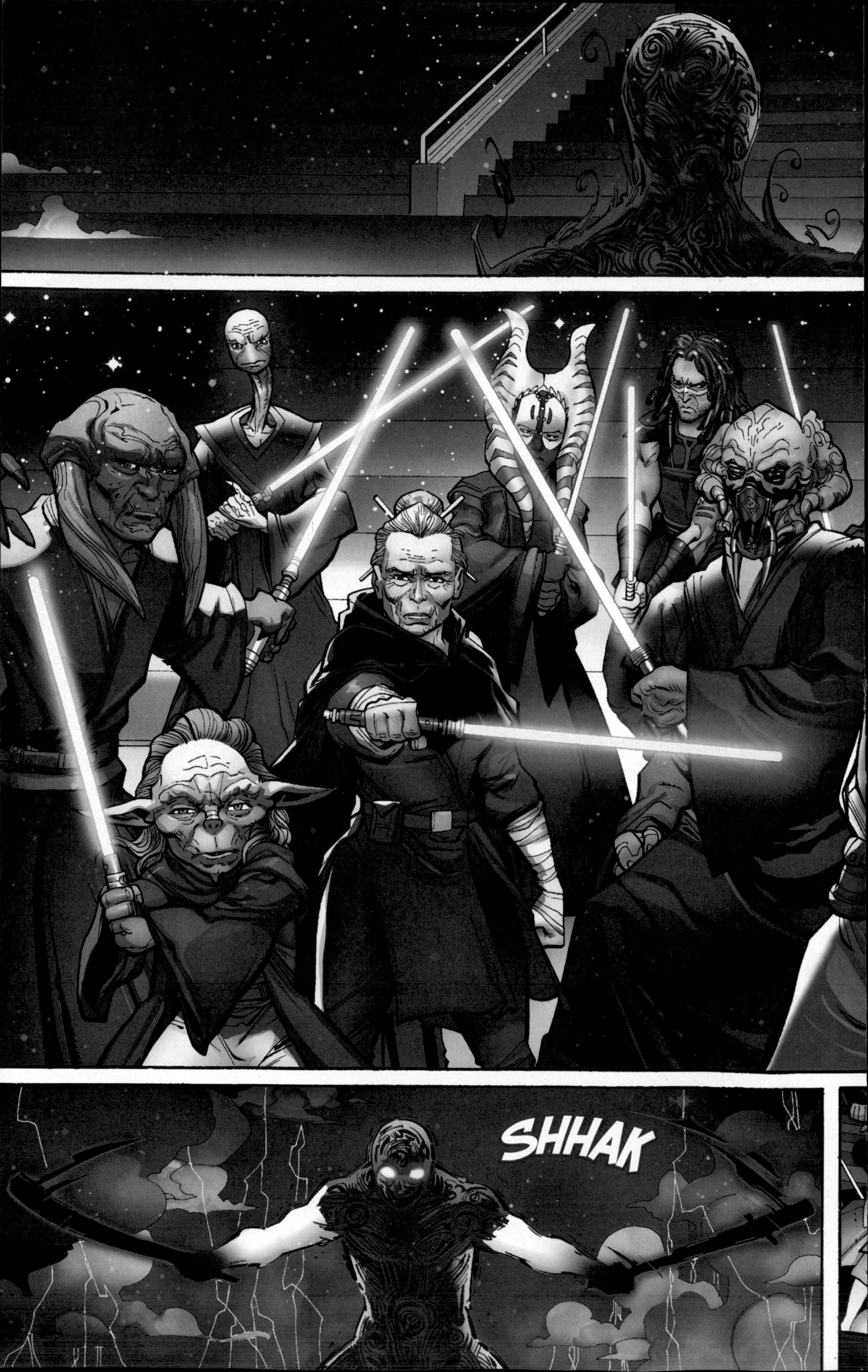
SHHAK

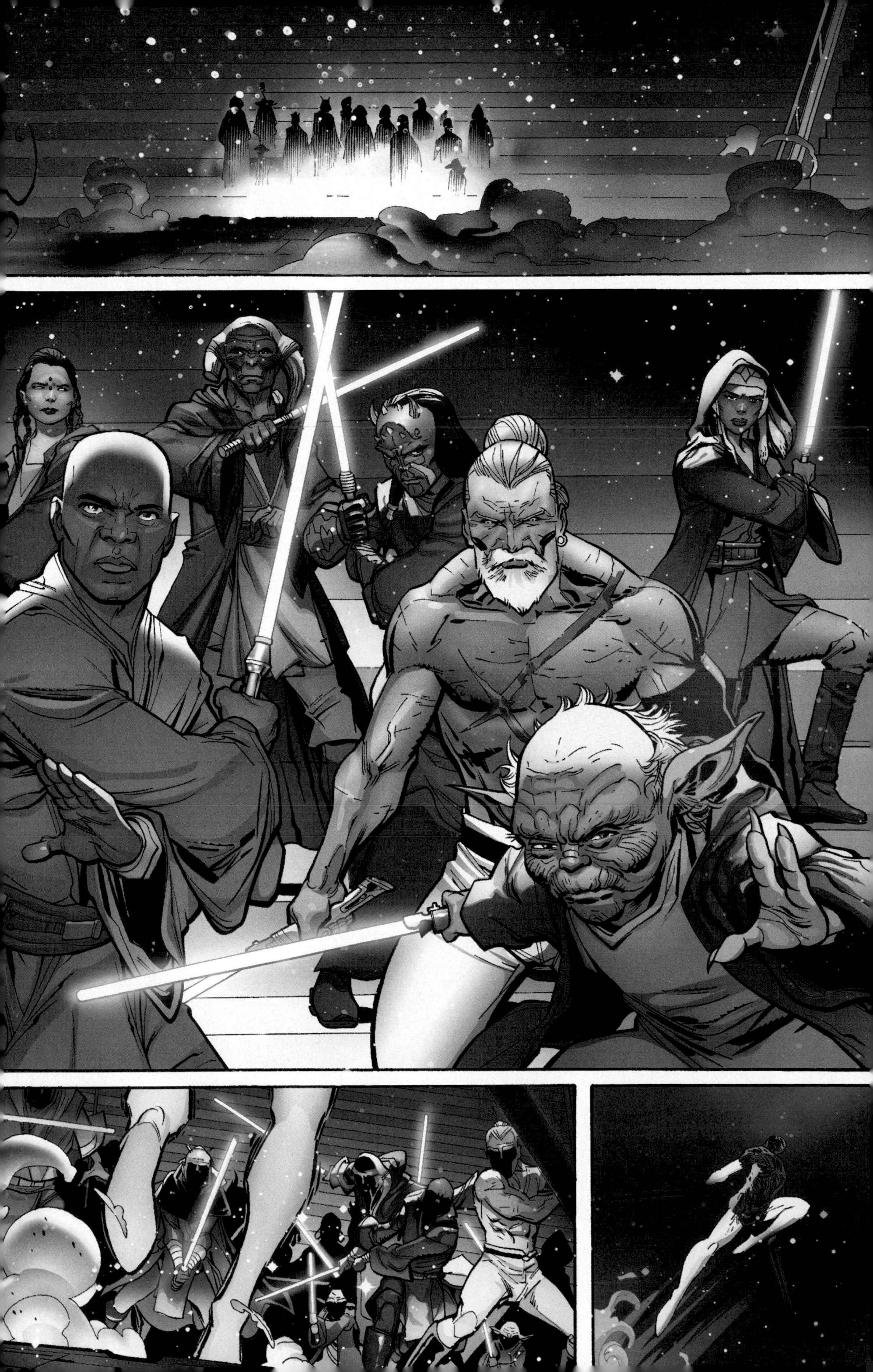

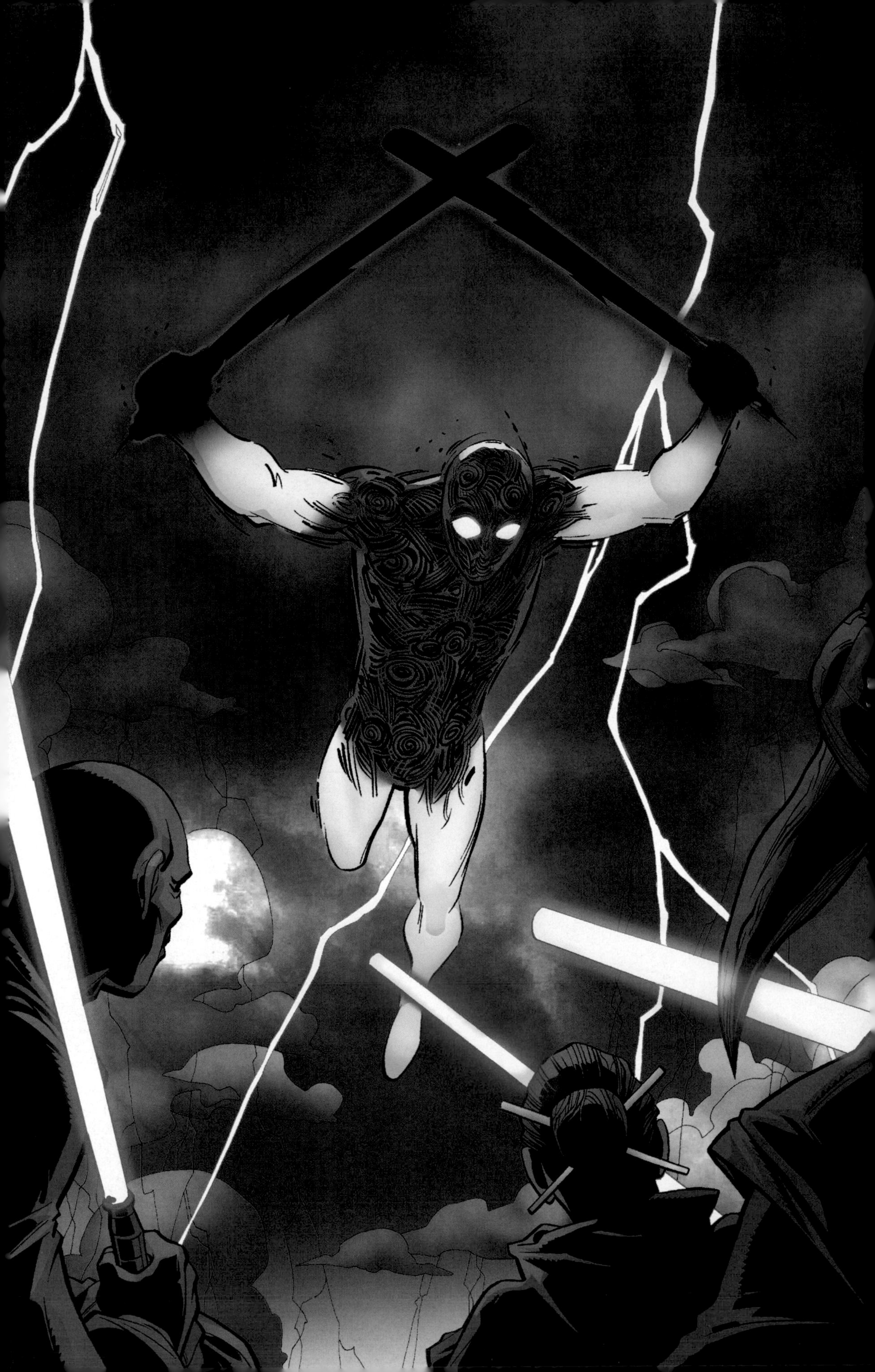

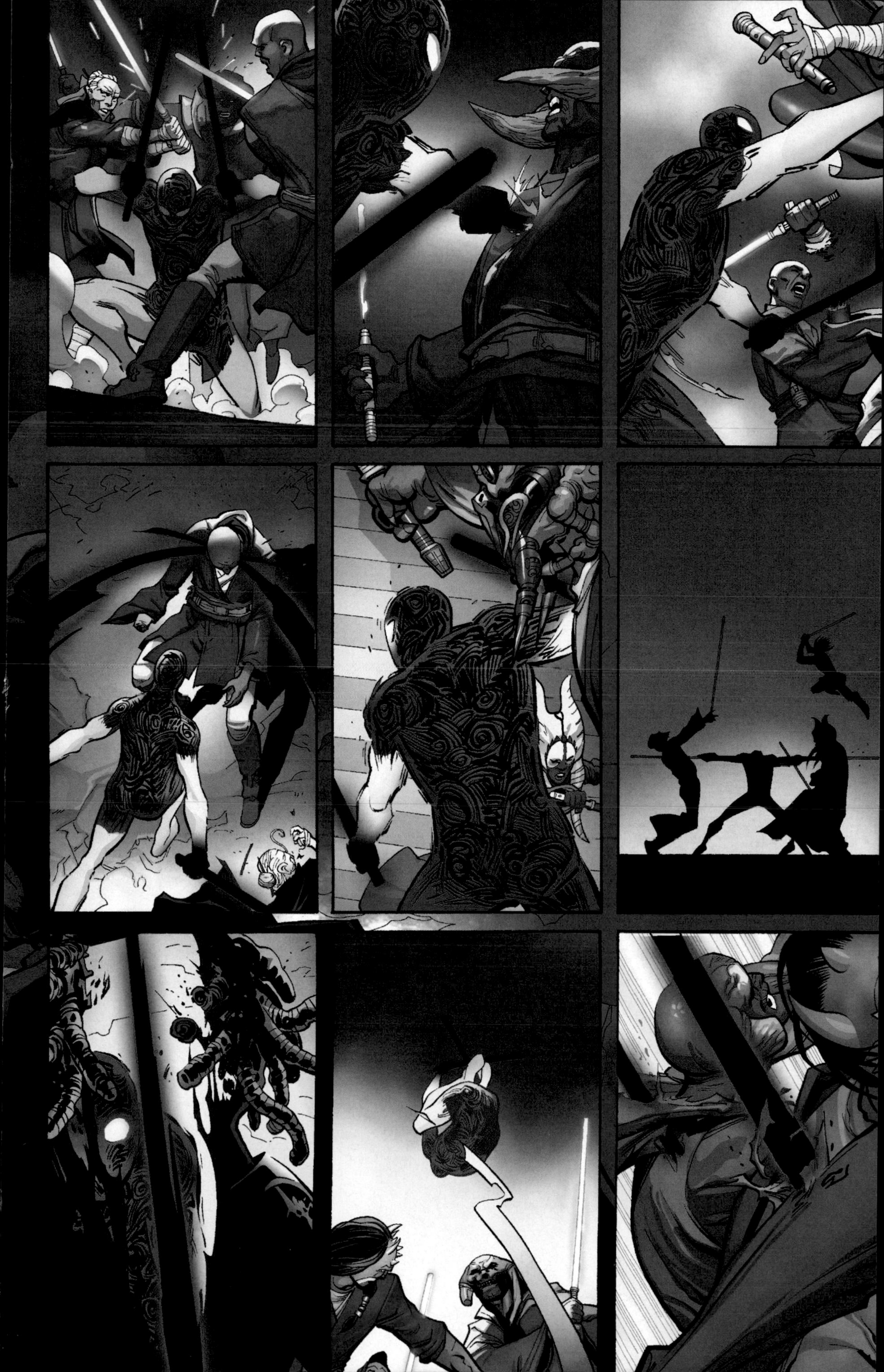

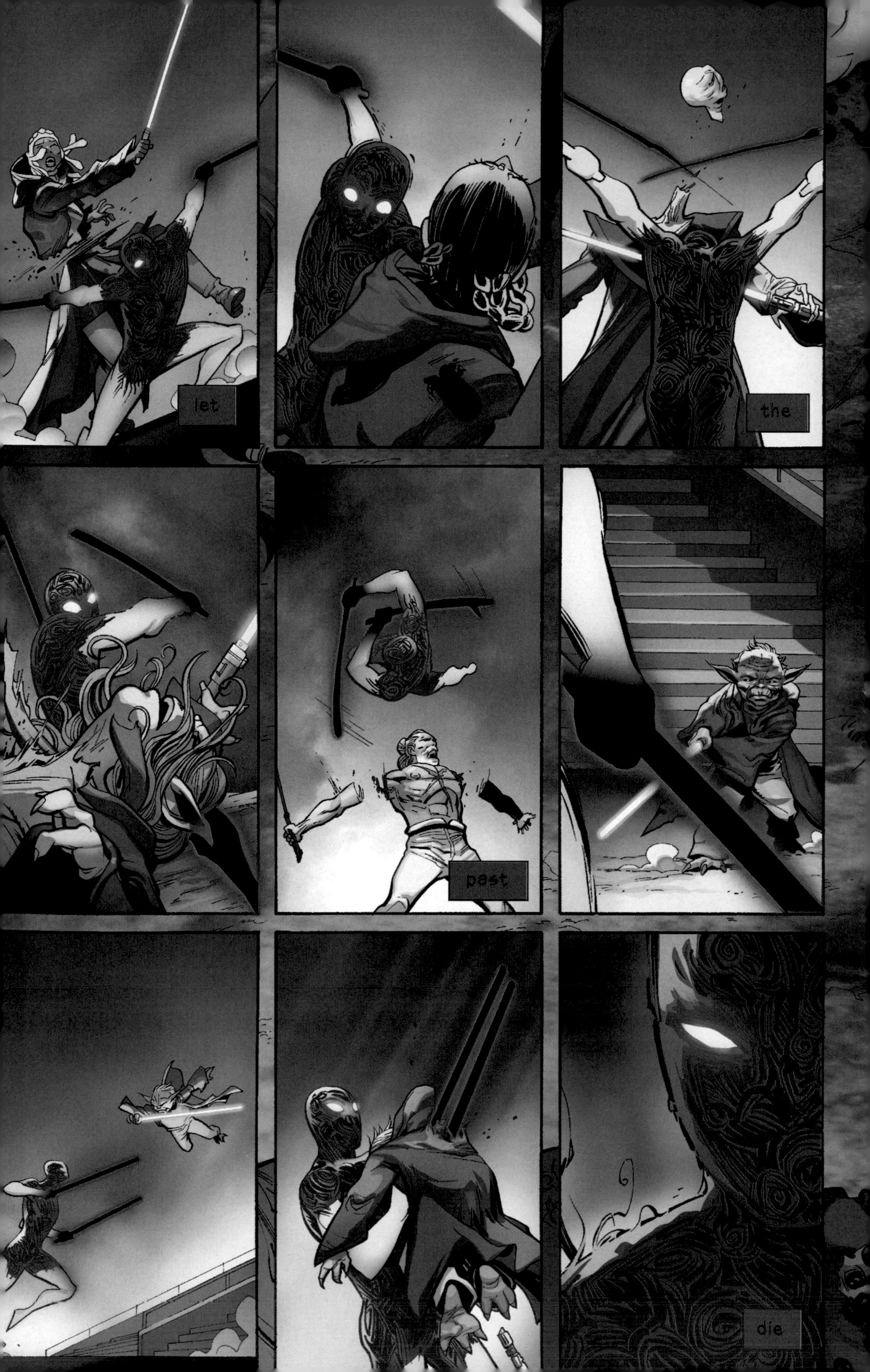
let
the
past
die

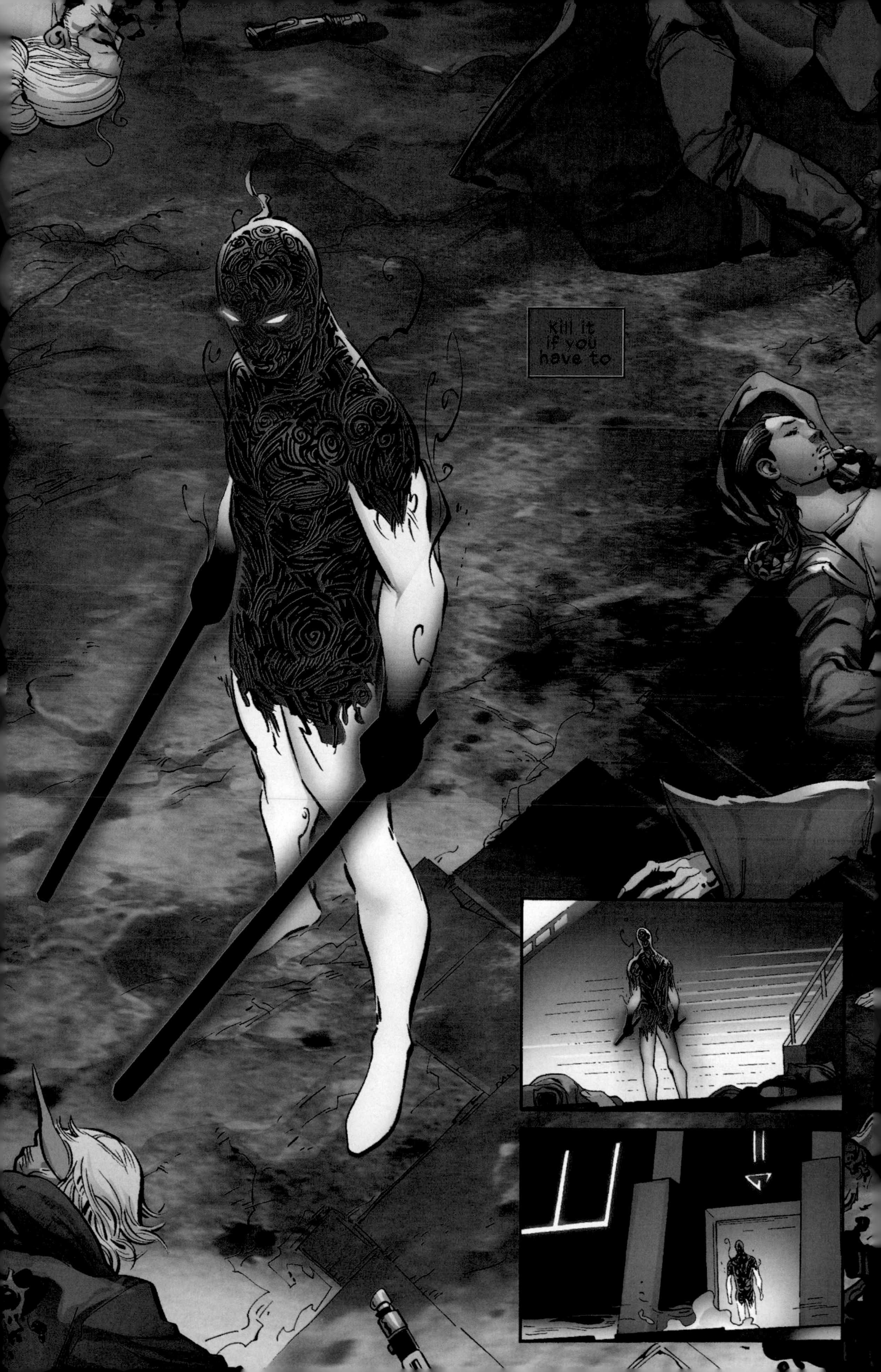
Kill it
if you
have to

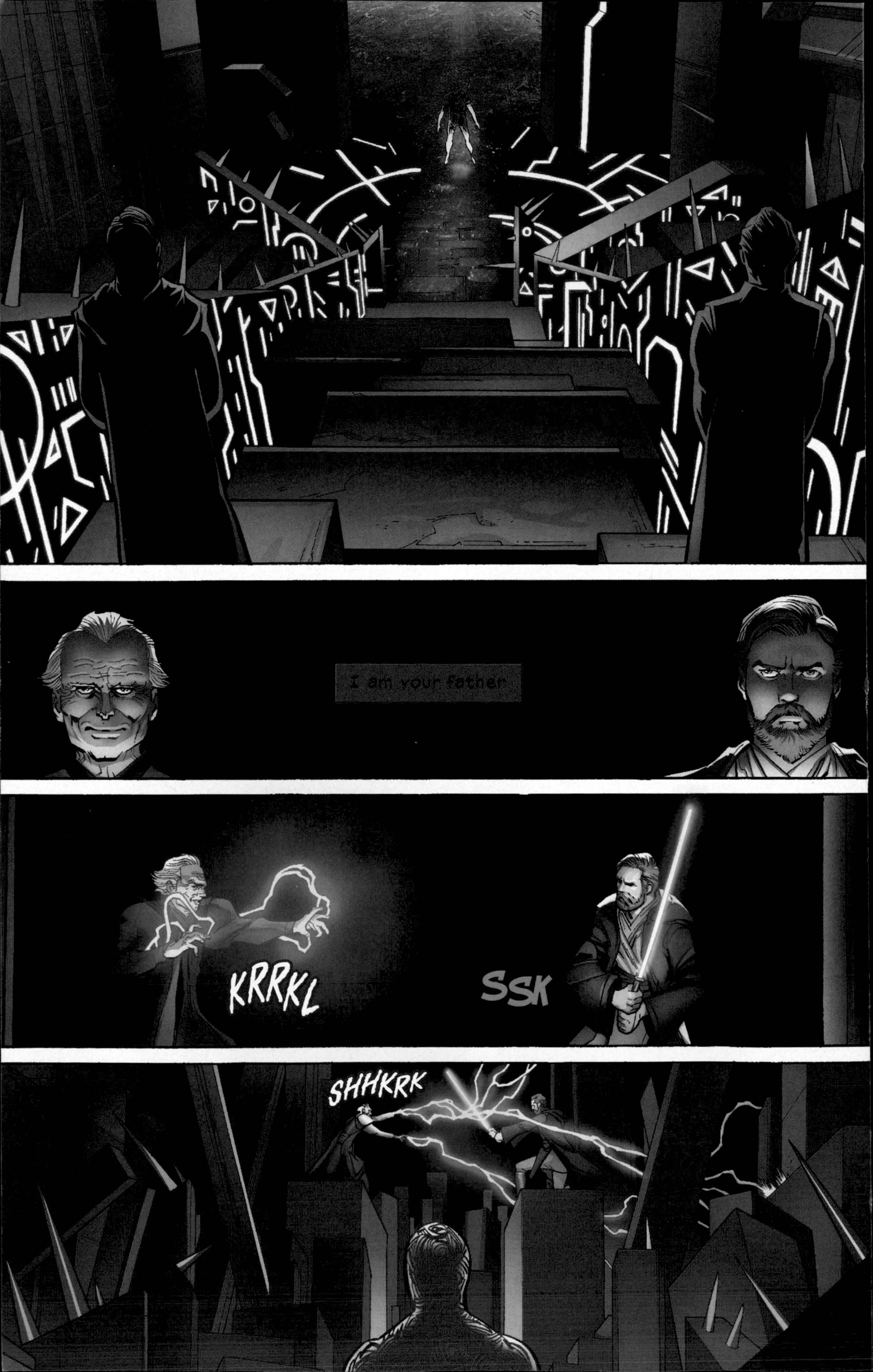
I am your father
KRRKL
SSK
SHHKRK

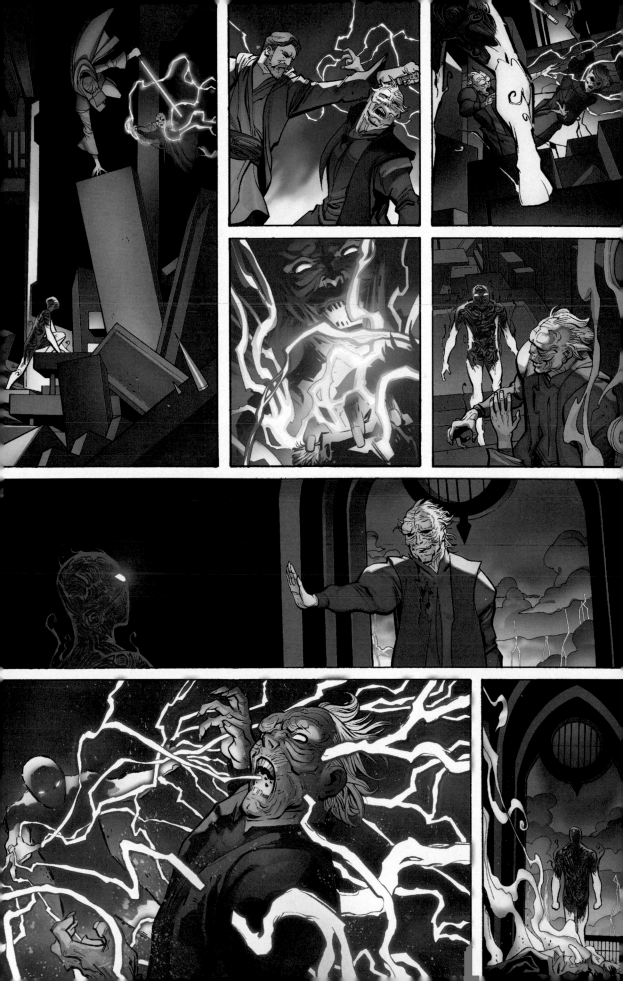

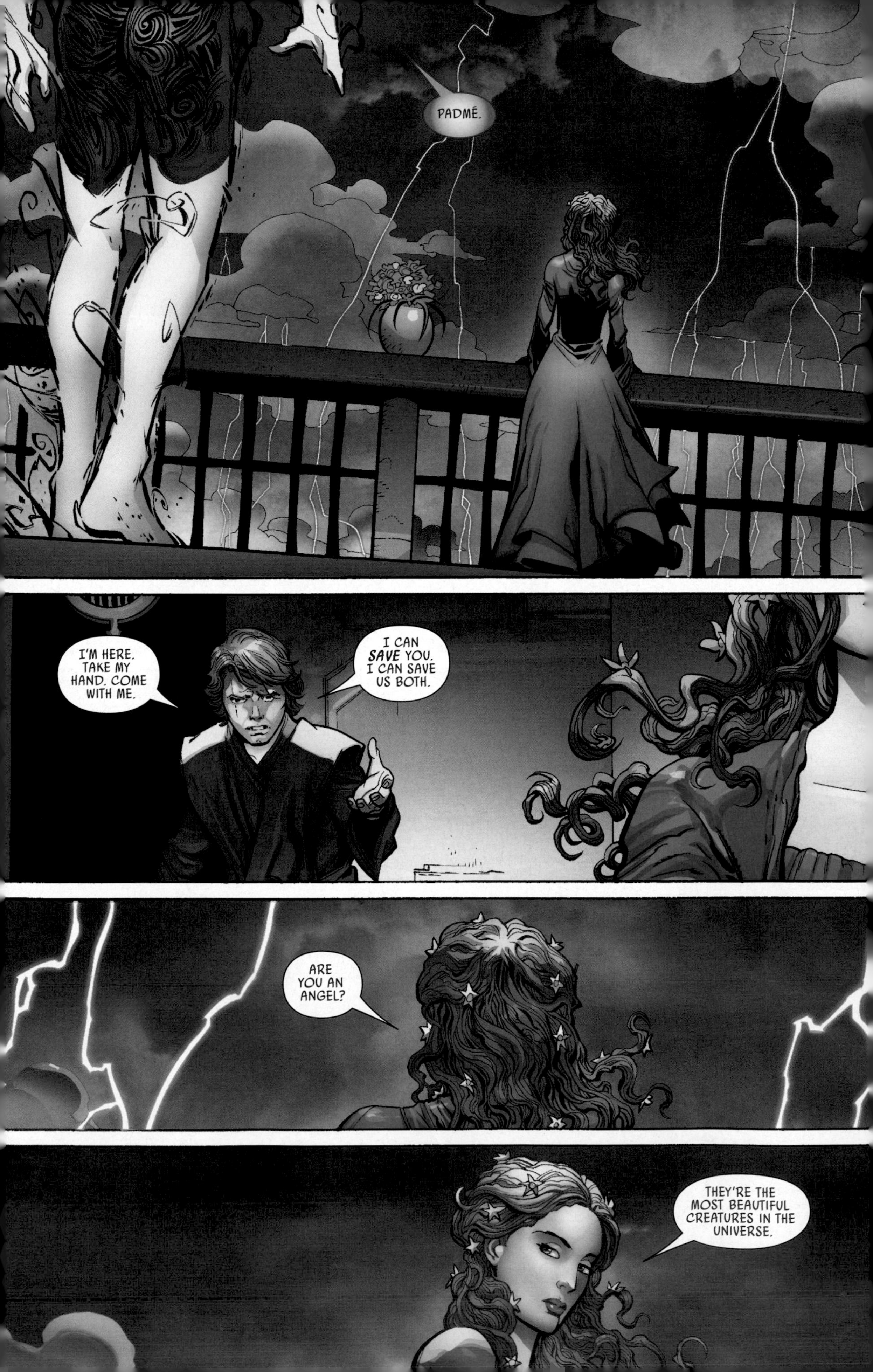
PADMÉ.
I'M HERE. TAKE MY HAND. COME WITH ME.
I CAN SAVE YOU. I CAN SAVE US BOTH.
ARE YOU AN ANGEL?
THEY'RE THE MOST BEAUTIFUL CREATURES IN THE UNIVERSE.

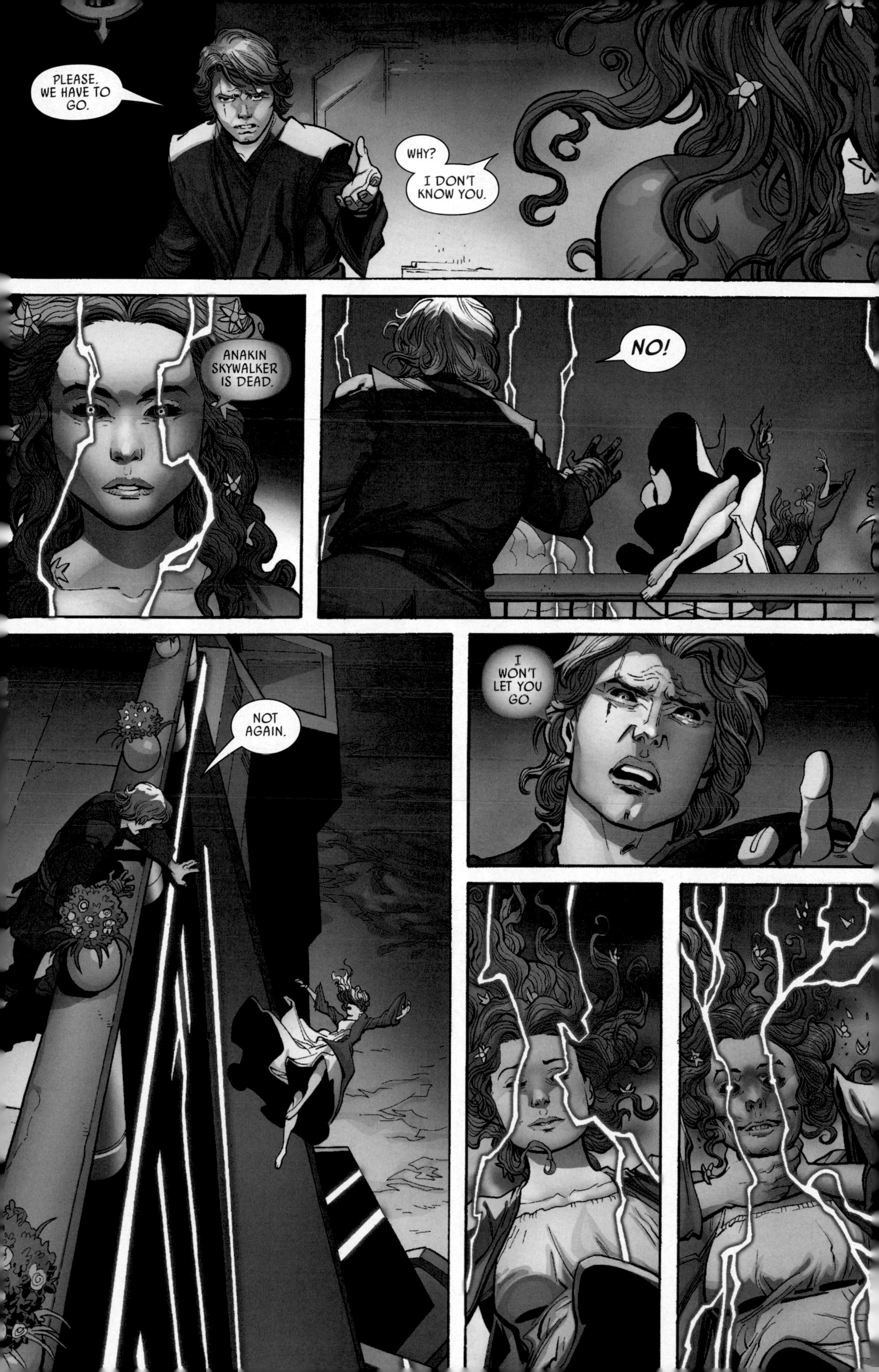
PLEASE. WE HAVE TO GO.
WHY?
I DON'T KNOW YOU.
ANAKIN SKYWALKER IS DEAD.
NO!
NOT AGAIN.
I WON'T LET YOU GO.

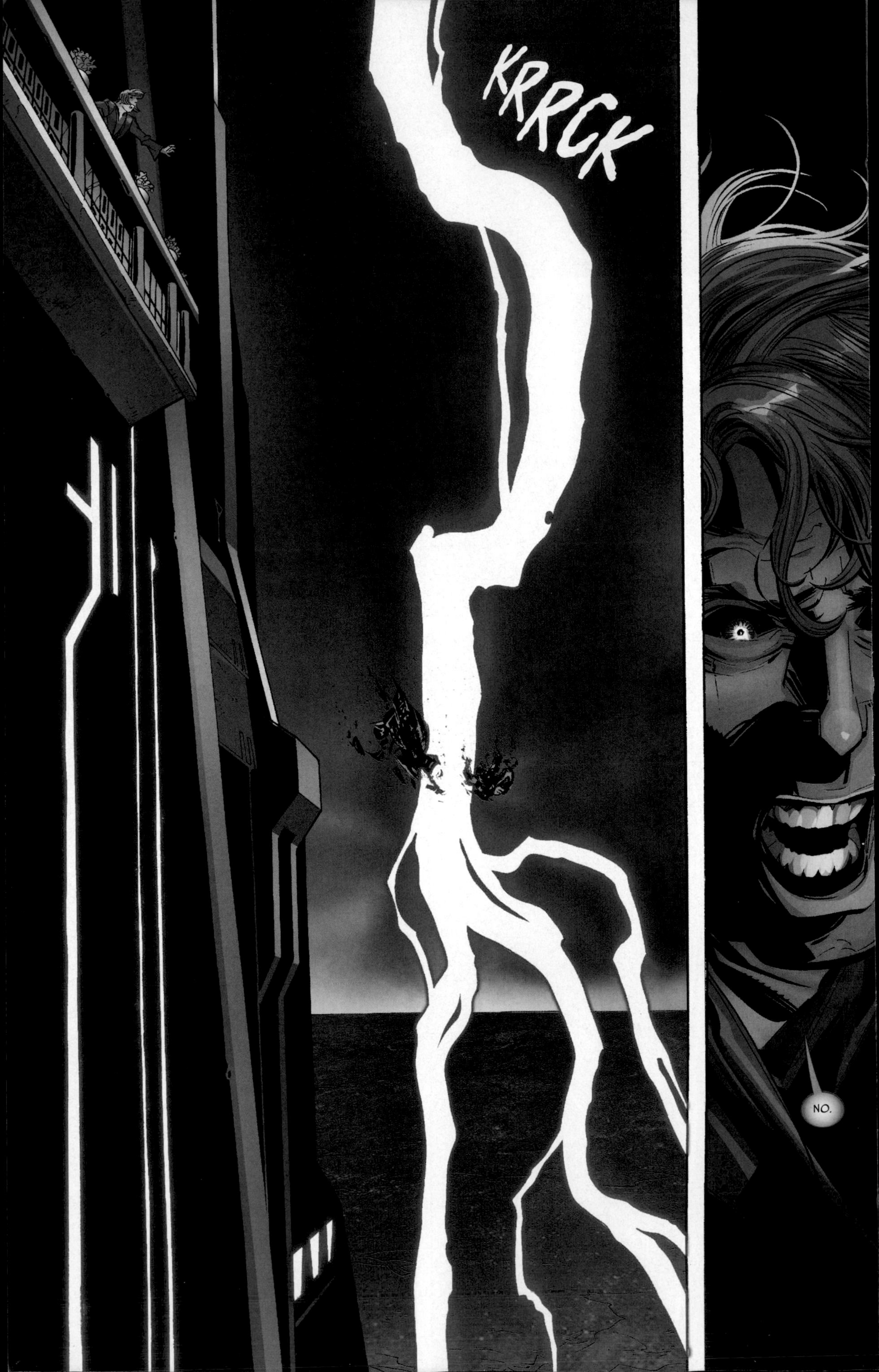
KRRCK
NO.

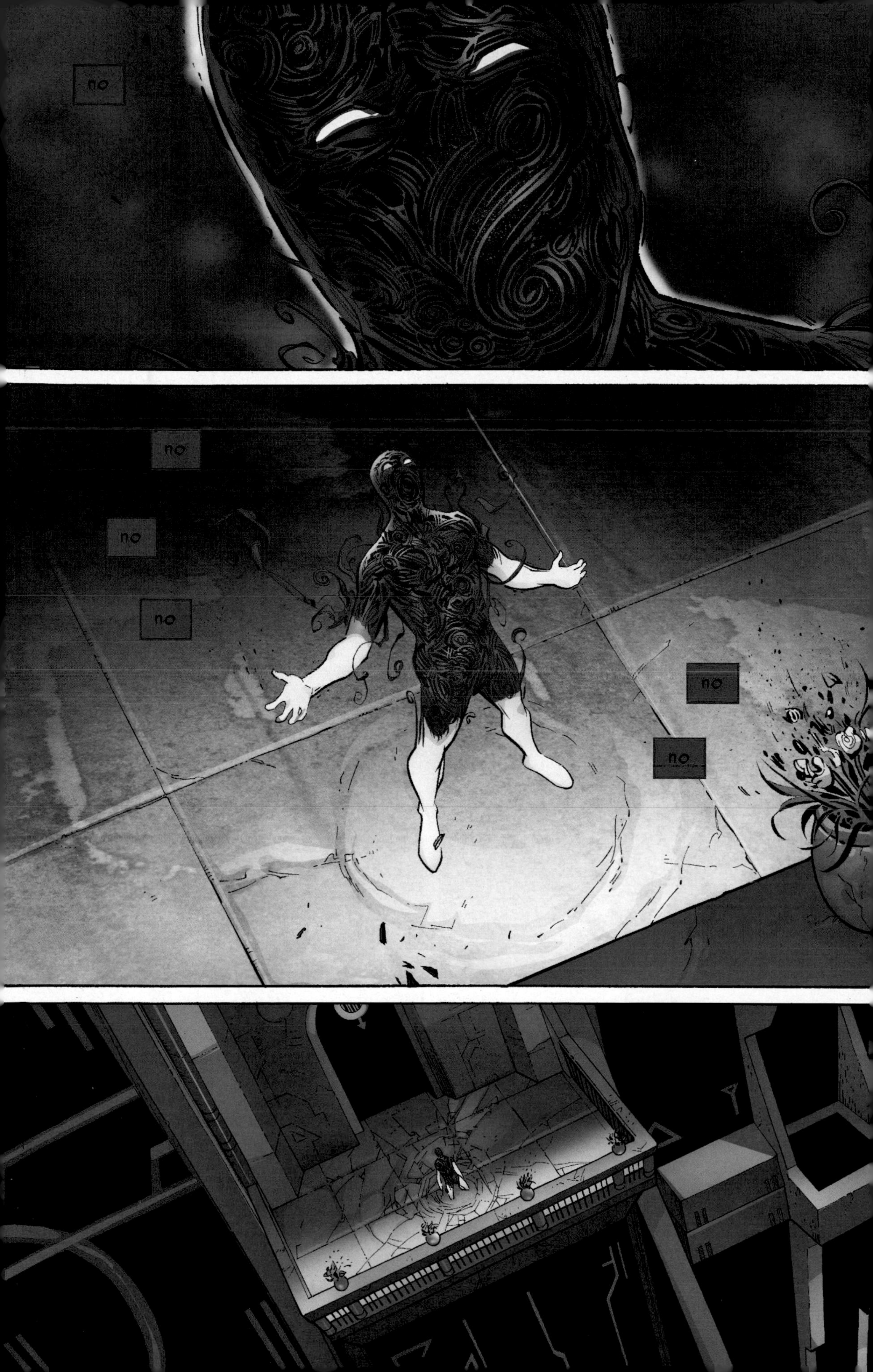

no
no
no
no
no
no

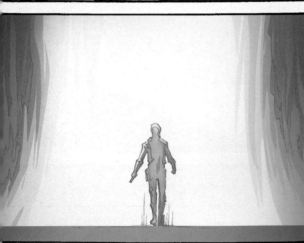

FIVSS

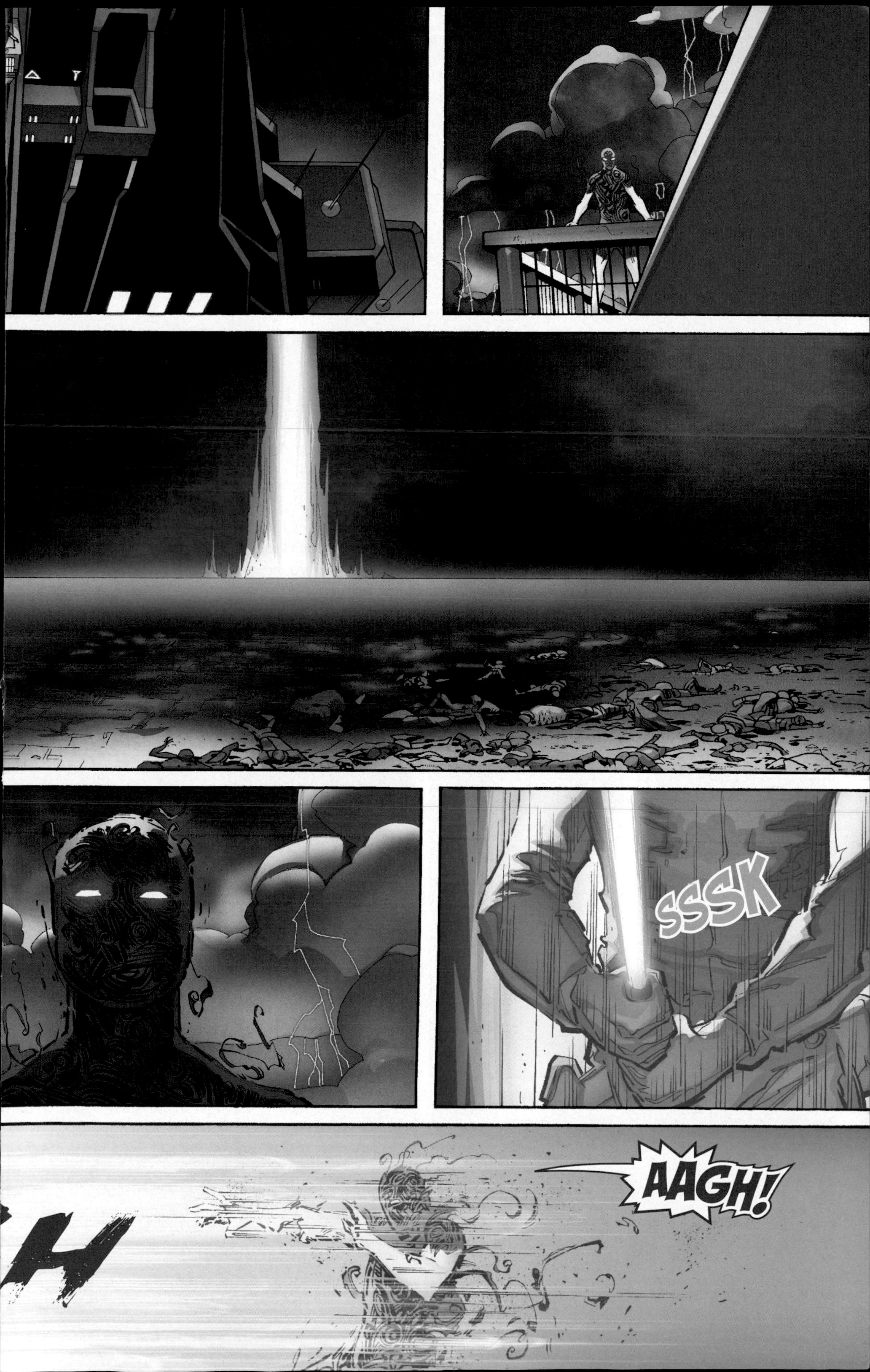
SSSK
AAGH!

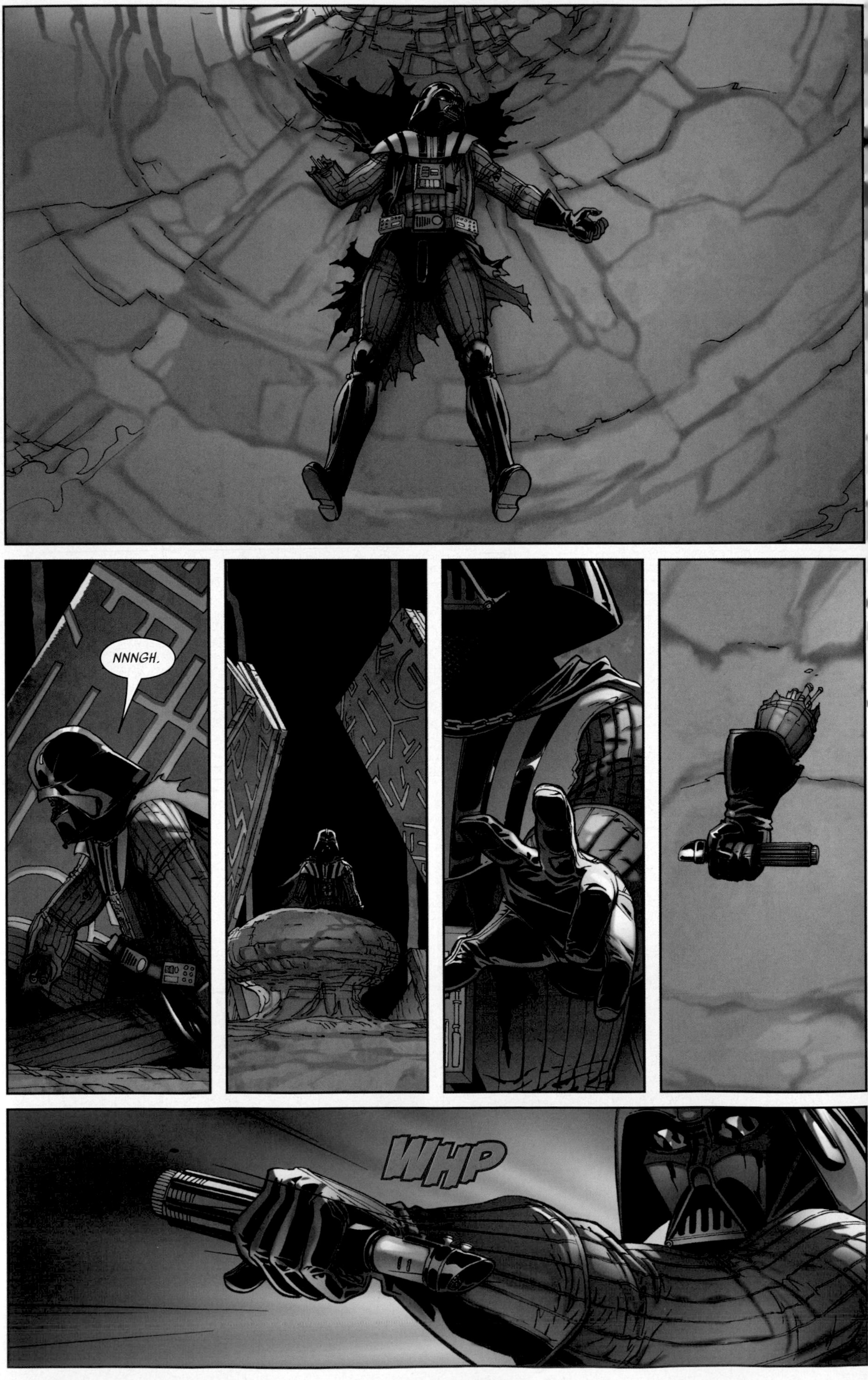
NNNGH.
WHP

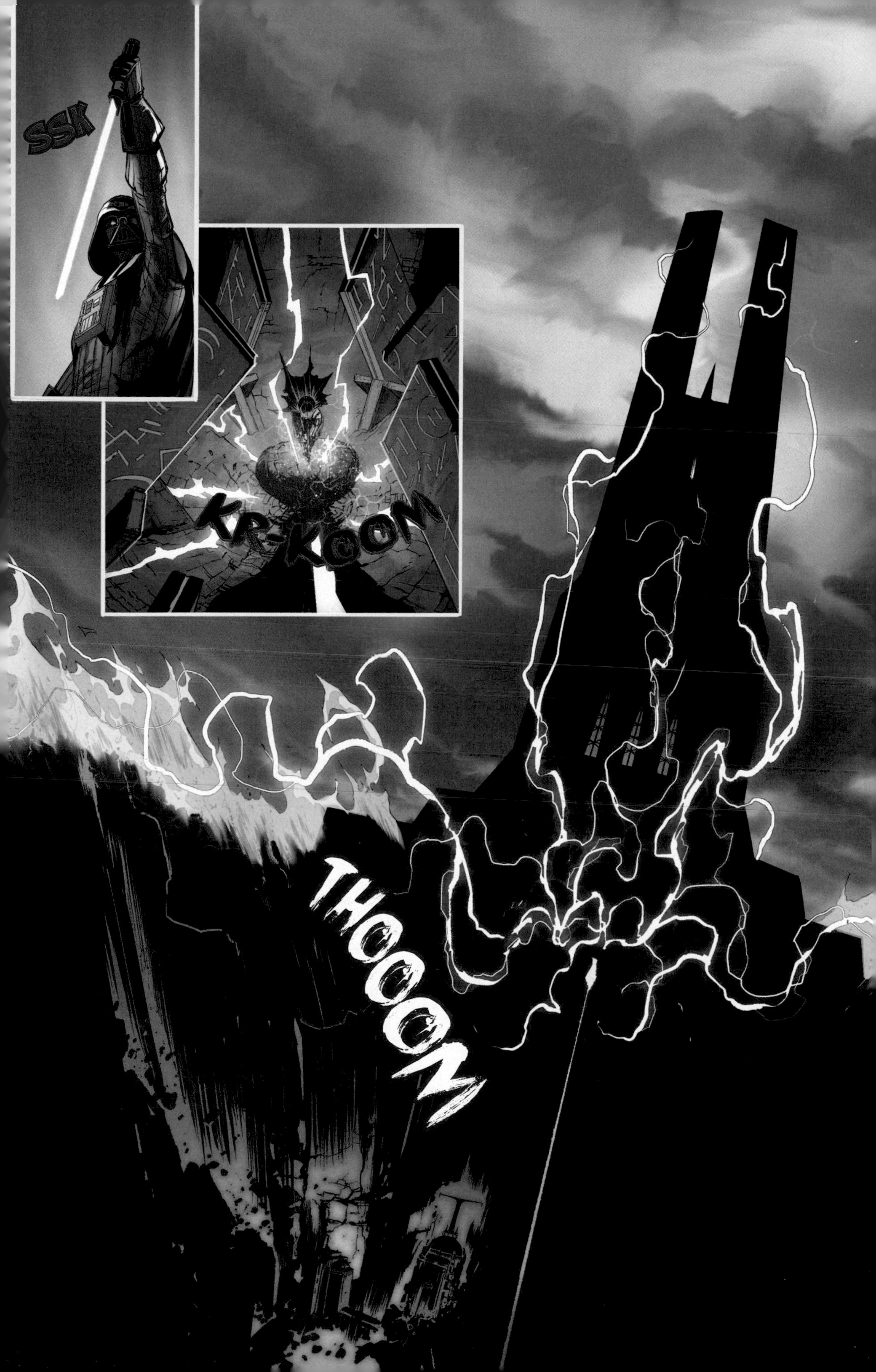
SSK
KR-KOOM
THOOOM

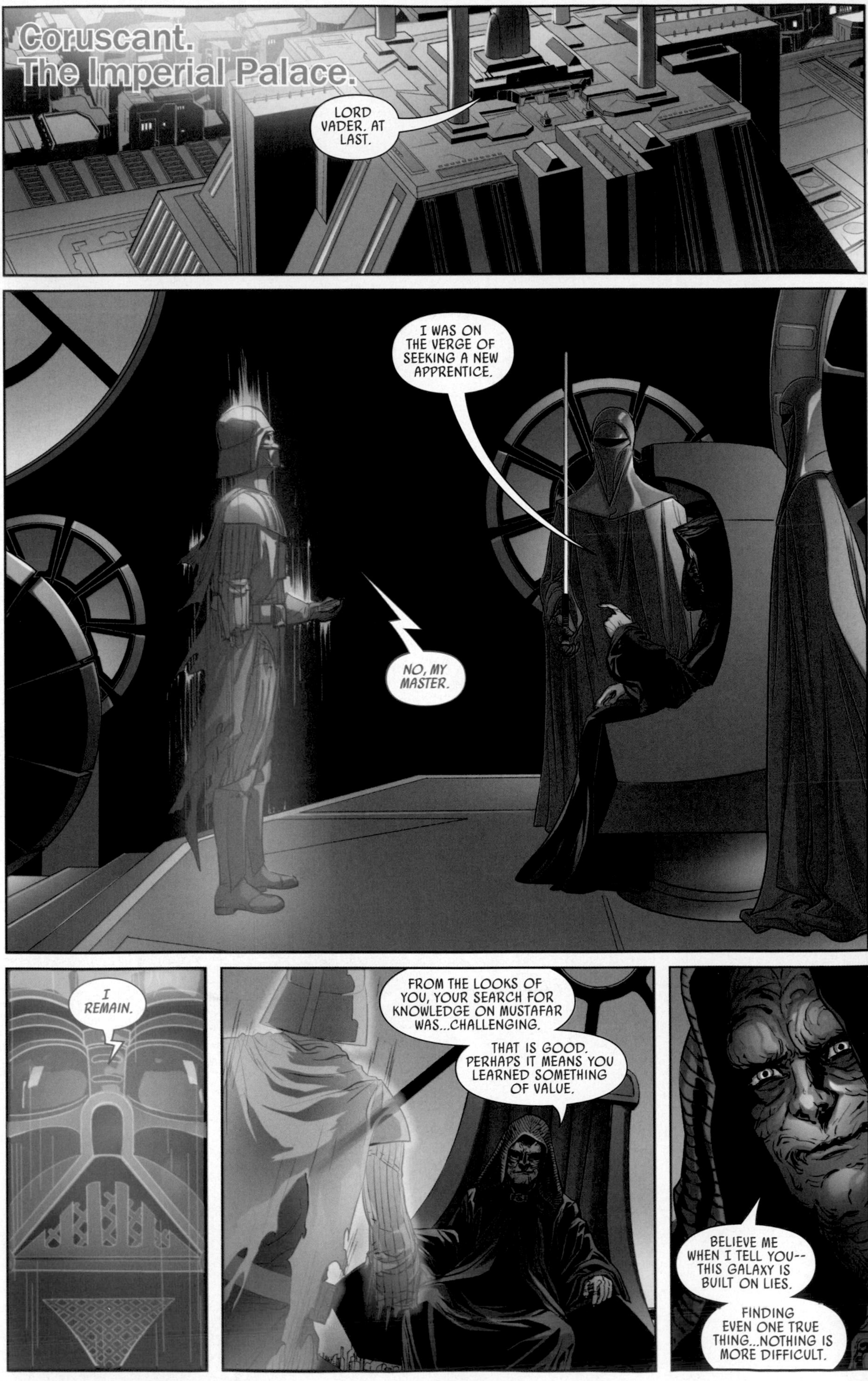
Coruscant.
The Imperial Palace.
LORD VADER. AT LAST.
I WAS ON THE VERGE OF SEEKING A NEW APPRENTICE.
NO, MY MASTER.
I REMAIN.
FROM THE LOOKS OF YOU, YOUR SEARCH FOR KNOWLEDGE ON MUSTAFAR WAS...CHALLENGING.
THAT IS GOOD. PERHAPS IT MEANS YOU LEARNED SOMETHING OF VALUE.
BELIEVE ME WHEN I TELL YOU-- THIS GALAXY IS BUILT ON LIES.
FINDING EVEN ONE TRUE THING...NOTHING IS MORE DIFFICULT.

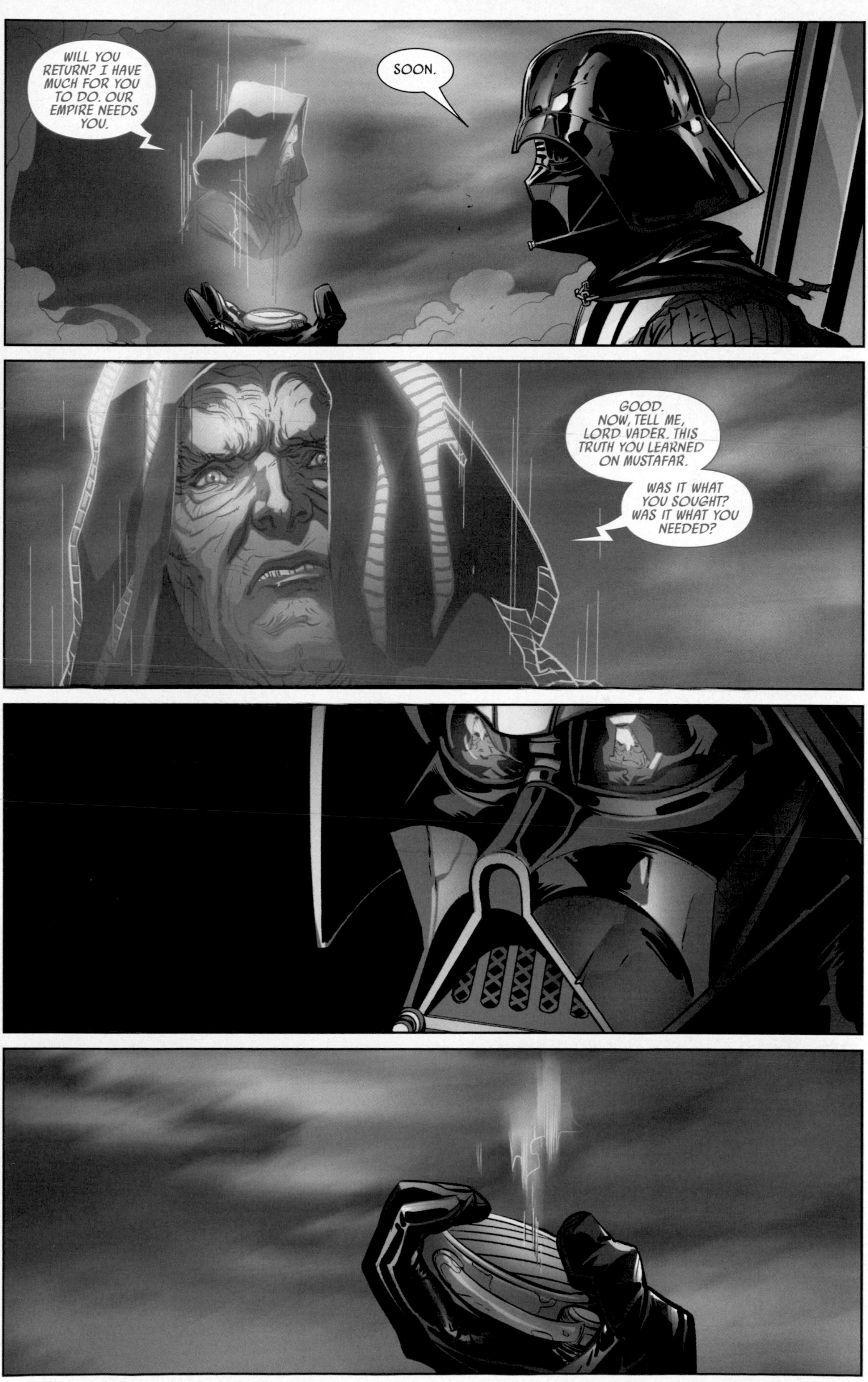
WILL YOU RETURN? I HAVE MUCH FOR YOU TO DO. OUR EMPIRE NEEDS YOU.
SOON.
GOOD. NOW, TELL ME, LORD VADER. THIS TRUTH YOU LEARNED ON MUSTAFAR.
WAS IT WHAT YOU SOUGHT? WAS IT WHAT YOU NEEDED?

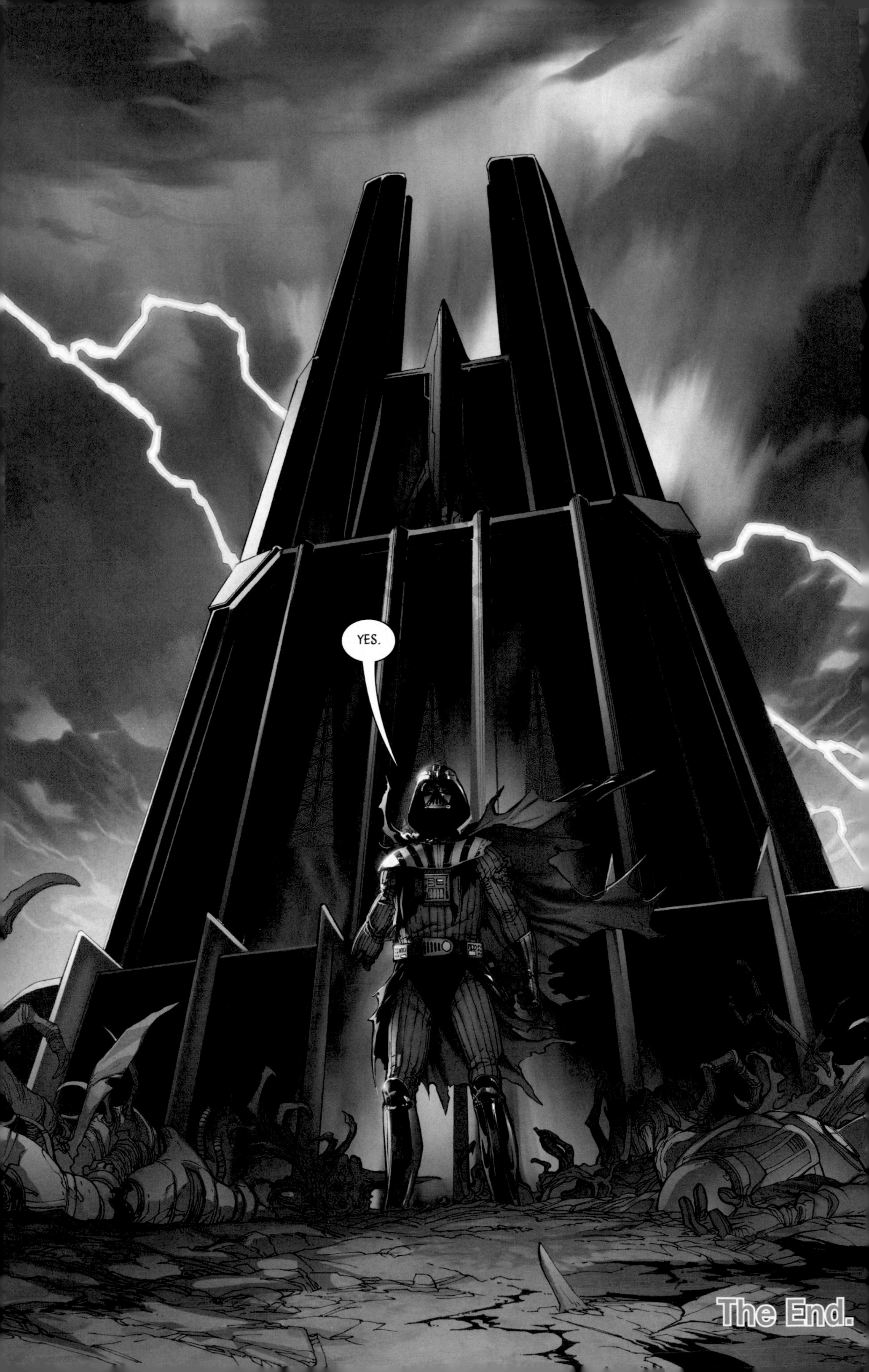
YES.
The End.

AFTER BARELY ESCAPING DARTH VADER WITH HER LIFE, DOCTOR APHRA SETS OFF IN SEARCH OF RARE AND DEADLY ARTIFACTS!

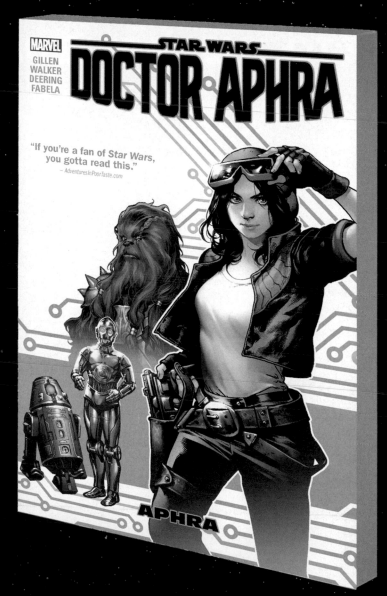

MARVEL
GILLEN
WALKER
DEERING
FABELA

STAR WARS. DOCTOR APHRA

"If you're a fan of Star Wars, you gotta read this."
— AdventuresInPoorTaste.com

APHRA

STAR WARS: DOCTOR APHRA VOL. 1 — APHRA TPB
978-1302906771

ON SALE NOW
AVAILABLE IN PRINT AND DIGITAL WHEREVER BOOKS ARE SOLD

TO FIND A COMIC SHOP NEAR YOU, VISIT COMICSHOPLOCATOR.COM

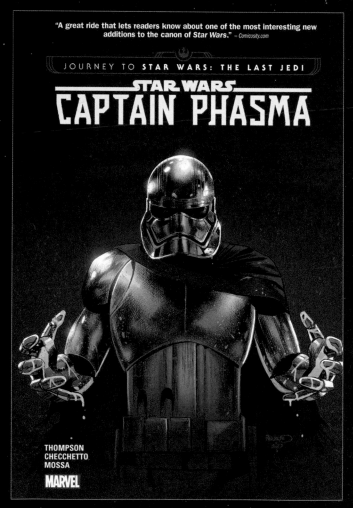